HIDDEN HISTORIES OF
BRITISH PSYCHOANALYSIS

BOOKS BY PROFESSOR BRETT KAHR

D. W. Winnicott: A Biographical Portrait (1996)

Forensic Psychotherapy and Psychopathology: Winnicottian Perspectives, Editor (2001)

Exhibitionism (2001)

The Legacy of Winnicott: Essays on Infant and Child Mental Health, Editor (2002)

Sex and the Psyche (2007)

Who's Been Sleeping in Your Head?: The Secret World of Sexual Fantasies (2008)

Life Lessons from Freud (2013)

Tea with Winnicott (2016)

Coffee with Freud (2017)

New Horizons in Forensic Psychotherapy: Exploring the Work of Estela V. Welldon, Editor (2018)

How to Flourish as a Psychotherapist (2019)

Bombs in the Consulting Room: Surviving Psychological Shrapnel (2020)

Celebrity Mad: Why Otherwise Intelligent People Worship Fame (2020)

On Practising Therapy at 1.45 A.M.: Adventures of a Clinician (2020)

Dangerous Lunatics: Trauma, Criminality, and Forensic Psychotherapy (2020)

Freud's Pandemics: Surviving Global War, Spanish Flu, and the Nazis (2021)

How to Be Intimate with 15,000,000 Strangers: Musings on Media Psychoanalysis (2023)

BRETT KAHR

HIDDEN HISTORIES OF BRITISH PSYCHOANALYSIS

FROM FREUD'S DEATH BED
TO LAING'S MISSING TOOTH

KARNAC
firing the mind

First published in 2024 by
Karnac Books Ltd
62 Bucknell Road
Bicester
Oxfordshire OX26 2DS

Copyright © 2024 by Brett Kahr

The right of Brett Kahr to be identified as the author of this work has been asserted in accordance with §§ 77 and 78 of the Copyright Design and Patents Act 1988.

All rights reserved. No part of this publication may be reproduced, stored in a retrieval system, or transmitted, in any form or by any means, electronic, mechanical, photocopying, recording, or otherwise, without the prior written permission of the publisher.

British Library Cataloguing in Publication Data

A C.I.P. for this book is available from the British Library

ISBN-13: 978-1-80013-190-3

Typeset by vPrompt eServices Pvt Ltd, India

Printed in the United Kingdom

www.firingthemind.com

www.freud.org.uk

FREUD MUSEUM LONDON SERIES

The Freud Museum London and Karnac Books have joined forces to publish a new book series devoted to an examination of the life and work of Sigmund Freud alongside other significant figures in the history of psychoanalysis, psychotherapy, and depth psychology more broadly.

The series will feature works of outstanding scholarship and readability, including biographical studies, institutional histories, and archival investigations. New editions of historical classics as well as translations of little-known works from the early history of psychoanalysis will also be considered for inclusion.

ALSO IN THE FREUD MUSEUM LONDON SERIES

Freud's Pandemics: Surviving Global War,
Spanish Flu, and the Nazis
by Brett Kahr

In memory of the late Miss Pearl King (1918–2015),

Distinguished psychoanalyst and historian,

With love and affection and admiration,

To whom I owe much gratitude.

Contents

INTRODUCTION
My Love of Deceased Psychoanalysts   xi

PART I
Sigmund Freud as an Englishman

CHAPTER ONE
"Zooming" in Old Vienna: How Sigmund Freud
Became an English-Speaking Psychoanalyst   3

CHAPTER TWO
Freud's London Death Bed: Notes on the "Invalid Couch"
at Maresfield Gardens   9

PART II
Unpublished Winnicottiana

CHAPTER THREE
Donald Winnicott's Wives: From Alice Buxton Taylor
to Clare Britton   15

CHAPTER FOUR
"The Piggle" Family Papers: Unpublished Archival Gems Regarding Winnicott's Most Iconic Case — 45

PART III
Dr and Mrs Bowlby

CHAPTER FIVE
"Half-Baked Pseudo-Scientific Rubbish": How John Bowlby Reinvented Child Psychiatry — 93

CHAPTER SIX
Ursula Longstaff Bowlby: The Creative Muse of Attachment Theory — 109

PART IV
Two Truly Unassuming Icons

CHAPTER SEVEN
Breakfast with Marion Milner: Reminiscences of the World's Oldest Psychoanalyst — 127

CHAPTER EIGHT
Enid Eichholz Balint: The Birth of Couple Psychoanalysis in England — 155

PART V
The Bad Boys of British Psychoanalysis

CHAPTER NINE
Rajah on the Couch: The Magnificence and Misery of Masud Khan — 179

CHAPTER TEN
R. D. Laing's Missing Tooth: The Secret Roots of Genius and Madness — 207

CONCLUSION
How to Be Intimate with a Corpse: The Role of Psychoanalytical Historiography — 225

Notes — 235
Original Sources of Chapters — 247
Acknowledgements — 255
References — 257
Index — 315

INTRODUCTION

My Love of Deceased Psychoanalysts

As a little boy, I developed a huge obsession with history. Indeed, I spent quite a lot of time memorising the names and dates of all the kings and queens of England; and thus, to my shame, I can still recall that Henry VIII ascended the throne on 21st April, 1509, without having to consult Wikipedia!

Everyone assumed that I would become a geeky, professional historian, and to a certain extent, I have done so. But I also decided at quite a young age that, irrespective of my love for the past, I wished to devote my life to something more immediately impactful, namely, the practice of depth psychology, helping to alleviate the suffering of souls in great distress.

In some respects, while studying psychology and psychotherapy and psychoanalysis, I became, I suppose, what I have come to refer to as a "clinical historian", namely, a historian who does not necessarily peruse the life and times of Henry VIII but, rather, one who delves into the archives of the history of my patients and thus often unearths important and long-forgotten data from the internal filing cabinets of the mind.

As it happened, although I have dedicated the last forty-plus years of my career to the field of mental health, I have never abandoned my love for history. In fact, after I qualified and set up my long-standing clinical practice, I then returned to university in my spare time and completed my formal training in historiography, specialising, in particular, in the medieval and early modern eras. Thus, I would now consider myself both a "clinical historian" and, also, an academic historian in the more traditional sense.

In some ways, I see little difference between the fields of psychoanalysis and history; in fact, I have always regarded psychoanalysis not only as a clinical discipline but, also, as a historical one, with a deeply rich and insufficiently explored past. And, from my undergraduate days as a baby student of psychology, I did my very best to meet and interview as many of the elderly grandees of psychoanalysis as possible, desperate to preserve their priceless memories of the olden days, and eager to learn as much as I could from these extraordinary pioneers.

While still in my mid-twenties, I had managed, somehow, to spend a most memorable afternoon with Professor Sigmund Freud's greatniece, Mrs Anne Marlé, who shared with me a wealth of unpublished stories about the family of this great man. I enjoyed both an extremely pleasant tea and, also, a most delicious supper with Dr John Bowlby, a pioneering child psychiatrist, who reminisced at length about his mentors from the 1930s, and who treated me to a vicious impersonation of his vexing clinical supervisor, Mrs Melanie Klein. And, after taking tea with Mrs Marion Milner, and talking at length with Mrs Enid Balint, and dining with Dr Ronald Laing, I began to embark upon a more focused and more extended research project about the life of one of my most profound heroes, the great child psychiatrist and psychoanalyst, Dr Donald Winnicott. Indeed, over the course of the next several decades, I succeeded in interviewing more than 900 people who knew this man personally, including his loyal and long-standing secretary, Mrs Joyce Coles, who bequeathed to me her unique archive of unpublished Winnicott papers and letters and drawings.

Although I had the privilege of training with a number of truly inspiring and amazing teachers—all eminent psychoanalysts and psychotherapists and psychiatrists and psychologists—I often found my time with those elderly octogenarians and nonagenarians far more engaging and, also, far more instructive than my formal seminars and supervisions with those in their fifties and sixties. Often, I learned more about psychopathology and psychotherapy from imbibing the writings of the early psychoanalysts of the 1910s and 1920s than I did from my own teachers and colleagues. Thus, to my great delight, the study of the history of this profession proved not only a rich research experience, but, moreover, my immersion in the Freudian past gave me a unique education and made me feel so very deeply at home while sitting in my consulting room.

Most of my contemporaries took little interest in the past and I knew no one else of my age who had taken the trouble to meet all of these remarkable personalities or who had studied their unpublished archives. In fact, during my early days as a fledgling researcher, only the late Miss Pearl King, a brilliant psychoanalyst and, also, the founder of the Archives of the British Psycho-Analytical Society, really encouraged me to pursue my historical interests; and, across many decades, she shared her knowledge with me in a most liberal fashion, regaling me with unpublished stories about her own training analyst, Dr John Rickman—one of Professor Sigmund Freud's patients—and, also, with tales of such colourful figures as Mrs Joan Riviere and the hugely controversial Rajah Masud Khan, with whom she had trained in the 1940s.

I absolutely fell in love with each of the elderly psychoanalysts whom I met in person and with the writings of those who had already died. Sadly, all of my ancient mentors have since passed away and I fear that I may well be the only person of my generation to have had personal contact with so many of these extraordinary grandparental figures of the previous eras.

In view of that fact, I have remained determined to pass on as much of the wisdom that I absorbed, not only from my personal encounters with the great and the good but, also, from their archives of papers. And I hope that, by sharing my passion for these ancient figures, I might encourage the next generation of mental health colleagues to benefit from the insights of our founding mothers and founding fathers, as I believe that I have done.

My obsessional interest in the history of psychoanalysis has exposed me to Berlin in the 1920s and 1930s, to Paris in the 1940s and 1950s, and, especially, to Vienna in the 1890s and 1900s and to the study of the early Austrian psychoanalysts who had trained with Freud. But, as someone who has lived most of my life in London, I have also developed a huge interest in the English school of psychoanalysis as well.

And, in the pages that follow, I hope to share a wide range of unknown, hidden stories about different aspects of psychoanalysis in the United Kingdom.

Although Sigmund Freud may have had little do with *British* psychoanalysis *per se*, I have chosen to launch this volume with two very brief essays about some rather tiny, but symbolically important, links to England. In the very first chapter, I will describe the rather unknown fact that, in 1919, Freud engaged an English teacher to help him spruce up his linguistic skills in order to receive patients from both Great Britain and the United States of America. This proved a very helpful decision indeed, as it permitted Freud to revive his flagging clinical practice, hard hit by the ravages of the Great War. I will also consider how Freud helped to foster the psychoanalytical movement in Great Britain through his treatment of such pioneering Englishmen as Dr David Forsyth.

In the following chapter, I shall discuss a much-overlooked detail about Freud's death in London. It will not be widely known that, on 23rd September, 1939, Freud died on a couch … *not* the famous psychoanalytical couch upon which his patients had prostrated themselves for decades but, rather, a very different couch, namely, a death couch or death bed, placed specially in his consulting room, only inches away from his carpet-covered psychoanalytical divan. This chapter will explore Freud's death bed in some detail and will help us to remember that although Freud lived most of his life in the Austrian empire, he did spend his very last months in Great Britain; hence, the story of his death bed does indeed constitute a small, but, nevertheless, interesting moment in the history of British psychoanalysis.

Thereafter, over the course of two chapters, I shall describe the private world of Dr Donald Winnicott, examining how his domestic circumstances impacted upon his professional life. In the first of these studies of little-known Winnicottiana, I will consider the nature of his marriage to Miss Alice Buxton Taylor, a talented, but troubled, woman; and, after chronicling his eventual divorce from his first wife, I shall explore the nature of his subsequent marriage to the social worker, Miss Clare Britton, a much sturdier individual who brought Winnicott far more happiness. In particular, I will investigate whether Winnicott's lengthy personal psychoanalyses with Mr James Strachey and Mrs Joan Riviere had helped him to overcome his wish to rescue an ill woman and thus forge a more mutually satisfying marriage to a stronger partner.

In the second of these Winnicottian essays, I shall reconsider the case of Donald Winnicott's most famous patient, namely, the little girl known as "The Piggle". During the 1990s, I had the privilege of meeting and interviewing "The Piggle" in person and I also engaged in correspondence with the father of "The Piggle" and enjoyed an informative telephone interview and a rich exchange of letters with the mother. In later years, "The Piggle" and her sister kindly permitted me access to their unpublished family archives. I have drawn upon all of these materials in order to help us understand this important and compelling story more fully.

After engaging with Dr Donald Winnicott's divergent marriages and with his remarkably rich and detailed child case history, I will then offer two chapters inspired by Winnicott's younger colleague, the visionary Dr John Bowlby, whom I first met in 1984 and who kindly permitted me to interview him and to engage with him on several subsequent occasions, prior to his death in 1990. In the first of my two Bowlbian essays, I shall describe the horrific way in which so-called experts would treat psychologically troubled children, from medieval times until the early twentieth century. Bowlby, like Winnicott before him, had the courage to challenge some of the cruel methods of neglect and punishment, which characterised much of the ethos of child psychiatry prior to the 1920s and 1930s; and in my historiography of child mental health, I will chronicle how Bowlby contributed hugely to the development of a depth-psychological approach to the treatment of emotional illness in the young.

In the second Bowlbian essay, I will provide an introduction to the great woman behind the great man, namely, Dr Bowlby's devoted spouse, Mrs Ursula Longstaff Bowlby. I first met Mrs Bowlby in 1995, several years after her husband's death, and she welcomed me warmly into the family home and generously shared with me a welter of stories about her marriage, and, also, her reminiscences of some of the early psychoanalysts such as Dr Ernest Jones, as well as Dr Edward Glover, Dr Adrian Stephen, Dr Karin Stephen, and so many more. A woman of tremendous modesty, Ursula Bowlby neglected to tell me about her own informative writings on the psychology of infancy, which I discovered only after her death and which I shall discuss in this survey.

Throughout the remaining chapters, I will provide glimpses into the professional and private lives of three extremely fascinating psychoanalysts from the post-Winnicott, post-Bowlby cohort, namely, Mrs Marion Milner, Mrs Enid Balint, and Rajah Mohammed Masud Raza Khan. I first met Marion Milner at a conference in Cambridge, back in 1985, and I enjoyed my growing friendship with her. She shared a multitude of reminiscences about the early pioneers of British psychoanalysis and offered unique encapsulations of the work of such celebrated figures as Dr Donald Winnicott, as well as vignettes concerning those whose contributions we have now forgotten, such as Mr Anton Ehrenzweig, Dr Margaret Little, and Mr Adrian Stokes. After exploring the life and work of Mrs Milner, I shall then offer an insight into the early years of the wonderfully inspiring Enid Balint, who, as Mrs Enid Eichholz (prior to her marriage to Dr Michael Balint), pioneered the development of couple psychoanalysis in Great Britain. And, after presenting these portraits of both Milner and Balint, I will offer an extremely frank summation of more than sixty unpublished encounters with those individuals who knew the infamous Masud Khan, undoubtedly the most controversial figure in the entire history of psychoanalysis.

I have also provided an account of the memorable day that I spent with none other than Dr Ronald David Laing, back in 1983. Although Laing had trained in London at the Institute of Psycho-Analysis, he always harboured a considerable loathing for many of his teachers, and he eventually removed himself from the formal British psychoanalytical community in order to develop the controversial, but game-changing, anti-psychiatric movement. Although many orthodox Freudians do not regard Laing as a member of the professional family, he does, nevertheless, hold a significant place within the history of British psychoanalysis, not least in view of his work on the meaning of madness; hence, I have included my memories of this genius who, rather like Khan, could also be quite troubling and damaging and, even, at times, somewhat broken.

Thus, across the nine historical cases described in this book, ranging from the brief study of Freud's death bed to the more lengthy examination of "The Piggle", I will reveal some of the hidden tales of British psychoanalysis which deserve to be told and which, I would argue, do *need* to be told. Many of these stories expose the ugly, shadow side of psychoanalytical life. And yet, if we do not discuss these stories and become more conscious of them, and if we fail to understand them, we run the risk of repeating the very errors that our predecessors had made years and years previously. Therefore, I hope that these engagements with Freud and Winnicott and Bowlby and Milner and Balint and Khan and Laing will offer not only some interest and inspiration and, also, some gossip, but, above all, that they will provide younger colleagues with an introduction to these significant figures, thus stimulating, I trust, a fascination with their contributions.

It would certainly please me greatly to know that the individuals featured in these historical essays might furnish us with some fine role models, and, moreover, with a sobering warning about how we might, at times, comport ourselves more sanely.

If I have enjoyed any success during the course of my career, I owe so much of that to my own training analyst, to my clinical supervisors, to my teachers, and to my colleagues within the mental health profession, all of whom have nurtured me and educated me and supported me in a great many ways. Moreover, I must also acknowledge my enormous debt to all of those wonderful pioneering figures, many of whom I have had the privilege of meeting in person and some of whom I have endeavoured to bring to life in the pages which follow.

My love and gratitude to all of the deceased psychoanalysts described herein remains huge, and I warmly encourage others to come to know the older generation and to learn from the incomparable wisdom of our ancestors.

PART I

SIGMUND FREUD AS AN ENGLISHMAN

CHAPTER ONE

"Zooming" in Old Vienna:
How Sigmund Freud Became
an English-Speaking Psychoanalyst

In March, 2020, the deadly coronavirus pandemic erupted on both sides of the Atlantic Ocean and changed our world immeasurably, causing huge disruption and terror and bereavement.

As the infection rate of this shockingly lethal disease skyrocketed with alarming rapidity, each one of us had to readjust our lives, both personally and professionally, in a desperate effort to ensure our physical safety and our psychological health.

After the outbreak of COVID-19, virtually every single mental health professional, myself included, had to alter the very physicality of our daily clinical work. In more normal times, those of us who practise psychoanalysis and psychotherapy would welcome our patients into a quiet, cosy consulting room and invite these men and women and children to sit in a comfy chair or, even, to recline upon the Freudian couch, perched only inches away from our own seat. But once the coronavirus began to spread, each of us had to transform our practices from such in-person intimacy to a more remote method of mental health care.

As someone who has never particularly embraced modern technology, I elected to communicate with my patients on the old-fashioned landline telephone, rather than via the computer. During the apex of the pandemic, I found this to be a surprisingly effective means of persevering with psychological treatment. The telephone certainly provided me and my patients with a successful method of engaging in rich, private conversations, and, in consequence, we could readily listen to one another on the landline with a laser-like intensity.

My more technologically sophisticated colleagues, by contrast, transferred their practices immediately to a laptop and quickly became pioneers of "Zoom psychotherapy" and "Zoom psychoanalysis". Most patients did agree to this new method of online therapeutic work, but many others dropped out of treatment, too exhausted by Zoom fatigue. Many of my fellow colleagues, even the younger ones, complained that, by staring at the screen all day, they had begun to experience unbearable pains and strains in their eyes. Nevertheless, the vast majority of clinicians ultimately found a way to meet their patients regularly and reliably online.

Sigmund Freud, the father of modern psychoanalysis and psychotherapy, died in 1939, long before the invention of the computer and the internet. If he had lived and worked today, I cannot imagine how he would have responded to the sheer fact that his creation of the intimate psychoanalytical conversation has become Zoomified in this way across the planet. Freud might have had to shrug his shoulders and lament that, in the wake of a pandemic, practitioners simply had no other option. But he might also have expressed great sadness that the extremely private and confidential conversations that he had helped to facilitate must now be practised with the assistance of such complicated electrical devices.

It may not be widely appreciated that Sigmund Freud harboured little affection for the technological developments of his time. According to his eldest son, Dr Martin Freud (1957), the father of psychoanalysis did not particularly like the telephone or the typewriter or the radio, or, even, the bicycle. Thus, had he lived through COVID-19, he might well have struggled to adjust to a Zoom platform.

But Freud did have to battle through the *Weltkrieg*—otherwise known as the Great War—and this global catastrophe affected his clinical practice hugely. Many of his patients could no longer afford psychoanalytical treatment, and many had to enlist in the armed services and could not, therefore, attend sessions with Freud on a daily basis. Hence, in the wake of the First World War, Freud and his loved ones suffered financially. And then, just as the war began to end, after more than four years of fighting, the deadly "Spanish flu" blighted our planet in 1918, 1919, and 1920, and devastated many families, claiming somewhere between 50,000,000 and 100,000,000 lives, and, perhaps, even more (e.g., Barry, 2004; Arnold, 2018). In view of these losses, many people struggled simply to stay alive, and few had the energy or the resources to pursue a lengthy, multi-frequency psychoanalysis.

Thus, in the wake of the war and the Spanish flu, Sigmund Freud knew that he would have to transform the very nature of his working day.

And he did so, *not* by installing Zoom, but, rather, by taking English lessons!

By the end of 1918, the world war and the viral pandemic had crushed the Austrian economy almost completely, and few, if any, Viennese could afford Freud's private clinical services. He sensed, and rightly so, that he would have to reconfigure the discipline of psychoanalysis from an exclusively German-language process with local patients to a more international practice for wealthy patients from Great Britain and from the United States of America.

At that time, psychoanalysis had become increasingly well known in English-speaking countries. And both of those Allied nations, winners of the war, had access to far greater monetary resources. Hence, British and American physicians began to write to Freud asking whether they might come to Vienna to train with him and to undergo a short period of psychoanalysis on his famous couch. Freud had no wish to turn down paid work; moreover, he strongly hoped to disseminate his important psychological discoveries worldwide, and thus, he knew that he would have to begin to practise the craft of psychoanalysis *in English*.

As a deeply well-educated man, steeped in the classics, and quite fluent in a range of foreign languages, Sigmund Freud already enjoyed a facility not only for German, his native tongue, but, also, for French and Italian and Spanish, and, additionally, for the ancient languages of Greek and Latin. Moreover, he had already developed a considerable knowledge of English as well, not least in view of the fact that his two elder half-brothers had relocated to Manchester and had offered the young Freud opportunities to visit (Jones, 1953). But, although he could read medical literature in English, he had not spent much time treating *native* English-speaking patients.

Thus, in 1919, Sigmund Freud (1919b) actually engaged an English teacher in order to spruce up his linguistic skills.

Fortunately, he did, indeed, begin to attract foreigners—former "enemies", in fact, from Allied countries—such as Dr David Forsyth, a British physician who specialised in children's medicine, and who came to the Berggasse to undergo a training analysis (Jones, 1919; Freud, 1919c, 1933; cf. Roazen, 2000). Freud offered Forsyth an English-language psychoanalysis, and, in due course, this became an increasingly common procedure among Viennese clinicians, eager to expand their flagging, post-war practices (e.g., Menaker, 1989). The father of psychoanalysis experienced so much gratitude towards Forsyth that, after the arrival of this new patient, Freud instructed Frau Beata Rank, the wife of the psychoanalyst Dr Otto Rank, to host a special dinner party in Forsyth's honour (Roazen, 2000; cf. Roazen, 1990).

We know from Freud's patient calendar (i.e., his clinical appointments diary) that Forsyth commenced treatment on Monday, 6th October, 1919, and attended for six sessions weekly—Mondays through Saturdays inclusive—until Tuesday, 18th November, 1919. In total, he participated in thirty-eight psychoanalytical sessions—a relatively short experience by contemporary standards but by no means unusual at that period of time, especially for foreigners who wished to acquire a taste of Freud (May, 2006, 2007a, 2007b).

Forsyth repaid Freud's kindness and attention with gratitude. Upon his eventual return to London, he became not only a progenitor of psychoanalytically orientated paediatrics, as well as a key early member of the British Psycho-Analytical Society, but, moreover, the author of a very loyal textbook, *The Technique of Psycho-Analysis* (Forsyth, 1922), and, also, an insightful paper on the use of Freudian methods in the understanding of paranoid dementia, published in the prestigious *Proceedings of the Royal Society of Medicine* (Forsyth, 1920).

Having undertaken lessons and having begun to offer foreign-language psychoanalysis proved a most wise strategy because, by October, 1920, fully five of Sigmund Freud's (1920b) nine patients had come to him from English-speaking countries, and many more would follow in due course (e.g., Freud, 1920a; Stern, 1922; Grinker, 1940; Wortis, 1940, 1954; H. D. [Hilda Doolittle], 1945a, 1945b, 1945c, 1945d, 1946, 1956; Eissler, 1952, 1953; Oberndorf, 1953, 1958; Winnicott, 1969b; Blanton,

1971; Khan, 1973; Dorsey, 1976; Kardiner, 1977; Burlingham, 1989; Cameron and Forrester, 1999; Forrester and Cameron, 2017). With deep relief, Freud (1919a, p. 340) could at last begin to see what he described as "The first window opening in our cage".

In fact, after a time, Freud had welcomed so many British and American patients into his consulting room that he often had no free spaces at all and had to refer keen individuals to his more junior colleagues. When the young London-born Mr Lionel Penrose, a budding geneticist, physician, and psychoanalytical enthusiast (and, in years to come, the father of the future Nobel Laureate, Professor Sir Roger Penrose), requested treatment from the founder of psychoanalysis, Freud had to refuse as he simply had no vacancies and, consequently, he referred Penrose to his talented colleague, Dr Siegfried Bernfeld (Roazen, 2000).

Thus, although Freud had crafted psychoanalysis in his native German language, he succeeded in reframing his daily professional life to become an honorary Englishman of sorts, thus filling his practice successfully and managing to support his family. In this way, he transformed his clinical work, much as my colleagues and I have endeavoured to do nowadays by transferring our practices to the telephone or the laptop, with many of us having had to become overnight experts in "Zoom psychoanalysis".

Freud undertook the reconfiguration of his German work into English in large measure to feed his family, but his Anglicisation of psychoanalysis produced very positive side effects. Two of his patients, Mr James Strachey, a Briton, and Mrs Alix Strachey, his American-born wife, became Freud's two most prominent translators, without whom we would never have enjoyed the privilege of immersing ourselves in the twenty-four volume collection of Freud's writings, *The Standard Edition of the Complete Psychological Works of Sigmund Freud*, published between 1953 and 1974 (Freud, 1953a, 1953b, 1953c, 1953d, 1955a, 1955b, 1955c, 1955d, 1957a, 1957b, 1958, 1959a, 1959b, 1960a, 1960b, 1961a, 1961b, 1962, 1963a, 1963b, 1964a, 1964b, 1966, 1974).

Furthermore, Freud had little sense that, by 1938, he and his family would, in due course, have to emigrate from Austria to Great Britain in order to escape the Nazi menace. Thus, one might argue that his English lessons of 1919 might well have proved indispensable on such numerous different fronts.

In the wake of the twenty-first-century coronavirus outbreak, many colleagues and I have had to make a complicated adjustment to our long-established practices, and, moreover, our patients have had to do so as well. Fortunately, most of us seem to have managed with remote therapy across this ongoing pandemic, especially during periods of lockdown restrictions. In fact, once it became apparent that patients need no longer attend the consulting room in person, several of my colleagues had even received referrals from patients who live overseas! In the olden days, if one wished to consult a psychotherapist in London, one actually had to live in the United Kingdom, but, nowadays, with the availability of Zoom and the telephone, the possibilities may well become limitless.

Let us hope that, with the ongoing survival and, moreover, expansion of psychoanalytical work across the world, those of us who continue to honour and practise Freud's legacy might be able to contribute to the improvement of everyone's mental health amid this tragically ugly chapter in world history.

CHAPTER TWO

Freud's London Death Bed: Notes on the "Invalid Couch" at Maresfield Gardens

It may not be widely appreciated that, on Saturday, 23rd September, 1939, Sigmund Freud died, not in a *bed* but, rather, on a *couch*.

Freud did not pass away on the famous psychoanalytical couch but, rather, he did so on a special "invalid couch", installed in his study.

As this less well-known couch has long remained in storage at the Freud Museum London, few psychoanalytical historians have ever seen Sigmund Freud's actual death bed. A close scrutiny of this "other" couch might seem rather fetishistic; nevertheless, it may be of some interest to contemporary psychoanalytical clinicians to learn more about Freud's final moments.

Sigmund Freud arrived in London on 6th June, 1938—a refugee from the Nazis—but he did not take occupancy of 20, Maresfield Gardens, in London's Swiss Cottage, until 27th September, 1938, having spent the previous months in Primrose Hill at 39, Elsworthy Road. In his new home, parallel to the Finchley Road, Freud ensconced himself in the combined consulting room and study on the ground floor, but he slept in a small bedroom on the first floor with *Frau Professor* Martha Freud, his devoted wife. As Sigmund Freud, then eighty-two years of age, struggled to ascend or descend the spacious staircase (Berthelsen, 1987), his son, Dr Ernst Freud, a skilled architect, arranged for the installation of a lift which transported the father of psychoanalysis from one level to the next (Roazen, 1993; cf. Kahr, 2021a).

In spite of his illness, Freud worked vigorously during the final months of 1938 and during much of 1939. He even treated a small number of psychoanalytical patients and he also continued to write. Moreover, Freud spent time lounging in his garden on a special hanging couch. However, as his cancer progressed, he became increasingly necrotic (Schur, 1972). By 1st August, 1939, Freud (1939) ceased clinical practice entirely and, not long thereafter, it became clear that he could no longer be shuttled upstairs in the lift, and that he would have to be cared for full-time in his more spacious and brightly lit, book-lined and antique-strewn study. This extraordinary room had now become a veritable sick bay (Jones, 1957; Schur, 1972).

Dr Ernest Jones (1957, p. 245), Freud's colleague and, ultimately, biographer, noted that the father of psychoanalysis benefited from having his sick bay downstairs, in the study, because it afforded a clear view into the garden and permitted him to gaze at his "beloved flowers"; whereas his upstairs bedroom, by contrast, looked out onto the road. Dr Max Schur (1972, p. 527), Freud's physician, reported that, at one point, in September, 1939—shortly after the eruption of the Second World War—Freud had to be moved to a so-called "safe zone" at Maresfield Gardens, in the centre of his study, thus repositioned away from the large garden windows, which could have shattered dangerously from potential bombings (Young-Bruehl, 1988).

The renowned psychoanalytical couch, which Freud had brought to London from Vienna, and which he had used in his practice for more than fifty years, would not have provided the dying man with sufficient orthopaedic support; hence, the family purchased a special "invalid couch" from J. & A. Carter, a well-known company, based on Great Portland Street in Central London, which specialised in the manufacture of furniture for the aged and the disabled.

J. & A. Carter supplied the Freud household with a suitable invalid couch, some 224.5 centimetres in length, 54 centimetres in height, and 77 centimetres in width, consisting of a dark, mahogany frame with turned feet, and an upholstered base attached to the upper side of the frame. This special invalid couch, one of the manufacturer's many types of patient furniture, also contained a special ratchet which permitted the head end to be lifted. Freud's new bed boasted a silk-trimmed seat and a cotton fabric covering, decorated with a floral pattern, and trimmed with blue, pink, and green silken cords on the seat and on the back.

The firm of J. & A. Carter, originally established in London circa 1880 by one John Carter, had become one of the leading suppliers of patient furniture, manufacturing not only invalid beds and chairs and appliances but, also, hospital surgical furniture, bath chairs, and, even, ambulances. Headquartered initially at 6A, New Cavendish Street, John Carter's company, which eventually came to receive a royal warrant, also produced revolving bed-tables, wheelchairs, invalid carriages, hand-lifters, stretchers, and perambulators. Furthermore, Carter created a patented "literary machine"—essentially a bookstand designed to help reduce the orthopaedic strain on Victorian scholars who had become fatigued from holding heavy tomes! In due time, John Carter amalgamated his business with that of Messrs. Alfred Carter of Holborn Viaduct and Shoe Lane, and they eventually came to trade as Messrs Carter and, later, as J. & A. Carter.

The particular type of invalid couch, which had now come to serve as Sigmund Freud's bed, had first become popular during the Regency period; and from the 1830s onwards, it would be fitted with springs and other mechanisms, which allowed for the adjustment of the patient's bodily position (cf. Kravis, 2017).

We do not know precisely when Freud moved into his study full-time and lay upon his invalid couch but, in all likelihood, he did so only a few weeks before his death. Sadly, at that time, the genius physician and psychoanalyst began to experience some memory loss (Roazen, 1995) as well as tremendous bodily pain from his long-standing carcinoma. Tragically, Freud's bones became more and more foetid and emitted a putrefying odour which frightened his beloved chow (Jones, 1957) and, also, attracted countless flies; consequently, his attendants had to cover his makeshift invalid bed with mosquito netting (Schur, 1972).

As all Freud scholars will know, during his final days, he read Honoré de Balzac's novel, *La Peau de chagrin: Roman philosophique*, in the original French, in an edition published in Vienna (Balzac, n.d. [1920])—a book about a man whose skin begins to decompose. As Freud remarked to his physician, Dr Max Schur, "This was the proper book for me to read; it deals with shrinking and starvation" (quoted in Schur, 1972, p. 528).

Illustration 1 Professor Sigmund Freud's death bed at 20, Maresfield Gardens, Swiss Cottage, London, reproduced by courtesy of the Freud Museum London.

In spite of his progressive emaciation and his excruciating pain, Freud bore his final days with fortitude. Indeed, his sister-in-law Minna Bernays remarked that a more ordinary man might already have killed himself by this point (Roazen, 1993).

Eventually, in the small hours of the morning of 23rd September, 1939, the eighty-three-year-old Sigmund Freud, assisted by an injection of morphine, died on his invalid couch, only a few feet away from the more famous carpeted and cushioned psychoanalytical couch.

To this day, Sigmund Freud's death bed or invalid couch remains in the possession of the Freud Museum London, carefully preserved in a small upstairs storage room, which also contains the many boxes of archived papers of both Sigmund Freud and Anna Freud. This precious piece of furniture—catalogue item LDFRD 4902—will, perhaps, one day be displayed to members of the general public. In the meanwhile, we must extend our thanks to the curatorial staff of the museum for permitting the publication of a photograph of this hugely resonant, even iconic, "other" couch—possibly the first time that such an image has appeared in print (see Illustration 1).

PART II

UNPUBLISHED WINNICOTTIANA

CHAPTER THREE

Donald Winnicott's Wives: From Alice Buxton Taylor to Clare Britton

A Syllabus Without Winnicott

Many years ago, as a young trainee at the Tavistock Marital Studies Institute (subsequently renamed as the Tavistock Centre for Couple Relationships and then, more recently, as Tavistock Relationships), I enjoyed the privilege of learning the art of couple psychotherapy from our nation's most clinically sophisticated specialist practitioners. I worked extremely hard during this training, and I did my best to develop a clinical muscle in order to engage with some very deeply troubled and traumatised couples.

Although I received tuition and clinical supervision from many of the United Kingdom's couple psychoanalytical superstars, I must confess that our reading seminars left something to be desired. Each week, we pored over papers written predominantly—almost exclusively—by Melanie Klein and her followers, but we *never* had the opportunity to explore a single essay by Donald Winnicott! This might seem rather strange to current-day students, in view of Winnicott's undisputed celebrity status within the psychoanalytical canon; but, back in the old days, the Tavistock Clinic, then home to the marital department, adopted an almost exclusively Kleinian emphasis, and many of its practitioners regarded Winnicott as rather a suspicious character who had dared to develop his own ideas. Indeed, it will not be widely known that, although Winnicott occasionally delivered guest lectures at the Tavistock Clinic during the 1950s and 1960s, he failed to receive the staff appointment for which he had applied (Dicks, 1970; cf. Kahr, 2023b).

Fortunately, in spite of the dearth of Winnicottian input on our course, I had already discovered the works of this great man quite independently, having benefited from a training analysis with one of Winnicott's protégés. Hence, in spite of the fact that my fellow trainees and I never studied Winnicott formally as part of the curriculum, I did, happily, develop a fascination for his work and, also, for his personal and professional life; and in 1996, I published the first biography of this heroic figure (Kahr, 1996a), whose contributions remain of the deepest interest to me.

The lack of tuition about Winnicottiana saddens me greatly because, even though Donald Winnicott never worked as a "couple psychoanalyst" or "couple psychotherapist" *per se*, he not only had more experience of consulting with parental couples than any other psychoanalyst in world history—having interviewed some 40,000 mothers and fathers over a long clinical lifetime (Winnicott, 1948b)[1]—but, moreover, his theories about a whole range of subjects have much to teach contemporary couple mental health professionals (as well as those who specialise in other branches of psychological practice).

In the context of a brief communication, one cannot in any way do justice to the myriad Winnicottian concepts which might be instructive for couple and family mental health workers. To hint at but a few examples, I have certainly enjoyed considerable honorary supervision from Winnicott (1960a, 1962f, 1963b, 1963h) by drawing upon his notions of dependency, as applied to couples, especially as we consult with so many fused and merged partners who often function more like mothers and absolutely dependent babies rather than as two sexually mature adults. Similarly, I have derived significant inspiration from Winnicott's (1955a, 1956a, 1960b) concepts of the true self and false self, aware that most couples spend a great deal of time pretending to be devoted and affectionate in both public and private settings when, in fact, each member often wishes to murder the other, and neither believes himself or herself to be inhabiting an honest and authentic marriage. And, of course, Winnicott's (1949b) incomparable notion of hate in the countertransference has proved to be especially helpful, as every couple practitioner must navigate the sadistic rage which often emerges in sessions (and which will be directed, frequently, towards the psychotherapist). Indeed, each of us must, somehow, find a way to contain and to process our hostile feelings—often projections of the patients' hostilities—rather than retaliate against the couple in an unconscious way. Thus, Winnicott has provided us with a cornucopia of clinical and theoretical writings which have the capacity to enlighten us and to support us as we endeavour to practise this challenging branch of psychotherapeutic work.

Over the last thirty years or more, I have devoted a considerable amount of time not only to a careful scrutiny of Winnicott's plethora of books and papers but, also, to his private and professional biographical journey. I have now read through the hundreds of thousands of pages of his unpublished correspondence and related documents in archives on both sides of the Atlantic Ocean, and I enjoyed the privilege of having interviewed nearly 1,000 people who knew Winnicott personally, ranging from family members and friends to colleagues and patients. Thus, as a couple mental health practitioner, I have learned a great deal about the marital relationship not only from having studied Winnicott's publications but, also, from having investigated his two private marriages.

In the pages that follow, I shall endeavour to share some highlights of this hitherto unknown biographical research about the domestic life of Donald Winnicott in the hope of discovering whether a careful immersion into the psychodynamics of his marital history may be of value to those of us who still have much to learn about the complexities of the spousal relationship. By reviewing what I have come to learn about his first marriage to Alice Buxton Taylor, which ended painfully in divorce and sadness, and about his second marriage to Clare Britton, which proved infinitely more gratifying, I will attempt to address a key question of unconscious marital choice, namely, *why* did Winnicott wed *these* particular women? I shall also explore the vital question as to whether Winnicott's extensive experience of personal psychoanalysis impacted upon him sufficiently and permitted him to learn from bitter life events.

The First Mrs Winnicott

On the morning of Saturday, 7th July, 1923, Dr Donald Woods Winnicott had every good reason to be jubilant. This young, attractive man had grown up in a prosperous family, in the peaceful, bucolic town of Plymouth,[2] on the coast of the county of Devon, doted upon by innumerable family members and servants. He had received a premier education at the Leys School, a private Wesleyan Methodist boarding school, followed by undergraduate studies at Jesus College in the University of Cambridge—one of the most venerable, long-standing educational institutions in the world. Thereafter, he completed his training as a physician at St. Bartholomew's Hospital Medical College in London—the oldest and most prestigious of Great Britain's medical colleges. As a "Bart's man", Winnicott would be assured of a rich career as a medical practitioner. Indeed, in 1923, not long after qualification, he obtained his first permanent post as Assistant Physician at the Paddington Green Children's Hospital in West London and would soon open a private office on Weymouth Street, near Harley Street, the epicentre of the nation's elite medical district. Above all, Winnicott had survived the Great War intact, with no physical injuries, in spite of having served on the naval destroyer HMS *Lucifer* (Kahr, 1996a), in which capacity he experienced active combat over several months (Clare Winnicott, 1978).[3]

Whether Winnicott paused on that July morning in 1923 to reflect upon his multiple good fortunes, while fixing his starched collar and tie, or while donning his tailcoat with a boutonnière, one cannot say. But it would not be unreasonable to suspect that he awoke full of excitement, before heading towards the parish church in Frensham, in the county of Surrey, where, later that day, he would marry his fiancée, Miss Alice Buxton Taylor—a good-looking woman with a most fetching, twinkly smile. A brilliantly intelligent natural scientist, and one of the first female graduates of the University of Cambridge, Miss Taylor also painted and sculpted with a high degree of skill and, moreover, wrote delightful poems and short stories. In many respects, this Renaissance woman epitomised the very essence of playfulness and creativity.

Although we know nothing of the bride's state of mind on that summer morning, Alice Taylor, too, may have enjoyed a private moment of triumph, not only for having become engaged to a handsome and promising young doctor but, even more so, for having found *any* husband *at all*, in view of the fact that a very substantial number of the men of her generation had died during the Great War. Indeed, both of Donald Winnicott's sisters, Violet and Kathleen—chronological contemporaries of Miss Taylor—remained lifelong spinsters, unable to attract male spouses, in spite of their tremendously pleasant personalities and their family wealth. Thus, finding a husband in 1923 often represented quite a remarkable achievement.

Viewing the rare photograph of the wedding party which survives, bequeathed to me by Alice Winnicott's family many years ago, one cannot help but smile with delight at the numerous happy faces. Donald Winnicott and his new bride each beam with considerable glee, as do so many of the relatives and friends who surround the young couple as a safe and protective cordon. The wedding portrait brims with privilege, not only monetary wealth, but, of greater importance, with what we would now refer to as psychological wealth. Indeed, the newly married Dr Winnicott and Mrs Winnicott stood on the brink of a glittering future.

I have endeavoured, thus far, to provide a snapshot of the newly married couple, based solely on confirmable, documentable facts. Donald Winnicott did, indeed, hail from a bountiful Devonian family, son of a former mayor of Plymouth who also owned one of the town's most successful businesses. In fact, Winnicott grew up in a vast home with a garden so huge that it consisted of no fewer than four separate levels (Clare Winnicott, 1978). And he did study at an exclusive boarding school followed by a studentship at an ancient university, and then, after a short stint in the navy, he matriculated to a prestigious medical school. Alice Winnicott, too, had studied at the University of Cambridge—at Newnham College—and had already begun to produce a copious number of appealing works of art in multiple media. Their public selves could not be bettered.

And yet, as every practising psychoanalyst or psychotherapist will appreciate, the image of the smiling Dr and Mrs Winnicott captured in their wedding-day picture—though seemingly quite genuine—reveals only a *part* of the story. Decades later, Donald Winnicott (1955a, p. 16) would, quite famously, introduce the notion of the "false self" into the canon of psychoanalysis—a concept which he developed in apposition to that of the "true self" (Winnicott, 1955a, p. 16). Naturally, one cannot help but wonder whether the wedding portrait represents the true marital selves of Donald and Alice, or whether each spouse simply imported his and her best false self for the photographer? In other words, every couple mental health worker must maintain the possibility that these seemingly blissful newlyweds might have struggled, or would come to struggle, with quite a considerable shadow side.

As marital psychotherapists will appreciate only too acutely, many, if not most, of the clients who consult with us will present themselves as impressive people by *day*—working as doctors, or accountants, or actors, or bankers, or parents—often quite successfully so—but, in due course, they will reveal their less impressive, more traumatised parts, which often manifest only at *night*, in the privacy of the sitting room or the bedroom. As couple psychotherapy unfolds, we invariably hear stories of spousal infidelity, of sexual addictions, of emotional betrayal, of psychological misattunement, of profound disappointment and, even, of physical violence. In fact, over the years, I have worked with numerous couples who lament at the very outset of the first consultation session, "If you met him at a party, you would think he was the most lovable, charming, amazing man. But he treats *me* like rubbish," or "If you met her socially, you would be completely captivated. Everyone loves her. But she treats *me* like a fucking piece of shit."

Couple psychotherapy and couple psychoanalysis did not exist as formal disciplines in Great Britain in 1923. Freudian practitioners would, from time to time, offer parallel, but separate, treatment sessions for husbands and wives. For instance, the Englishman, Mr James Strachey, and his American-born wife, Mrs Alix Sargant-Florence Strachey, underwent psychoanalysis with Professor Sigmund Freud in Vienna during the early 1920s; but each party attended for separate sessions in Freud's consulting room on the Berggasse at different times of day (e.g., Roazen, 1995). To the best of our knowledge, Freud never treated both Stracheys in the same room at the same time. Several of the couples who worked with Freud in this arrangement, which automatically split the two partners, either gravitated towards divorce or ended up in a state of emotional stagnation (cf. Kahr, 2017a).

But, if modern-day, Tavistock-style couple psychotherapy—in which two spouses attend for the very same session—*had* existed in England in 1923, and if Dr and Mrs Winnicott *had* agreed to a joint consultation, one must wonder what private information might have emerged? Indeed, what do we know about Donald Winnicott's marriage, about his capacities as a spouse, and about his most private sexual thoughts and his deeper inner world?

In many respects, it would be absolutely foolhardy to attempt a reconstruction of the marital dynamics of this couple, never having met either of these rich and engaging people, as Alice Winnicott died in 1969, and Donald Winnicott passed away not long thereafter in 1971. But, in spite of the fact that I had no direct, first-hand experience of the Winnicotts, I have, over the last forty years, interviewed a very large number of individuals who did, in fact, know Donald Winnicott personally—including many of his colleagues, his patients, his family members, his private secretary, and even his tailor, as well as his cardiologist. Far fewer of these men and women knew Alice Winnicott, but quite a number of them had, indeed, met her and knew her extremely well, not least two of her nephews and two of her nieces, each of whom provided copious memories and, sometimes, plentiful archival materials about the personal life of the first Mrs Winnicott. Furthermore, I have had the privilege of studying hundreds of thousands of pages of family letters and other documentation preserved in various archives—both public and private—including a rare cache of Donald's correspondence with Alice.

Thus, on the basis of this extensive research, both oral historical and archival, I shall now attempt to offer a fuller portrait of the intimate marital life of Donald Winnicott, exploring some questions which, I hope, may be of relevance to the contemporary couple psychoanalytical practitioner.

If Donald and Alice walked into the headquarters of Tavistock Relationships today, I suspect that most of the staff clinicians would be extremely impressed by their warm demeanour, by their significant professional capacities in their respective fields of psychoanalysis and art, and by their well-mannered graciousness of character. But as the sessions unfolded, it would not be unreasonable to suspect that the false selves of these two talented spouses would, eventually, begin to crumble, allowing their true selves to be revealed more fully over time.

But what, precisely, might have emerged? What do we know about Donald Winnicott's first marriage?

After their wedding in 1923, the Winnicotts established a home in Surbiton, in the county of Surrey, on the outskirts of London, a town to which Donald referred, with characteristic playfulness, as "Suburbiton" (quoted in Kahr, 1996e). Although he and Alice created a pleasant life together and often played music together, Donald also abandoned his wife quite frequently, travelling into London not five but, rather, six days per week, in order to engage in his medical work with ill children and their families.

Although Winnicott boasted an impressive curriculum vitae as a Cambridge and Bart's graduate, just beneath that surface, he did, I strongly suspect, struggle with great shame. It will not be widely known or appreciated that Winnicott had barely eked his way through medical training. First of all, he undertook his pre-clinical undergraduate studies at the University of Cambridge between 1914 and 1917, during which time a great many of the senior teachers had enlisted in the fighting forces; thus, as a young student, Donald Winnicott had access to merely a reduced pre-medical curriculum, delivered under the most horrifically deprivational and terrifying of wartime circumstances. Furthermore, although medical students did receive exemption from military service during the early days of the Great War, many of the hardier young men joined up, nevertheless. Thus, one wonders whether Winnicott experienced a sense of inadequacy and insufficiency for not having received a robust training in the sciences and for not having served his country as virtually all of his classmates did, many of whom then lost their lives in combat (Stirland, 1963; Howard and Houghton, 1991; Kahr, 1996a). Inadequately educated during these appalling wartime conditions, Winnicott did not engage with his studies in a satisfactory manner, and he graduated with only a third-class degree (*Cambridge University Reporter*, 1917).

Towards the very end of the war, Donald Winnicott enlisted as a temporary probationer surgeon in the Royal Naval Volunteer Reserve, but he did so for only a few short months, before progressing to St. Bartholomew's Hospital Medical College. Although clearly sufficiently adept to have received a place at this premier institution, he soon found himself outclassed in every respect by the many brainbox medical trainees who overshadowed him. With classmates such as Christopher Andrewes, a future virologist of note, who would also become both a Fellow of the Royal Society and, additionally, a Knight Bachelor, Winnicott did not distinguish himself at all from an academic perspective; indeed, according to hospital records, he never received a single prize or merit or distinction of any kind. Once again, he simply ambled through his studies with unremarkable, albeit passable, results. And while the other contemporaries often published serious medical contributions in the *St. Bartholomew's Hospital Journal* (e.g., Andrewes, 1921), Donald Winnicott, by contrast, produced merely a handful of poems and other ditties (e.g., Winnicott, 1918a, 1918b, 1919). Furthermore, during his tenure as a medical student, Winnicott (1949c) spent approximately three months on one of the wards at St. Bartholomew's Hospital as a *patient*, suffering from an extremely serious mediastinal pleurisy—possibly a result of the Spanish flu pandemic—which interrupted his studies hugely and which may have dented his confidence and his sense of bodily potency (Kahr, 2020c, 2021c, 2021d, 2021e).

In view of his meagre, barely good-enough performance, it soon became clear that he would never receive patronage from either the leading specialists in internal medicine or in surgery—then considered the apex of British medicine—and, consequently, he had no alternative but to embrace a much-neglected and much-denigrated speciality, namely, that of children's medicine. Although the United Kingdom now provides highly impressive clinical services for young people, facilitated by the Royal College of Paediatrics and Child Health, during Winnicott's tenure at St. Bartholomew's Hospital, children rarely received medical treatment in hospitals as most parents simply could not afford the fees in the era preceding the creation of socialised health care. At that time, Great Britain did not boast a royal college for the study and treatment of sick children; indeed, British physicians did not even use the word "paediatrics". During the 1910s and 1920s, many English medical practitioners considered this term to be a vulgar Americanism. Instead, those few men who undertook service in children's hospitals referred to themselves as physicians in children's medicine rather than as paediatricians (e.g., Winnicott, 1937; Cameron, 1955; cf. Royal Society of Medicine, Section of Paediatrics and Child Health: Symposium on the History of Paediatrics 2000, 2000).

To compound matters, Winnicott embraced not only one of the least glamorous areas of medicine, but he also began to pursue private readings in an even more seemingly bizarre form of medical practice, namely, psychoanalysis. Winnicott's tutor in psychiatry, Sir Robert Armstrong-Jones (1917, p. 216), lambasted Freudian psychoanalysis as a "repulsive" Jewish psychology fit only for Austrians and certainly not for Britons. Perhaps Armstrong-Jones' absolute condemnation of depth psychology had piqued Winnicott's curiosity or had even excited his mischievous fervour and, gradually, the young medical student began to explore psychoanalysis in his spare time. Thus, as someone who chose to specialise in children's medicine, and as someone who admitted to a growing interest in Freudian psychology, Winnicott did *not*, for the most part, inspire confidence among the senior physicians of the era. And when, in 1923, Winnicott finally set up in practice, he had few, if any, private patients, as his colleagues had not yet come to respect him significantly; thus, to avoid being shamed by the porter at his private medical office on Weymouth Street, Winnicott would actually pay some of his impecunious hospital patients to travel to his consulting room so that he could hold up his head with pride (Clare Winnicott, 1978).

Thus, although Donald Winnicott seemed to enjoy a life of medical privilege on the outside, just beneath the surface he struggled with a sense of professional impotency, reminding one of the famously chilling riddle: "What do you call a man who graduated at the bottom of his medical school class? A doctor!"

A sense of inadequacy dogged Winnicott not only in the workplace but, also, in his marriage to Alice Winnicott, because, as I have come to learn from interviews with family members, he simply could not penetrate his wife sexually. Whether Winnicott had actually attempted to engage in copulation and failed, or whether Alice had resolutely refused him access to her body, we certainly do not know. But, according to the reminiscences of several of Alice's relatives, the Winnicotts slept in separate bedrooms (Kahr, 1995e, 1996e), and Alice confessed to at least one family member that she had never, ever, experienced sexual intercourse and that she would die a virgin (Kahr, 1995f).

In a state of desperation in both his professional and private lives, Winnicott craved assistance, and thus, already quite familiar with the potentialities of psychoanalysis from his copious readings, he arranged for a consultation with Dr Ernest Jones, the founding President of the British Psycho-Analytical Society and, also, Freud's leading disciple in London. In a little-known, virtually forgotten radio interview, Winnicott actually reminisced about his first meeting with Dr Jones, claiming that the Welsh-born psychoanalyst understood his "illness" rather well (quoted in Jones and Ferris, 1959). Indeed, when describing Jones, many years later, Winnicott (1968c) recalled that, "Ernest Jones had the largest desk I have ever seen", a reflection, no doubt, of Winnicott's admiration of Jones' huge potency and sense of command. In view of these comments, and of the long-standing professional relationship which would ensue between these two men over the next thirty-four years or more (e.g., Jones, 1944; Kahr, 2023b), it would not be unreasonable to suspect that Jones provided Winnicott with a very helpful experience, and that he earned Winnicott's gratitude for having encouraged the younger man to embark upon a course of full psychoanalysis—then practised six days weekly, from Monday to Saturday inclusive—in Gordon Square, in the heart of Bloomsbury, Central London, with the newly qualified James Strachey, freshly returned from his own apprenticeship in Vienna with Sigmund Freud.

Winnicott's analysis on Strachey's couch proved to be a very rich and sustaining experience; indeed, he would remain in treatment for no less than ten years—a length of time virtually unheard of in the 1920s and 1930s. Sadly, in spite of the affection and dedication which both analyst and analysand shared during this lengthy process, Strachey did breach Winnicott's confidence on multiple occasions and described some of the intimate details of Winnicott's analysis to his own wife, Alix Strachey. From the correspondence which has survived, we know that James Strachey communicated to his wife about Winnicott's inability to engage in copulation. In fact, Alix Strachey, then resident in Berlin, Germany, undergoing personal analysis with Dr Karl Abraham, actually wrote to her husband, enquiring about the progress of Winnicott's treatment. She even dared to wonder whether this young man might ever "f-ck his wife all of a sudden" (Alix Strachey,[4] 1924, p. 166). In view of James Strachey's own extensive history of homosexuality during his youth—having indulged in "obscene loves" (Stephen, 1909, p. 63; cf. Sherman, 1983; Deacon, 1985)—one cannot help but wonder whether Alix Strachey's curiosity about penetrativity referred solely to Donald and Alice.

Assuming that Winnicott had, in fact, told Strachey the truth about his sexless marriage, how can we come to understand this situation?

Those of us who work with sexually troubled and anaesthetised spouses might well be able to offer a multitude of hypotheses as to the reasons why couples become asexual. Perhaps one or other of them had struggled with homosexual impulses and fantasies as a result of particular early parental identifications and hence experienced little or no heterosexual desire. Perhaps one or other of them had suffered from bodily maltreatment or abuse which made the sight of exposed and vulnerable genitalia deeply frightening. Perhaps one or other member of the couple became burdened by unresolved Oedipal attractions and experienced a deep unconscious sense of loyalty towards a revered parental figure which prevented any spousal intimacy.

It would, of course, be irresponsibly presumptuous to do more than speculate as to why Donald and Alice could not copulate; consequently, I must underscore that we cannot possibly know the full reason, or reasons, for the failure of Donald and Alice Winnicott to have done so.

Although the inability to engage in a penetrative sexual relationship would evoke strong concerns among those of us living in the twenty-first century, during the 1920s—approximately one hundred years ago—the sexless marriage proved by no means unusual, as many religious, post-Victorian Britons regarded physical intimacy as both unclean and, also, as un-Christian, giving rise to a widespread phenomenon of unconsummated marriages (Friedman, 1962).

Perhaps a richer investigation of the early life of Alice Buxton Taylor Winnicott might help us to appreciate more fully what apprehensions and fears she might have brought to the marital bed at 89, Ditton Hill Road, in Surbiton, Surrey. On the surface, Alice seemed to have it all. A bright woman, skilled in both the sciences and the arts, she had held a research post at the National Physical Laboratory in Teddington, Middlesex, during the Great War (*Newnham College Register: 1871–1950. Volume I. 1871–1923*, 1963), where she undertook important work on optical glass (Pyatt, 1983), which would be used in the manufacture of rangefinders and other types of essential wartime equipment (Magnello, 2000). An excellent painter and potter who played the recorder and who enjoyed socialising, she seemed, at least on the surface, an ideal spouse.

Although quite competent, if not gifted, as a scientist, Alice Winnicott had suffered tremendously in her private life. Her father, Professor John Taylor, an extremely distinguished gynaecological surgeon and, also, a religious fanatic, may have terrorised his children. Professor Taylor (1894c, p. 344) specialised in the treatment of carcinoma of the vulva and other forms of "fatal vulvo-vaginal disease" as well as syphilitic elephantiasis of the vulva, and he wrote numerous medical papers on genital cancers and upon their surgical extraction (e.g., Taylor, 1894a, 1894b, 1894c, 1895). One can readily imagine a literate, intellectually curious girl such as Alice stumbling upon her father's papers and photographs in his study, and one cannot help but wonder whether her understanding of the female genitalia of adult women thus became a fearful one—something disease-ridden, waiting to be cut with a knife. Perhaps Alice even experienced her husband Donald—also a doctor—as having a knife-like penis which could inflict some horrific damage upon her. Although one of John Taylor's three daughters, Mary Taylor, did marry and did produce children, the other two did not, and Alice became a lifelong virgin, while her sister, Pauline Taylor, known widely as "Paul", became lesbian, and avoided any contact with the male genitalia entirely.

Not only might Professor Taylor have intimidated his daughter due to his devotion to gynaecological surgery but, moreover, he and his wife, Mrs Florence Maberly Taylor, failed to provide a model of couple unity for their children, as Professor Taylor elected to share a house with his own sister, rather than cohabit with his wife and five children (Kahr, 1995e).

In addition to her fears of genitalia and, furthermore, her possible loathing of sex, Alice had other struggles as well. As a young researcher at the National Physical Laboratory, she suffered a significant head injury when struck by a large metal pendulum (Taylor, 1941; Bradshaw, 1996). Although we have no proper neuroimaging data about the precise nature of her condition, we do know that she began to experience narcolepsy sometime thereafter which may, or may not, have resulted from the head trauma. But, as time progressed, she also began to hallucinate and to suffer from obsessional states of mind. Indeed, according to several witnesses, Alice Winnicott would imagine that she could see and hear the famous military officer and adventurer Thomas Edward Lawrence—better known as "Lawrence of Arabia"—in her bedroom (Kahr, 1995e).

Thus, in spite of Alice's many lovable and admirable qualities, she also had the capacity to become mentally and physically absent and distracted on innumerable occasions, giving rise to accusations of being dotty (Kahr, 1996e) or, indeed, fully mentally ill (e.g., Khan, 1987). According to Alice Buxton Taylor Winnicott's nephew, the late Professor Anthony Bradshaw, she drove her family "completely and utterly mad" (quoted in Kahr, 1995e; cf. Kahr, 1996c).

What drew Donald Winnicott to a woman of so much strength, ability, and intelligence but, also, such fragility, at the very same time?

As it happens, both of Winnicott's parents could be described as simultaneously potent and, also, impotent. Donald's father, Frederick Winnicott, ran a successful business, became mayor of Plymouth twice, and fathered two daughters and a son, while also devoting considerable time and energy to the Wesleyan Methodist church. His wife, Elizabeth Winnicott, proved to be the ideal consort to her mayor husband and attended innumerable official functions and, even, set up a support group for local mothers and their children. But, after hours, Frederick Winnicott struggled with learning difficulties, never having received a formal education, and this remained an area of great sensitivity (Winnicott, n.d.). In similar vein, Elizabeth Winnicott suffered with her own distress and seems to have succumbed to intermittent depressions, prompting her son Donald to recall her as "weeping / weeping / weeping" (Winnicott, 1963j, p. 29) during his childhood (cf. Winnicott, 1963k). In view of Elizabeth Winnicott's fight against depression, the young Donald Winnicott may have experienced his mother as having a psychological head injury of sorts, just as his future spouse, Alice, also had a head injury, albeit of a different type.

On a conscious level, Donald chose Alice as a woman from a similar social class, professional background, and educational milieu, whom he found physically pleasing, intellectually stimulating, and playfully entertaining. Consciously, she proved the perfect candidate. Unconsciously perhaps, he had selected a symbolic version of a parent, both stable and fragile at once, prompting us to speculate that Donald gravitated towards Alice in order to fulfil what Freud (1910, p. 396) would have referred to as a *"Rettungsphantasie"*—a "rescue phantasy"—of becoming the doctor to his own ill mother. While Winnicott could not cure Elizabeth, Lady Winnicott, of her depression, or of the catarrhal pulmonary illness which finally claimed her life at the age of sixty-three years, he may well have wished, perhaps, that he could help Alice, victim of a head injury and, moreover, of a frightening father. Alice may well have found Donald's status as a medical man quite appealing, hopeful that he might become the safe version of the doctor whose scalpel would never eviscerate her vulva.

Throughout the 1920s and the 1930s, Alice and Donald did, to the very best of our knowledge, remain loyal to one another, in spite of the complete sexual anaesthesia which had become institutionalised between them. Nevertheless, as the years unfolded, both Dr and Mrs Winnicott began to abandon one another physically and emotionally. Winnicott completed his ten-year analysis with James Strachey and, also, his intensive training in both adult psychoanalysis and child psychoanalysis at the Institute of Psycho-Analysis in London, and he became increasingly active within the British Psycho-Analytical Society as a committee member and as a frequent scientific contributor. His pioneering work on the interface between paediatrics and psychoanalysis and, also, his contributions to the development of psychoanalytical child psychiatry, as well as to the practice of adult psychoanalysis, became so profound and popular that he received many invitations to lecture, both nationally and internationally. Winnicott even held the distinction of having become the first psychoanalyst in Great Britain to broadcast regularly on the radio (e.g., Winnicott, 1949a; cf. Kahr, 2015d, 2018, 2023a). Consequently, he arranged his life in such a way that he had very little time for his wife.

Alice, too, became successful in business, and she opened up her own pottery in Kent and soon began to manufacture earthenware which she sold to some of the largest shops in London, such as Heal and Son on Tottenham Court Road. Collectively, the Winnicotts began to lead loyal but, in fact, quite parallel—even separate—private lives.

Across the 1930s, in particular, Donald Winnicott's professional potency grew by leaps and bounds. Having begun his career with a notion of himself as a marginal physician, working in a very unpopular, denigrated area of clinical practice, he eventually progressed to become a leader within the burgeoning field of psychoanalysis. Though his old colleagues in medicine and surgery did not rate his psychoanalytical contributions at all during that point in history, the members of the international Freudian community certainly did, and Winnicott soon came to occupy a place of enormous privilege, renowned for his theoretical brilliance, his vast clinical experience with children, and his compelling public lecturing style. Indeed, it will not be fully appreciated that the child psychoanalytical training at the Institute of Psycho-Analysis and the treatment of young people at the London Clinic of Psycho-Analysis flourished almost entirely because of Winnicott, as virtually all of the patients who attended for treatment did so upon his recommendation, owing to the fact that Winnicott had numerous cases to refer through his position at the Paddington Green Children's Hospital. Thus, although completely undistinguished as a medical student at Jesus College in the University of Cambridge and at St. Bartholomew's Hospital Medical College, Winnicott had, at last, acquired a more profound sense of capability, fuelled, in large measure, as a result of a very lengthy and stable analysis with James Strachey.

By the 1940s, Winnicott, no doubt sexually frustrated, had begun to test his newfound psychological potency with other women, and he became extremely flirtatious and seductive with his secretary, "Mrs Gladys Watson-Dixon",[5] and with at least one of his colleagues, Mrs Marion Milner, who developed a huge erotic attraction towards him, which he inflamed, not least when he became her psychoanalyst and treated her, *not* in his consulting room on Queen Anne Street in Central London but, rather, in her own home on Provost Road in Chalk Farm (Kahr, 2011, 2015a, 2023b). Although once a rather undistinguished member of the medical community at St. Bartholomew's Hospital, Donald Winnicott had since become arguably one of the more outstanding people within the British psychoanalytical establishment. Although Dr John Bowlby (1951a) would soon come to rival, if not surpass, Winnicott in terms of international impact through impressive work commissioned by the World Health Organization in the early 1940s, Bowlby had not yet achieved the extent of the prominence which lay in wait; hence, of his generation, Winnicott certainly held pride of place.

During the Second World War, Winnicott worked as a Consultant Psychiatrist to the Government Evacuation Scheme in Oxfordshire and Berkshire, helping to care for emotionally ill children who had to flee from London to avoid the *Blitzkrieg*. In that context, he met an extremely compelling young social worker, Miss Clare Britton, with whom he came to collaborate increasingly closely. Miss Irmi Elkan (1995), a child care officer who later became a psychoanalyst, recalled seeing Donald and Clare together during the war years, and could appreciate at once the smouldering attraction between the married, older physician and the unmarried, younger social worker. Miss Britton, quite deeply smitten, harboured such a protective crush on Dr Winnicott that she regarded Miss Elkan as a potential rival and treated her, at first, in rather a frosty manner.

Donald Winnicott's new lover seemed to have made quite an impact. In later years, after she had begun to teach social work trainees, one of her former students described her to me as a "bombshell" (Roberts, 1994; cf. Kahr, 1996a), while the noted Jungian analyst, Dr Michael Fordham, remembered her as something of an "anima woman" (quoted in Kahr, 1994c; cf. Kahr, 1996a) or *femme fatale*. Donald Winnicott may have found these seductive qualities irresistible, and hence, the relationship blossomed. Before long, he embarked upon a full-fledged extramarital affair with Clare Britton. Thus, Winnicott may well have lost his virginity, at last, shortly before his fiftieth birthday.

In view of Dr Winnicott's growing discontent with Alice and his burgeoning attraction to Clare, he certainly contemplated ending his marriage. But, at that point in time, most British people disapproved of divorce wholeheartedly as a violation of the sacred marital bonds. One need merely recall the huge scandal evoked by the former British monarch, Edward VIII, for having embarked upon a relationship with an American *divorcée*, Mrs Wallis Warfield Simpson. Consequently, Donald Winnicott found himself trapped by his own religious upbringing and by the disapproval of his elderly father, Sir Frederick Winnicott, who, like many spiritually observant Britons of the period, regarded divorce as sinful.

Thus, the newly potent Donald Winnicott found himself in a true dilemma. He had fallen in love with Clare Britton; but, as a full-time psychoanalyst and as a man who had enjoyed long-term attachments across the course of his lifetime—consisting of a ten-year relationship with his first analyst, James Strachey, followed by a six-year or seven-year commitment to his second analyst, Joan Riviere—he certainly did not abandon intimate relationships lightly. Winnicott still loved his wife Alice, but he also harboured resentments towards her, no doubt, as he might well have felt emotionally neglected by her, just as she might well have experienced psychological abandonment from him.

Their childless marriage, though by no means a problem inherently, began to vex both Donald and Alice at a more symbolic level. During the war, Alice came to work in a voluntary capacity with psychiatric patients at Napsbury Hospital on the outskirts of St Albans in Hertfordshire, and there she befriended a very ill schizophrenic woman whom she invited home to the Winnicott residence on Pilgrim's Lane in Hampstead, in North-West London.[6] Before long, this troubled individual, "Susan", began to live in the Winnicotts' spare bedroom on a full-time basis. Donald, too, brought many patients home with him, including, most famously, the little vagrant boy about whom he came to write in his famous paper on "Hate in the Counter-Transference" (Winnicott, 1949b). Across the 1940s, Donald and Alice became honorary parents to several psychiatric patients and turned their house into a prescient and pioneering therapeutic community of sorts. Desperate to save some of these individuals from the cruel somatic treatments then offered by psychiatrists, such as leucotomies and electroconvulsive shocks, the Winnicotts transformed their domestic residence into what they hoped would be a safe haven (Kahr, 2011, 2015a, 2023b). But they did so at great cost to themselves. Alice, untrained in psychology, had to undertake the bulk of the caretaking of these "inpatients", as Donald worked all day with his own patients in London and, also, in Oxfordshire and Berkshire.

Before long, the marriage between Alice and Donald had reached a point of crisis and, in 1949, he succumbed to a near-fatal coronary. Donald spent several months convalescing in his bedroom at Pilgrim's Lane but, alas, Alice did not care for him at all well and, according to the testimony of Winnicott's private secretary, Mrs Joyce Coles, Alice would often spend hours in her pottery and would somehow forget to check on her husband or bring him food and drink (Kahr, 1994g). On several occasions, Alice, quite unconsciously, even caused a fire in the house when her pottery kiln exploded; and, on another occasion, she nearly killed both herself and Joyce Coles by falling asleep at the wheel of her automobile (Kahr, 1994g).

In many respects, Mrs Coles' description of Pilgrim's Lane during the time of Winnicott's cardiac convalescence serves as a chilling symbolic portrait of the inner marital world shared by Donald Winnicott and Alice Winnicott, namely, one of simultaneous explosion and neglect.

Not long after Winnicott's recovery, he resumed clinical consultations with patients, but his marriage still vexed him. At one point, he invited Alice to lunch and told her that he had fallen in love with someone else and that he no longer wished to be married to her. He then returned to his consulting room to treat a patient. Distraught, Alice eventually barged into his private office suite on Queen Anne Street and began to pound on the door of her husband's consulting room in rage and tears. Joyce Coles, the secretary, had to bar the door bodily to protect her employer, Dr Winnicott, then mid-session with a patient, and, in consequence, she had to drive Alice back home to Hampstead. Mrs Coles, a gracious lady who never spoke viciously about anyone, did, however, confess that she thought Donald quite cruel to have ended his marriage with Alice over a meal in a public restaurant (Kahr, 1994g).

Not long thereafter, Alice Winnicott instituted formal divorce proceedings and, eventually, the couple parted after more than twenty-eight years of marriage.

The Second Mrs Winnicott

On 28th December, 1951, Donald Winnicott, freshly divorced from Alice Winnicott, wed Clare Britton and launched upon a new life in a large house in Belgravia, in South-West London, not far from Buckingham Palace. This happy new couple would remain married to one another for the next nineteen years until Winnicott's death from heart disease on 25th January, 1971. Virtually everyone who knew Donald and Clare as a couple spoke about the depth of their love, the tenderness and playfulness of their interactions, and the warmth of their marriage (e.g., Kahr, 1996c). They travelled together; they held successful parties together; they read each other's writings; they took an extremely detailed interest in one another's professional lives; and they stayed up late into the night painting, or watching television, or, even, making love.

Although Donald had already reached his mid-fifties at the time of their marriage, he and Clare did endeavour to make a baby, albeit unsuccessfully. Joyce Coles, the secretary, confirmed that she had seen various medical papers which indicated that the couple had, in fact, undergone fertility testing (Kahr, 1995g).

The second Mrs Winnicott proved to be a very attentive, creative, stable, and loving spouse, to whom Dr Winnicott remained devoted. Plagued by cardiac illness, Donald claimed that without Clare he would have died twenty years sooner (Tizard, 1971). Indeed, Clare offered such comfort to Donald that he once underscored to the psychiatrist Dr Lawrence Goldie (1994)—somewhat inaccurately—that he had experienced all of those coronaries during his marriage to Alice and none during his relationship with Clare.[7]

Perhaps Clare Winnicott summed up the marriage best when, in 1983, she reminisced in an interview with the medical historian Michael Neve, "somebody came to our house one day—stayed a weekend in our house—and said to me, 'You and Donald play, don't you?'" (quoted in Neve, 1983, p. 182). This male guest then explained, "You play with all kinds of things. My wife and I, we don't play." (quoted in Neve, 1983, p. 182). Mrs Winnicott elaborated that, "We did play with arranging our furniture—chucking this out or … with books, with reading, with—and going out. We had our Saturdays always for play. No work was done by either of us on Saturdays, except enjoying ourselves and thinking what to do" (quoted in Neve, 1983, p. 182; cf. Clare Winnicott, 1978).[8]

So, how did Donald Winnicott manage to make a better second marriage? As we know, the divorce rate for second marriages tends to be *much* higher than that for first marriages. Like many of our patients, Donald could, certainly, have had a salacious fling with Clare, then wed her and, ultimately, come to regret the decision. But, in fact, he had chosen extremely well, and both Dr Winnicott and the second Mrs Winnicott enhanced one another's lives tremendously.

We must wonder, of course, why Donald Winnicott did not simply repeat the disappointments of his first marriage to Alice with his second wife. Why did he not engage in what Sigmund Freud (1914a, p. 487) referred to as the "*Zwang zur Wiederholung*"—"compulsion to repeat" (Freud, 1914b, p. 150)—and marry yet another psychiatrically compromised person?

Once again, it would be far too presumptuous to claim that we might truly understand the internal workings of the private mind of a man who died more than half a century ago and whom almost none of us had met in person, let alone in the context of the psychoanalytical consulting room. But, in view of the copious surviving biographical and interview data, we can, at least, offer a considered hypothesis as to how and why Donald Winnicott chose a more stable, second spouse later in life.

I wish to propose that Winnicott's extremely lengthy first analysis with James Strachey, and his reasonably lengthy second analysis with Joan Riviere, may well, in all likelihood, have saved him from a further marital disaster.

As we know, James Strachey, the first of Donald Winnicott's personal psychoanalysts, breached the clinical confidentiality of his patient by relating some of the intimate details of Winnicott's analysis to his own wife, Alix Strachey; nonetheless, in spite of such a professional transgression, he did provide his patient with a long-standing, stable experience which lasted for many years. Although the precise content of those analytical sessions remains mostly a mystery, we do know that Winnicott spoke to Strachey in great detail about his inner world and even revealed his pleasure in urinating while he swam in the sea (James Strachey, 1924). Thus, it seems very probable that Winnicott felt sufficiently safe with Strachey's essentially boundaried and regular approach to psychoanalysis, and that, as a patient, he could readily confess to his deepest fears and fantasies.

All told, Winnicott attended psychoanalysis with Strachey for approximately ten years, six times weekly, and spent somewhere in the vicinity of 2,500 hours on the couch—a truly extensive analysis by anyone's standards.

I wish to suggest that, even *if* Strachey had remained silent for much of the time and had failed to offer any brilliant interpretations (and we have no reason to suspect that he practised in such a manner), the sheer experience of being able to narrate one's story for some 2,500 hours would have allowed Winnicott an unparalleled opportunity to engage in catharsis, thus divesting himself of the burden of pathogenic secrets, and thereby finding his voice, one which became increasingly powerful through his writings and public talks. Consequently, the Strachey analysis allowed the previously undistinguished physician to become the exceptionally distinguished psychoanalyst whose memory we continue to venerate.

I propose that Winnicott internalised Strachey as a good, benign object; indeed, the two men became warm associates in later years, and Winnicott proved a great advocate of, and ally for, Strachey's multi-decade commitment as chief English-language translator of the works of Sigmund Freud. In fact, in 1966, during Winnicott's second presidential term at the British Psycho-Analytical Society, he had the pleasure of hosting a banquet in honour of his former training analyst to mark the approaching completion of the publication of *The Standard Edition of the Complete Psychological Works of Sigmund Freud* (Kahr, 2017b).[9]

But if Winnicott had such a lengthy and fruitful analysis with James Strachey, why, during the late 1930s, did he commence a further tranche of analysis with Joan Riviere?

Once again, we cannot answer this question with any degree of certainty. In part, Winnicott seems to have sought out Mrs Riviere—a trusted colleague of Mrs Melanie Klein—as a means of gaining favour and patronage from Klein herself, who, as a progenitor of child psychoanalysis, became Winnicott's (1962h) clinical supervisor and his most important theoretical and technical mentor at that time. An analysis from Riviere would ensure Winnicott a place among the pantheon of anointed Kleinians within the British Psycho-Analytical Society.

But whatever Winnicott's *professional* reasons for embarking upon a re-analysis from Riviere, we know that, by the late 1930s, his marriage with Alice Winnicott had begun to founder, and it may be that Winnicott needed psychological support. It might also be the case that he felt compelled to work closely with a *woman*, as opposed to a *man*, as his first analysis may not have exposed him to the same transferential dynamics which would emerge more starkly with a female practitioner, especially one who had developed an expertise in being provocative and difficult. And with Joan Riviere, Winnicott had selected unquestionably the most difficult female in the British psychoanalytical community.

Certainly, we cannot do justice to the complexity of Joan Riviere's character; but we do know that this woman, once a patient of both Ernest Jones and then, later, Sigmund Freud, struggled with her own mental vulnerabilities and developed quite a reputation for being both vexing and exacting. I had the privilege of interviewing quite a number of elderly psychoanalysts—all now deceased—who had worked with Mrs Riviere, many of whom described her as a "bully"—the term used most frequently. For instance, Dr Hanna Segal, renowned for her own toughness and, in earlier years, for smoking cigars, revealed that, on one occasion, as a young trainee, due to transport difficulties, she had arrived late for a clinical supervision session, only to receive a shrill response from Riviere, who berated Segal, exclaiming that she would not tolerate such "manic" (quoted in Segal, 1995) nonsense, and promptly evicted her from the consulting room. Likewise, Dr Charles Rycroft reminisced to me that he found Mrs Riviere to be absolutely "terrifying" (quoted in Kahr, 1993). In view of these reports, it will hardly surprise us that Mrs Riviere struggled to keep domestic servants in her employ, as her staff kept bolting (Hughes, 1995)!

With such a difficult, bullying personality, how, then, did Joan Riviere behave with her analysand Donald Winnicott?

Riviere wrote many letters to Winnicott, both during the analysis and afterwards, which survive to this day in archives on both sides of the Atlantic Ocean and which reveal, only too clearly, the agitated and strained relationship between analyst and patient (e.g., Riviere, 1936, 1937a [sic] [1936], 1937b, 1938, 1958a, 1958b). As I have already described the tumultuous relationship which unfolded between Riviere and her patient Winnicott in my earlier biographical study (Kahr, 1996a), and as I have completed a fuller exploration of this relationship in my forthcoming study of Winnicott's wartime years (Kahr, 2023b), I shall not elaborate upon the specificities at this point, except to report that, in her work with Winnicott, Riviere broke many classical boundaries, which included not only the expression of her regret that she had charged him only one guinea per session rather than two guineas (Riviere, 1936), but, moreover, the revelation of a great deal of information to Winnicott about her own physical ailments (e.g., Riviere, 1937a [sic] [1936], 1938). Strikingly, Mrs Riviere (1938) even confessed to her patient that she suffered from "trouble in an ear"—arguably the least confidence-inspiring confession that a psychoanalyst could impart to an analysand.

We can speculate *ad infinitum* as to why Winnicott persevered in treatment with Riviere over the course of several years. He may have done so for the very same reasons that he had remained with Alice Winnicott for decades, perhaps due to a masochistic vulnerability or, perhaps, because he found the fight to be a useful one, which gratified certain aggressive needs. Whatever Donald Winnicott's motivation for working with Joan Riviere, it may be that she also afforded him an ongoing experience of having to stand up to a difficult female psychoanalyst and, ultimately, to develop his ability to walk out on her and to leave the treatment. Of course, in spite of being a bullying and terrorising woman, Riviere, who had studied with both Jones and Freud, also enjoyed a profound grasp of the unconscious, and in spite of her somewhat callous interpersonal style, she may have perceived something profound about Winnicott's object relations. Hence, she might well have understood Winnicott's own unconscious sadomasochistic struggles which she then helped to render more conscious.

Perhaps, in a somewhat perverse way, the prototypically difficult Joan Riviere permitted Donald a greater sense of private potency, stimulated by his need to defend himself; and this newfound state of mind may have contributed to his ultimate boldness in leaving his first wife, Alice.

Thus, all told, Donald Winnicott benefited from approximately one and a half decades of personal psychoanalysis. Clare Winnicott also enjoyed a great deal of psychological support, having undertaken her first analysis with Dr Clifford Scott and her second analysis with Mrs Melanie Klein. Although we know little of the first experience, and we know that the latter experience proved rather difficult at times (Grosskurth, 1981), it may well be the case that Donald Winnicott's second marriage benefited hugely, both during his courtship and during the actual marital years themselves, from the internalised support of so much in-depth psychoanalysis on the couch. Alice Winnicott, the first wife, also undertook some psychoanalytical treatment from Dr Clifford Scott (Winnicott, 1938, 1939b; King, 2002; cf. Taylor, 1938), but, according to the best archival evidence available, her encounter with Scott came too late in the day to save her marriage with Donald.

Whatever the roots of Winnicott's attraction to Clare Britton, and whatever the psychological forces which facilitated his late-in-life marital proposal to a new woman, it remains absolutely certain that Winnicott chose a more healthy wife the second time round, and that he enjoyed a far richer and infinitely more stable relationship with Clare than with Alice. Indeed, not long after his divorce from the first Mrs Winnicott, he revealed to Miss Ruth Thomas, a fellow psychoanalyst, that he had married his second wife because, "I felt I had to have some real happiness for the rest of my life" (quoted in Thomas, 1971).

Clare Britton proved a sturdy companion. In fact, in her brief tribute to her husband, published some years after his death, she noted that she and Donald had managed to exist as two separate adults in one union, rather than as a merged infantile pair. As she explained, "What we could take for granted was something more basic that I can only describe as our recognition and acceptance of each other's separateness. In fact the strength of our unity lay in this recognition" (Clare Winnicott, 1978, p. 30). She also underscored that, "Our separateness left us each free to do our own thing, to think our own thoughts, and possess our own dreams, and in so doing to strengthen the capacity of each of us to experience the joys and sorrows which we shared" (Clare Winnicott, 1978, p. 30). One could not ask for a more coherent and more mature assessment of a marital pairing.

The Implications of Winnicott's Marriages

Fellow couple clinicians will appreciate only too clearly how much we struggle to divine the very complex unconscious psychodynamics of intimate spousal relationships. When I began my career as a couple practitioner, I often described the work to colleagues in other branches of the mental health profession as an experience rather akin to watching the finals of Wimbledon. But today, decades on, I would revise that characterisation. As I have become more adept at facilitating couple psychoanalysis, helping spouses to reach the deeper bedrocks of their shared misery, I now refer to the process not as a genteel Wimbledon final but, rather, as something more closely resembling a World Boxing Federation championship.

Grasping the nettle of the intimate life of a couple remains one of the most intellectually and emotionally challenging experiences of my professional work, which becomes even harder over time, rather than easier, as one comes to appreciate more and more fully the true complexity of someone else's marriage.

In view of the difficulty of understanding the intimate partnerships of one's own patients, whom one meets quite regularly in a profound manner, one must struggle even more greatly to grapple with the hidden unconscious marital dynamics of long-deceased historical personalities whom one has *not* met at all. Nonetheless, in my defence, although

I never made the acquaintance of Donald or Alice or Clare, I have studied their lives for a longer period of time than I have those of any of my patients. And I have examined their private, handwritten letters and photographs, and have sought independent testimony from eyewitnesses, something which I have never done with real patients, and will never do for reasons of privacy and clinical antisepsis.

Thus, in many respects, the long-deceased Winnicotts have taught me rather a lot about the unfolding of marital choice and marital struggle which one cannot always appreciate so clearly amid what Winnicott once referred to as the "white heat" (quoted in Elmhirst, 1996a) of the consulting room. I have, therefore, learned a great deal about the psychodynamics of intimacy from studying historical personages in such depth.

Although Donald Winnicott never became a couple psychoanalyst or couple psychotherapist *per se*, he did recognise the vital role of the primary intimate relationship between two adults most profoundly; similarly, he came to appreciate, perhaps more fully than any other clinician hitherto, the essential nature of the coupling between a mother and a baby, which may be the most important "marriage" in our entire lives. And Winnicott utilised this knowledge of the mother–infant relationship as a template for the marriage between the psychoanalyst and the patient.

True, Winnicott did not work with marital couples in the way in which we do nowadays, by offering ongoing, open-ended spaces in which each partner may discuss concerns in complete privacy, but he did, however, meet with parental couples, especially when treating their troubled children. In that respect, he might qualify, retrospectively, as a pioneer of couple psychoanalysis.

Certainly, Winnicott recognised only too clearly that not all difficulties within the adult marital relationship stem from the burden of caring for babies and young children and adolescents. He knew, quite well, from both his private experiences with Alice and, also, from his professional work, that couples must navigate complex sexualities. In a very little-known piece of writing, namely, the "Foreword" to a text on *Any Wife or Any Husband: A Book for Couples Who Have Met Sexual Difficulties and for Doctors. Second Edition*, published in 1955, Winnicott (1955b, p. v) opined that, "The majority of educated people, nowadays, know that most difficulties inherent in a marriage relationship are produced by psychological rather than physical factors."

In spite of his growing understanding of marriage and his interest in couple relationships, Winnicott never overstepped his professional competency or expertise, and although qualified in both adult psychoanalysis and in child psychoanalysis, he did not rush to treat divorcing couples. When, for instance, Miss Dorothy Gardner, a pioneering colleague who taught for many years at the Institute of Education in the University of London, asked Winnicott to offer a consultation to a man with a psychiatrically ill wife threatening divorce, Winnicott (1951) refused the case, and he recommended that the prospective patient seek assistance from either Dr Lothair Rubinstein or Dr Sonny Davidson, two adult psychoanalysts with extensive experience of treating psychotic individuals.

It may be that Winnicott's greatest contribution to the development of couple psychotherapy remains his work supporting Mrs Enid Balint, the progenitor of couple psychoanalysis in the United Kingdom today. In 1946, in the wake of the ravages of the Second World War, Enid Balint, then known as Mrs Enid Eichholz, established a series of family discussion bureaux under the auspices of the Family Welfare Association, which offered pioneering marital counselling, informed by depth psychology. These family discussion networks became the precursor to Tavistock Relationships. Through this paradigm-shifting work, Enid Eichholz and her staff provided psychotherapeutic interventions of increasing dynamic sophistication to untold numbers of couples in distress over more than seventy years (Kahr, 2017a, 2019f).

Enid Eichholz undertook her own training analysis with the venerable psychoanalyst Dr John Rickman, but he died, alas, mid-treatment, and, not long thereafter, Winnicott then became her second analyst and nurtured her professional development, ultimately supporting her candidacy to become a training analyst at the Institute of Psycho-Analysis. Enid Eichholz eventually divorced her first husband and then married a Hungarian-born psychoanalyst, Dr Michael Balint, and she became better known by her new name, Enid Balint. Indeed, in view of the fact that Mrs Balint worked ferociously long hours establishing the marital department within the Tavistock Institute of Human Relations, Winnicott sometimes offered her private psychoanalytical sessions at weekends. Thus, in many respects, he became the honorary grandfather to British couple psychoanalysis.

Strikingly, both Donald Winnicott and Enid Balint had each endured painful first marriages but, in the wake of their own experiences of personal psychoanalysis, both went on to enjoy much more successful second marriages.

As I indicated at the outset of this chapter, many of Winnicott's theoretical and technical contributions remain of great relevance to couple mental health practitioners and, perhaps, none more so than that of the apposition between the "true self" and the "false self". Indeed, as many of our couple patients present to us with complaints about a lack of authenticity and intimacy in their marriages, it might behove us to consider speaking not only about a "false self" but, also, about a "false self couple"[10] or a "false self marriage", and that through our ongoing, painstaking work, we might endeavour to help our couples reclaim the "true self marriage" upon which they had once embarked, years previously, during their hopeful courtships.

Winnicott (1955a) did not publish his work on the true self and false self until 1955, a mere few years into his marriage to Clare Britton. Perhaps the joy of his new marital situation helped him to appreciate the difference between a false self marriage and a true self marriage. Indeed, in 1962, in his paper on "The Aims of Psycho-Analytical Treatment", he wrote, quite famously, about the development of his clinical technique, "I am not like what I was twenty or thirty years ago" (Winnicott, 1962g, p. 169). This statement certainly does apply to Winnicott's technique with patients, which evolved over time from a more interpretative Kleinian stance to one which cherished the patient's capacity simply to *be*. But his comment might also refer to the development of his own sense of a marital self. In 1962, he certainly did not occupy the same marital space as he had done previously, during the time in which his partnership with Alice Winnicott had already begun to deteriorate.

Did psychoanalysis facilitate a healthy marital choice for Donald Winnicott and permit him to manage the transition from Alice to Clare? Although only Donald Winnicott could answer this question, aided perhaps, by thoughts from James Strachey and Joan Riviere, I would argue that, having embarked upon approximately fifteen years of psychoanalysis, at a time when most analyses lasted little more than one year at best (e.g., Forsyth, 1922; Kardiner, 1977), Winnicott enjoyed the privilege of well over 3,000 sessions on two different couches. These precious and unparalleled opportunities for emotional growth and self-reflection cannot but have helped Donald to extricate himself from the constant caretaking burdens of life with Alice and thus move towards a more mutually satisfying personal and professional partnership with Clare.

Although Sigmund Freud occasionally advised his analysands to refrain from marriage until after they had completed their psychoanalyses (Roazen, 1995), contemporary practitioners dare not be so prescriptive, not least as an analysis nowadays might often require a very long time indeed. But even though we cannot advise our newer patients to refrain from embarking upon what could well become a rocky marital relationship, one wonders whether there might be merit in preventing patients from rushing into marriage, at least until the analysis has helped to unmask the potentially dangerous masochistic, sadistic, or sadomasochistic phantasies that might propel someone to marry for the *wrong* reasons rather than for the *right* ones.

CHAPTER FOUR

"The Piggle" Family Papers: Unpublished Archival Gems Regarding Winnicott's Most Iconic Case

Section One: Dinner with "The Piggle" at Kettner's

One afternoon in March, 1996, long before the omnipresence of cell phones, I picked up the receiver of my old-fashioned plastic telephone, placed squarely on the desk of my office in London's Regent's Park, and I dialled the home number of a young woman, once known as "The Piggle"—certainly one of the most famous patients in the entire history of psychoanalysis.

I must confess that, never having spoken to this person before, I reached out to this iconic psychoanalytical celebrity with more than a bit of trepidation.

The Piggle answered my call and we spoke directly, and I introduced myself as a biographer of Dr Donald Winnicott. I found The Piggle to be both sweet and straightforward, and she expressed an interest in my research and agreed to be of assistance with any reminiscences about her former psychoanalyst. Towards the end of our short telephone conversation, I invited her to join me for supper, at her convenience; and, to my delight, The Piggle agreed to the plan.

As I intended to take The Piggle for a meal at a lovely restaurant tucked away down a little side street, I suggested that we might meet in front of the more visible Palace Theatre nearby, in the very heart of London's

West End, then home to the long-running musical *Les Misérables*, at 7.00 p.m. on Tuesday, 2nd April, 1996. I explained to The Piggle that, for ease of identification, I would be standing outside the theatre, clutching a copy of one of Donald Winnicott's classic tomes.

At the appropriate time, The Piggle arrived, recognised the book in question, and we greeted one another warmly. I then walked with her to Kettner's, one of my very favourite restaurants, located on Romilly Street, not far from the theatre. I chose that particular venue not only for its excellent food and friendly, convivial atmosphere but, also, for its psychoanalytical significance, because, some forty-four years previously, on 30th March, 1952, the noted psychoanalyst, Mrs Melanie Klein, had celebrated her seventieth birthday at this restaurant in the presence of a handful of carefully selected guests, including such distinguished clinical colleagues as Dr Michael Balint, Dr Paula Heimann, Dr Ernest Jones, Mrs Marion Milner, Dr Sylvia Payne, Mrs Joan Riviere, Dr Herbert Rosenfeld, Mr James Strachey, and none other than the paradigm-shifting genius Dr Donald Winnicott (Grosskurth, 1986).

Only after I put down the receiver of the telephone did I appreciate fully that I had arranged to meet with The Piggle on 2nd April, 1996, literally five days in advance of Donald Winnicott's centenary on 7th April of that year.

But how on earth did I manage to obtain the home telephone number for The Piggle? And how, indeed, did I discover her real name?

Merely a few weeks before meeting The Piggle in person, I had published my very first book (Kahr, 1996a)—a biography of Dr Donald Woods Winnicott, upon which I had first embarked some years previously.

As part of my research for the Winnicott biography, designed to appear in print in time for the great man's one hundredth birthday, I had the privilege of studying many of his unpublished manuscripts and much of his private correspondence, buried in various archives; and, additionally, I had undertaken a very extensive series of oral history interviews with literally hundreds of elderly colleagues and family members who had known Winnicott personally. As a young clinician and historian, I took tea with Mrs Marion Milner; I lunched with Dr Hanna Segal; and I enjoyed a memorable supper with Dr John Bowlby. I also corresponded with Mrs Francesca Bion (the widow of

Dr Wilfred Bion); I had the privilege of spending a morning in the company of Mrs Enid Balint; I lingered for hours on the telephone with Professor Elliott Jaques; and, moreover, I even took a train to the wilds of Kent, in the South-East of England, to meet Dr Margaret Little. Additionally, I interviewed quite a number of Winnicott's nephews and nieces and cousins, not to mention his long-standing secretary, Mrs Joyce Coles, as well as his cardiologist, Dr Michael Rosenblüth, and, even, his bespoke tailor, Mr Cyril Rosenberg.

I got rather carried away by my overly enthusiastic attempt to meet every single surviving person who had ever encountered Donald Winnicott (however briefly); and, across many years, I succeeded in interviewing more than 900 people who had known him personally, including approximately fifty of his former patients.

Sadly, as time has unfolded, virtually all of these great figures from the history of psychoanalysis have since passed away, with only few exceptions. Fortunately, The Piggle, born in 1961, remains alive and thriving at the time of this writing—a mere stripling in her early sixties.

I had certainly never suspected that I would ever meet The Piggle in person, as I did not know her true identity. Moreover, even if I had access to her contact details, I doubt that I would have approached her out of the blue, because, as a clinician, I would have considered such a request as potentially quite intrusive. As a one-time patient of Dr Winnicott, The Piggle had previously enjoyed a private, confidential experience in his consulting room at 87, Chester Square, in the Belgravia district of London. Although I had met many of Winnicott's other patients, in virtually all instances *they* had contacted *me* first, through various channels, offering assistance with my research, once they had discovered that I had begun to write Winnicott's biography; or, in certain cases, mutual colleagues or acquaintances had thoughtfully facilitated an introduction. But I had never reached out to any of Winnicott's former patients directly.

At that time, in the 1990s, I did strongly suspect that The Piggle might still be alive and well—a woman in her mid-thirties—but I had absolutely no means of engaging her, and I presumed that we would, therefore, never meet in person.

However, towards the latter part of 1995, one of my interviewees—a kind and helpful elderly lady who still worked in the mental health profession and who had, during the 1960s, come to know Winnicott reasonably well—told me, quite unexpectedly, that she had once enjoyed an acquaintance with none other than the *mother* of Winnicott's famous child patient and asked whether I might wish to meet the woman to whom I shall refer, hereafter, as "Mrs Piggle". Naturally, I expressed great interest, subject, of course, to Mrs Piggle's agreement. Thankfully, within a mere matter of days, my interviewee provided me with a postal address for Mrs Piggle, whereupon I wrote her a formal letter of introduction on 7th November, 1995, describing my credentials and the nature of my research project (Kahr, 1995a).

Shortly thereafter, I received a handwritten letter in the post from Mrs Piggle, explaining that she would be very pleased to speak to me and suggested that I should telephone her at her home in Oxfordshire. Mrs Piggle's penmanship struck me as Continental, rather than as traditionally British in handwriting style, and I sensed that she had probably grown up and had learned her letters in a foreign country.

Cheered by Mrs Piggle's willingness to be interviewed, I then rang her directly and we talked on the telephone at great length (Kahr, 1995h).

I found Mrs Piggle to be a delightfully friendly person—very openhearted, very generous with her time, and very eager to talk. She spoke with a distinctly German accent.

As an interviewer, I did not have to do much at all on that occasion. Mrs Piggle needed little prompting and she communicated in a fluid manner, having absolutely no difficulty articulating the entire story of how and why she had arranged for her daughter to undergo child analysis with Dr Winnicott more than three decades previously. I sat quietly in my office, holding the receiver of my landline telephone in my left hand, with a pen in my right hand, and, with the blessing of Mrs Piggle, I took detailed notes of the entire conversation.

I had assumed—incorrectly, in fact—that Mrs Piggle had first discovered Dr Winnicott through his writings or radio broadcasts and that, as a mother in Oxfordshire, she had reached out for professional help when she discovered that her daughter suffered from various anxieties and symptoms in the wake of the birth of her younger sister, "Susan". But, to my surprise, I learned that Mrs Piggle had actually known Winnicott personally for many, *many* years, and that she had worked in the mental health profession and had even attended Winnicott's famous child psychiatric clinic at the Paddington Green Children's Hospital in West London and had watched him in action, interviewing young people and their families. (I subsequently discovered that not only had Mrs Piggle met Winnicott on many occasions, but so, too, had her own mother—the *grandmother* of The Piggle—who had visited the Paddington Green Children's Hospital not long after the Second World War.[1])

In fact, at some point during the 1950s, Mrs Piggle had even arranged for Winnicott to deliver a lecture at her workplace. She recalled that Winnicott had, alas, received rather a frosty reception from her colleagues, some of whom regarded his ideas with suspicion as he, unlike many of his other London colleagues, did not insist that each child *must* undergo *five-times-weekly* psychoanalysis. Most of the stodgier child mental health professionals, steeped in the work of both Miss Anna Freud and Mrs Melanie Klein, considered Donald Winnicott somewhat heretical for having adopted a more open-minded and creative stance, which included the fact that he offered to treat children according to their needs, rather than subscribing to a predetermined protocol of frequency. Mrs Piggle herself had trained in the Kleinian tradition and remained a dedicated supporter of the work of Melanie Klein throughout her career; nevertheless, she admired Winnicott and chose him, rather than a Kleinian child psychoanalyst, to consult with her daughter ("The Piggle", 2020).

Mrs Piggle explained that, over time, she and Donald Winnicott developed a warm association and that he often visited her at her home in Oxford, a city to which Winnicott travelled from time to time, particularly as he and his wife, Mrs Clare Winnicott, enjoyed a warm friendship with Miss Lucy Faithfull—a noted social worker and child advocate (and, subsequently, a baroness), who happened to live quite close by.

Thus, although it will not be widely known, Winnicott first met The Piggle at the family home in Oxfordshire, rather than in his consulting room in Chester Square. In fact, Winnicott enjoyed a long-standing association not only with Mrs Piggle—a fellow mental health colleague—but, also, with her husband, whom I shall call "Mr Piggle", and with The Piggle and her younger sister as well.

Mrs Piggle spoke entrancingly about her early association with Winnicott and then told me that she found him to be a most charming man, so much so that he conquered the hearts of many of those whom he had encountered. She also stressed that Winnicott enjoyed the capacity to help people discover parts of themselves that they had not known about previously. Consequently, in view of her high regard for this distinguished psychoanalyst, then in his late sixties, she had no hesitation in writing to him to arrange an appointment for her daughter, The Piggle, having become concerned for her child's well-being in the wake of the birth of her second baby, Susan.

I talked at great length with Mrs Piggle on several occasions thereafter and we engaged in further written correspondence as well. With extreme generosity, she even sent me one of the Christmas cards that Winnicott had hand-painted for her family decades previously. Eventually, having come to appreciate my very serious and respectful passion for Winnicott's work, Mrs Piggle asked me, "Would you like to meet my daughter?" I replied that I would be delighted and honoured to do so, but only if The Piggle had no objections. Mrs Piggle assured me that her daughter would be happy to speak to me. And thus, I rang The Piggle and arranged our supper at Kettner's restaurant.

On that Tuesday evening in April, 1996, The Piggle and I enjoyed a very delicious meal. Although she appeared a bit nervous at first, she soon relaxed and began to talk and to reminisce. Rather like her mother, she seemed quite keen to help me with my biographical research (Kahr, 1996h). I warmed to The Piggle immediately and I found her to be a very pleasant person.

Because The Piggle had attended Chester Square for a small number of consultations throughout 1964, 1965, and 1966, from the age of two years and five months until the age of five years and two and three quarter months, she could remember very little of the content of those psychoanalytical sessions, not least as she found it somewhat difficult to differentiate her direct memories from what she had subsequently read about the experience in the published version of Winnicott's (1977) now legendary book, *The Piggle: An Account of the Psychoanalytic Treatment of a Little Girl*, first published in 1977, some nineteen years prior to our supper at Kettner's. But although she could not recall many of the intricate details of her child analysis as such, she did, however, remember some seemingly insignificant pieces of information about the physicality of Winnicott's consulting room, and continued to do so across the years, including the fact that his office boasted brown Bakelite-covered electrical plugs—a piece of data that one will not find in any published accounts ("The Piggle", 2017).

I felt very blessed to be in the presence of such a friendly and helpful young person and one who had enjoyed such a psychologically intimate experience with one of the great heroes of world mental health.

As our supper unfolded, The Piggle reminisced further about the pleasant atmosphere that Dr Winnicott had created in his office, and she described him as a kindly and decent soul towards whom she had developed a great affection.

Although The Piggle did not remember much of the actual dialogue and playfulness that she had experienced with Winnicott between the ages of two and five, she reminisced far more clearly that, as a nine-year-old girl, she burst into tears after her mother told her the sad news of Winnicott's death on 25th January, 1971, at the age of seventy-four years.

The Piggle proved most gracious and generous with her memories. She also put me in touch with her father, Mr Piggle, with whom I then embarked upon a correspondence. Over the intervening years, The Piggle and I developed a warm association and we have continued to meet for supper from time to time. I would describe her as a most engaging and convivial dinner companion.

Even though The Piggle did not remember Donald Winnicott in the same detailed way in which Mrs Piggle had done—owing to their age differences at the time of their association with the great psychoanalyst—I nevertheless had a strong sense that Winnicott had helped The Piggle tremendously. Certainly, the woman with whom I dined at Kettner's on that memorable evening struck me as a person of considerable mental sturdiness, warmth, compassion, and intelligence. And while we cannot attribute all of these qualities solely to The Piggle's handful of consultations with Winnicott, I had suspected that her extraordinary experience at Chester Square might well have contributed greatly to the development of her impressive personality structure and the socially minded professional career in which she has since flourished.

Many years later, in 2011, while dining with The Piggle once again, she told me that she and her sister had recently discovered a large collection of old letters and photographs from their childhood, which contained much correspondence between her parents and Donald

Winnicott. The Piggle had also unearthed the very first unpublished draft of the book, encased in an ageing and slightly crumpled binding, which ultimately became enshrined in psychoanalytical history as Winnicott's most celebrated case study.

With great trust and generosity, The Piggle, knowing of my interest in pursuing further research on Donald Winnicott, kindly loaned me a very large and weighty box of documents and pictures, which I studied carefully over several years. I returned this box to The Piggle in 2017 with tremendous gratitude.

In the pages which follow, I shall endeavour to draw upon this unique archive of family papers, which I have come to call "'The Piggle' Papers", as well as my several decades of research in the various Winnicott archives, to offer a more comprehensive and more fully contextualised account of this landmark case in the history of child psychoanalysis and to explore at greater length the nature of Winnicott's remarkable achievement.

Section Two: Donald Winnicott at Sixty-Seven Years of Age

The Piggle attended for her very first formal consultation with Donald Winnicott on Monday, 3rd February, 1964.

What did Donald Winnicott look like, physically, at that point, in the early months of 1964? What sort of life did he lead at that time? And what, if anything, do we know about his state of mind and about his preoccupations, whether professional or, indeed, personal?

In 1964, Winnicott had every reason to be utterly exhausted, having worked tirelessly and unrelentingly in the health professions since the Great War. Throughout the 1920s and beyond, he always toiled full-time as a clinician and made a considerable contribution by having introduced dynamic psychology into the field of children's medicine (e.g., Winnicott, 1931a, 1931b, 1932, 1933, 1939a); moreover, he helped to pioneer the new disciplines of both child psychiatry and child psychoanalysis in Great Britain (e.g., Winnicott, 1940, 1942, 1945a, 1948a, 1948b, 1953, 1963c, 1963i, 1965c, 1966a, 1967a, 1968a; cf. Kahr, 2015b, 2019e). Not only did he engage in psychoanalytical work with children and their parents, but he also maintained a thriving practice with adult patients as well. Additionally, he distinguished himself as a lecturer, a supervisor, a teacher, an administrator, a writer, and a broadcaster—a behemoth set of achievements which might rival those of Professor Sigmund Freud.

Unsurprisingly, such unrelenting workaholism exerted a heavy toll, not only upon his marriage to Miss Alice Buxton Taylor, whom he had wed in 1923, but, also, upon his physical health. In 1949, both his marital relationship and his heart suffered dangerous explosions, and, after a perilous coronary episode—the first of many more to come—he nearly died (Kahr, 2019b, 2023b). By 1951, he had divorced his first wife, and then he married Miss Clare Britton, a talented and engaging social worker who trained, subsequently, as a psychoanalyst in her own right; and, moreover, he moved from his long-standing home in Hampstead, in North-West London, to a large, rented house in a luxurious section of Belgravia in South-West London (Kahr, 1996a).

The love and care and affection that Winnicott received from his second wife certainly helped to fortify him and, also, to re-energise him. And throughout the 1950s, he became even more creative than ever before, publishing several influential books (e.g., Winnicott, 1957a, 1957b, 1958a), and serving as President of the British Psycho-Analytical Society.

Throughout this time, Winnicott maintained his long-standing post as a physician at the Paddington Green Children's Hospital in West London, which became his principal clinical laboratory. Although Winnicott had trained as a child psychoanalyst and had treated quite a number of young people on a five-times-weekly basis in traditional Freudian style, he certainly could not offer such regular and intensive treatment to the many thousands of troubled children and families who attended his specialist clinic at Paddington Green; hence, he had to develop a capacity for offering one or two therapeutic consultations only, during which he would endeavour to identify a core anxiety within the child or family which could then be interpreted, rendered conscious, and, in many instances, even allayed or cured (e.g., Winnicott, 1968b, 1971).

Donald Winnicott remained passionately devoted to Paddington Green since he had begun to work there in 1923. But shortly after his sixty-fifth birthday, on 7th April, 1961, he knew that he needed to retire. Indeed, on 3rd July, 1961, Winnicott (1961f) wrote to his younger colleague, the child psychiatrist Dr Gordon Levinson, "At the present minute I feel that if I survive till the middle of September it will be quite a feat."

To mark his retirement, Winnicott wrote a very short essay for the *St. Mary's Hospital Gazette*, the newsletter of St. Mary's Hospital, London, which served as the umbrella body of several local healthcare facilities, including the Paddington Green Children's Hospital. In this communication, Winnicott reflected upon the establishment of his very specialist unit, which he named "The Paediatric Department of Psychology", where he had, over the decades, deployed psychoanalytical concepts in order to treat both paediatric and child psychiatric cases. In the unpublished draft of his article, Winnicott (1961e) took a swipe at some of his more orthodox medical colleagues who would, occasionally, perform leucotomies upon patients, but, on further reflection, he removed this potentially inflammatory criticism from the final, published version of the piece (Winnicott, 1961b), eager, perhaps, to avoid being provocative after so many years of gratitude towards the institution.

The *St. Mary's Hospital Gazette* published not only Winnicott's essay about his unique paediatric department but, also, a special tribute to him, designed to commemorate his many decades of dedicated service to the institution. Mr Gershon Hepner (known to all as "Gershy"), a Leipzig-born refugee to England and, subsequently, a senior medical student who had worked at Paddington Green, conducted an interview with Winnicott in preparation for this article. Nearly half a century later, I had the privilege of interviewing Dr Gershy Hepner, then a retired physician in his own right, who still recalled his visit to Chester Square almost fifty years earlier, and who remembered Dr Winnicott as "very engaging" (quoted in Kahr, 2009c) with a "winning personality" (quoted in Kahr, 2009c), explaining that he could happily have talked with the esteemed psychoanalyst for hours.

In his article, published anonymously, Hepner described Winnicott as "one of the greatest living child psychiatrists" (Anonymous [Gershy Hepner], 1961, p. 137). Unsurprisingly, Winnicott deeply enjoyed this public praise, so much so that he then ordered six copies of the magazine at the cost of one shilling and three pence each (Hepner, 1961).

In further recognition of his retirement, the hospital organised a special leaving party for Donald Winnicott and, also, for a fellow medical colleague, the noted paediatric surgeon, Mr Frederick William Markham Pratt, who had worked at Paddington Green since 1933. As a gesture of the institution's deep appreciation, Winnicott (1961g) received what he described as an "astonishingly fat" voucher from Harrods department store.

Needless to say, like many hard-working, creative people, Winnicott discovered that "retirement" from his part-time post at the Paddington Green Children's Hospital simply afforded him more opportunities to undertake *additional* work. In September of 1961, he flew to Helsinki in Finland to present a paper on "Psycho-Neurosis in Childhood" to the Scandinavian Orthopsychiatric Congress; then, in November of 1961, he delivered a talk on "A Child Psychiatry Case" to the Oxford University Mental Health Association, and, in that same month, he spoke to the Royal Medical-Psychological Association on "Example of a Therapeutic Consultation with a Child". He also published numerous pieces in professional journals (e.g., Winnicott, 1961a, 1961c) and in popular magazines (e.g., Winnicott, 1961d).

In 1962, Donald Winnicott immersed himself even more fully into the professional mental health community, both nationally and internationally. For instance, he maintained his long-standing commitment as a lecturer for students at both the Institute of Education in the University of London, and, moreover, at its sister organisation, the London School of Economics and Political Science, also part of the University of London. Additionally, he continued to undertake committee work for the British Psycho-Analytical Society, and he persevered as a speaker at conferences, not only in the United Kingdom, but, also, overseas. For instance, in May, 1962, he travelled to Paris, France, in order to address the Société Psychanalytique de Paris [Paris Psycho-Analytical Society] about regression in clinical work; and, in the autumn, he journeyed to Los Angeles, California, for a multi-week American lecture tour, during which time he spoke to numerous organisations, including, *inter alia*, the Los Angeles Psychoanalytic Society, the San Francisco Psychoanalytic Institute, the Topeka Psychoanalytic Society, the Menninger School of Psychiatry (also located in Topeka, Kansas), the Beth Israel Hospital, in Boston, Massachusetts, as well as the Boston Psychoanalytic Society and, additionally, the Division of Psychoanalytic Education at the State University of New York in the Bronx, New York.

Throughout 1962, he not only lectured, supervised, attended conferences, and composed professional papers (e.g., Winnicott, 1962a, 1962b, 1962c, 1962d, 1962e), but he also persevered with his treatment of private patients in his consulting room at Chester Square. Moreover, in spite of his official retirement, Winnicott refused to leave Paddington Green completely and still made regular visits as a Consulting Physician to that institution virtually every Monday afternoon, during which time he continued to conduct clinics.

In view of Winnicott's multi-decade attachment to the Paddington Green Children's Hospital and to his unique expertise in psychoanalytical child psychiatry, one can readily appreciate his reluctance to remove himself from the institution completely. We can only begin to imagine the sadness that he must have felt when, one day, circa 1963, he pitched up at the hospital for a visit, and the new receptionist, who did not recognise him, announced to his successor, Dr Susanna Isaacs, "There is a Dr Winnicott to see you" (quoted in Kahr, 1994e).

Eventually, Winnicott ceased his visits to the Paddington Green Children's Hospital entirely and devoted most of 1963 to other professional pursuits, including numerous lectures, not only throughout England and Scotland but, also, in Rome, and in Stockholm, as well as overseas, visiting various American states, such as Connecticut, Georgia, Maryland, Massachusetts, New York, and Pennsylvania. Naturally, he persevered with writing and publication (e.g., Winnicott, 1963a, 1963b, 1963c, 1963d, 1963e, 1963f, 1963g), and, furthermore, he received honorary membership in the British Paediatric Association (Hart, 1963), an organisation whose annual conferences he had attended quite regularly over several decades.

Fortunately, Winnicott seemed to manage his ongoing cardiac illness quite well across the early 1960s, and he remained in reasonably good health, aided, perhaps, by his more complete retirement from the British National Health Service in 1963.

Although Donald Winnicott did enjoy a respite from his near-deadly coronary crises of the late 1940s and early 1950s, he did, however, navigate a serious health scare at some point during the 1960s, namely, a significant injury to one of his eyes.

In 1997, not long after my first meeting with The Piggle, a colleague introduced me to a gentleman to whom I shall refer as "Mr Edmund

Fothergill" (a pseudonym), one of Winnicott's patients in the 1960s. Mr Fothergill—a generous person—very kindly agreed to speak to me about his sessions with Dr Winnicott. Blessed with a very vivid memory, Fothergill shared many useful details about Winnicott, including the fact that, during one of his appointments, the two men spoke at length about Fothergill's complex relationship to violence. In the midst of their discussions, Winnicott revealed to his patient that, sometime previously, during a psychotherapeutic consultation with an autistic child, he had focused too much attention on the child's mother, at which point this angry autistic youngster grabbed a sharp instrument, possibly a pencil, used for drawing squiggles, and stabbed Winnicott in the eye! Fortunately, Winnicott did not lose his vision in that eye, but he told Fothergill that his eye continued to cause him great pain (Kahr, 1997; cf. Kahr, 2020a).

To the best of my knowledge, no one has ever written about this physically burdensome and truly horrifying episode in Winnicott's life; indeed, I came to know about this injury solely from my interview with Edmund Fothergill. I have a strong reason to believe this reminiscence to be completely true, because we do have independent evidence that, in 1963, shortly before Winnicott first met The Piggle, he did visit the noted London ophthalmological surgeon, Mr Frank Law (1963), who maintained a private office at 36, Devonshire Place, in the heart of London's elite medical district.

Moreover, I subsequently discovered another unpublished source, written in 1965, in which Winnicott revealed that a very long-standing female patient—an adult—also poked him in the eye. For reasons of confidentiality, I cannot provide a precise bibliographical reference to this paper, contained within public archives, as that would breach the patient's name, but I can confirm the truth of this episode.

Thus, in view of these two separate instances of ocular injury, one of which occurred just prior to the meeting with The Piggle and the other which may have occurred at roughly the same period of time, we can now acquire a much greater understanding of why Winnicott kept bottles of Optrex in his consulting room and why he made so many references to these objects throughout the text of *The Piggle: An Account of the Psychoanalytic Treatment of a Little Girl*.

Donald Winnicott's full retirement from the Paddington Green Children's Hospital, after some forty years of service, created much more physical space in his diary and, no doubt, much more mental space as well, which allowed him to provide an opportunity to work with The Piggle at the very start of 1964. But these tragic and no doubt highly frightening injuries to his eye—a little known, indeed *unknown*, fact of Winnicott's biography—peppered their various meetings across the years.

Let us now explore the interweaving lives of Donald Woods Winnicott and The Piggle throughout the time of their occasional consultations and beyond, drawing predominantly upon unpublished archival materials and unpublished oral history interviews.

Section Three: Two Interweaving Biographies, 1964–1971

1964

Born on Friday, 18th August, 1961, The Piggle grew up in the English county of Oxfordshire, the eldest child of two intelligent, concerned, and reliable parents. But her life changed dramatically when, during her twenty-first month—not quite two years of age—the mother, Mrs Piggle, gave birth to a second baby, Susan, and, in consequence, The Piggle (also referred to in the published version of the case history as "Gabrielle"), like many youngsters, grappled with profound sibling rivalry. Indeed, The Piggle began to scratch her own face and she became preoccupied with blackness and often struggled to sleep. Moreover, The Piggle experienced significant distress and boredom, and she would often fall down, cry, and feel hurt. In consequence of these regressive behaviours and these strong psychological concerns, the parents decided to seek the assistance of Donald Winnicott, whom Mrs Piggle had already encountered on several occasions as part of her work in the mental health field (as we have noted previously). When the mother spoke to her elder daughter about the possibility of meeting with Winnicott, The Piggle replied, "Mummy take me to Dr Winnicott" (quoted in Winnicott, 1977, p. 7), whereupon the parents wrote to the great doctor at his home-office in Chester Square on 4th January, 1964, requesting a consultation ("Mr. Piggle" and "Mrs. Piggle", 1964a).

At the start of that New Year, Donald Winnicott had quite a lot on his mind. On 3rd January, the day before Mrs Piggle penned her note, hoping for an appointment, Dr Winnicott had paid a final visit to his very elderly medical mentor, Professor Sir Francis Fraser, a physician under whom he had worked at St. Bartholomew's Hospital in London, during the early 1920s, and who now suffered from a serious illness and would die several months thereafter. Additionally, Clare Winnicott—his second wife—had received an invitation to attend a very important interview on 8th January at the Home Office—a seminal ministerial department of the government—to determine whether she would assume the hugely responsible post as head of the Central Training Council in Child Care.

Also, during this same month, one of Winnicott's long-standing analysands, Mrs Jane Shore Khan, the former wife of yet another one of his sometime patients, fellow psychoanalyst Mr Masud Khan, married for the second time. Winnicott proved quite instrumental in helping Jane Khan to recover from her complex and painful marriage to the ever-controversial Masud Khan (Hopkins, 2006; cf. Kahr, 2009d).[2] But in spite of the success of his work with Jane Khan, Winnicott may have experienced considerable guilt that his analysand and colleague—the infamous Masud Khan—had treated his wife so unfaithfully (cf. Kahr, 2003).

In addition to these potentially emotionally evocative encounters—bidding goodbye to one of his most crucial medical teachers, supporting his wife during a stressful job interview, and having to dwell upon the complex marital woes of not one, but two, of his analysands—Winnicott also attended to other more regular tasks during January, 1964, including delivering several lectures to child care students at the London School of Economics and Political Science, participating in meetings of both the British Psycho-Analytical Society and, also, the Medical Section of the British Psychological Society, as well as travelling to Oxford on 29th January to dine with members of the Oxford Union Society, and to present a paper on "The Concept of the False Self" as part of a conference on "Crime: A Challenge", held at the university's distinguished All Souls College (Winnicott, 1964c).

On Saturday, 1st February, 1964—only two days before his first official professional in-person encounter with The Piggle—Winnicott met up with two of his nieces by marriage, Miss Alison Britton and Miss Celia Britton, at Peter Jones—a large department store in the Chelsea district of London—at 11.00 a.m.; and then, at 4.00 p.m., he spent the late afternoon with two of his long-standing producers at the British Broadcasting Corporation, Mrs Isa Benzie and Miss Janet Quigley, each of whom had facilitated his career as a psychological expert on the radio (e.g., Kahr, 1996a, 2018, 2023a; Karpf, 2014). Alas, on Sunday, 2nd February, Winnicott could not even permit himself a day of rest because he had to conduct an emergency session with a very psychiatrically ill private patient. The ageing psychoanalyst often filled his weekends in this way.

Thus, Winnicott may well have felt somewhat fatigued by Monday, 3rd February—the day on which he facilitated his very first consultation with The Piggle.

According to his unpublished diaries, carefully preserved in the Archives and Manuscripts division of the Wellcome Library, part of the Wellcome Collection in London, Winnicott met with The Piggle and her parents at 4.00 p.m. on that very afternoon.

What would The Piggle have experienced upon walking into the large and stately house at 87, Chester Square, in London's Belgravia? Fortunately, we know a great deal not only about Winnicott's physical appearance at the time but, also, about the details of his consulting room.

In all likelihood, Winnicott answered the front door himself. Although he employed a conscientious and devoted full-time secretary, Mrs Joyce Coles, to attend to his correspondence and typing and other administrative chores, including household tasks, and although she did answer the door from time to time (Anonymous, 2000), on the basis of my interviews with many of Winnicott's former patients, I can confirm that, on most occasions, he greeted the patients by himself in the foyer and then ushered them into his office.

Upon entering Chester Square, accompanied by both her mother and her father, The Piggle would have encountered a somewhat balding psychoanalyst, some 5'6" or 5'7" in height (Kahr, 1995c), with a rather wizened face marked by prominent crow's feet around his eyes (e.g., Kahr, 1994d, 1994f, 2009b, 2010b). Winnicott always dressed in finely tailored suits of clothing, which often became quite worn around the knees. As his wife, Clare Winnicott (1982), explained, her husband "had exceptionally strong powers of concentration when he was with patients. In analytic sessions he sat forward on a low straight chair with his elbows on his knees. (For a long time I could never understand why his trousers split across at the knees.)"

Thus, Winnicott may well have appeared both elegant and a bit ragged at the same time.

After a brief conversation in the consulting room among Winnicott and all three members of the family, the parents then returned to the nearby waiting room, while Winnicott invited his somewhat reluctant new child patient back into the ground-floor double-length office for what would prove to be the first of sixteen clinical consultations.

Donald Winnicott maintained a beautiful, carpeted office, heated by a gas fire, which contained a psychoanalytical couch, several chairs (one blue in colour), a desk, a small table for taking notes, as well as several bookshelves, which boasted a smattering of titles on psychology as well as various volumes devoted to art and literature (Guntrip, n.d.). The consulting room overlooked Chester Square itself, with curtains draped across the windows, not to mention many plants, including a box of crocuses. Winnicott adored plants, and one could actually see his blessed roof garden through the back window of his office. He also hung pictures on his consulting room walls, including a portrait of a little girl aged six or seven years, who looked rather serious. As a child psychoanalyst, Winnicott kept a generous stash of toys in his office, often secreted underneath one of his bookshelves. His collection consisted of numerous delights, including little cars and boats, a train, a box, a tractor, some tiny houses, pieces of wood, crayons, a small electric light bulb, soft toys, such as a lamb and a faun, as well as more complex toys which included a donkey and cart, not to mention a figure of a little boy pulling a little girl on a sleigh. He also carried a pair of scissors in his pocket, no doubt used for cutting paper or string (Winnicott, 1977).

Dr Winnicott had long appreciated that toys, in particular, will offer the child many great advantages in the course of psychoanalytical treatment. As early as 1935, in his brief essay on "The Manic Defence", he expressed his appreciation to his own mentor, Mrs Melanie Klein, for having recognised the vital role of such objects. As Winnicott (1935, p. 139, fn. 2) underscored, "Mrs Klein's introduction of the use of a few very small toys was a brilliant plan, because these toys give the child support in regard to contemptuous devaluation and make omnipotent mastery almost a fact. The child is able to express deep fantasies by means of the little toys at the outset of a treatment and so to start with some belief in his own inner reality." Certainly, Winnicott knew, at the outset, that offering toys would be an essential component of his work with The Piggle.

Thus, The Piggle met Donald Winnicott at the height of his career, as a senior clinician with vast experience, safely lodged in the secure space of his pleasantly furnished, familiar consulting room in his home of long standing, tucked away in an elegant and expensive part of London.

During the first of these encounters, The Piggle inspected Winnicott's consulting room; she played with some toys; and she began to become familiar with this important new setting. In his published account, Winnicott (1977) noted that some of the regressed behaviour of this little girl might well be indicative of her own wish to be a baby and thus take the place of her tiny sister, towards whom she experienced a strong sense of rivalry.

The Piggle felt quite safe in Winnicott's presence, and, after the first consultation, she agreed to return for a second meeting, held several weeks later, on Wednesday, 11th March, 1964, followed by a third consultation on Friday, 10th April, and, then, a fourth consultation on Tuesday, 26th May.

Throughout these subsequent encounters, Winnicott became increasingly aware of the extent of the little girl's hatred for her annoying new sister Susan. In fact, in the midst of the second consultation, The Piggle announced, "Put the baby in the dustbin" (quoted in Winnicott, 1977, p. 29). After the third meeting, Winnicott (1977, p. 39) had engaged in such significant contact with his new child patient that he could already begin to see improvements, noting that The Piggle had begun to appear "less tense than before" and, moreover, that she had developed a "New ability to *play at* (thus coping with) rather than *to be in* the frightening fantasy" (Winnicott, 1977, p. 47). Treatment seemed to be working.

After several months, Winnicott and The Piggle had established a deeply engaged relationship, so much so that Mrs Piggle (1964, p. 63) wrote to Winnicott, "The Piggle has asked several times to see you."

In response to the mother's request, Winnicott then facilitated a fifth encounter with The Piggle, exactly one week later, on Tuesday, 9th June, 1964.

Reading through the published version of Winnicott's text, one would cheerfully assume that, by having met The Piggle on five occasions, and by having worked with her in such an engaging manner, analysing the meaning of her play and her many communications in great detail, he had become her definitive psychoanalyst, and, moreover, that he would remain her chosen physician. However, owing to the fact that the child lived in Oxford, some fifty miles north-west of London, he had already agreed to the plan that The Piggle might visit him only as needed, on a so-called "on demand" (Winnicott, 1977, p. 2) basis.

But reading through the unpublished correspondence in "'The Piggle' Papers", one finds a letter written by Winnicott (1964d) to Mrs Piggle on 25th June, 1964, not long after the fifth consultation, indicating that he had thought seriously about the real challenge posed by geographical distance, which prevented the child from visiting him more frequently. In consequence, Winnicott had considered the possibility of referring his new, young child patient to a colleague, Dr Donald Meltzer, an American-born physician who had immigrated to Great Britain in order to undertake a training analysis with Melanie Klein (Grosskurth, 1986). During the early years of Meltzer's career as a psychoanalytical practitioner, Winnicott rated him highly, in part because of his willingness to work with psychotic patients. As time progressed, however, the relationship between these two men became increasingly strained. Meltzer created quite a stir among his colleagues in the British Psycho-Analytical Society by having become possibly the first practitioner to work part-time in London and part-time in Oxford, before moving his office to Oxford on a full-time basis, and this raised many eyebrows (owing to rumours that he encouraged his patients to undergo psychoanalysis by dividing their time between these two separate cities). Nevertheless, in view of Meltzer's proximity to The Piggle and her family in Oxfordshire, it made great sense for Winnicott to have considered this option. In the end, he decided against facilitating such a referral.

Winnicott and Mrs Piggle also discussed the possibility that he might attempt to engage The Piggle by telephone—perhaps an early precursor to "Skype therapy" or "Zoom therapy" (!)—but, in the end, Winnicott (1964d) dismissed this suggestion, having noted, "I too think that conversations by telephone are liable to go awry." Thus, Winnicott opted for in-person, London-based sessions at Chester Square, recommending that, "It is much better to think in terms of natural recovery with an occasional visit to me helping things along a bit."

In his letter of 25th June, 1964—only part of which appears in the published version (cf. Winnicott, 1964d)—Donald Winnicott (1977, p. 74) concluded that a "full-scale analysis" of five sessions weekly would not be possible, but that, nevertheless, The Piggle could see him for "an occasional visit". Thus, after five consultations, spaced over several months, the so-called "on demand" treatment contract became established more formally between Winnicott and the parents.

Throughout 1964—the first year of Winnicott's sessions with The Piggle—the ageing psychoanalyst remained characteristically busy, leading a full professional life. He continued to deliver lectures at both the Institute of Education and, also, at the London School of Economics and Political Science, which had become a regular feature of his working week for many years. He also devoted considerable energy to the British Psycho-Analytical Society, attending Wednesday night Scientific Meetings and serving on committees. Additionally, Winnicott contributed to other professional organisations such as the Child Psychiatric Section of the Royal Medico-Psychological Association (the precursor to the Royal College of Psychiatrists).

On 27th March, 1964—Good Friday—between his second and third assessment sessions with The Piggle, Winnicott flew to Rome in order to present a paper on "The Neonate and His Mother" at a symposium on "Problemi neurofisiologici, neuroclinici e psicologici del neonata a termine e prematuro" ["Neurophysiological, Neuroclinical and Psychological Problems of the Full-Term and Premature Neonate"], organised by a distinguished Italian psychoanalyst, Professoressa Renata Gaddini (1996)—a woman whom he admired greatly. In his paper, eventually published in the periodical *Acta Paediatrica Latina*, Winnicott (1964b) described a very psychiatrically ill patient with whom he had worked for an extremely long period of time. Quite independently of my research on The Piggle, I have come to learn the identity of this particular patient, in part, through one of my many interviews with Winnicott's secretary, Joyce Coles (Kahr, 1994g), and, in part, through having studied much of Winnicott's unpublished correspondence; and I know that this highly troubled woman caused Winnicott immense stress, anxiety, and concern.

Not only did Winnicott preoccupy himself with that particularly challenging psychotic person, but, also, he had to treat at least one *other* psychotic patient during the early months of 1964, who required institutionalisation, and whom Winnicott visited in hospital on *at least* one occasion, if not several times. Although psychoanalytical work with small children can often be quite taxing and physically demanding, especially for the nearly seventy-year-old clinician, one suspects that Dr Winnicott might well have experienced his intermittent sessions with The Piggle—an occasionally troubled, though essentially highly sweet and eminently helpable, young person—as rather relaxing by comparison to his other much more burdensome and worrisome patients.

After his return to London from Rome, Winnicott delivered a range of further talks, including a speech on "The Origins of Violence" to the Cambridge University Campaign for Nuclear Disarmament, as well as a presentation on "The Psycho-Somatic Dilemma" before the Society for Psychosomatic Research.

Perhaps of greatest importance, the distinguished British publishers, Penguin Books, produced an omnibus edition of Winnicott's talks and broadcasts for members of the general public, which had originally appeared in two volumes, back in 1957, as *The Child and the Family: First Relationships* (Winnicott, 1957a) and *The Child and the Outside World: Studies in Developing Relationships* (Winnicott, 1957b). The new collection—an amalgamation of these texts—bore the now famous title *The Child, the Family, and the Outside World* (Winnicott, 1964a), and this paperback volume soon became the largest-selling of all of Winnicott's many publications. Priced initially at four shillings and six pence, the book actually sold an impressive 12,939 copies in the first year alone (Palmer, 1967).

Also, in 1964, Winnicott offered much assistance to the budding psychoanalytical society in Finland. Dr Maxwell Gitelson (1963), the President of the International Psycho-Analytical Association, invited Winnicott to meet the growing community of Finnish Freudian practitioners, in order to ensure that their training conformed to the exacting standards of other institutions worldwide. Winnicott made several trips to Finland and Sweden during the 1960s to supervise this process; and, to his delight, he helped the Finns to receive official recognition (Zetzel, 1964; King, 1997). It will not be widely known that Winnicott undertook this task of vetting the Finns, not only with characteristic generosity, but, also, with tremendous vigilance; and when he discovered that one of the Scandinavian psychoanalysts went on holiday with a patient, Winnicott recommended that this person's membership should be revoked (Kahr, 2005).

Furthermore, in 1964, Winnicott became a patron of the Peredur Appeal—a pioneer scheme for emotionally insecure school leavers. In this honorary role, he sat alongside such distinguished fellow patrons as His Grace the Duke of Norfolk (Bernard Fitzalan-Howard)—Earl Marshal to Her Majesty Queen Elizabeth II—as well as the actor Sir Laurence Olivier and the musician Yehudi Menuhin (Birt, 1964). Although Winnicott accepted this position as a patron, he turned down numerous other opportunities and he refused lecture invitations from such distinguished organisations as the Howard League for Penal Reform, the Board of Extra-Mural Studies at the University of Cambridge, the Institute of Youth Employment Officers, the Association of Workers for Maladjusted Children, the Northern New England District Branch of the American Psychiatric Association, the Massachusetts Society for Research in Psychiatry, the Boston Society for Psychiatry and Neurology, and many others besides.

In spite of having retired from four decades of service at the Paddington Green Children's Hospital, Donald Winnicott still had little time to spare during the 1964 calendar year. Indeed, Winnicott often could not see all of the potential patients who had requested consultations; and, owing to his crowded timetable, he had to turn down innumerable clinical referrals. We know from his unpublished correspondence that he maintained a list of some trusted junior psychoanalytical colleagues, including, *inter alia*, Dr Herman Hardenberg, Dr James Armstrong Harris, Mr Masud Khan, Dr Margaret Little, Dr Peter Lomas, and Dr Barbara Woodhead, and he would recommend these individuals to prospective patients, many of whom no doubt experienced a deep sense of disappointment that they would not be able to work with the great man himself.

Thus, the parents of The Piggle, and the little girl too, might have felt very pleased that Winnicott had generously agreed to approximately monthly consultations, especially in view of his packed schedule.

Certainly, without his embrace of "on demand" therapy, Winnicott would not, in all likelihood, have had the capacity at that point in his career to provide ongoing treatment for his new child patient. Fortunately, "on demand" treatment proved particularly attractive to Winnicott, not only due to his appreciation of both The Piggle's geographical location and her clinical needs, but, moreover, because of his growing recognition of what he could or could not manage from a practical, timetabling point of view.

Contemporaneously, Mrs Clare Winnicott did, in fact, receive the appointment as Director of Child Care Studies in the Children's Department of the Home Office—a very important government position which she would hold until 1971. Thus, not only did Donald Winnicott struggle with a hugely overburdened timetable in 1964, but so, too, did his wife. In consequence, the Winnicotts had to refuse many social invitations. Indeed, in 1964, he wrote to Mr Michael Duane, the head of the Risinghill School in North London, describing himself as "frantically overloaded" (Winnicott, 1964e).

As 1964 unfolded, The Piggle continued to make great progress in her very unique form of psychoanalysis, so much so that the appreciative parents wrote to Winnicott that, "on the occasions that Gabrielle is well, she is very well indeed" ("Mr. Piggle" and "Mrs. Piggle", 1964b, p. 97).

By the end of that first calendar year, The Piggle had visited Chester Square on fully eight occasions. During this time, Winnicott facilitated much play therapy with The Piggle and, also, encouraged conversation about a whole range of matters. Among the many striking themes discussed by Winnicott and The Piggle, one appreciates the focus on the little girl's sense of her own vulnerability. Indeed, in the eighth consultation, held on Tuesday, 1st December, 1964, The Piggle expressed her wish that one day she would be powerful, so much so that, "When I am big I will get old before Mummy's old, before she is old" (quoted in Winnicott, 1977, p. 103). The Piggle also acquired the ability to speak directly about her complex feelings towards her baby sister. She admitted, "I'm scared of the black Susan; so I play with your toys. I hate Susan. Yes I hate her very much" (quoted in Winnicott, 1977, p. 103).

Needless to say, Winnicott had long known about the perils of sibling rivalry. Indeed, even before he had completed his training as a psychoanalyst, Winnicott (1931a, p. 98) underscored, in his textbook on *Clinical Notes on Disorders of Childhood*, that, "it is very common for a child of 2–3 years old to be very upset at the birth of a baby brother or sister", and that elder siblings might readily develop a range of psychosomatic symptoms, which could include, "enuresis, temper, sickness, constipation, nasal congestion" (Winnicott, 1931a, p. 98), not to mention several other varieties, such as "an attack of pneumonia, whooping cough, gastro-enteritis" (Winnicott, 1931a, p. 98), as well as a loss of appetite. Thus, he had known for many decades about the importance of speaking to children about this normal, but vexing, aspect of family life.

Fortunately, through play and through verbalisation, Winnicott helped The Piggle to experience a growing sense of catharsis and to develop a greater capacity for robustness.

Winnicott capped the calendar year by sending a special Christmas card to The Piggle with a hand-drawn picture of a donkey inside!

1965

Throughout 1965, The Piggle attended for only five consultations. It may well be that Winnicott offered fewer appointments during this second year of treatment, in part because he had to endure quite a number of medical and professional burdens of his own. Indeed, a footnote appeared in the published version of his book on The Piggle, which revealed, "The summer of 1965 was an exceptionally demanding time and included a period of illness" (Ramzy, 1977b, p. 145, fn. 3). In all likelihood, the editor of the book had inserted this footnote after his death, thus offering further insight about the burdens of Winnicott's life at that time. Whatever Winnicott's preoccupations, we might also suppose that The Piggle had begun to develop successfully and, thus, had become better able to manage her sibling rivalry and other ordinary challenges of childhood, and, hence, may not have required quite as many consultations as she had received during the previous year.

Although Winnicott maintained contact with The Piggle, now three years of age, he also enjoyed an extensive correspondence with each of the parents, who wrote to him frequently. We know from an inspection of the family archive that Mrs Piggle, in particular, would prepare numerous handwritten drafts of her letters before sending a more polished version to Dr Winnicott. By studying the original documents, including these multiple drafts with many crossings-out, one can readily see how much energy Mrs Piggle devoted to her correspondence with Winnicott, and one can certainly imagine the important "holding" function that

Dr Winnicott offered not only to The Piggle but, *also*, to the parents. After all, Mrs Piggle had known Winnicott over many decades; hence, he occupied a vital position in her mind, and he may also have served as an honorary psychoanalyst of sorts to her as well.

In terms of Donald Winnicott's wider professional commitments, 1965 proved to be an even more crowded year than 1964. Of greatest importance, he published two of his most impressive books—each a volume of carefully curated collected papers—namely, *The Family and Individual Development* (Winnicott, 1965a) and, also, *The Maturational Processes and the Facilitating Environment: Studies in the Theory of Emotional Development* (Winnicott, 1965b), which has since become a classic in the history of psychoanalysis. The first of these books, *The Family and Individual Development*, produced by Tavistock Publications, appeared in the early part of 1965 and sold for thirty shillings. The even more substantial successor, *The Maturational Processes and the Facilitating Environment: Studies in the Theory of Emotional Development*—released by the Hogarth Press in collaboration with the Institute of Psycho-Analysis of London, as part of "The International Psycho-Analytical Library" series—became available for purchase in the summer of 1965 at the cost of forty-two shillings. This text contained no fewer than twenty-three chapters (many of which had not appeared in print previously) and would, in all likelihood, have exhausted the author in the process.

Winnicott worked extremely hard to prepare these two significant volumes for publication. In consequence, he had little time for social encounters or for meetings with colleagues, lamenting to his longstanding psychoanalytical contemporary, Dr Roger Money-Kyrle, "It is sad that we meet so seldom, and life slips away, but somehow it can't be helped—this job we are in takes so much of our time and emotional energy" (Winnicott, 1965e).

Amid this flurry of creative activity, Winnicott's fame continued to spread, even to Africa. Indeed, a student from Rhodesia, Miss Pam Gabriel (1965a), wrote to him asking for references about the psychology of the only child. Winnicott (1965i), overwhelmed by work, took two months to reply to this woman but, eventually, he did so, prompting her to enthuse, "I was honoured to receive a letter from such a distinguished person" (Gabriel, 1965b). By the mid-1960s, Winnicott's reputation had become so potent that one of his London colleagues, Dr Martin James

(1965), enthused, "You see, you have become a commercial proposition like the Beatles ("let me be your Brian Epstein" etc)." One cannot help but wonder whether the parents of The Piggle considered themselves quite fortunate that Great Britain's most distinguished psychoanalyst had carved out any time for them at all.

Throughout 1965, Winnicott persevered with his teaching and lecturing. On 25th February, he delivered a talk on "The Price of Disregarding Research Findings" at a distinguished conference on "The Price of Mental Health", sponsored by the National Association for Mental Health. Winnicott (1965d) took to the stage immediately after the Right Honourable Kenneth Robinson (1965), the Minister of Health, who had spoken about the heavy financial cost of mental illness.

In May, 1965, Winnicott travelled to Copenhagen, in Denmark, to continue his work as one of the sponsors of the developing Scandinavian psychoanalytical community. Additionally, Winnicott continued to teach extensively. He had kindly offered to deliver as many as nine lectures on "A Clinical Approach to Family Problems" to students attending the Applied Social Studies Course at the London School of Economics and Political Science in the University of London, during the summer term of 1965, for which he received a fee of eleven pounds and ten shillings per lecture (Caine, 1964). Likewise, in June of 1965, he presented two further lectures at the Institute of Education, also part of the University of London, and, moreover, in that same month, he addressed the Medical Section of the British Psychological Society, and then, in July of 1965, he spoke at the British Psycho-Analytical Society—all hugely time-consuming activities. And later that very month, he travelled to Amsterdam, in the Netherlands, to participate in the congress of the International Psycho-Analytical Association and talked about a case of obsessional neurosis (Winnicott, 1966b).

After such enormous professional commitments, Winnicott suffered from exhaustion. Indeed, on 2nd August, 1965, he wrote to his psychoanalytical colleague, Dr Ronald Markillie, emphasising his urge to have a summer holiday, having described himself as "panting to forget everything" (Winnicott, 1965h).

Of greatest importance, Winnicott stood for election as President of the British Psycho-Analytical Society, a post of enormous responsibility, having already occupied this seminal role once before, between 1956 and 1959. In 1965, Donald Winnicott ran against colleagues Dr Paula Heimann, Dr Herbert Rosenfeld, and Dr Lothair Rubinstein, and he beat all three of them. Miss Pearl King, Winnicott's sometime supervisee, became his Deputy President, having served previously as his Secretary during his prior term of office. A woman of immense administrative reliability and capability, Miss King (2001a) undertook a vast amount of the tedious paperwork on behalf of this professional organisation, thus permitting Winnicott to attend to the more ceremonial tasks. Nonetheless, in spite of the assistance of his Secretary, Winnicott had to deal with many responsibilities, and, in view of the huge commitments that he had already undertaken as a clinician, supervisor, teacher, lecturer, and writer, many had come to regard him as administratively negligent and incompetent to a certain extent (Kahr, 2010a).

Throughout this time, Winnicott continued to treat The Piggle successfully and he maintained his vital correspondence with Mr Piggle and Mrs Piggle, especially the latter, who continued to rely upon the great psychoanalyst for her own containment and reassurance. On 12th July, 1965, not long after his eleventh consultation with the young girl, Winnicott (1965f, p. 145) wrote to Mr Piggle and Mrs Piggle, "Children do have to work through their problems at home and I would not be surprised if Gabrielle is able to find a way through the present phase" (cf. Winnicott, 1965f).[3]

The Piggle continued to engage with the safe-making and delightful elderly psychoanalyst, and one senses that she paid very close attention to his every movement. As I indicated earlier, at some point during the early 1960s—very probably in 1963—Winnicott endured one or more injuries to his eyes and had to consult an ophthalmologist. He suffered considerable pain, and, in consequence, he kept a bottle of Optrex eyebath in his consulting room at Chester Square. Whereas most psychoanalysts would secrete their medications in a drawer, Winnicott needed to soak his eyes with this fluid on such a regular basis and, consequently, The Piggle became quite drawn to this very visible and most unusual object. As early as 11th March, 1964—the second of her consultations— the child picked up this blue bottle and enquired, "What's this?" (quoted in Winnicott, 1977, p. 23). Before Winnicott had a chance to reply, The Piggle had already begun to preoccupy herself with a toy train. But later in this same session, The Piggle began to speak about eyes and, after handing Winnicott an electric light bulb, she chirped, "Put in more eyes and more eyebrows" (quoted in Winnicott, 1977, p. 26).

References to eyes and to Optrex would continue to punctuate the treatment. On Saturday, 10th October, 1964—the seventh consultation—Winnicott noted that The Piggle played with the bottle of Optrex once again. And during the following meeting on Tuesday, 1st December—the eighth consultation—The Piggle played with the Optrex for at least the third time and asked her psychoanalyst directly, "What is this for?" (quoted in Winnicott, 1977, p. 103). Immediately thereafter, she began to speak about her mother becoming older. One cannot help but wonder whether The Piggle sensed that Dr Winnicott used the Optrex because of his own ageing eyes, or, indeed, whether he might have deployed them in her presence on one or more occasions.[4]

The Piggle continued to engage with the eyebath bottle and did so, yet again, in the ninth consultation on Friday, 29th January, 1965. In fact, during this session, she toyed with the bottle several times across the psychoanalytical hour and even put it into her mouth, producing "sucking noises" (Winnicott, 1977, p. 118) in the process, which Winnicott (1977, p. 118) described as "very near to a generalized orgasm."

In his published account of the tenth consultation of Tuesday, 23rd March, Winnicott took great pains to inform his readers that the toys in his consulting room had remained constant throughout the analysis of The Piggle, but that he had introduced the Optrex eyebath between the first and second appointments. We might well hypothesise that Winnicott's injury occurred during mid-1963, and that he placed the Optrex in his office, on ophthalmological advice, during the early part of 1964.

By Wednesday, 16th June—the eleventh appointment—Winnicott boasted not one, but two, Optrex eye cups in his consulting room. Unsurprisingly, The Piggle became extremely curious and began to play with these items even more extensively, staring at the world through one of the blue glasses and placing the other one on top of a toy truck. In the twelfth consultation, on Friday, 8th October, The Piggle used a red crayon to draw a picture of a lamp lady, which she then crowned with an Optrex cup as a hat of sorts.

One imagines that The Piggle might well have engaged with the Optrex on numerous other occasions, although Winnicott may not have written about each and every one of these episodes in this relatively short study of his child patient. But, certainly, the Optrex may well have represented a part of Winnicott's body to The Piggle, which she might have wished to touch and swallow and incorporate. For Winnicott himself, the Optrex bottle and eye cups served as a constant reminder of his potentially great physical pain and suffering—a fact never previously reported in the literature.

Amid these five consultations of 1965, Winnicott continued to overcommit himself professionally. In the autumn of that year, he delivered ten more seminars for child psychiatrists at the Mary Ward Settlement about "Therapeutic Consultations in Child Psychiatry", sponsored by the National Association for Mental Health and the Institute of Child Health. He also undertook further talks at the London School of Economics and Political Science. Nevertheless, in spite of all of these diary obligations, Donald Winnicott continued to remain loyal to The Piggle and her family and certainly did not interrupt the treatment at all. Nevertheless, by learning about Winnicott's overcrowded diary, one can understand his championship of so-called "on demand" consultations even more fully.

1966

Throughout the year 1966, this ageing man continued to work with some very disturbed adult psychiatric patients who taxed him considerably (Winnicott, 1966c). Undeterred, he performed his duties as President of the British Psycho-Analytical Society, and he also persevered with his foreign travels. In early February, 1966, he lectured extensively in Geneva, in Switzerland, and then, in Milan, in Italy; and later that month, he flew to Leiden, in the Netherlands, to deliver several more talks.

On Thursday, 7th April, 1966, Winnicott turned seventy years old. His former trainee, Dr Peter Tizard, who subsequently became a distinguished professor of paediatrics, telephoned Winnicott to offer him happy birthday greetings. As a scientific researcher, Tizard then clarified his well wishes, noting, "I should say the anniversary of your birthday" (quoted in Tizard, 1981, pp. 267–268). As Tizard recalled, "You certainly should," said Winnicott, "thank Heavens one doesn't have to undergo *that* experience more than once!" (quoted in Tizard, 1981, p. 268).

Some weeks later, on Saturday night, 30th April, 1966, the British Psycho-Analytical Society hosted a party at its headquarters on New Cavendish Street, in Central London, in honour of this landmark birthday, for approximately 250 guests (Montessori, 1968), including Winnicott's very first psychoanalyst, the scholarly Mr James Strachey—one of Professor Sigmund Freud's analysands and, of course, translators—whom Winnicott had first consulted, decades previously, in 1923 (Kahr, 2010c; cf. Kahr, 1996a).

In 1966, The Piggle attended for her final three sessions with Donald Winnicott. In the fourteenth consultation, on Friday, 18th March, the child—now four and a half years of age—began to play with a very new toy, namely, a figure of "a little boy pulling a sleigh with a little girl on it" (Winnicott, 1977, p. 180). One might well surmise that this child who, as a two-year-old girl, could not bear the thought of sharing space with a younger sibling, had, by now, succeeded in enjoying her play with a single toy composed of two people working as a pair, rather than as rivals.[5]

Most touchingly, in her penultimate session—the fifteenth—held on Wednesday, 3rd August, The Piggle reached for the Optrex glass bottles once again. This time, she placed the cups over her own eyes. Winnicott, in truly spontaneous mode, tensed his orbicularis muscles and succeeded in holding the eye baths on his face without the aid of his hands. After some practice, The Piggle managed to follow suit and would clutch one of these glass objects with one of *her* eye muscles. Afterwards, she confessed to Winnicott, "I'd like to take them home with me" (quoted in Winnicott, 1977, p. 190). No doubt, at this point, Winnicott may well have felt satisfied that The Piggle could imitate him, identify with him, and even incorporate him. She had begun to consolidate her internalisation of this child psychoanalytical process—an indication that she had achieved success and could begin to manage without his concrete physical presence, so much so that, at the end of her sixteenth and final session on Friday, 28th October, 1966, he pronounced this five-year-old child as "psychiatrically normal" (Winnicott, 1977, p. 198).

Of course, it would be sheer idealisation to presume that Winnicott's work with The Piggle unfolded in a magical fashion, marked by constant improvement along the way. Throughout the course of treatment, Winnicott possessed the ability to disappoint The Piggle and she certainly enjoyed the capacity to express her displeasure. The unpublished letters from the archives of The Piggle's family reveal that, on one occasion, the little girl told her mother that she felt aware of the presence of a "policeman" (quoted in "Mrs. Piggle", n.d. [d]) in her mind—perhaps a transferential reference to the ever-monitoring psychoanalyst. Upon hearing this, Mrs Piggle asked her daughter whether she might wish to share this information with Dr Winnicott; but The Piggle replied, "No, he does'nt [sic] understand" (quoted in "Mrs. Piggle", n.d. [d]).

Also, in my very first interview with the mother, Mrs Piggle, in 1995, she revealed that although she held Winnicott in high esteem, it saddened her that, from time to time, Winnicott's health situation interfered with the treatment and that, on at least one occasion, he upset The Piggle greatly by not being able to meet with her for a period of time, having promised the child that he would be available. Apparently, The Piggle experienced Winnicott's absence as very painful indeed (Kahr, 1995h).

But on the whole, the treatment worked extremely well. And in one of the mother's untitled notes, contained in "'The Piggle' Papers", we learn that, on another occasion, Mrs Piggle asked her daughter directly what she thought of Winnicott. The little girl responded, "he can make me better" (quoted in "Mrs. Piggle", n.d. [a]); and when the mother requested further clarification and wondered which part of The Piggle now felt better, the little girl pointed to her head!

In having undertaken this extraordinary piece of clinical work with The Piggle, Donald Winnicott made a vital contribution to child psychotherapy and child psychoanalysis. He allowed his patient considerable time in which to communicate not only through language but, also, through play. In each consultation, he paid extremely close attention to The Piggle's words and gestures, as demonstrated by his carefully written notes and by his foregrounding of detail.

Winnicott also devoted much attention to the trauma of sibling rivalry—a very classical notion—and came to appreciate the little girl's struggle with her new baby sister, Susan. Moreover, he granted considerable authority to The Piggle herself by permitting her to request an "on demand" session with him when it most suited her.

With tremendous clinical intelligence, Winnicott also recognised that the roots of The Piggle's symptoms may have stemmed not only from the recent birth of her younger sibling but, also, from earlier, intra-familial factors within the Piggle household more generally. Indeed, in his write-up of the twelfth session with The Piggle, he included a letter from Mrs Piggle in which she confessed to Winnicott that she, too, had endured a considerable experience of sibling rivalry during her own childhood with a brother whom she disliked. As Mrs Piggle noted, "My anxieties were very intense at the time of Susan's birth—I forget whether I told you that I have a brother, whom I greatly resented, who was born when I was almost exactly the same age as Gabrielle was when Susan was born" ("Mrs. Piggle" (n.d. [b] [1965], p. 161).

Throughout the text, Winnicott made no overt reference at all to the fact that Mrs Piggle grew up in a Jewish family. Perhaps he disguised such biographical information for reasons of confidentiality. But, certainly, he would have appreciated from Mrs Piggle's real name and from her vocal accent and, also, from their many conversations, her status as an émigré from a persecuted background. Moreover, as I indicated earlier, Winnicott had also known Mrs Piggle's mother—the grandmother of The Piggle—and, together, she and Winnicott had once discussed the case of a little boy whose parents died in the Holocaust.[6]

Thus, although Winnicott undertook this treatment long before the explosion of knowledge about what we would now conceptualise as the intergenerational transmission of trauma (e.g., Krugman, 1987), he certainly remained sensitive to the historical precursors of The Piggle's struggles, some of which might be rooted in her ancestry.

In view of the richness of the case and the successful outcome of his work, it should hardly surprise us that, in due course, Winnicott began to consider sharing this material with his clinical colleagues and with a wider audience.

Donald Winnicott's Final Years

Winnicott conceived the idea of writing up his consultations with The Piggle for publication at least as early as 1965. In an unpublished letter addressed to Mrs Piggle, he opined, "Dont [sic] let this idea of the book get in the way of our ordinary inter-communicating" (Winnicott, 1965j). And only weeks thereafter, he penned a letter to the mother encouraging her to record her own observations: "I am very pleased to get notes if you feel like writing any" (Winnicott, 1965k).

Unsurprisingly, as the intimacy between Winnicott and The Piggle developed throughout the mid-1960s, so, too, did the closeness of his relationship with the parents themselves. In 1964, he always wrote to them as "Mr Piggle" and "Mrs Piggle",[7] but, by 1966, he began to address them by their forenames. Throughout the treatment, the family maintained ongoing contact with Winnicott both by post and, also, by telephone. Dr Winnicott even paid a number of visits to the family home in Oxfordshire. The Piggle proved sufficiently important to Winnicott that, even after the conclusion of the treatment, he continued to correspond with her from time to time. In a delightful letter of 21st April, 1967, Winnicott (1967d) wrote to his former child patient after having received a drawing from the little girl: "Thank you for your letter and for the lovely picture of me. I am afraid I am not really as beautiful as all that, but as I seem to be crying in the picture I expect that means that I am sad because I have not seen you for so long."

The case had obviously captivated Winnicott sufficiently, and, even before the end of the treatment in 1966, he embarked upon the process of transforming his notes into a book. Having published his sturdy text on *The Family and Individual Development* (Winnicott, 1965a) during the early months of 1965, followed by his profound collection of essays, *The Maturational Processes and the Facilitating Environment: Studies in the Theory of Emotional Development* (Winnicott, 1965b), which appeared by the summer of 1965, Winnicott suddenly found himself with some breathing space, at least in terms of his writing commitments. With his seventieth birthday looming, he no doubt felt keen to craft his legacy with all due speed. In fact, Winnicott completed the "Introduction" to his draft book about The Piggle on 22nd November, 1965, almost exactly one year *prior* to the conclusion of the formal sixteen consultations with The Piggle, at 10.30 a.m., on the morning of 28th October, 1966.

Throughout the mid-1960s, Winnicott continued to refine his typescript, aided by his long-standing and efficient secretary Joyce Coles. Moreover, he collaborated with Mr Piggle and Mrs Piggle, each of whom provided some additional comments (Winnicott, 1977). Gradually, Winnicott produced a complete text, in pretty good shape; and I had the privilege to consult the original typescript, preserved in "'The Piggle' Papers".

It remains unclear precisely why Winnicott did not then insist upon a swifter publication during the late 1960s, especially as he already had a virtually perfect typescript to hand. Perhaps he planned to see how The Piggle would develop over the next few years, in order to be certain that his sixteen consultations actually proved efficacious in an ongoing way. No clinician would wish to boast that he or she had cured a patient successfully only to discover soon thereafter that the patient then suffered from a debilitating relapse (as proved to be the case with Dr Josef Breuer's famous patient, Bertha Pappenheim, better known as "Anna O" (Breuer, 1882, 1895; Freud, 1932; cf. Freeman, 1972; Forrester and Cameron, 1999; Skues, 2006)).

Winnicott may also have delayed publication because he might have intended to elicit feedback from his psychoanalytical colleagues, especially as his unusual "on demand" arrangement with The Piggle challenged the orthodoxy of five-times-weekly treatment. Consequently, on Wednesday, 15th March, 1967, he presented an informal paper, "Discussion Around a Clinical Detail", at a Scientific Meeting of the British Psycho-Analytical Society on New Cavendish Street in London and offered a preview of his work with this captivating child patient. Apparently, Winnicott had not prepared a formal talk on this occasion, as he had kindly and helpfully agreed to step in at the last minute because of the unexpected illness of a colleague already booked to present a paper on that evening. After he delivered his remarks, Winnicott (1967b) wrote to the parents of The Piggle that, having discussed the case with psychoanalytical colleagues, he had come to appreciate the necessity of generating pseudonyms for the patient and her family in order to protect confidentiality.

Some years ago, while researching in the Archives of the British Psycho-Analytical Society, I had the privilege of listening to a very scratchy, uncatalogued tape recording of this talk, which revealed that, in spite of Winnicott's tremendous seniority at the time, several of his colleagues expressed their doubts about the nature of his work. The impact of this evening among his more staunchly conservative colleagues may also have contributed to Winnicott's hesitation regarding a more immediate publication.

After speaking to his fellow psychoanalytical practitioners about The Piggle in March of 1967, Donald Winnicott undertook many further professional commitments during the remainder of that calendar year. Across 1967, he persevered with his treatments of a large cohort of patients, as well as with his teaching commitments, not to mention quite a number of organisational contributions. For instance, in addition to his ongoing work at institutions such as the British Psycho-Analytical Society, the London School of Economics and Political Science, and the Institute of Education, he assumed the vice-presidency of the National Association for Mental Health (Appleby, 1967; Winnicott, 1967c). He also embarked upon a lecture trip to New York City and to Boston, Massachusetts. Winnicott toiled so relentlessly that, in spite of having departed for London from Boston's Logan Airport on Sunday, 16th April, 1967, at 8.00 p.m., arriving in England the following morning, on Monday, 17th April circa 8.10 a.m., he resumed his clinical sessions almost immediately and even met with a patient that very evening at 8.00 p.m.—no doubt an unbearably tiring timetable for a man of seventy-one years of age.

His workaholism proved so profound that on 2nd May, not long after his exhausting international trip, Winnicott actually delivered *three* separate talks. At 12.00 p.m., he spoke to students at the London School of Economics and Political Science in the University of London. Several hours afterwards, at 7.15 p.m., he presented material to a seminar on autism, sponsored by a pharmaceutical company. And then, later that very night, he taught a group of candidates at the Institute of Psycho-Analysis.

I cannot do full justice to the extent of Winnicott's professional commitments in 1967, but I can report that, during this calendar year, the septuagenarian psychoanalyst not only lectured to numerous London-based organisations but, also, he travelled extensively throughout Great Britain, speaking in Winchester in the county of Hampshire; in Standlake in the county of Oxfordshire; in Plymouth in the county of Devon; and in Radlett in the county of Hertfordshire. In addition to his teaching trips to both New York City and Boston, he also delivered presentations about his work to colleagues in Copenhagen in Denmark, and in Paris in France, as well as in Wiesbaden in Germany; and, he even returned that year for a second lecture trip to Boston. Due to sheer exhaustion, he cancelled trips in 1967 to both Italy and Spain.

Amid all of these commitments, Winnicott continued to prepare his typescript about the treatment of The Piggle. And, shortly after Christmas, 1967, Winnicott (1967e) wrote—somewhat hastily—to Mr Piggle and Mrs Piggle, with glee, boasting, "I've nearly finished the book. Its [sic] terriffic [sic]."

The following calendar year, 1968, proved even more burdensome for the seemingly tireless and always productive Donald Winnicott. Across the months, he continued to toil incessantly as he had done in previous years. And on 7th November he flew—economy class—to New York City, once again, to deliver several more professional papers. Winnicott already suffered from a cold while on board the outbound flight, which no doubt placed him in a physically vulnerable position (Kahr, 1996b). And then, quite tragically, while in Manhattan, he succumbed to a virulent strain of Asian influenza—the so-called "Hong Kong Flu"—and, also, experienced another very serious coronary episode with pulmonary oedema, a frequent complication of valvular heart disease, from which he nearly died. Winnicott required immediate hospitalisation and thus had to spend many weeks in the Lenox Hill Hospital on the Upper East Side of Manhattan and could not fly home to London until 20th December, 1968 (Kahr, 1996a, 2020c, 2021c, 2021d, 2021e).

Although this frail psychoanalyst did manage to resume sessions with patients on 6th February, 1969, he could not work at full capacity and became increasingly debilitated. He did, however, maintain contact with The Piggle and her family and, on 3rd March, Winnicott (1969c) sent a letter to his former patient, underscoring that, "I'm getting well now and I like to write to you from time to time." Winnicott (1969c) also promised, "One day I shall be coming along again for a cup of tea or coffee + to see you all."

To the best of our knowledge, Winnicott did not meet personally with any members of the family of The Piggle after his serious illness in Manhattan, and, although he maintained correspondence by post, he could not manage another consultation or visit.

At some point in 1969, the ailing psychoanalyst completed a full draft of his typescript about his child patient, entitled *The Piggle: Her Psychoanalytic Treatment*; and in March of that year, he sent a copy to the parents along with a note, which read, in part, "You are invited to write all over these pages" (Winnicott, 1969d). But in spite of having nearly finished the book, his almost fatal illness in November of 1968 prevented him from progressing the typescript through the time-consuming complexities of publication. Hence, in spite of his multi-year work, the book did not appear in print during Donald Winnicott's lifetime.

He died at approximately 4.00 a.m. on Monday, 25th January, 1971 (Khan, 1971b), at the age of seventy-four years, from left ventricular failure and myocardial infarction (Kahr, 1996a).

Section Four: Veering Towards Publication

Following Winnicott's death, Clare Winnicott (1971), his grieving widow, wrote to both Mr Piggle and Mrs Piggle to inform them of the sad news. It seems that through their interconnections with the mental health community, the family already knew of Winnicott's decease and had even managed to attend the funeral.

Sometime later, on 4th June, 1973, Clare Winnicott convened with both parents at her home in Chester Square to discuss the publication of the long-percolating book about their daughter. Previously, these three individuals had not met in person—a testament to Donald Winnicott's protection of the family's privacy and confidentiality. Afterwards, Mrs Winnicott (1973a) corresponded further with Mr Piggle and Mrs Piggle, explaining, "I know Donald gained so much from working with you, and it would be good if others could learn from the experience that you all shared."

As discussions about the publication unfolded, Clare Winnicott (1973b) consulted the parents about what name could be used to refer to her late husband's former child patient. The little girl, now twelve years old, agreed that the book should, in fact, bear the supratitle *The Piggle*.

Mrs Winnicott enlisted the services of Dr Ishak Ramzy to assist her with the editing and preparation of the final typescript of her late husband's work. Born in 1911 in the city of Zagazig in the Nile delta of Egypt, Ishak Ramzy studied psychology in Cairo and then moved to England in order to undertake his doctoral studies at the University of London and to train at the Institute of Psycho-Analysis. He then returned to his native Egypt for several years more, after which Ramzy relocated to Topeka, Kansas, in order to work for the distinguished American psychiatrist and psychoanalyst Professor Karl Menninger. Ramzy would remain in the American Midwest until his death in 1992.

Winnicott knew Ramzy reasonably well from their mutual involvement in the British Psycho-Analytical Society, and, in 1965, Winnicott chaired a Simultaneous Session at the International Psycho-Analytical Congress of the International Psycho-Analytical Association, in Amsterdam, in the Netherlands, at which Ramzy delivered a paper on "Factors and Features of Early Compulsive Formation". The two men remained in contact over the years; and when Ramzy discovered that Winnicott had almost died while lecturing in New York City, he sent him a box of "Holiday Feast" chocolates as a present (Ramzy, 1969a), decades before most members of the public had come to realise that such sugary foods might be inadvisable for cardiac patients.

Certainly, Winnicott held Ramzy in sufficiently high regard because, four years later, in 1969, he invited Ramzy to supervise him publicly on his work with The Piggle, at a Pre-Congress gathering of the International Psycho-Analytical Association in London, prior to a larger meeting of this bi-annual psychoanalytical congress in Rome. Just as Winnicott had challenged the Freudian orthodoxy of five sessions of child analysis per week in his treatment of The Piggle, so, too, did he subvert the traditional model of supervision in which an older clinician will comment upon the work of a more junior clinician. Ramzy (1969b), some fifteen years younger than Winnicott, accepted this unusual offer to supervise the case and he wrote to Winnicott, "much as it fills me with awe and timidity, neither can submerge the excitement over the fantastic idea of role-reversal". Winnicott also invited Ramzy (1971) to assist with editorial work on the typescript as early as 1969. Thus, after Dr Winnicott's death, Ramzy became the ideal person to support Mrs Winnicott with the completion of the book.

Clare Winnicott, the widow, maintained quite a vigilant watch over the entire proceedings and, in 1976, she even revised Ishak Ramzy's (1977a) "Editor's Foreword", in spite of her own health struggles, which, at that time, included the eruption of shingles (Clare Winnicott, 1976),[8] and, more severely, a malignant melanoma on her foot, which resulted in many surgical procedures and even prompted her doctors to consider amputation (Elmhirst, 1996b).

Ishak Ramzy also became a confidant to Mrs Piggle, in particular. In a draft letter to Dr Ramzy, written circa 1973, Mrs Piggle revealed that, in her estimation, Dr Winnicott did not always engage with the full extent of her daughter's struggles. As she confessed, "I would have a few criticism [sic] (which I did not keep from Donald)—to do with the dark aspects of the child's feelings, that may sometimes have appeared to have been slurred over" ("Mrs. Piggle", n.d. [c] [c. 1973]). However, in spite of this reservation, she still proclaimed Winnicott's treatment of her daughter as "a marked success" ("Mrs. Piggle", n.d. [c] [c. 1973]).

As a result of this collaboration among Clare Winnicott, Ishak Ramzy, Mr Piggle, and Mrs Piggle, all of the relevant adults eventually approved the final text of Donald Winnicott's typescript. Although The Piggle did agree to both the supratitle and the plan to publish the book, she did not read the final typescript at that time ("The Piggle", 2020).

The carefully copy-edited version of this now classic text, entitled *The Piggle: An Account of the Psychoanalytic Treatment of a Little Girl* (Winnicott, 1977), finally appeared in print just before Christmas, 1977 (Clare Winnicott, 1977), in an American edition, wrapped in a light blue cloth binding and a simple dust jacket, produced by the long-standing psychoanalytical publishing house International Universities Press, based in New York City. With much satisfaction, Clare Winnicott (1977) wrote to Mrs Piggle, "Here it is at last. I do hope you will be happy with it, and feel secretly proud of it, as you are really entitled to!" Not long thereafter, a 1978 British edition, published by the Hogarth Press of London, in association with the Institute of Psycho-Analysis, bound in green cloth, became available for purchase at the cost of six pounds and fifty pence per copy (Winnicott, 1978). The British version formed a part of the series, "The International Psycho-Analytical Library", then under the editorship of Winnicott's one-time analysand Masud Khan. A special "Preface", authored by Clare Winnicott and her psychoanalytical colleague Mr Raymond Shepherd (Winnicott and Shepard [sic] [Shepherd], 1977;[9] Winnicott and Shepherd, 1978)—both members of the Winnicott Publications Committee— appeared alongside Ishak Ramzy's (1977a, 1978) "Editor's Foreword" in each edition, as well as a charming sketch of Donald Winnicott's working space at 87, Chester Square, drawn by Miss Elizabeth Britton, sister-in-law to the deceased psychoanalyst.

Section Five: A Winnicottian Masterpiece

Having embarked upon his medical training as an undergraduate at the University of Cambridge in 1914 (during which time he helped to treat soldiers wounded during the Great War), and having worked with patients until his death in 1971, Winnicott had encountered literally tens, if not hundreds, of thousands of patients across the course of his long and rich clinical career. And although he wrote many brief accounts of a great many of his paediatric, child psychiatric, child psychoanalytical, and adult psychoanalytical cases, he produced only two book-length case histories, namely, his study of The Piggle and, also, a far less well known summary of an adult psychoanalysis of a male patient, only parts of which appeared during his lifetime (Winnicott, 1954a), with longer versions published only after his decease (firstly as a 200-plus page chapter on "Fragment of an Analysis" (Winnicott, 1972) and, subsequently, as a full-length book, *Holding and Interpretation: Fragment of an Analysis* (Winnicott, 1986a)).

It remains unclear why Winnicott chose to present The Piggle as his sole single-case, book-length documentation of his child psychoanalytical endeavours. Certainly, Winnicott could well have written innumerable comprehensive child case histories throughout his long career as he had no shortage of clinical material at his disposal. Although we cannot provide a clear answer to this question, I have often wondered whether Winnicott, who commenced his work with The Piggle at the age of sixty-seven years, strongly identified with his one-time teacher and one-time clinical supervisor, the legendary Melanie Klein (1961), who, in spite of her immense psychoanalytical experience, published only one book-length case study of her own, *Narrative of a Child Analysis: The Conduct of the Psycho-Analysis of Children as Seen in the Treatment of a Ten Year Old Boy*, which appeared in print shortly after her death. Perhaps Winnicott also wished to bequeath a detailed, post-mortem child case history, just as Klein had done one decade earlier.

We must also consider whether Winnicott, approaching death, began to lament the fact that he had never become a biological parent in his own right, even though he "parented" thousands and thousands of infants and children and adolescents across his very lengthy career. Perhaps The Piggle became something of a symbolic daughter or granddaughter to Winnicott, worthy of the deep investment of his time and of his passion.

Whatever Donald Winnicott's motivation for writing up this particular case of The Piggle, he has, with the facilitation of Clare Winnicott and Ishak Ramzy, and with the blessing of both Mr Piggle and Mrs Piggle, gifted a remarkable text to mental health workers worldwide.

With the possible exception of Dr Josef Breuer's (1895) iconic case of "Anna O" and of Professor Sigmund Freud's legendary patients, known in the English-speaking world as "Dora" (Freud, 1905a, 1905b), "Little Hans" (Freud, 1909a), the "Rat Man" (Freud, 1909b), and the "Wolf Man" (Freud, 1918), as well as the case of the German jurist Daniel Paul Schreber (about whom Freud (1911) wrote in some detail in spite of never having met this man in person), the little girl nicknamed "The Piggle" may well be the most well-recognised patient thereafter in the entire history of psychoanalysis.

Other clinicians or scholars will no doubt extol the many virtues of Winnicott's work with The Piggle, emphasising its pathbreaking nature, its epitomisation of empathy and clinical intelligence, its foregrounding of sensitive play therapy, its compassion, its humility, and so many other fine achievements. One need not look far in order to appreciate the innumerable virtues and lessons contained within this magnificent work of psychological prose. In many respects, the fact that The Piggle has grown into a remarkably sane and sensitive woman—I can attest to this from my personal acquaintance with her over more than twenty-five years—provides the best evidence that Winnicott undertook something very special and very lasting, supporting and helping and containing not only The Piggle but, also, her very emotionally sensitive and concerned parents.

Of course, we must not underestimate the fact that, subsequent to her psychoanalytical experience with Winnicott, The Piggle embarked upon a rich and full life and will, no doubt, have received much positive support from family and friends and colleagues and, even, perhaps, from further psychoanalysis in adulthood. Certainly, her foundational work with Dr Winnicott may well have provided a unique opportunity for greater solidity and understanding throughout her childhood.

But Winnicott's monograph also posed a very *vital challenge* to classical psychoanalysis, while, paradoxically, maintaining a very *firm allegiance*.

During the early years of the twentieth century, most clinical psychoanalysts insisted upon meeting with their analysands six days per week, from Mondays to Saturdays inclusive. Sigmund Freud (1913) pioneered this deeply intensive model of treatment, which proved to be such a contrast to the more conventional psychiatric practice of the nineteenth century when physicians consulted with their patients only on an occasional and irregular basis (cf. May, 2006, 2007a, 2007b). By codifying this clinical procedure in such a predictable and intensive manner, Freud created something very containing for his patients, providing a true experience of reliability and safety.

Some of the pioneers of psychoanalysis would, even, from time to time, treat patients on Sundays as well, thus creating a seven-day psychoanalytical week. For instance, the distinguished Viennese-born practitioner Professor Paul Schilder, who emigrated to the United States of America, worked with one of his patients, Dr Alexander Reid Martin (1975), from Mondays to Sundays *inclusive*. More recently, the British psychoanalyst Dr Leslie Sohn, who specialised in treating highly psychotic patients, believed that those very vulnerable individuals simply could not tolerate the breaks at weekends, and so he, too, consulted with some of his extremely ill patients every single day of the week (Minne, 2019).

Child psychoanalysts such as Anna Freud also championed the intensive treatment of young people, establishing five sessions per week as the gold standard. When Winnicott began to work with little boys and girls at the Paddington Green Children's Hospital, often providing only one or two consultations in total, and, subsequently, when he conducted "on demand" psychoanalyses, he succeeded in irritating Anna Freud, in spite of her affection for the man (cf. Freud, 1968; Kahr, 2023b). According to Miss Freud's long-standing colleague Dr Martin James (1991), she actually spoke scathingly of Winnicott's technique, especially his espousal of the "on demand" approach.

Even though colleagues questioned Winnicott's (1962g, p. 168) embrace of his model of occasional consultations, to which he sometimes referred as "modified analysis", he continued to champion the fact that, as a child psychiatrist as well as a child psychoanalyst, he could certainly appreciate that not everyone will require a full analysis and that not everyone would enjoy such opportunities. As he wrote in his essay on "The Aims of Psycho-Analytical Treatment", presented to colleagues in the British Psycho-Analytical Society on 7th March, 1962, "In analysis one asks: how *much* can one be allowed to do? And, by contrast, in my clinic the motto is: how *little* need be done?" (Winnicott, 1962g, p. 166). Indeed, not long thereafter, Winnicott described his briefer, consultative, "on demand" work as "snack-bar psychotherapy" (Winnicott, 1963b, p. 344)—often practised from his clinic at the Paddington Green

Children's Hospital, to which he referred as his very own "Psychiatric Snack Bar" (quoted in Clare Winnicott, 1978, p. 28)—suggesting that not every patient will require a full five-course meal and that some might well satisfy their cravings with just a little snack!

But in spite of Winnicott's capacity to raise some eyebrows and concerns among his psychoanalytical colleagues for not always conducting five-times-weekly child or adult treatment, let us recall that he certainly did *not* invent this more flexible model of "on demand" psychotherapy. Apparently, Sigmund Freud himself would, from time to time, meet with patients on an occasional basis. Indeed, according to his disciple Dr Theodor Reik, Freud referred to this arrangement as "Fractured Analysis" (quoted in Freeman, 1971, p. 96). Reik, likewise, employed fractured analysis in the treatment of his own patient, Lewis Namier, whose political career prevented him from attending psycho-analysis regularly, as he kept bouncing back and forth among Vienna, London, and Geneva (Freeman, 1971).

Other Freudian clinicians followed suit. For instance, during the 1930s, Dr Ruth Mack Brunswick, the American-born psychoanalyst who worked in Vienna, would permit her analysand, Dr Muriel Gardiner, to attend on an occasional basis towards the end of her regular treatment. As Gardiner (1983, p. 81) revealed in her memoir, she participated in psychoanalytical sessions "only when I asked for an appointment".[10]

Likewise, in New York City, the German émigré psychoanalyst, Dr Karen Horney, also acknowledged the need for an "on demand" model, especially for those individuals who might live outside major cities. In her popular book, *Self-Analysis*, Horney (1942, p. 28) spoke of the possibility of offering "occasional checkups" for certain patients.

Even as late as 1950, Dr Ernest Jones (1950), a devoted follower of Freud, referred to "fractional analysis" when corresponding with Winnicott about a lengthy treatment.

Thus, Donald Winnicott certainly cannot claim credit for the notion of shortened or occasional sessions—"on demand" psychotherapy—although he certainly foregrounded its possibility and, indeed, its desirability in many instances.

In some ways, Winnicott's treatment of The Piggle, which consisted of sixteen formal London-based consultations, as well as home visits, not to mention frequent correspondence by post, as well as telephone calls with Mr Piggle and Mrs Piggle, may well seem rather a hefty treatment by comparison to some of his other work. For instance, in the case of "John", the youngster who stole from his parents and from shops, Winnicott (1956b) never even met the child in question and worked exclusively with the mother, in part because the father objected to psychology on religious grounds; consequently, through his discussions with the mother, Winnicott successfully advised her on the unconscious meaning of her son's behaviours.

Donald Winnicott's embrace of the "on demand" method of treatment developed from many sources, including the fact that, as a hospital physician with thousands of patients entering his clinic, he simply could not provide intensive multi-frequency psychoanalysis or psychotherapy for each of them; therefore, he had to develop a model of more occasional therapeutic consultations. Winnicott found this approach to be of great use, recognising that young people will often benefit quickly from brief interventions.

But in addition to Winnicott's clinical justification of the "on demand" style of treatment, he also practised this particular method for personal medical reasons, especially towards the end of his life. For instance, in 1970, not long before his death, a patient, whom I shall designate as "Miss Arabella Bagshawe", approached Winnicott for psychoanalytical treatment; but, owing to his fading physical health, he refused to agree to ongoing, open-ended work and offered "on demand" sessions instead, which proved most useful to the patient, who, years later, spoke to me enthusiastically of her experience with the seventy-four-year-old man (Kahr, 1996g; cf. Kahr, 2020b).

Not only did Winnicott promulgate "on demand" treatment in his relationship with The Piggle, but he also developed what he came to call "psychoanalysis *partagé*" (quoted in Winnicott and Shepard [*sic*] [Shepherd], 1977, p. viii)—a neologistic English-French phrase meaning "shared psychoanalysis", referring to the fact that, in his work with The Piggle, he also shared his psychoanalytical knowledge with the parents and, consequently, the whole family cooperated and collaborated in the treatment in different ways. In other words, Winnicott believed that one should communicate some of the material to the parents, without breaching the child's confidentiality *per se*. He also insisted that "psychoanalysis *partagé*" should in no way be confused with family therapy. Winnicott did not intend to "treat" the entire system but focused, instead, on the child with the support of the parents.

Once again, just as Winnicott cannot receive full credit for "on demand" work, he also cannot claim to be the progenitor of "psychoanalysis *partagé*". Most obviously, Sigmund Freud (1909a) had created a shared arrangement many years previously in his work with Herbert Graf, the little boy who suffered from a phobia of horses. Freud had met not only with Herbert Graf but, also, with the child's father, Max Graf. Freud also knew the mother, Olga Hönig Graf, extremely well, as she had undergone her own psychoanalysis with him years previously (Wakefield, 2007). Thus, in many respects, Freud pioneered this particular model of treatment, although Winnicott elaborated upon it with his tremendous compassion and talent.

Winnicott barely refers to the famous case of "kleine Hans" (i.e., "Little Hans") in his writings (e.g., Winnicott, 1960a), but it may well be that Freud's detailed analysis of the child's precise dialogue and language might have propelled Winnicott towards writing a comparable case by quoting the exact words used by The Piggle. Throughout the history of psychiatry, most case reports simply summarised what the patient had spoken, but in Winnicott's text, as in Freud's, more than half a century earlier, the precise voice of the little child still shines through.

Conclusion

Donald Winnicott's book, *The Piggle: An Account of the Psychoanalytic Treatment of a Little Girl*, published posthumously, remains one of the most important and enjoyable texts in the entire history of psychoanalysis.

This playful book reminds us of the extraordinary healing powers of the talking cure and of the ways in which a clinician of deep experience and profound compassion and creativity can facilitate the growth of an individual in distress.

Winnicott's text provides clear evidence of the importance of tracking the child's words and gestures and play, and the necessity of interpreting their meaning in a helpful manner, thus facilitating emotional growth and stability. The book also confirms the crucial need for collaborating with the wider system when conducting work with vulnerable populations, whether children, the disabled, the mentally ill, and so forth.

When one studies the life of Donald Winnicott in some detail, one soon comes to appreciate that the treatment of The Piggle unfolded amid a time of great physical distress for this extraordinary psychoanalyst. He not only had to navigate his seventieth birthday and all the developmental vicissitudes of the life cycle, but, moreover, he had to work in spite of having already endured a number of coronary crises, with several more to come, as well as significant ocular pain from at least two patient-induced injuries. A man of considerable sturdiness, Donald Winnicott managed to access his professionalism, his playfulness, and his joy for living, in order to transmit these qualities to The Piggle, in spite of his own quite significant medical struggles.

The case of The Piggle remains a source of engagement and interest and provides the leaping-off point for much creative discussion among child and adult mental health practitioners alike. In this day and age, the need for evidence that psychological treatment really does work certainly predominates. Thus, we may all benefit from the fact that in view of the current-day robustness of The Piggle as a full-grown adult, who daily offers her own compassionate contributions to the world, we have important confirmatory data that Donald Winnicott's support of this one-time little girl and her parents has made a truly lasting impact.

PART III

DR AND MRS BOWLBY

CHAPTER FIVE

"Half-Baked Pseudo-Scientific Rubbish": How John Bowlby Reinvented Child Psychiatry

Look back at 1939
—Dr John Bowlby, 1979
(quoted in Dinnage, 1979, p. 325)

Charles Darwin will be remembered for all eternity as the progenitor of the theory of evolution, Albert Einstein as the architect of the theory of relativity, and Sigmund Freud as the creator of the theory of psychoanalysis.

The late Dr John Bowlby may not *yet* enjoy quite the celebrity of this trio of Titans, but those who do recognise his name admire him hugely for his many rich contributions to the psychological sciences and, most particularly, for the body of knowledge that has come to be known as "attachment theory". Indeed, Bowlby's detailed conceptualisation of the nature of the interactions between infants and their caregivers, his delineation of the consequences of ruptured affectional bonds, and his elucidation of the implications of this work for psychotherapeutic practice remain of inestimable value.

But in spite of my deep regard for Bowlby's (1969, 1973, 1980) seminal researches on attachment and loss, on the links between maternal care and mental health (Bowlby, 1951a, 1951b), on the application of ethology to child development (Bowlby, 1957, 1958), on the making and breaking of affectional bonds (Bowlby, 1979), and on the establishment of a secure base (Bowlby, 1988), I wish to propose that his numerous foundational publications from the 1940s through to the 1980s, which serve as the bedrock of the ever-burgeoning field of attachment studies, may, in fact, be by *no* means his most important legacy but, only, his *second* most important.

Speaking as a historian, I wish to propose that, during the 1930s, Edward John Mostyn Bowlby made a much *bigger* contribution to the human sciences.

My story begins, however, not in the 1930s but, rather, in the twelfth century.

The Vespasian manuscript, written in Latin, and carefully preserved in the British Library, provides an excellent description of English child psychiatry circa 1159. In a section entitled "*Of a certain little boy that was mad*" (*The Book of the Foundation* [...],[1] 1923, p. 51), we learn of a young lad who "had lost all sense of reason since the day of the festival of the blessed Laurence the Martyr" (ibid.). According to this medieval text, the boy, "on account of his madness, from which he suffered terribly, was even to his mother herself burdensome and past bearing with, and, as she said, he had been carried round to many places of the saints already, but had nowhere obtained any cure" (ibid.). A woman of considerable persistence, the mother continued to seek help for her mad son, and, in desperation, brought him to the relatively newly founded church of St. Bartholomew's in London, and kept vigil, praying to "the most godly apostle of Christ" (ibid.). Fortunately, this medieval spiritual psychotherapy seems to have worked quite well, and, as we know from the ancient text, the mother "secured joy for herself and health for her boy, and she showed him sound to all the people on the following Lord's Day" (ibid.).

Regrettably, child psychiatry did not progress much beyond this point over the centuries which followed; in fact, it worsened quite considerably as suffering became increasingly medicalised throughout the eighteenth and nineteenth centuries, mirroring the frequently cruel treatment of young people at that time (deMause, 1974, 1990, 1991; Kahr, 1991a; cf. Berke, 1977). Many children of yesteryear lived in horrific conditions (e.g., Despert, 1965; Pinchbeck and Hewitt, 1973;

Pollock, 1983; Taylor, 1985); indeed, in 1839, Dr James Phillips Kay (1839), the Assistant Poor Law Commissioner, reported that toddlers of only two years of age could be encountered, quite frequently, in grim workhouses across England and Scotland. In 1842, a landmark government inspection revealed that many children as young as five years of age laboured long hours in treacherous coal mines (*First Report of the Commissioners: Mines*, 1842), many of whom would fall down the mine shafts and would either drown or be crushed to death (*Appendix to First Report of Commissioners: Mines. Part I. Reports and Evidence from Sub-Commissioners*, 1842; cf. *Appendix to First Report of Commissioners: Mines. Part II. Reports and Evidence from Sub-Commissioners*, 1842). Not until the introduction of the Mines and Collieries Act 1842 would English children aged nine years and younger be prevented from toiling underground.

Fortunately, during the latter half of the nineteenth century, the plight of British children improved greatly due to the pioneering efforts of such reformers as philanthropist Anthony Ashley-Cooper, the seventh Earl of Shaftesbury (e.g., Hodder, 1886a, 1886b, 1886c; Battiscombe, 1974), as well as Dr Thomas Barnardo (e.g., Williams, 1943; Wagner, 1979) and, also, Charles Dickens (e.g., Ackroyd, 2002; Waters, 2006; Reed, 2010; Tomalin, 2011), whose collective contributions to child psychiatry remain ill-appreciated to this day. Gradually, the "Oliver Twist"–like conditions of poverty began to improve substantially, and charitable institutions became increasingly better at sheltering orphans and unwanted children from the harsh realities of the streets (cf. Pankhurst, 1935). But these nineteenth-century pioneers focused their efforts solely on improving the *physical* conditions of children's homes. They did not, in the main, lobby for greater emotional succour, unsurprisingly so, in view of the fact that the field of child psychology would not emerge for yet another half-century.

Children's medicine—still a relatively new discipline in health care— left much to be desired. Dr Charles West, Senior Physician at the Royal Infirmary for Children in London, and, subsequently, founder of the Hospital for Sick Children on Great Ormond Street and a man whom many considered to be the veritable father of children's medicine in Great Britain, regarded the fears of young boys and girls as manifestations of physical illness. Indeed, West (1848, p. 131) conceptualised anxieties as "the result of sympathetic affection of the brain through the medium of the abdominal viscera", and, in consequence, he recommended that youngsters should be treated with castor oil, tepid baths, and Dover's powder—a combination of ipecacuanha and opium—as well as the careful control of diet.

Indeed, our nineteenth-century predecessors had such little appreciation for the special needs of young people that child patients would regularly be housed on adult wards—a practice that persisted well into the 1920s, at least—long before the development of specialist paediatric services (Bourne, 1963).

Of course, not all Victorians neglected infants and children quite so completely. In 1877, Dr Silas Weir Mitchell, the noted American-born physician, recommended that young girls suffering from hysteria should be treated with rest, massage, and overfeeding and, also, with stimulation by electrical currents. But even Mitchell (1877, p. 35), one of the more enlightened medical practitioners of that era, nonetheless described the hysterical girl in condemnatory fashion as "a vampire who sucks the blood of the healthy people about her".

During the course of researching the biography of John Bowlby's long-standing colleague, Dr Donald Winnicott (Kahr, 1996a), I discovered some shocking advice in the pages of *The Lady*, a popular magazine read by women of refinement. On 9th April, 1896, only two days after Winnicott's birth, the author of an article entitled "Healthy, Happy Nurseries" counselled, "Have your nurseries at the top, or as near the top of the house as possible, both for your own comfort and the children's good—for your comfort in that you will hear no noise" (Anonymous, 1896, p. 498). It seems remarkable that both Winnicott, born in 1896, and Bowlby, born only a few years later in 1907, developed the capacity to progress so very much beyond the climate in which they had grown up, and could succeed in repositioning the nursery from the top of the house to its very centre.

Bowlby, Winnicott, and others forged a profession of child mental health with virtually no support from the wider medical community. Indeed, during Bowlby's youth and throughout his training as a physician, publications on children's medicine barely existed, let alone those on child psychiatry. The few medical textbooks written during Bowlby's growing years which *did*, in fact, make reference to the treatment of childhood psychopathology generally dismissed the subject quite quickly. The great Professor William Osler, Regius Professor of medicine at the University of Oxford from 1905 until his death in 1919 (and, from 1911, a baronet, to boot), recommended that "neuropathic" (Osler, 1905, p. 1128) (i.e., psychologically unwell) children "should not be pampered" (Osler, 1905, p. 1128) and should, instead, be subjected to a process of "psychic hardening" (Osler, 1905, p. 1128), insisting that, "Complaints of children should not be too seriously considered" (Osler, 1905, p. 1129).[2] Indeed, he recommended that, whenever possible, children with psychological illnesses should be removed from their homes (Osler, 1905; cf. Osler and McCrae, 1930).

Dr Leonard George Guthrie, Winnicott's predecessor at the Paddington Green Children's Hospital in West London, had to admit that physicians of the late nineteenth century had learned precious little about young people throughout their medical education. As he confessed, "In days gone by, our training as medical students did not include more than a text-book acquaintance with the diseases to which children are subject" (Guthrie, 1907, p. 1). However, this restriction did not prevent Guthrie from recommending, in 1907, that boys and girls who suffered from *pavor nocturnus*—namely, night terrors— should be treated with five to ten grains of bromide of potassium, or two and a half to five grains of chloral hydrate, and that those who walked in their sleep should be tied to their beds. As for enuretic youngsters—bed-wetters—Guthrie (1907, p. 159) had no objection to such children being slapped by "the nurse's palm", and he advised that more intractable cases should be treated with a tincture of hyoscyamus (a type of henbane), combined with citrate of potash (potassium carbonate) and an infusion of buchu (a South African shrub). Guthrie (1907) also practised digital stimulation of the bladder *per rectum*, as well as faradism, namely, electrical stimulation, accomplished by the insertion of a probe into the child's urethra.

Other British physicians, such as Dr John Neil Leitch, a licentiate of the Royal College of Physicians of London and a member of the Royal College of Surgeons of England, recommended either the passage of time, or, if need be, the prescription of belladonna as a cure for childhood bed-wetting. Dr Leitch, a specialist in the use of faradic currents in the treatment of various medical conditions (e.g., Leitch, 1920a), also advocated electrotherapy, administering sixty shocks per minute, for twenty minutes, two or three times each week, from an electrode placed in the centre of the perinaeum (the region between the genitalia and the anus). As he explained, "The strength of current was in each case as strong as the patient could comfortably bear" (Leitch, 1920b, p. 162).

Perhaps no one held more sway in the field of children's medicine during the years of Bowlby's youth than Dr Edmund Cautley, a Senior Physician at the Belgrave Hospital for Children in London. Cautley maintained a private practice off Park Lane, and had, in 1911, served as President of the Society for the Study of Disease in Children and, subsequently, in 1929, became one of the very first presidents of the fledgling British Paediatric Association. His hugely influential textbook on *The Diseases of Infants and Children* provided very few guidelines on the treatment of neuroses in the young, but advised, nonetheless, with clarity and certainty, that all of the "inherited" (Cautley, 1910, p. 772) emotional problems in boys and girls could best be relieved by two methods. First, Dr Cautley prescribed pharmacological remedies, including bromides, hypnotics, laudanum, purgatives, apomorphine, trinitrin, pilocarpin, erythrol tetranitrate, ergot, calcium salts, asafoetida, and valerian. And second, since Cautley (1910, p. 777) believed that children had inherited their neuroses, classifying hysteria as a "cerebral" affliction, he advised that in order to provide *truly* effective treatment, one should send children away from their homes and from their long-suffering parents. As Cautley (1910, p. 780) pronounced, "Separate the child from neurotic parents or attendants," underscoring that, "Intentional neglect is advisable in convulsive affections, and indeed for most symptoms" (Cautley, 1910, p. 780).

Some more enlightened physicians advocated ordinary bed rest, but, nevertheless, would often enforce this practice *in extremis*. As Dr William Gillespie (1971, p. 228) reminisced, it would not be uncommon for a depressed child in the 1930s to be sent to bed for weeks or even *months*, a strategy long regarded as "orthodox treatment". But the vast majority of physicians of the early twentieth century dismissed psychologically troubled children as diseased, as *"morally weak-minded"* (Hollander, 1916, p. 211) and, often, beyond real hope.

Thus, one might reasonably conclude that during John Bowlby's youth and throughout his medical training, a specially demarcated field of child psychiatry simply did not exist. Classic, compendious textbooks of medicine not only neglected to offer advice on how to treat mentally unwell children but they failed to offer information on how to cure *any* children at all. Even as late as 1930, the fourteenth edition of *Taylor's Practice of Medicine* (Poulton, Symonds, Barber, and Gillespie, 1930)—some 1,074 pages in length—appeared, containing not a single chapter on children nor, indeed, any reference to children's medicine or to paediatrics in the "Index". The authors of this textbook, all leading physicians at Guy's Hospital in London, neglected the special medical and psychological needs of young people completely in an otherwise meticulously comprehensive and scholarly work.

Many of Bowlby's contemporaries regarded any expression of ordinary kindness towards children as unhelpfully indulgent. As Bowlby reminisced, "'You'll spoil him, you'll spoil him,' was the regular cry. That was not just the conventional wisdom of the twenties and thirties, it was the conventional wisdom of the forties" (quoted in Dinnage, 1979, p. 323).

In view of the fact that most senior physicians in the field of children's medicine during the 1910s, 1920s, and 1930s prescribed belladonna, purgatives, emetics, electricity, neglect, and separation from parents as treatments of choice, John Bowlby faced a gargantuan dilemma. Having already worked for a time as an unpaid teacher at The Priory Gate School in rural Norfolk for troubled children, under the supervision of the progressive educators Theodore Faithfull[3] and John Alford (Senn, 1977; Karen, 1994; van Dijken, 1998), Bowlby had already begun to sense that children's problems could not, and should not, be dismissed as inherited cerebral illnesses but might be understood, by contrast, as the sequelae of family traumata (Senn, 1977).[4]

But how could the young John, a mere stripling in his early twenties, challenge the received wisdom of his new profession?

Bowlby had already become well aware of the vitriol directed towards Winnicott (1931a), some eleven years his senior, who angered the medical profession upon the publication of his textbook, *Clinical Notes on Disorders of Childhood*, in which he observed that many of the apparently physical illnesses of the young could be explained as consequences of anxiety and depression. In claiming a role for intra-familial psychological factors, Winnicott had to endure much hatred from fellow physicians (e.g., Cautley, 1932; cf. Tizard, 1981) and, indeed, "risked his whole professional reputation in the interests of the children, for had one of them died this would doubtless have been ruined" (Gillespie, 1971, p. 228).

Fortunately, Bowlby possessed sufficient independence of mind that he began to develop the capacity to report his own clinical observations, irrespective of the consequences, and became committed far more to scientific truth than to the prospect of popularity. Thus, during the 1930s, Bowlby began to synthesise his preliminary observations about the role of family factors in the development of childhood psychopathology, long before he came to publish his two-part paper on the forty-four juvenile thieves (Bowlby, 1944a, 1944b; cf. Bowlby, 1945–1946, 1946), described erroneously, on at least one occasion, as "His first publication" (Senn, 1977, p. 1). In spite of the fact that most professionals regarded child psychiatry, especially "analytically oriented" (quoted in Senn, 1977, p. 4) child psychiatry, as "very novel and peculiar" (quoted in Senn, 1977, p. 4) and, also, as "very controversial" (quoted in Senn, 1977, p. 4) and in need of "academic justification" (quoted in Senn, 1977, p. 4), Bowlby persevered even though he held his psychiatric colleagues in slight regard, confessing, "I don't think they had a great deal to offer" (quoted in Senn, 1977, p. 8).

In 1939, as the world went to war, so, too, did Bowlby, who became a major in the Royal Army Medical Corps. But Bowlby initiated another far more unique battle by launching a creative challenge to his medical colleagues and, also, to the British government. And in 1939, he published two small contributions, both overlooked, indeed, often forgotten, which, in my estimation, outshine his subsequent compendious tomes on attachment and loss.

Of course, Dr Hermine von Hug-Hellmuth (Hellmuth, 1912; von Hug-Hellmuth, 1914; Hug-Hellmuth, 1919, 1922) and Fräulein Anna Freud (1927, 1928) had already begun to pioneer the fledgling field of *Frühanalyse*—child psychoanalysis—in Vienna, and Frau Melanie Klein (1923, 1924, 1927a, 1927b, 1928, 1932a) had begun to do so as well, first in Berlin and, subsequently, in London. But those applying psychodynamics to the treatment of neurotic children proved to be a very tiny force indeed. And Klein's unpublished appointment diaries reveal that she never worked with more than a handful of children at any time, many the offspring of fellow psychoanalysts (e.g., *Walker's Diary for 1929*, 1929; cf. Grosskurth, 1984, 1986; Frank, 1999). Professor Esther Menaker, a trainee social worker who subsequently became a noted psychoanalyst, recalled that, circa 1930, she knew of only one psychoanalytically trained child mental health professional in the whole of New York. Indeed, she even remarked that, "by all standards one could scarcely consider the field threateningly competitive" (Menaker, 1988, p. 375).

Although Bowlby had trained as a psychoanalyst and had practised during the war in this capacity (e.g., Bowlby, 1984), and, moreover, had always remained indebted to his Freudian forebears, he now endeavoured, nonetheless, to create a much bigger splash.[5]

First of all, Bowlby contributed an essay to the very first book ever published in Great Britain with the phrase "Child Psychiatry" in its title. Prior to the appearance of Dr Ronald Gordon's (1939) edited text, *A Survey of Child Psychiatry*, the field of child mental health enjoyed no formal recognition whatsoever. One must remember that neither the Association of Child Psychotherapists nor the Association of Child Psychoanalysis existed at that time, nor did any of the child-related sections within either the British Psychological Society or indeed the Royal Medico-Psychological Association—the forerunner of the Royal College of Psychiatrists. Certainly, the formal posts of Consultant Child and Adolescent Psychiatrist and of Consultant Child and Adolescent Psychotherapist would not be created for decades to come. Thus, by having joined forces with Dr Ronald Gordon, and with fellow chapter-writers Dr Emanuel Miller, Dr Donald Winnicott, and others, Bowlby gave organisational shape to the field of child mental health for the very first time in British history, acknowledging that youngsters do suffer from profound psychological distress and that such misery can be alleviated conversationally through the new dynamic psychotherapies inspired by the work of Sigmund Freud and others.

Bowlby's (1939a) chapter in this textbook, entitled "Hysteria in Children", explored the lives of youngsters who displayed symptoms ranging from fits, fugues, and giddiness, to diarrhoea, constipation, and indigestion, to anxiety, pain, vomiting, and lack of appetite.

On the surface, Bowlby's essay strikes one as an exercise in traditional psychiatric writing, with section headings such as "Symptomatology", "Diagnosis", "Course and Prognosis", "Psychopathology", and "Treatment", all described in clean, sparse prose with typical Bowlbian clarity. But beneath this seemingly ordinary exterior, Bowlby advanced two shocking hypotheses.

First of all, on the basis of his growing clinical experience, Dr Bowlby (1939a, p. 84) dared to aver that hysteria cannot be conceptualised as an organic condition but, rather, that it should be regarded as completely "psychogenic" in origin. Years earlier, Dr Josef Breuer and Dr Sigmund Freud (1895) had made a similar observation in their landmark book, *Studien über Hysterie*, but they spoke solely about adult patients. Bowlby now applied that same style of thinking to young children, arguing that the range of complex hysterical symptomatology results entirely from family-related causes.

Moreover, Bowlby surpassed Breuer and Freud, not only by exploring the psychogenesis of *childhood* hysteria but, also, by expanding the range of potential aetiological factors. Certainly, Bowlby's essay reveals all the hallmarks of a man who had undertaken a psychoanalytical training. For instance, he presented the case of a child who developed a headache "after something particularly pleasant has happened" (Bowlby, 1939a, p. 83) and argued that the headache might represent an unconscious attack on the child's experience of success. Although Bowlby failed to cite Freud in this instance, colleagues will immediately recognise Bowlby's line of thought as precisely that conveyed some twenty-three years previously by Freud (1916a) in his essay "Einige Charaktertypen aus der psychoanalytischen Arbeit" ["Some Character-Types Met with in Psycho-Analytic Work" (Freud, 1916b)] in which he articulated that symptoms often develop in the wake of success and pleasure as a means of mastering our unconscious guilt at having surpassed our parents.

Bowlby recognised not only the importance of unconscious forces, as Freud had done but, also, he introduced something quite novel into the discourse. Unlike Freud, Bowlby did not examine the role of sexual trauma substantially as a possible aetiological ingredient—a subject which, I would argue, Freud understood far better than Bowlby. Nevertheless, the Englishman extended the work of Freud profoundly by having foregrounded *separation* as a key causal element in childhood hysteria for the very first time.

Bowlby advanced his preliminary views on the role of separation with particular vividness in his discussion of the case of a thirteen-year-old hysterical boy called "Robert A.", who suffered from excruciating pains in his abdomen, his eyes and, also, in his right arm, for which no organic basis could be found. Robert experienced so much discomfort from his symptoms that he would often scream. It soon emerged that various real-life triggers had induced these multitudinous pains. In the midst of traditional psychotherapeutic work, Bowlby learned that, during Robert's early childhood, his father suffered from chronic respiratory illness, and, also, that Robert's mother bade her children to keep quiet so that the father could rest. But on one occasion, Robert, then only four years of age, happened to smash an electric light bulb which made considerable noise. Robert's father died shortly thereafter and, consequently, the poor boy, having internalised his mother's injunction to be silent, began to suffer from the fantasy that he had killed his father.

Through further investigation, Bowlby discovered that not only had Robert experienced a deep childhood bereavement with attendant guilt-laced fantasies but, also, that he had endured other losses too, each of which precipitated a subsequent hysterical attack. One of Robert's worst bouts of hysterical pain developed in the wake of the death of his pet rabbit; and another series appeared owing to the fact that his mother had left him alone in the house, whereupon a neighbour threatened to report this woman to the National Society for the Prevention of Cruelty to Children. And yet a further set of hysterical symptoms emerged in the immediate wake of Robert's mother having nearly died after an omnibus whooshed by her.

This essay on "Hysteria in Children", published as early as 1939, contains, in my estimation, every one of the principal ideas that Bowlby would come to elaborate so brilliantly in his subsequent, manifold contributions. Alas, I cannot ever remember seeing a single citation to this essay in the writings of any Bowlbian colleagues, an observation confirmed all too painfully by a computerised search of PEP-Web, the Psychoanalytic Electronic Publishing database.[6] And yet, this virtually unknown chapter by John Bowlby[7]—only fourteen and a half pages in length—represents his first challenge to both the neglect of children and to the organic psychiatric practitioners.

Bowlby unleashed a second salvo that year, in a very short letter, dated 6th December, 1939, co-authored by Emanuel Miller and Donald Winnicott, and published in the "Correspondence" section of the *British Medical Journal*, entitled, quite simply, "Evacuation of Small Children". On 31st August, 1939, the Ministry of Health, in an effort to protect British children from the threat of bombing by the Luftwaffe, authorised widespread evacuations which commenced the following day, on 1st September, 1939 (Gardiner, 2005). Bowlby, Miller, and Winnicott (1939, p. 1202), three prescient doctors, supported the plan to keep children safe from bombing, but expressed tremendous concern that the evacuation of youngsters to the countryside, separated from parents and other caregivers, might, perversely, result in "major psychological problems". The authors shared a particular apprehension about the fate of those children aged two to five years who, they argued, would be most devastated by the evacuation experience.

These three pioneers of British child psychiatry referenced Bowlby's as yet unpublished work at the London Child Guidance Clinic, arguing that those boys and girls who suffered early separations would be more likely to become delinquent in later years, and they concluded that, "separation was the outstanding aetiological factor in these cases" (Bowlby, Miller, and Winnicott, 1939, p. 1202). Bowlby and his colleagues underscored their concerns by exclaiming that if the evacuation plan should proceed, young children would run the risk of suffering not only "emotional 'black-out'" (Bowlby, Miller, and Winnicott, 1939, p. 1202) but, also, "severe disturbance of the development of the personality which may persist throughout life" (Bowlby, Miller, and Winnicott, 1939, p. 1202), cautioning that evacuated children could suffer from "radical harm" (Bowlby, Miller, and Winnicott, 1939, p. 1203), and could become "seriously warped" (Bowlby, Miller, and Winnicott, 1939, p. 1203).[8]

Although Bowlby, Miller, and Winnicott did not provide any detailed case studies in their short communication to the *British Medical Journal* about the emotional anguish experienced by evacuees, one need not search far and wide in order to acquire primary testimony of the profound impact of separation from parental figures upon youngsters.

Perhaps little Rose Kops, a Jewish girl from London's East End, best encapsulated the anguish of children in 1939, when, upon being sent away with an identity label and gas mask hanging around her neck, screamed at her mother, "I want to stop with you. I want to get killed with you" (quoted in Gardiner, 2005, p. 20). Within the first three days of evacuation, approximately 1,900,000 British children had to leave their family homes forcibly, and many of those who went as far away as Canada or the United States of America would not see their parents for another six years until after the war had ceased (Gardiner, 2005).

One cannot help but note that as the short, but punchy, letter written by Bowlby and his colleagues in the medical press unfolded, their prose became increasingly menacing. Indeed, the authors concluded their remarks by warning fellow medics that, "If these opinions are correct it follows that evacuation of small children without their mothers can lead to very serious and widespread psychological disorder. For instance, it can lead to a big increase in juvenile delinquency in the next decade" (Bowlby, Miller, and Winnicott, 1939, p. 1203).[9]

Although one might regard my foregrounding of this often overlooked book on child psychiatry and this *cri de coeur* in the *British Medical Journal* to cease the desperate, though misguided, evacuation programme as merely harbingers of the more important work to come, I wish to suggest that, by 1939, Bowlby had already made his greatest achievements by laying down the foundations for the child mental health profession, by creating formal institutional structures, and by alerting us all to the dangers of breaking affectional ties between young people and their caregivers.

Some of my colleagues may not agree with my assessment that Bowlby had reached an important peak in 1939. But John Bowlby certainly would have done.

In a little-known interview granted to the distinguished American paediatrician Professor Milton Senn of Yale University, John Bowlby actually proclaimed that, by 1929, while working on the staff of The Priory Gate School for maladjusted children, he had already discovered virtually everything that he would need to know in order to fortify himself for the rest of his career. As Bowlby expounded, "when I was there, I learned everything that I have known; it was the most valuable six months of my life, really" (quoted in Senn, 1977, p. 2).[10]

Thus, although the John Bowlby who created secure bases (Bowlby, 1988), and who consulted to the World Health Organization (Bowlby, 1951a, 1951b, 1953), and who collaborated with Mr James Robertson and Mrs Joyce Robertson on the pioneering films which transformed the nature of paediatric hospitals (e.g., Bowlby and Robertson, 1953; cf. Robertson and Bowlby, 1952), and who worked with Dr Mary Salter Ainsworth on the classification of attachment typologies (e.g., Bowlby, Ainsworth, Boston, and Rosenbluth, 1956; cf. Ainsworth, 1962), and who wrote a groundbreaking psychobiography of Charles Darwin (Bowlby, 1990) as well, remains very much in the forefront of the Bowlby legend, one might argue that the more youthful, less publicised, but perhaps much bolder Bowlby—the brash young man who had an idea—deserves to be remembered and celebrated. Quite simply and yet quite profoundly, the Bowlby of 1929 and the Bowlby of 1939 taught us that madness develops in the family, particularly when parent–child bonds become severed, and thus we need a large and creative cohort of mental health professionals to offer psychotherapy and, above all, prevention.

Everything else which followed from 1940 to 1990 might be regarded as an elaboration of these brilliant early insights and observations. Indeed, round about 1939, John Bowlby engaged in a most revealing conversation with his spouse, Mrs Ursula Bowlby. As he recalled some forty years later, "My wife asked me during the war what I was going to do afterwards, and I said I was going to do research on separation. She said, what else? I said, that'll keep me busy for the rest of my life" (quoted in Dinnage, 1979, p. 323). And this indeed proved to be the case.

John Bowlby had the courage to fly against convention. It will not be widely known that this prototypical English gentleman who comported himself with tremendous courtesy and diplomacy could, also, in private life, swear "like a trooper" (quoted in Kahr, 2014b). In fact, as Bowlby's daughter, Mrs Mary Gatling, revealed to me, his university friends used to call him "Bugger Jack" (quoted in Kahr, 2014b). And with this capacity to curse and to damn the consequences, he created a veritable paradigm shift in our approach to the child and the family. No wonder that, during the Second World War, people often quipped, "Major Bowlby goes flat out / Whatever his goal be" (quoted in Kahr, 2014b).

The online encyclopaedia, known as Wikipedia, has described John Bowlby as the pioneer of "attachment theory" (Anonymous, 2022), and many would, of course, agree with this assessment (cf. Kahr, 2022b). But I hope that I have demonstrated that if we reduce Bowlby simply to a buzz phrase, as school children do when they describe Darwin as the father of evolutionary theory and Einstein as the inventor of the theory of relativity, we do him a great disservice, and we run the risk of forgetting the path-breaking work that he undertook during the 1930s by helping to establish the modern psychologically orientated child mental health profession in the first place.

John Bowlby had little patience for fools, and when he encountered odious professional practices, he had no difficulty in speaking out against them, especially in his detestation of the cruel Truby King–style of regimented infant care which prohibited mothers from holding their crying babies for hours at a time (Dinnage, 1979; cf. King, 1916).[11]

Ursula Bowlby shared her husband's philosophy and supported his work to the full, and she, too, decried barbaric treatment methods such as electrical stimulation of the urethra, manual stimulation of the rectum, and enforced separation from parents, which, today, we would refer to as child abuse. And I should like to leave the last words, not to John, but to Ursula. In the typescript of Mrs Bowlby's (c. 1948a, p. 48) unpublished book, *Happy Infancy*, she wrote of the so-called "baby experts", urging, "May they be forgiven for the mothers they have led astray by their half-baked pseudo-scientific rubbish" (Bowlby, c. 1948a, p. 48) and for having misled many "well-meaning mothers" (Bowlby, c. 1948a, p. 48), who "half-unwillingly followed 'official advice' instead of their own instincts" (Bowlby, c. 1948a, p. 48).

CHAPTER SIX

Ursula Longstaff Bowlby: The Creative Muse of Attachment Theory

Professor Sigmund Freud had an extremely devoted wife. Although not widely known, Freud's long-standing spouse, *Frau Professor* Martha Freud, pledged herself *so* slavishly to her husband that she even put the toothpaste on his toothbrush, to save the great man precious seconds before bedtime which could be used instead for writing and research (Berthelsen, 1987; Roazen, 1993, 1995; cf. Kahr, 2021a).

Dr John Bowlby, like Freud, also benefited from the care of a deeply faithful wife, Ursula Longstaff Bowlby, whom he married in 1938. But although Mrs Bowlby endeavoured to make her husband's life extremely comfortable, she certainly had a mind of her own, and could in no way be described as subordinate.

Miss Ursula Longstaff met the thirty-year-old Dr John Bowlby in 1937, shortly after he had ended his romance with Lady Prudence Mary Pelham—the daughter of Jocelyn Brudenell Pelham, the sixth Earl of Chichester—whom he had almost married.[1] Dr Bowlby and Miss Longstaff fell in love during the course of a shooting holiday in Ireland, and they wed on 16th April, 1938. In spite of the fact that her own parents had divorced, Ursula remained an extremely devoted wife to John Bowlby until the latter's death on 2nd September, 1990, enjoying more than fifty-two years of committed marriage.

Although I had the privilege of meeting Dr John Bowlby on quite a number of occasions, and had the pleasure of hosting his visit to the University of Oxford in 1984 (e.g., Kahr, 1984, 2004a, 2009a), I did not meet Ursula Bowlby properly until several years after her husband's death. I did, however, have the opportunity to sit near her at a performance of *Jazz for John Bowlby* at Burgh House in Hampstead, in North-West London—a memorial musical event created by the players from the group Jazzindo, shortly after Bowlby had died. And not long thereafter, I saw her once again, in Herringham Hall, at Regent's College, London—now Regent's University London—at the first-ever John Bowlby Memorial Lecture, which has since become an annual fixture sponsored by The Bowlby Centre. But, back then, I had neither the excuse nor the temerity to approach Mrs Bowlby directly. Indeed, none of us within the growing London attachment-based psychoanalytical community knew much, if anything, about Ursula Bowlby at that time, except the fact that those colleagues who *had* talked to her had found her kindly and appreciative and, also, grateful that we had organised an eponymous lecture in her husband's honour.

Finally, in late 1994, I plucked up the courage to write to Mrs Bowlby, asking her whether she had any memories of her late husband's psychoanalytical colleague Dr Donald Winnicott that she might wish to share, as I had, by that point, become Winnicott's biographer (Kahr, 1996a), and I endeavoured to follow up all potentially helpful research leads, interviewing as many first-hand witnesses as I could. With extreme promptitude and courtesy, Mrs Bowlby (1994) wrote to me by return of post, explaining that, "I met Winnicott many times, liked him, and we always got on very well." With great generosity, she then invited me to have coffee with her at the Bowlby family home at Wyldes Close Corner, in Golders Green, North-West London, on Sunday morning, 29th January, 1995.[2] As a long-standing admirer of the work of John Bowlby, and as a teacher at the Institute for Self Analysis (subsequently renamed as the Institute for Self Analysis Centre for Attachment-Based Psychoanalytic Psychotherapy, and then as the Centre for Attachment-Based Psychoanalytic Psychotherapy, and, ultimately, as The Bowlby Centre), I entered the home with a sense of reverence and awe, acutely aware that, somewhere in this house, Dr Bowlby (1969, 1973, 1980) himself had written the masterworks on parent–child relations which would eventually become codified as "attachment theory", a paradigm which has since changed the course of modern psychology.

Mrs Bowlby greeted me at the door, and she instantly put me at ease with her graciousness of spirit. She then invited me to sit round the dining room table, and there we chatted for many hours, with Mrs Bowlby serving refreshments and reminiscing in an animated fashion. No doubt she had hosted many dozens (if not hundreds) of similar interviews with historians and mental health professionals over the years (e.g., van Dijken, 1998), but she never revealed a trace of impatience, or weariness, or boredom. She responded to my questions about Winnicott with tremendous engagement. In fact, she had even taken the trouble to do some homework prior to our interview, and had scoured her copious archives, as well as those of her husband, in search of any letters or other documents that might be of value to my investigation. In this respect, she reminded me greatly of John Bowlby himself, who, in spite of his international stature and his weighty professional commitments, never failed to answer letters personally without any irritation or delay (Kahr, 2009a).

In our correspondence, and later, in the interview, Mrs Bowlby told me that she had, of course, known Dr Donald Winnicott, and that she regarded him as someone with similar views to those of her husband. As we will appreciate, Winnicott and Bowlby came to share comparable philosophies of child psychology, emphasising the role of actual parenting in the development of mental health and mental illness. Indeed, when I interviewed John Bowlby in 1986, he explained to me that he regarded himself and Winnicott as "singing from the same hymn sheet" (quoted in Kahr, 1986). Although Bowlby and Winnicott never enjoyed a deep friendship or emotional intimacy, the two men remained warm and mutually respectful colleagues to one another throughout their professional lives. Dr Bowlby told me that he considered Winnicott to be something of an artist, whereas he, Bowlby, thought of himself as a scientist.

Mrs Bowlby certainly knew that both men had struggled against some of the more conservative forces at the Institute of Psycho-Analysis where Winnicott had trained in the late 1920s and early 1930s, and where Bowlby had trained some years later, each undergoing psychoanalytical treatment with Mrs Joan Riviere, one of the key figures in the early British psychoanalytical movement, and a leading disciple of Mrs Melanie Klein. In fact, both men had fallen foul of the Training Committee of the Institute of Psycho-Analysis at various points, as neither toed the party line completely, and each had already begun to manifest evidence of creativity of mind and independence of thought (*Training Ctte Minutes: 24.3.1926—29.10.1945*, 1926–1945; cf. Kahr, 1996a, 2004b, 2009a).[3]

Regrettably, although she had searched her husband's archives prior to my visit, Mrs Bowlby found very little information about Winnicott contained therein. She did tell me, however, that she knew Winnicott's first wife, Mrs Alice Buxton Taylor Winnicott, a formidably talented artist and potter, whom various Winnicottian authors have dismissed, unfairly, as mad (Khan, 1987; cf. Rodman, 2003). The first Mrs Winnicott did indeed struggle psychologically in many respects, but it would not be accurate to diagnose her in such a manner. Alice Winnicott ran a very successful pottery business for many years, and she engendered great affection among many of those who knew her (cf. Kahr, 2019b). In my more substantial Winnicott biography, currently in progress, I intend to re-examine the traditional portrait of Alice Winnicott. Ursula Bowlby certainly remembered her, albeit not well. She did recall, quite affectionately, that Alice Winnicott dressed in an arty, bohemian manner, which Mrs Bowlby characterised as very "Hampstead" (quoted in Kahr, 1995b).

During my earlier investigations of Winnicott's unpublished correspondence in the Archives of Psychiatry in The Oskar Diethelm Library of the History of Psychiatry at the New York Hospital–Cornell Medical Center in Manhattan, I had discovered a lovely letter which Mrs Bowlby had written to Dr Winnicott, shortly after the publication of his popular book, *The Child and the Family: First Relationships* (Winnicott, 1957a), in which she reported, "I just wanted to let you know how much I've enjoyed reading 'The Child and the Family'. As you know, I had already read 'The Ordinary Devoted Mother and her Baby' and admired it so much—indeed it has been the only English book which I've felt able to recommend when mothers have asked me for the name of a good baby-book. But that was some time ago and I've very much enjoyed re-reading it, and I find it just as recommendable and good" (Bowlby, 1957).[4] In fact, Mrs Bowlby (1957) then offered further congratulations, "Now I am busily recommending the book to all my friends and relations, because it seems a tradition nowadays that every educated mother should read at least one baby-book, and I am all in favour of their reading a really good one." I reminded Mrs Bowlby that she had written to Dr Winnicott nearly forty years previously, but, unsurprisingly, she had no clear memory of having done so. Nevertheless, that generous letter from Ursula Bowlby certainly indicates the degree of respect and collegiality between the Bowlby and Winnicott families.

Having told me as much as she could about Winnicott, I then took this precious opportunity to speak to Mrs Bowlby about her late husband and, also, about some of the other key figures from the early British psychoanalytical movement whom she would have known. We began our interview by discussing Bowlby's training analyst Joan Riviere, a complex personality who had come to psychoanalysis as a very ill woman, and who, in spite of having received treatment from both Dr Ernest Jones and Professor Sigmund Freud, never quite managed to lose her abrasive qualities[5] (cf. Hughes, 1991, 1995; Segal, 1995; Kahr, 1996a).[6] Amusingly, Mrs Bowlby recalled that her husband would refer to his analyst as "Mrs. Rivi" (quoted in Kahr, 1995b). Dr Bowlby had, in fact, told me that he and Mrs Riviere used to have supper together after the conclusion of his lengthy analysis (Kahr, 1984), but Mrs Bowlby had no memory of this, though she certainly acknowledged that it might well be true. She did intimate, however, that Bowlby had had a challenging time in his increasingly Kleinian analysis with Riviere, and that he seemed pleased when, at last, he had ended his cumbersome training. She believed that, after many years, her husband had spent quite long enough in analysis on Riviere's couch. Although Mrs Bowlby did not know much about the content of her husband's analysis, she, as the wife of a young doctor in training, certainly recognised the great financial cost, and she worried whether Bowlby would be able to keep both a wife *and* an analyst as, in the end, Bowlby spent most of his capital funding his clinical training (Kahr, 1995b).

Ursula Bowlby also reminisced about two early members of the British psychoanalytical movement, now increasingly forgotten, namely,

Dr Adrian Stephen, the brother of Virginia Woolf, and his wife, Dr Karin Stephen, the niece of Bertrand Russell. The Bowlbys lived nearby to the Stephens and saw them frequently, and Ursula Bowlby remembered Karin Stephen, in particular, as quite mad. In many respects, the early psychoanalysts, especially those who had come to Freud through the Bloomsbury group, as the Stephens had done, struggled with often enormous psychological difficulties. Karin Stephen bore the additional burden of being extremely deaf, a crippling handicap for a traditional psychoanalyst who saw all of her patients on the couch, while she sat behind them, thus making lip-reading nearly impossible (Kahr, 1995b). More than ten years previously, John Bowlby told me that Karin Stephen used to listen to her patients through a large ear trumpet, and that she required her analysands to place an amplification voice-box on their chests in order to improve their audibility (Kahr, 1984, 2012b; cf. Bowlby, 1984, 1985).

Bowlby joined forces with Dr Adrian Stephen and others during the so-called "Controversial Discussions" which beset the British Psycho-Analytical Society during World War II. Adrian Stephen, in particular, resented the stranglehold that Dr Ernest Jones and his amanuensis Dr Edward Glover maintained on the organisation, with Jones having served as its President uninterruptedly since its foundation in 1919. Bowlby, Stephen, and others objected greatly to this oligarchy, and they helped to stage what Ursula Bowlby described to me as the "palace revolution" (quoted in Kahr, 1995b), attempting to usher in a more democratic style of governance, with regular elections and with a more egalitarian distribution of power (cf. King and Steiner, 1991).

Ursula Bowlby responded to my queries and offered supplementary information in a very straightforward manner. I had no sense that she had become excited by gossip for its own sake. I also experienced her as offering no observations of a gratuitous nature. Nevertheless, she could be quite frank when she needed to be, and she provided a brief, but searing, encapsulation of Melanie Klein, whom she described as a "wicked old woman" (quoted in Kahr, 1995b). Mrs Bowlby also reminisced about Dr Esther Bick, whom Dr Bowlby had hired to develop the child psychotherapy training at the Tavistock Clinic.[7] With uncharacteristic venom in her voice, Ursula Bowlby described Dr Bick as "an absolute snake" (quoted in Kahr, 1995b). Both of these snapshots stood in stark contrast to the other portraits that Mrs Bowlby had painted for me, underscoring the growing sense of animosity between her husband and the Kleinians, and of Bowlby's resentment that the Kleinian subgroup could not seem to appreciate the importance of his work. Indeed, when Klein supervised one of Bowlby's child-analytical cases in the 1930s, he despaired that Klein understood nothing about the realities of that particular youngster's home environment, nor did she seem to take much interest in the fact that the child's mother had entered a psychiatric hospital and, therefore, could no longer transport this little patient to sessions (Kahr, 1984, 2009a). The Kleinian animosity towards Bowlby will be well known from the comments recorded in Professor Phyllis Grosskurth's (1986) biography of Klein (cf. Grosskurth, 1982a, 1982b), wherein we learn that many of Klein's acolytes came to regard Bowlby as a traitor. It should not surprise us, therefore, that Ursula Bowlby harboured a certain resentment towards the Kleinians in kind, evidence that the infighting and rivalry among the psychoanalysts persisted for many decades.

Above all, Mrs Bowlby seemed keen to reminisce about her remarkable husband, whom she loved so very deeply. Although she talked happily about Winnicott and Klein and the others, it soon became clear that she yearned to speak about John above all else, and she took great delight in leafing through numerous photograph albums which she had placed carefully on the dining room table in anticipation of my visit. She treated me to a remarkable collection of memorabilia, sharing many black-and-white snapshots of John Bowlby as a little boy perched alongside members of his family, and then she displayed more pictures of Bowlby at boarding school, looking very sad indeed. With her uncompromising frankness, she told me that she objected greatly to the institution of boarding school and to its disruption of the potential for security of attachment between a child and his or her parents. In this context, Mrs Bowlby reminisced that her son "Ricky" (later Sir Richard Bowlby) had once asked his father why he had become a child psychiatrist. Apparently, Bowlby replied that he had endured difficulties in his own childhood—boarding school among them—but that he did not have *such* a bad time that he could not help others.

She also spoke of her husband as a scientist, and revealed to me that Bowlby never read for pleasure. In part, he confined himself to necessary scientific works because of his relentless pursuit of psychological research; but, also, Mrs Bowlby told me that John suffered from dyslexia, which made reading difficult, although Bowlby himself hotly denied this, even though several other members of the Bowlby family had become dyslexic since (Kahr, 1995b).

Additionally, Mrs Bowlby reminisced about her husband as a clinician and, to my surprise, she confessed that John did not have a particular interest in practising psychotherapy clinically, nor did she believe that he could boast an especially strong aptitude for psychotherapeutic work. In fact, Bowlby often described the day-in, day-out ministration to patients in intensive psychoanalytical treatment as an activity best undertaken by women (Kahr, 1995b).

After several hours, I left the Bowlby house at Wyldes Close Corner, immensely grateful to have spent such an informative afternoon with such a warm-hearted woman. She provided me with important nuggets of historical information, and she did so in a truly kind and illuminating manner. Above all, Mrs Bowlby furnished me with a wonderful glimpse into the private atmosphere in which John Bowlby flourished for more than fifty years, from his marriage in 1938 until his death in 1990. Ursula Bowlby impressed me as a person of deep intelligence, passionate loyalty, huge competence, and an unwavering belief in the importance of solid family attachments. In many ways, I found her to be the living embodiment of what attachment theory represents. Moreover, Mrs Bowlby struck me not only as the loving and supportive wife of Dr Bowlby but, above all, as a substantial person in her own right, and one who, had she decided to devote herself to a career outside the home, would have succeeded in manifold ways.

Although I had formed a very warm and favourable impression of Ursula Bowlby back in 1995, I had absolutely no idea of the full extent of her remarkable contributions. Apart from her family and a small number of close colleagues, I suspect that few people knew what a brilliant mind she possessed and how much of a role she played in facilitating, supporting, and encouraging the development of her husband's work and in forging her own contributions likewise. In fact, it would take me another twenty years to discover something more about the true nature of Mrs Bowlby's creative capacities.

In the wake of John Bowlby's death in 1990, Ursula donated her husband's many papers and files to the Contemporary Medical

Archives Centre at The Wellcome Building in London, now housed in the Wellcome Library. Between 1991 and 2001, various members of the Bowlby family bequeathed additional materials, including tape-recorded interviews and other memorabilia. After a very extensive cataloguing process, which took quite a number of years, the "(Edward) John (Mostyn) Bowlby (1907–1990) Collection" became available to scholars for inspection, and I had the privilege of being among the first to consult the vast holdings in the library's Rare Materials Room on the Euston Road.

The hundreds of thousands of pages of text in the Bowlby archive, spanning the years from 1887 until 2000, fill up no fewer than 144 deep archival boxes as well as one additional oversized container. In the era before emails and text messages and mobile telephones, any professional of repute had to communicate with colleagues by old-fashioned letter writing; therefore, this collection includes copies of virtually every piece of correspondence that John Bowlby had ever received, along with carbon copies of a very substantial number of the letters that he had sent, aided by his long-time and devoted secretary at the Tavistock Clinic, Miss Dorothy Southern. Each of the 144 archive boxes brims with countless correspondence and notes and other literary outpourings, such as draft manuscripts, conference programmes, as well as photographs. Depending upon the thoroughness with which one studies any particular box, it would not be unreasonable for a serious scholar to spend several days working on each container. Progressing through all 144 boxes and the oversized container would require months, if not years. But as a keen historian, I nevertheless carved out many hours over a long period of time to read through Bowlby's professional and personal papers, as much of it proved quite relevant to my ongoing Winnicott research.

During my initial archival visits, I did *not*, however, make time to peruse the fourteen boxes of Ursula Longstaff Bowlby's papers, spanning the years 1926 to 2000, nor a fifteenth box, containing eight files—many heaving with documents—located therein, brimming with drafts of the manuscript of a book about infancy that Mrs Bowlby had written during the late 1940s and which she had revised during the early 1950s. Even though I had spent a lovely morning with Ursula Bowlby in 1995 and found her to be highly engaging, I lacked sufficient space in my timetable to study Ursula's papers as well as John's while researching at the Wellcome Library. Fifteen boxes would, I knew, require days and days and days of research. And so, I left this task rather unattended.

Until more recently …

Several years ago, I had decided to assemble a collection of essays about some of the less well-known figures in the history of psychoanalysis whom I had met and interviewed during the course of my research about Donald Winnicott. Over many decades I had encountered a number of very interesting characters and I thought it would be regrettable if they became lost in the mists of time. And so I started to pursue this work, and I thought that a write-up of my 1995 meeting with Ursula Bowlby might be of some small value to future researchers. I soon realised that I would be able to compose a far more authentic and detailed tribute if I actually studied her private papers first; and so, I preserved several windows in my diary and, at long last, began to plough my way through the fifteen boxes.

I suppose I had thought that by reading Ursula Bowlby's papers I might come to encounter a rather traditional, English version of Martha Freud: a loving, loyal, helpful spouse, who devoted herself to the facilitation of her husband's productivity. I did not, of course, expect to discover that Ursula put paste on John's toothbrush, as Martha Freud had done, but in view of Mrs Bowlby's age, I thought it might be possible that she, like many women of her era, had lived in her husband's shadow.

I could not have been more mistaken.

With each new box of Ursula's papers, I became increasingly familiar with, and delighted by, a woman of prodigious intelligence, staggering literary abilities, and possessed of a fine absorptive mind, who read prodigiously and who wrote about everything. In fact, although Ursula Bowlby chronicled virtually every step of John Bowlby's career, adding her personal thoughts, footnotes, impressions, corrigenda, and reminiscences along the way, her unpublished diaries and papers reveal that she wrote far more about her own adventures, travels, readings, thoughts, impressions and, even, recipes.

Certainly, I never anticipated that, among Ursula's voluminous papers, I would find the manuscript of a remarkable book on infancy, written in her very own hand, as well as the typescripts of many other as yet unpublished books to boot. Indeed, it would not surprise me if we came to discover that Ursula's literary output—virtually all unpublished—came to exceed that of John's.

Ursula Bowlby wrote extensively and clearly and frequently, chronicling almost every moment of her life. The Wellcome Building contains her daily diaries, her memoirs, her short stories, her recipe books, her drawings, her poems, her reminiscences of her husband's colleagues, her maps, her lists of the books that she had read, her lists of the books that she had loaned out to family and friends, and so much more. A woman with tremendous literary capacities, Ursula Bowlby has bequeathed a true legacy, which, hitherto, has remained virtually unknown and unappreciated outside the bosom of her family.

In the confines of such a brief essay, I cannot possibly provide a sufficiently comprehensive biography of the late Mrs Bowlby. Certainly Ursula deserves a significant tribute in her own right. But on this occasion we can offer solely a glimpse of this smart, engrossing woman as both a personality and, also, as a writer that will, I trust, be of interest to clinical practitioners, attachment theorists, and historians of psychotherapy and psychoanalysis, as well as to feminist historians researching outstanding women of the twentieth century. The holdings in the Wellcome Library include, beyond doubt, enough data for several extensive biographical portraits.

Born on 6th March, 1916, at "Ridgelands", the home of her paternal grandparents in Wimbledon, in South-West London (Bowlby, 1962), the third of the seven daughters of Dr Tom George Longstaff— a physician, mountaineer, and explorer—and his first wife, Mrs Dora Mary Hamilton Scott Longstaff, the young Ursula Longstaff grew up in the quaintly named Picket Hill, in Ringwood, located in the New Forest in the county of Hampshire (Gatling, 2015). Ursula's father had not only qualified as a physician from the medical school of St. Thomas' Hospital in London, but he also pursued his lifelong love of mountain climbing, and, on 12th June, 1907, he ascended Trisul in the Kumaon region of the Indian Himalayas, to an elevation of 23,360 feet. At that point in history, no other human being had, to the best of our knowledge, ever climbed higher. Ursula's mother, Dora Longstaff, undertook charitable works, and served as a Poor Law Guardian for the Ringwood Workhouse in

Ashley, in the New Forest of Hampshire, where the Longstaff children grew up (Bowlby, 1992).

Ursula enjoyed a privileged childhood, looked after by her mother, to whom she remained deeply close throughout her life, and, also, by a fleet of devoted household servants. Clearly a young person with strong intelligence, Ursula began writing poetry at least as early as eight years of age. In fact, her grandmother, Mrs Mary Longstaff, published some of Ursula's juvenilia in a book, printed privately for family members. One untitled poem, written at the age of eight years, still survives, and deserves to be published as evidence of Ursula Longstaff's (1926, p. 11) extremely precocious and sensitive linguistic abilities:[8]

> Sun come out
> And play about.
>
> Oh wind do sing,
> And I'll feel like a king.
>
> Oh fir-tops do sway,
> Come and dance little fay.
>
> Oh bees do hum,
> And it will be rum,
> And very great fun.
>
> Oh birds do chatter,
> And I shall grow fatter,
> But that doesn't matter.
>
> Oh sun do shine,
> And sway columbine,
> Then I shall get up,
> And the hens with cluck,
> For I cannot stay in
> When the sun is shining.

Ursula eventually matriculated to the University of Edinburgh to study foreign languages, especially French and German, but, owing to the break-up of her parents' marriage, she abandoned her studies in order to spend more time with her mother. One senses that if Ursula Longstaff had attended university during the 1970s or thereafter, rather than during the 1930s, she would not only have taken a bachelor's degree but, owing to her love of learning and to her capacity for writing, she might well have pursued postgraduate studies in one or more fields of higher education.

As I indicated earlier, Ursula Longstaff met the young psychiatrist Dr John Bowlby in 1937, and she married him the following year, in the All Saints' church in Broad Chalke, in the county of Wiltshire, on Saturday, 16th April, 1938. Evan Durbin, a long-standing friend to John Bowlby (and a future parliamentarian of prominence)[9] served as best man, and Dr Ignacio Matte Blanco, a Chilean psychiatrist who had come to London to train at the Institute of Psycho-Analysis, and who knew Bowlby in that context, participated in the ceremony as one of the ushers (Ursula Bowlby, 1938).[10] In the characteristic tradition of the Bowlby family, known for its ongoing attachments, both Ursula and John maintained lifelong friendships with the Durbin family and with the Matte Blanco family. Sadly, no one could have foreseen on this happy wedding day that, within only a decade, Evan Durbin would die in a drowning accident. Both Ursula, and especially John, who had collaborated with Evan Durbin on an important book, *Personal Aggressiveness and War* (Durbin and Bowlby, 1939), grieved deeply.

Ursula Bowlby became not only a stalwart wife and mother, bearing two daughters and two sons, but, additionally, she worked hard to disseminate her husband's ideas by having crafted a full-length manuscript about caring for a newborn baby, entitled *Happy Infancy*, which John Bowlby had helped to edit. Dr Bowlby suggested that Ursula should entitle her manuscript *Broken Hearts and Broken Rules: A Book About Babies*. Unfortunately, the text never appeared in print, particularly since one of Bowlby's acquaintances considered the book as too much of a mutual admiration society between the doctor and his wife (van Dijken, 1998).

Intrigued to discover that Mrs Bowlby had written her own book—arguably a brave undertaking for a full-time wife and mother in such markedly pre-"feminist" times, not least for the spouse of a well-established author such as Dr Bowlby—I began to read through the various drafts of *Happy Infancy* preserved at the Wellcome Library (Bowlby, c. 1948a, c. 1948b). Quite honestly, I did not know what to expect from a typescript by Mrs Bowlby but, within only a few moments, I found myself deeply absorbed, hugely impressed, and even a bit entranced by the sheer brilliance of this neglected, undiscovered, never-before-published treasure.

Ursula Bowlby seems to have begun the project round about 1948 and then continued to revise it many times over the course of the next few years, its composition triggered, perhaps, by the arrival of Robert Bowlby, her fourth and final child, born at that time. Essentially, *Happy Infancy* serves a multiplicity of functions. First and foremost, Ursula wrote this treatise in very warm, very friendly, very approachable language, aimed specifically at new mothers. And in the short chapters contained therein, she provided her readers with sensible advice on the art of breastfeeding, nappy-changing, bathing the baby, preparing meals, and so forth. But Mrs Bowlby wrote her book with an even higher purpose in mind.

During the 1940s, large numbers of British mothers had found themselves gripped by the very popular pedagogy espoused by the New Zealand child care "expert" Dr Truby King (1916), who, as readers of this book may well know, campaigned for strict, tightly-timetabled regimes of feeding, bathing, and bedding the baby (King, 1948). The influential Dr King opposed the more naturalistic approach, and he objected to excessive cuddling and other forms of physical contact. Many mothers who reared their babies in accordance with King's obsessional and restrictive approach to child care would put their babies in a cot, in a closed-off room or at the end of the garden, and would not return to check on the baby for several hours! Of course, today, such a stingy, if not deprivational, approach to parent–baby interaction would be virtually unthinkable to those with empathy for the constant twenty-four hour needs of their babies; but in the pre-World War II period, and immediately thereafter, Truby King exerted an enormous influence.

Ursula's book, *Happy Infancy*, challenged the Truby King model of pedagogy in a clear, bold, and blunt manner. Backed up by her child psychiatrist husband and, even more so, by her own experience as the mother of four youngsters, Ursula Bowlby crafted the text of *Happy*

Infancy as a veritable manifesto, warning her readers of the dangers of Truby King's philosophy. In contrast, she encouraged mothers to trust, instead, in their own maternal instincts, and to regard themselves as the true experts. In this respect, her philosophy of child care very much mirrored that of her husband's colleague Dr Donald Winnicott who, at that time, broadcast regularly on the radio (e.g., Winnicott, 1949a), encouraging mothers to honour their own capabilities (cf. Kahr, 1996a, 2015d, 2018, 2023a).

Mrs Bowlby (c. 1948a, p. 1) began her typescript with a revolutionary salvo, proclaiming the necessity for a modern philosophy of parenting: "This book is an attempt to present a new attitude towards babies and their management—new, that is, according to present day traditions. What I am urging is that mothers should act to a great extent upon their instincts of affection and solicitate for their babies." In many respects, this opening remark serves as the very foundation stone of all of her subsequent writings, which bear not only the influence of her husband but that of Donald Winnicott as well.

Furthermore, *Happy Infancy* provides a great deal of evidence of Ursula Bowlby's tremendous sensitivity and affection, and of her deep experience as a mother and, moreover, of her anti–Truby Kingian recognition that each newborn has a distinct personality and must be engaged with accordingly, rather than in a formulaic fashion. In sympathy with both her husband and, also, with Winnicott, she vehemently opposed the notion that "babies are machine-like creatures who should spend their lives in eating and sleeping at regular intervals" (Bowlby, c. 1948a, p. 2), and staunchly critiqued the idea that "feeds must take place with military punctuality" (Bowlby, c. 1948a, p. 6).

One cannot do justice to the beauty and complexity of Mrs Bowlby's book in the confines of such a brief communication, and I urge those interested to read her text, *Happy Infancy* (Bowlby, c. 1948a, c. 1948b), as this will provide a richer, fuller appreciation of the work of this heretofore unsung heroine of child care studies.

Having now examined all of the Ursula Bowlby boxes in the archives, I feel enriched at having had the chance to meet such a deeply cultivated, emotionally sensitive, and engaging personality. Not only have I enjoyed the opportunity to come to know Mrs Bowlby in this way, but, also, I believe that I now possess an even greater admiration for the work of her husband. And consequently, I have come to appreciate much more fully how her fascination with her husband's research, her commitment to his burgeoning ideas, and her efforts to care for their four children and their two homes (in London and in Scotland) permitted John Bowlby the time, the space, the protection, and the "secure base" upon which he could come to construct his paradigm-shifting body of theory.

Although Ursula Bowlby may not have ministered to her husband as Martha Freud seems to have done, she nonetheless created a warm, stable home in which a family could grow and flourish creatively and in which a great psychologist and scientist could complete his important life's work. In this respect, it would not be unreasonable to proclaim Ursula Bowlby as the vital muse behind the body of work that has subsequently come to be known as "attachment theory".

I wish that I had known Mrs Bowlby better during her lifetime. After our interview in 1995, we wrote to one another from time to time, and she expressed generous interest in the progress of my biography of Winnicott. She certainly held my research about Winnicott firmly in her mind and, occasionally, to my delight and surprise, she would even unearth another Winnicott-related letter from her archives and would send such documentation to me most generously. I thank her greatly for her care and for her thoughtfulness.

On 3rd February, 2000, Ursula Bowlby died after a short illness at the Garden Hospital in Hendon, in North-West London, at the age of eighty-three years (Bowlby, 2000; cf. Kahr, 2000a). I feel very honoured to have had the privilege of meeting such a kindly and intelligent and engaging person.

PART IV

TWO TRULY UNASSUMING ICONS

CHAPTER SEVEN

Breakfast with Marion Milner:
Reminiscences of the World's
Oldest Psychoanalyst

On 4th January, 1985, as a very young postgraduate student, I had the honour of presenting a paper at a two-day conference at Trinity College in the University of Cambridge, hosted by a small, now long defunct, organisation—the Cambridge Psychoanalytical Society.

Although I had already delivered a number of lectures by this point and did not experience too much nervousness at public speaking, on this occasion, however, I became quite anxious and my knees began to buckle as soon as the chairperson of the conference whispered to me, just before the start of my talk, "Brett, do you see that old lady in the front row? That's Marion Milner."

"Marion Milner?" I gawped. "But she lives in London. Has she really come all this way to Cambridge on a snowy day?"

The chairperson replied, "She has indeed. But don't be thrown. I understand she's very nice."

In spite of my trepidation, I then presented my paper on the topic of working psychotherapeutically with schizophrenic patients, no less—the subject of Mrs Milner's (1969) classic book, *The Hands of the Living God: An Account of a Psycho-analytic Treatment*, published roughly sixteen years previously. I spoke at some length about my clinical sessions with

Illustration 2 Marion Milner's book inscription to Brett Kahr, 1986.

a male schizophrenic patient who had suffered profound sexual abuse in childhood and whose delusional material contained many disguised references to anal penetration by an older male.

During the coffee break, Marion Milner approached me and thanked me for my talk and told me that she particularly appreciated the fact that, unlike the previous speaker, I had communicated in a sufficiently clear and audible voice. She explained that, as an octogenarian, her hearing had begun to suffer; but, happily, she understood every word of my paper. She also complimented me on some of the psychoanalytical interpretations that I had made during my sessions with this particular patient. Mrs Milner's gracious and generous response to my lecture and her kindly interest in the clinical material touched me tremendously and I fell in love with her straightaway.

In the midst of our conversation, I told Mrs Milner that I had, of course, read her classic book, *The Hands of the Living God: An Account of a Psycho-analytic Treatment*, and that I had found it extremely useful. I then asked her whether the patient about whom she had written, known pseudonymously to readers as "Susan", had ever experienced childhood sexual abuse, as my male schizophrenic patient had done. Mrs Milner looked very puzzled, as though she had not ever entertained this possibility, and she told me that she would be happy to dig out her old case notes and reconsider her clinical material.

For a woman of Marion Milner's age—only weeks shy of her eighty-fifth birthday—to respond in such a modest and engaging manner impressed me hugely. As a budding psychoanalytical historian, I had, at that point, already begun to conduct interviews with quite a number of the last surviving members of the British psychoanalytical community of the 1930s and 1940s, but Mrs Milner stood out as quite exceptional. Unlike many of her more obstreperous and competitive colleagues, Milner's kindness shone through in a most sincere and authentic manner and I became a massive fan.

All of the guests and delegates at this two-day conference stayed overnight in student rooms in Trinity College, as the new academic term had not yet begun; and the following morning at breakfast, in the grand, sprawling medieval dining hall, I noticed Marion sitting at a long wooden table, all by herself. This surprised me greatly. Perhaps the other conference participants felt too intimidated to approach such an iconic psychoanalyst. But having already had the pleasure of a brief and convivial conversation with Mrs Milner the previous day, I asked whether I might join her, and with a warm smile and an elegant hand gesture, she invited me to do so.

As we sipped our coffee and buttered our toast—back then no one had heard of cholesterol—in preparation for a second day of psychoanalytical papers, I expressed a curiosity as to why Mrs Milner had taken the trouble to travel all the way to Cambridge, by train, in the middle of such dreadfully cold weather. In my youthful ignorance, I presumed that most old people in their eighties would prefer to sit at home, and I also suspected that Mrs Milner already knew everything about psychoanalysis and could not possibly learn anything more from yet another conference. But Marion smiled and simply told me that she continued to find psychological ideas most fascinating indeed and that she had certainly made the right decision to attend the conference, in spite of the uncomfortable nature of the journey in the midst of a particularly ugly British winter.

In view of the fact that I had just delivered a talk on schizophrenia and that Milner had already worked with an ostensibly schizophrenic woman in multi-decade psychoanalysis, our conversation soon veered in that direction and we talked about the cruel way in which many British psychiatrists would simply dismiss their patients with heavy doses of antipsychotic medication and would make no attempts to engage these individuals in ongoing dialogues about their childhood histories or private lives.

At that point, Milner told me, with a twinkle in her eye, that, years previously, she had served as the clinical supervisor to the famous anti-psychiatrist and one-time psychoanalytical candidate, Dr Ronald David Laing, a man whose work I admired tremendously in spite of the fact that he had since developed a reputation for being a rather pugnacious individual (Kahr, 1994a). According to Milner, this man, better known as "R.D. Laing", or, indeed, as "Ronnie", had succeeded in alienating quite a number of the older teachers at London's Institute of Psycho-Analysis, many of whom found him rather unsuitable as a candidate, but Milner explained that she rated him highly and respected his work; consequently, both she and the great Dr Donald Winnicott championed Laing and argued that he should not be removed from the training. Although Laing eventually parted company with the traditional psychoanalytical establishment, she remained in contact with him, and, years later, Milner (1985) even referred a patient to him, someone whom she described as an "intractable" case—in other words, a person who seemed to be very untreatable indeed. With a glint in her eye, Milner told me that Laing agreed to work with this individual but quoted a sessional fee of £60—a sum which Milner regarded as shockingly expensive, at a time when most analysts charged no more than £10 per hour. As Mrs Milner really wanted to obtain help for this patient, she arranged to pay Laing's fee herself.

Marion also reminisced about Donald Winnicott, with whom she had enjoyed a very long-term set of interconnections. With a huge smile on her face, she told me that Winnicott's widow, fellow psychoanalyst Mrs Clare Winnicott, once quipped that her husband suffered from "delusions of benignity" (quoted in Milner, 1985), imagining everyone to be kindly first and foremost, rather than brimming with envy and evil.

Mrs Milner explained that her fascination with Winnicott remained fervent across the decades and that she had recently become active in a newly formed organisation called The Squiggle Foundation. With tremendous kindness, she asked me to write my name and address on a piece of paper so that she could instruct the administrator to place me on the mailing list. She also engaged with my evident interest in the history of psychoanalysis and told me that she had just participated in a series of talks about the early years of child analysis, organised by Dr Susanna Isaacs Elmhirst, and she wondered whether I should write to Dr Elmhirst to discuss publication possibilities, as I had earlier revealed to her that, one day, I hoped to produce a book on the origins of this esteemed profession. Little did I know at that point in time that, in due course, I would become a regular attendee of events at The Squiggle Foundation (and, ultimately, a patron) and that the brilliant Sue Isaacs Elmhirst would become one of my most venerated and enlightening clinical supervisors.

As our breakfast unfolded, Milner kept regaling me with many truly wonderful stories about herself and her colleagues, all related in a soft but musical voice, and I felt extremely fortunate to be able to sit at the feet of such a magnificent person. At one point, I noticed that Mrs Milner had stopped eating her food and that she still had a full plate of eggs and sausage in front of her. With time ticking and with the first of the morning conference papers about to begin, I asked Mrs Milner whether she had had enough to eat, whereupon she told me, very touchingly, that, owing to the rheumatic arthritis in her hands, she found it difficult to cut her food. Naturally, I offered some practical assistance. Happily, she then ate a few little bites of her breakfast to fortify herself for another long day of scholarly presentations.

I then escorted Mrs Milner into the lecture theatre, and we navigated our way through a second day of psychoanalytical talks, most of which Marion could not hear clearly, owing to the fact that many of the presenters mumbled, in characteristic British fashion. I did my best to serve as her translator and whispered little summaries whenever I could. One of the lecturers, the noted Cambridge academic, Dr John Forrester, spoke at length about Marion Milner's work throughout his presentation, but, alas, she could understand very little of his paper, in spite of being seated in the front row. She gently elbowed me for some assistance, and so, I took out a notepad and began to jot down little quotations from Forrester's speech, in which he expressed his appreciation of Milner's early book, *A Life of One's Own*, written under the pseudonym of Joanna Field (1934). Mrs Milner beamed with delight to know that a distinguished Cambridge historian would have taken the time to read a book that she had written more than fifty years previously.

During the morning coffee break, one of the conference participants approached me, having clocked that I had very evidently fallen in love with Marion Milner. Discreetly, this woman whispered to me that, years ago, she had referred a highly autistic member of her family to Marion for psychoanalytical treatment, and, happily, Mrs Milner cured this individual completely. As a young man, contemplating a career in the psychoanalytical community, it pleased me greatly to learn that Freudian-style treatment really *does* work and that Marion Milner might well be one of its most skilled practitioners.

As the conference drew to a close, Mrs Milner kindly enquired if I ever came to London (as I lived in Oxford at that time), and when I told her that I did, she smiled and chirped, "Oh good, do come and visit me, won't you?" She then gave me her home telephone number. I promised that I would ring her in due course to arrange a cup of tea.

Extraordinarily, while sifting through old boxes of papers, I recently discovered my notes from that 1985 conference, held many long decades ago. It surprised me not at all that I had described Mrs Milner as an "utterly charming and fascinating woman" (Kahr, 1985b). But I also jotted down a few further observations at that time, namely, "Her expression betrayed a certain loneliness; her husband has been dead for quite some time, and I began to conjure up images of a single woman sitting alone, in despair" (Kahr, 1985b). In just two days, I had enjoyed a privileged glimpse of the benign, curious, engaged, playful, and warm-hearted side of Mrs Milner, yet I could also see the more isolated parts, struggling with ageing and with the preparation for death.

I departed that Cambridge conference feeling quite blessed that I had met such a special person who, in just a short space of time, taught me so very much, welcomed me into the fold, and gave me a master class in growing old, helping me to appreciate that if, and when, one does reach her grand age, one can still participate in the world, in spite of rheumatism and hearing loss.

I returned to Oxford and, not long thereafter, a parcel arrived from The Squiggle Foundation, courtesy of Marion Milner, containing all sorts of information about upcoming events. I felt very touched that Marion had taken the trouble to pass along my contact details to the administrator. Soon thereafter, I telephoned Mrs Milner and arranged to visit her at her home on Saturday, 16th February, 1985, at 5.00 p.m.

* * *

On the day in question, I travelled by train from Oxford to Paddington Station in London, and then hopped on the Underground, alighting at Chalk Farm tube station, only a stone's throw away from Marion's long-standing residence at 12, Provost Road. I rang the bell punctually and Mrs Milner greeted me with a handshake. She sported a wispy skirt and blouse, thick glasses on her nose, and very prominent hearing aids in her ears, which, I believe, she had not worn one month previously when we had met in Cambridge.

I presented her with a bouquet of flowers, although I did so somewhat sheepishly as, owing to the horrific winter weather, I could not find any truly robust floral tribute in the local shops, and the ones I offered looked a little frazzled from the wind and the rain. Marion accepted the bouquet with a sweet smile and then invited me inside her home and suggested that I place my overcoat on the banister of her staircase. She then ushered me into the ground floor lounge and told me to look outside at her snow-covered garden, while she walked down the stairs into her kitchen in order to fetch the tray of tea.

As I began to glance round the lounge, I noticed not one, but, rather, two psychoanalytical couches, and I soon came to appreciate that Mrs Milner must have used this room for her clinical practice, although I could not be certain which of the couches she reserved for her patients. One of the couches resembled that rather iconic piece of furniture deployed by Sigmund Freud in his consulting room on the Berggasse in Vienna, with a slightly curved back; the other seemed to be a much flatter bed with a chair parked behind. Surprisingly, Milner had placed both this couch and chair in the middle of the room, rather than more comfortably and snugly, perhaps, up against the wall.

The room struck me as incredibly laden with dust and clutter, which seemed unsurprising in view of Mrs Milner's physical frailty. I doubted whether she had either the energy or the inclination to scrub and clean on a regular basis.

I then treated myself to a closer glance at the furnishings and the decorations, and I soon became quite absorbed by her library—only two shelves of books—which struck me—a trainee bibliophile—as rather sparse. I presumed that a psychoanalyst of Milner's age and distinction would have accumulated a heaving library with hundreds of tomes covering every single wall.

Most of the volumes on the top shelf of Mrs Milner's tiny bookcase boasted those familiar shiny green spines, indicative of the titles published in "The International Psycho-Analytical Library" series, a joint venture between the Hogarth Press and the Institute of Psycho-Analysis. Milner's collection included some of the works of Mrs Melanie Klein (1932b, 1948, 1961), as well as a copy of Klein's book, jointly authored with Mrs Joan Riviere, the now classic *Love, Hate and Reparation: Two Lectures* (Klein and Riviere, 1937). Milner also possessed copies of Dr Donald Meltzer's (1967) *The Psycho-Analytical Process*, as well as Dr Charles Rycroft's (1968a) tomes on *Anxiety and Neurosis* and, also, *Imagination and Reality: Psycho-Analytical Essays. 1951–1961* (Rycroft, 1968b), not to mention a first edition of Dr R. D. Laing's (1961) sturdy text, *The Self and Others: Further Studies in Sanity and Madness*, personally inscribed to his former clinical supervisor, as well as a copy of Laing's book on *Reason and Violence: A Decade of Sartre's Philosophy. 1950–1960*, co-written by Dr David G. Cooper (Laing and Cooper, 1964). The bottom shelf consisted entirely of the twenty-four-volume collection of Sigmund Freud's writings in English. Each book seemed to be covered in a very visible layer of dust.

Mrs Milner's lounge also contained a desk, a low table with a telephone perched upon it, as well as a prominent mantelpiece, strewn with letters and invitations. I could not help but notice that she had placed my letter, confirming our meeting, on display, no doubt as a reminder. She also exhibited an invitation to attend the next meeting of the 1952 Club, a small cohort of psychoanalysts who gathered from time to time to discuss their work.

On the whole, this musty room struck me as somewhat neglected and by no means lavish or elegant. But it also appeared rather homey and welcoming at the same time.

As I waited upstairs in the combined lounge and consulting room, I could hear much rattling of spoons and the opening and closing of cabinet doors downstairs as Marion prepared our tea. Eventually, she began to mount the staircase, with heavy tray in hand, and I quickly sensed that she found herself struggling with the physicality of the task, and so, I offered to help, but Mrs Milner insisted that she could manage. Slowly and carefully, she climbed up the old wooden steps with the tray jiggling back and forth in her rheumatic hands. Happily, Marion reached the top of the stairs and then placed the tea tray on the sofa, nearly toppling the teapot in the process. With great difficulty, she then poured the tea, laced with milk which, alas, looked somewhat curdled and which tasted foul. I made a bold attempt to take a few small sips.

Of most importance, we then embarked upon a rich and lengthy conversation. Mrs Milner began by explaining that she had lived in this house, at 12, Provost Road, for fully fifty-two years. She stressed that, during the mid-1930s, no psychoanalysts resided in that part of London, whereas subsequently, from 1938 onwards, after the arrival of the Freud family in nearby Maresfield Gardens, the villages of Chalk Farm, Swiss Cottage, Belsize Park, and Hampstead—the four communities comprising the NW3 postcode—ultimately became the very epicentre of British psychoanalysis. She then spoke about her home in more detail and confessed that she really needed to contract a gardener.

Naturally, we reminisced about our first meeting in Cambridge, some weeks previously. Marion explained that she had come to that psychoanalytical conference quite by happenstance. She revealed that she had really little interest in some of the papers, several of which focused on the work of Dr Jacques Lacan, a man whom she did not rate particularly highly; but, with a twinkle in her eye, she confessed that she had always harboured a secret wish to visit the majestic Trinity College, founded in the sixteenth century.

Mrs Milner then began to reminisce about some of her old psychoanalytical friends and repeated several of the same stories that she had told me only a few weeks earlier. She took particular delight in reminding me of Clare Winnicott's observation that Donald Winnicott suffered from delusions of benignity. Perhaps Marion also struggled with benignity!

Our conversation soon turned to books. With much excitement, Mrs Milner explained that Yale University Press had approached her recently about the possibility of republishing some of her classic titles. But she had no guarantee that this offer would ever materialise. She told me that she possessed a collection of beautiful colour plates of many of her own paintings and she deeply hoped that someone would reproduce those in book form, although she appreciated that such a volume would be, potentially, quite expensive. Mrs Milner did have greater reassurance from the Hogarth Press and from Chatto & Windus that they would publish her collected papers as the very first volume in a new monograph series about psychoanalysis. This book would eventually appear in print some two years hence under the title *The Suppressed Madness of Sane Men: Forty-Four Years of Exploring Psychoanalysis* (Milner, 1987b), released by Tavistock Publications. Another book would be launched contemporaneously under the title *Eternity's Sunrise: A Way of Keeping a Diary* (Milner, 1987a) by Virago Press.

Milner then talked about her pleasure in holidays, underscoring how the little things in life—such as trips abroad—really do matter. In many respects, by speaking in this way, she certainly epitomised the Winnicottian notion of the importance of play.

Throughout our discussion, I asked Mrs Milner many questions, inviting her to elaborate on all of the topics that she had introduced. Although most of the conversation and questions focused entirely on Marion, she did, throughout our dialogue, have the graciousness to ask about my own work and she seemed particularly interested when I told her that, a short while previously, I had founded an organisation called The Oxford Psycho-Analytical Forum, which sponsored weekly or, sometimes, twice-weekly lectures and seminars on psychoanalysis. Over the last year or more, I had invited such stalwarts as Dr John Bowlby, Dr Muriel Gardiner, Dr Robin Skynner, Professor Albert Solnit, and, even, Dr Ronald Laing, to speak at the University of Oxford, an institution which, at that time, regarded psychoanalysis with tremendous scorn. Milner found this most fascinating. We also discussed my ongoing interest in learning more about the history of psychoanalysis, and she helpfully suggested that I should contact two of her senior colleagues, in particular, Miss Pearl King and, also, Miss Charlotte Balkányi. Although I had not met either of those women at that point in time, Pearl King, in particular, would eventually become a great mentor and, ultimately, a much cherished friend, as well as a true source of inspiration who held Marion Milner in very high regard.

Throughout our discussions, I found Milner to be very liberal-minded, with a great capacity for mutual conversation. At one point, she asked me to enlighten her about the work of the French psychoanalyst Jacques Lacan. Although I have certainly never become a "Lacanian", I had met some of the early British Lacanians, and I did my best to illuminate what I had come to understand about their very particular approach to psychological work.

After discussing my interest in the history of psychoanalysis and my fledgling clinical work in Oxford, Milner told me that I would enjoy the meetings of the 1952 Club—a gathering which she described as "exclusive" (quoted in Kahr, 1985c)—and that I might also appreciate the discussions of the group known as "Imago", run by her psychoanalytical colleague Dr Harold Maxwell, designed to explore a wide range of interesting Freudian topics. Milner explained that several members of Imago had expressed a particular fascination for the contributions of the Chilean psychoanalyst Dr Ignacio Matte Blanco, whose work I had not yet encountered. Milner confessed that she struggled to understand Matte Blanco's extremely complicated theories.

At this point, our focus shifted to further discussion about her famous patient "Susan", whose tragic but, also, hopeful, case history Milner had described in great detail in her aforementioned book *The Hands of the Living God: An Account of a Psycho-analytic Treatment*. In the midst of our discussion, Marion stood up from her seat and showed me a large selection of small plasticine sculptures of a pig and a zebra, which Susan had made as part of the treatment process.

Marion then revealed an important psychoanalytical secret. She explained that, during the early years of Susan's sessions at Provost Road, this very psychiatrically challenged woman, only recently discharged from a mental asylum, actually lived nearby in the Hampstead home of Dr Donald Winnicott and his first wife, Mrs Alice Winnicott. The Winnicotts provided a secure space in which Susan could live safely and then attend psychoanalysis with Milner nearby. Marion spoke very highly of Donald Winnicott; but she described Alice Winnicott, the spouse, as somewhat "dotty" (quoted in Kahr, 1985c) and recalled that, after the couple divorced, Alice moved to Wales where she then died in isolation.

At the time of our conversation in 1985, Milner had not yet revealed *publicly* that Susan had once lived in the Winnicott family home. The following year, on 8th April, 1986, she wrote to the American historian Professor Judith Hughes about this matter (Milner, 1986a), who then published this intriguing information in her book on *Reshaping the Psychoanalytic Domain: The Work of Melanie Klein, W.R.D. Fairbairn, and D.W. Winnicott* (Hughes, 1989).

Apparently, Susan required quite a great deal of extra-analytical looking-after in addition to her formal psychoanalytical sessions. Not only did the Winnicotts care for Susan for a period of time but, so, too, did a certain religious couple known as the Craxtons, at least one of whom worked as a minister.

Milner then reminisced most generously about the details of Susan's treatment. For instance, she told me that Susan had had to endure rather primitive electroconvulsive shock treatments while in hospital and that Susan claimed that these bodily assaults actually produced many dreadful side effects and, consequently, ruined her life. Milner agreed with Susan's assessment of the horrific nature of primitive 1940s electric shocks.

Marion talked with affection about Susan and revealed that her long-standing patient still attended for sessions, after more than forty years. Unsurprisingly, at the outset of treatment, Susan referred to her psychoanalyst as "Mrs Milner", but, over time, she began to call her "Marion".

On the basis of my conversation with Mrs Milner, it seemed that Susan had, in fact, made considerable progress as a result of psychoanalysis, and, in more recent years, had even managed to hold down an intellectually demanding job and, also, maintain a relationship with a partner. At the time of my meeting with Marion, she explained that Susan had recently begun to date a priest. Marion also reported that Susan always boasted a very good sense of humour and that whenever Marion would enquire, "How's your man?", Susan would reply, "Which one?".

After many years of work, Susan retired from her institutional post, and Marion helped her to arrange for a pension. Clearly, the lives of these two women became very deeply intertwined. Marion confessed that the great American psychoanalyst Professor Harold Searles had once written to her offering his view that not only had Marion become therapeutic for Susan but, also, that Susan had proved to be therapeutic for Marion. Mrs Milner told me that she certainly agreed with Professor Searles' assessment.

Milner explained that, across the years, a number of psychoanalysts from overseas had corresponded with her about this now famous case history. Although Milner had always conceptualised Susan as having suffered from "schizophrenia", some American psychoanalysts had suggested that "borderline personality disorder" might be a more appropriate diagnosis. Winnicott (1969a), however, did subscribe to the diagnosis of schizophrenia, having known Susan intimately for quite some time.

Throughout our conversation, Marion kept referring to Susan—the pseudonym used in the publication—by her real name. Whenever she did so, she apologised immediately for having mistakenly revealed the patient's true identity, but I have certainly never repeated those details and I did not record Susan's actual name in my notes (Kahr, 1985b). Mrs Milner also told me that Susan, in spite of her improvements, still suffered from agoraphobia after many years and had to seek specialist treatment elsewhere. Also, Marion explained that Susan would often speak very scornfully about the lack of cleanliness of the house on Provost Road, and that she would frequently criticise Marion for living in such a grotty residence.

At no point did Marion mention any of her own family members, so, at that time, I did not know whether she had any children or grandchildren. But it did surprise me that no family members and no colleagues seem to have offered her help or guidance with basic dusting and tidiness.

When Marion Milner and I first met in Cambridge, after I delivered that paper on the role of child sexual abuse in the aetiology of schizophrenia, I asked her whether Susan had ever suffered such experiences as a youngster. At that time, Mrs Milner claimed not to remember and promised that she would consult her notes. During my visit to Provost

Road, I asked Milner about this matter once again and, on this occasion, she told me that she *had*, in fact, reviewed her old case notes and could now confirm that Susan had succumbed to child abuse of some sort. Marion seemed most unclear as to why she had not included this information in her memorable book—a true indication of how very few psychoanalysts in the 1960s could think about the horrors of parental sadism in a clear manner.

Milner then asked for more clarification about my own burgeoning clinical work in Oxford and even revealed that one of her patients had once attended the Warneford Hospital in Headington, just outside of Oxford town centre. We continued to speak at length about schizophrenia and we enjoyed discussing some of the psychodynamic aspects of this most severe form of psychosis.

Between the time of our first meeting on 4th January, 1985, and our subsequent meeting on 16th February, 1985, Marion Milner had celebrated her eighty-fifth birthday. It surprised me that a woman of this grand age would still be working psychoanalytically with patients, but Marion explained that, in addition to her occasional consultations with Susan, she continued to treat three analysands on a regular basis. She then revealed that, although most of her patients have enjoyed the couch, one of her current patients— a man—came to experience the couch as a sadistic object and would refuse to lie down. Milner underscored that she would often shift the precise position of her chair in order to face this man more directly during sessions.

Mrs Milner also talked to me about some of her trainee analysands, and she expressed concern that, over the years, two candidates from the Institute of Psycho-Analysis had proved to be particularly unsuitable for training and that she had to terminate their treatments. Milner made no mention of the names of these two disappointing psychoanalytical students and she provided no information which would have constituted a breach of confidentiality in any way.

Milner then turned her attention to some of her London colleagues. I did not have to prompt her at all. I suspect that Marion might have appreciated the fact that a young man with an interest in the history of her profession had come to visit and that she could speak in great detail, sensing that I would listen carefully.

Mrs Milner began to reminisce at considerable length about the controversial Indian-born Mr Masud Khan, then sixty years of age. Marion explained that she met Khan shortly after his arrival in England and that she had even attended his wedding to Miss Jane Shore. Milner lamented that Khan had become increasingly alcoholic and, also, quite sadly, that he had developed a cancer and recently had a lung removed. She had, apparently, seen Khan not long ago, after he had delivered a lecture to The Squiggle Foundation—his first public appearance in quite some time—and he seemed very pleased to know that he could still command an audience. Milner expressed much sadness that, as a result of her own hearing difficulties and of Khan's vocal struggles (a sequela of his cancer), it had become extremely difficult for the two of them to engage in basic conversation.

She then spoke very fondly about Dr Margaret Little, a fellow elderly psychoanalyst who had moved from London to Kent. I later discovered that Little (1985) had undergone psychoanalysis with Winnicott and, consequently, the two women had a great deal in common. Milner underscored that she would sometimes visit Dr Little in the countryside, to offer support to this aged and isolated woman, but that she could only manage the journey to the countryside during the summer and not in the winter, owing to the lack of a platform at Sevenoaks station, which made walking in the cold rather more difficult. Helpfully, Marion suggested that I should hop onto a train to Sevenoaks in order to interview Dr Little (which, in fact, I would do later that year, and, as a result of that conversation, I learned a great deal more about the history of post-war British psychoanalytical politics (Kahr, 1985d)).

In addition to gossiping about Masud Khan and Margaret Little, Mrs Milner also shared her thoughts about Dr William Gillespie and his wife, Mrs Sadie Gillespie. Marion told me, perhaps somewhat brashly, that she regarded Dr Gillespie as a dour old Scot who would always toe the line; nevertheless, the two remained in contact and she had come to learn that Dr Gillespie had recently begun to write his autobiography.

As our conversation unfolded, Marion continued to chat and to reminisce freely, regaling me with stories and anecdotes about such noted figures as Madame Janine Chasseguet-Smirgel, the distinguished French psychoanalyst, and, also, Dr André Green, whom she dismissed as far too academic and not sufficiently clinically empathic in her estimation.

Milner then explained that, in recent years, French psychoanalysts, especially those of a Lacanian persuasion, had begun to take an increasing interest in her work, not least Lacan's very own son-in-law, Monsieur Jacques-Alain Miller. Apparently, Miller had sent one of his Lacanian publications to Mrs Milner, but she confessed that she could not understand it at all and passed it along to a colleague who spoke French far better than she could manage. Monsieur Miller had asked Marion to consent to an interview, but she told me that she refused his invitation as, two years previously, she had made a decision not to grant any more interviews. Upon hearing this, I felt rather fortunate that Mrs Milner had agreed to meet with me at all.

After chatting about colleagues, both British and French, Milner revealed that, at present, she had become preoccupied with only one major task, namely, the completion of her collected papers. Apparently, she had only just begun to craft an introductory essay but admitted that she struggled to find an overarching theme that would link all of her papers together. Mrs Milner explained that she hoped to finish this gargantuan writing task before too long so that she would then be able to invest far more time in her truly profound and playful passion for painting.

In the middle of our conversation, the telephone rang, and Marion rose slowly from her chair and walked towards the phone, perched on a nearby table. She picked up the receiver, and, in that characteristic mid-twentieth-century English manner, she announced, "722 2112", thus reassuring her caller that he or she had, in fact, dialled the correct number. Marion spoke very briefly to the person on the other end of the line, explaining that she had company and could not talk at length.

Mrs Milner then sat down and revealed the caller to be none other than Mr Alexander Newman, a former priest who gravitated towards psychotherapy and psychoanalysis in order to support his parishioners. Newman then went on to create The Squiggle Foundation, an organisation devoted to an exploration of the work of Donald Winnicott. Apparently, Newman had become very friendly with Milner and, also, quite concerned about her, and it seems that he would check up on her regularly, especially after meetings, to ensure that this increasingly frail octogenarian lady would have arrived home safely. Milner also explained that Alexander Newman's wife, Mrs Miriam Rapp, often assisted her with the typing of her papers. It pleased me greatly to know that this Winnicottian couple took such an interest in Mrs Milner's well-being.

When I first arranged to meet with Marion at her home, I presumed that I might stay for merely an hour or so, but my gracious hostess revealed no signs of fatigue and she continued to talk. I sensed that she might have become quite lonely by this point in her life and that she may have welcomed the opportunity to chat with someone with a tremendous admiration for her work and with a great fascination for her professional community.

Somehow, our discussion veered towards the First World War. Milner lamented that she had lost many friends and acquaintances in the Great War and that this stirred a ferocious anger which, she admitted, none of her own psychoanalysts had ever helped her with in any significant way. I must confess that I found this revelation rather surprising. I would have thought that psychoanalysts would have discussed warfare quite extensively, but it may be that, in the early days, practitioners focused more on the private biography of the patient rather than upon the traumatogenic impact of broader social and political explosions. In spite of the fact that I barely knew Mrs Milner, she did inform me that, at some point, she had consulted a psychodramatist and then participated in psychodrama sessions, which certainly helped her to process the horrors of the 1914–1918 war more fully. She revealed such a respect for the discipline of psychodrama that she would, at times, recommend this method of treatment for her patients. Marion then told me that she needed to locate a good London-based psychodramatist for one of her patients and wondered whether I knew of any. I did, in fact, have an acquaintance—one of the leaders of the British psychodrama movement, whom I had met recently at a conference in Oxford—and I believe that I passed on the name of this colleague to Marion.

Thereafter, we began to chat about the Swiss-born psychoanalyst, Dr Alice Miller, who, in the late 1970s and early 1980s, had become increasingly popular in the English-speaking world, especially in view of her emphasis on the realities of child abuse and, also, parental insensitivity (e.g., Miller, 1981). We talked about Alice Miller's notion that many psychological workers often enter the mental health profession as a covert way of dealing with their own depressed mothers (cf. Miller, 1979). Mrs Milner considered this hypothesis to be very sensible and explained that she regarded her own mother as having suffered from a significant depression, though not clinically so.

Our dialogue seemed to be unending, with no shortage of fascinating topics. But as the sun had set by this time, and evening had approached, I wondered whether I should excuse myself in order to allow Mrs Milner some rest. She, however, seemed keen to continue our chat and so I remained perched in my chair. Surprisingly, Marion asked me if I gardened. As I lived at that time in student accommodation, I explained that I had little opportunity for either planting or pruning. She then spoke more extensively, and with great delight, about her love of gardening, perhaps hoping to inspire me to do likewise.

At this point, Marion continued to reminisce further about some of her old psychoanalytical companions. She explained that she would often attend painting classes with both Masud Khan and, also, with Mr Anton Ehrenzweig, a good friend and scholar of art and music whom she met through their mutual passion for psychoanalytical theory (cf. Ehrenzweig, 1949, 1953, 1967). Apparently, Ehrenzweig, a Viennese refugee to Great Britain, attended the meetings of the Imago group along with the writer Mr Adrian Stokes—one of Melanie Klein's long-term analysands. According to Milner, both Ehrenzweig and Stokes engaged in frequent verbal combat with one another, often in quite a rivalrous manner. On one occasion, Ehrenzweig telephoned Milner to complain that Stokes would no longer speak to him. When Milner enquired why that should be the case, Ehrenzweig revealed that he had actually told Stokes to go to hell!

Unlike many of the elderly psychoanalysts whom I interviewed during the 1980s, I did not experience Marion as pathologically narcissistic in any way. Certainly, she talked about herself with pleasure, but, throughout our conversation, she continued to turn the lens onto me and took a serious interest in my work, which I found rather sweet and kindly. I discussed my research post in a psychiatric hospital, as well as my first forays into professional writing (having begun a book on the psychodynamics of schizophrenia), and, also, my own small efforts to organise psychoanalytical lectures in Oxford. When I told her that R.D. Laing had come to speak on one occasion, Milner asked immediately whether he had arrived drunk—which, in fact, he *had* done—thus, she clearly knew all about his alcoholism (cf. Kahr, 1994a). We also discussed the psychopathology of wife-battering and other forms of domestic violence, as one of my very first patients had to endure much physical abuse from her husband. As I recall, Milner and I had a most interesting conversation about the potential role of unconscious masochism in such cases.

I believe that I asked Mrs Milner whether she had entertained any plans to retreat fully from clinical work. She told me that many of her colleagues had already urged her to set a formal retirement date, owing to her advancing age. But Milner insisted that she still had work to undertake and that she had no plans to retire *in toto*. She underscored that a psychoanalytical practice progresses very slowly indeed but that her patients do, eventually, make great strides. Marion insisted that she would endeavour to remain very active in the psychoanalytical community and that, in the upcoming week, she hoped to attend a meeting of training analysts at the Institute of Psycho-Analysis, to keep herself engaged and stimulated.

As I prepared to depart Provost Road and return to Oxford, I told Mrs Milner that I regarded her as quite an inspiring and courageous woman who had made such a huge contribution to mental health. I exclaimed that she deserved a Festschrift or some other written tribute which should examine her work in detail. She rather liked this idea, but she could not think of anyone who might have the capacity to prepare such a testament on her behalf.

I then bade Mrs Milner farewell, expressing the hope that I would meet her again in the future. As I reached for my overcoat, which I had hung on the hallway banister, I noticed Marion's walking stick, which she kept in a bucket placed not far from the front door—a powerful reminder of her age and her physical struggles. I shook her hand warmly before braving the cold weather of Chalk Farm.

I then walked back to the Tube station and hopped onto the London Underground, whereupon I began to write up detailed notes from my lengthy encounter with Marion (Kahr, 1985b, 1985c). Subsequently, upon my arrival in Paddington, with time to spare before boarding the train, I popped into a nearby restaurant, and I continued to record as much of the conversation as I could recall, which still remained quite fresh in my mind (Kahr, 1985b).

Mulling on this very unique encounter, I felt both inspired by Marion but, also, saddened by her widowed state and by her loneliness, and I wished that I had brought her a more useful present than some unimpressive flowers. I jotted down pages and pages and pages of notes, by hand, and I concluded my write-up with the following summation: "What a lovely woman" (Kahr, 1985b).

Several months thereafter, I travelled abroad on a visiting fellowship, but I remained in communication with Marion by old-fashioned letter writing. I shall never forget that, on one occasion, perhaps in early 1986, I sent her a draft of a very lengthy paper that I had prepared on the psychoanalytical approach to schizophrenia—an elaboration of the talk that I had delivered the previous year at Trinity College in Cambridge. To my utter surprise and delight, Milner read this juvenile typescript rather carefully and she even took the time to write back with some extremely detailed comments.

Upon my return to the United Kingdom one year later, I registered for a weekly Saturday morning course of lectures about the work of Donald Winnicott, sponsored by The Squiggle Foundation; and to my great surprise, I discovered that Mrs Milner also attended every single one of these talks quite regularly (Fielding and Newman, 1988). Although delighted to see Marion, it stunned me that she would wish to devote every Saturday morning to these basic seminars about Winnicott when she had known the man personally over many decades and, in all likelihood, could have delivered each of these introductory talks in her sleep. But clearly, her affection for Winnicott persisted long after his death in 1971, and she certainly enjoyed being part of this vibrant Winnicottian community.

The other students on the course regarded Mrs Milner as a historical object of veneration and did not dare to approach her. Rather like those conference delegates in Cambridge who left Marion sitting alone during breakfast in the great hall of Trinity College, my fellow Winnicottian seminar participants kept their distance. Indeed, young people often find very old people somewhat frightening as few have yet begun to prepare themselves for the possibility of death, at least not in a mature, well-processed manner. But, having come to know Marion already, I took great delight in sitting with her after each of the talks for a cup of tea. We chatted about anything and everything and I found her to be a joyful woman, full of warmth and curiosity. Throughout our association during the 1980s and 1990s, these Milnerian characteristics never wavered.

On one memorable occasion, we began to speak in more detail about the particularities of her relationship with Winnicott. Obviously, owing to our age difference and to the fact that she and I had met in a professional context, she did not tell me *everything* about her feelings towards Winnicott. For instance, I did not know at that point that he had treated her late husband, Mr Dennis Milner, or that she, herself, had undergone a period of analysis with Winnicott and that he had actually conducted *her* psychoanalysis in her very own lounge at Provost Road—the room that I had visited in 1985—in order to save her travelling time to and from his office (Milner, 2012), or that she harboured a very strong erotic transference towards him (Milner, n.d.). Most of that information became known to me only after I had read the unpublished correspondence between these two historical psychoanalytical figures years later, much of which will be documented in a forthcoming book (Kahr, 2023b). Back in the late 1980s, I knew none of that.

But Marion did tell me something about Winnicott which no one else had ever known or appreciated, namely, that this extraordinary king of psychoanalysis harboured a secret wish to write an operetta in the style of Gilbert and Sullivan (Milner, 1987c).

I must confess that I found Milner's musical reminiscence to be quite striking. Why on earth would Great Britain's most famous, most productive, and most path-breaking psychoanalyst yearn to be a lyricist and composer in the tradition of Sir William Gilbert and Sir Arthur Sullivan?

Milner did not elaborate much on this aspect of the man to whom she referred, rather intimately, as "Donald", having known him so well. But, in my subsequent archival research in years to come, I uncovered a fair bit of confirmatory evidence which has supported Milner's reminiscence about this aspect of Winnicott's profound musicality (Kahr, 2023c). Winnicott did, indeed, derive much joy and inspiration from the wit and wisdom of these two magnificent progenitors of the English operetta.

I certainly cannot do justice to the significance of Winnicott's interest in Gilbert and Sullivan in this brief context, although I will, in due course, publish a study elaborating this thematic in more detail (Kahr, 2023c); however, I can state succinctly that, in many ways, Winnicott's passion for Gilbert and Sullivan epitomised his love of play and joy and humour and wit—in a deeply serious manner—because, in my estimation, no two musical writers had ever encapsulated the seriousness of play more successfully than that pair of nineteenth-century gentlemen.

* * *

In 1986, shortly after the opening of the Freud Museum—the former London home of both Professor Sigmund Freud and Dr Anna Freud—I became the Deputy Director of the International Campaign for the Freud Museum, having chosen to pause my postgraduate studies for a year in order to pursue this unique opportunity to work in the Freud house and to help establish the museum in its early days. Naturally, I hoped that I might be able to invite Marion to the museum for a special private viewing.

As a young woman, Marion had attended seminars conducted by Anna Freud in the famous double-length study on the ground floor, but she had not visited 20, Maresfield Gardens, in London's Swiss Cottage, during Anna Freud's later years. Shortly after the museum opened its doors to the public in the summer of 1986, Marion did pay a visit as an ordinary tourist but, as she told me, owing to her failing eyesight, she could not see much of Freud's famous collection of antiquities in any proper detail, as she, like all the other members of the public, had to stand somewhat far away, behind the cordon.

It brought me great satisfaction that, in my new role, I could arrange a bespoke tour of the Freud Museum, just for Marion, and I even obtained permission from the head of security, Mr Alexandre Bento, to turn off the burglar alarms for a short while and to remove the cordon in the study so that Marion could examine Freud's priceless archaeological collection up close. And so, on 27th October, 1986, I arrived at Marion's home at Provost Road in a taxi and I then escorted her personally to Maresfield Gardens for this private viewing. Happily, Marion enjoyed herself immensely, and she especially loved walking round Freud's incomparable consulting room without any ropes to restrict her movements. Marion reminisced about having attended a particular seminar in that truly iconic study many decades previously when the psychoanalyst Dr Augusta Bonnard, one of Anna Freud's associates, delivered a paper. At that very moment, Marion brought the past back to life in such a vivid manner and she became a true messenger of the early history of psychoanalysis, resurrecting all of those wonderful, pioneering characters.

As Marion gazed at the objects in the study up close, she became particularly preoccupied with the small, lacquered Chinese statuette of an old Daoist sage, perched on the little card table adjacent to Freud's wooden desk (Davies, 2019). Upon seeing this piece of artwork, Milner (1986b) exclaimed with delight, "Oh look, he's got a little cap on." Marion's evident pleasure in this small detail of one of Freud's art objects reminded me of her whole philosophy of living, which she had outlined in her book, *A Life of One's Own* (Field, 1934), published some fifty-two years earlier—all about the ways in which we might find pleasure and engagement in tiny moments and miniscule details, thus embracing the canvas of life to the fullest.

I believe that I refrained from revealing to Mrs Milner that this statuette of the Chinese sage, which Freud himself used to greet every day (Fichtl, n.d.), is actually a modern piece of art, not an ancient one (Gamwell, 1989), as many had suspected—unlike most of the other multi-thousand-year-old objects in the study—but, had I done so, I doubt that Mrs Milner would have minded.

Marion's playful engagement with this little figure from Freud's collection produced a huge smile on my face. I remember thinking that, in all likelihood, many near-nonagenarians might have become so jaded that simply glancing at a tiny little statuette would have little impact; but Marion still had the great capacity to imbibe Freud's study and the objects contained therein with a lively, almost childlike, sense of wonderment, which inspired me greatly.

While ambling through Sigmund Freud's famous office with Marion, I told her that I had brought a copy of her book, *On Not Being Able to Paint* (Field, 1950), with me to the museum, and I wondered whether she would do me the honour of autographing my inexpensive paperback version of her classic text. The original cloth publication bore the pseudonym of "Joanna Field" on the title page, but my edition, published in 1984 and purchased for £4.95, boasted the author's real name, "Marion Milner" (Milner (Joanna Field), 1984). To my delight, Marion agreed to sign my copy but explained that she would need to sit down in order to do so.

At that moment, she asked me whether she might perch herself on Freud's office chair and sign the book at the great man's desk. It seemed quite fitting and appropriate that this *grande dame* of British psychoanalysis should be permitted to spend a few moments in Freud's chair, and I thus bade her do so.

Marion then seated herself on the leather chair, specially designed by Felix Augenfeld, a friend to Freud's youngest son, the architect Ernst Freud (Augenfeld, 1974; Molnar, 1992; cf. Welter, 2012). Happily, Marion kept a pen in her handbag, which she extracted, and then she began to write an inscription.

But just at that moment, a member of the curatorial staff of the museum came rushing into the study, no doubt having observed me and Marion on the security camera, and this vigilant colleague explained that, owing to the tremendous delicacy of the Augenfeld chair, no one must be allowed to touch it, let alone to sit upon it. To my great shame, although I had worked at the museum for some months by this point, none of the curatorial team had ever told me that we must *never, ever* touch Freud's chair. (Indeed, the desk and chair would ordinarily be roped off, but, owing to Marion's exalted status, she and I did have special permission on this occasion to approach each object at closer range.)

I expressed my regret to Marion that I had granted her permission to sit on Freud's chair without having appreciated that this might not be permissible. But, undaunted, Marion then kneeled on the floor, albeit with some orthopaedic difficulty, and she then placed the book on Freud's desk and signed my copy thus: "For Brett with all best wishes and thank you Marion" (see Illustration Number 2).

After Mrs Milner and I had explored Freud's study in some depth, the museum's convivial press officer, Mrs Karen Booth, very kindly prepared a special tea for us on the unique, sunlit half-landing where Martha Freud, the *Frau Professor*, used to entertain her visitors. It pleased me greatly that my colleagues at the Freud Museum treated Marion so graciously and afforded her this unique opportunity to explore Sigmund Freud's consulting room at close range and then to enjoy a tea in Martha Freud's special space. I know of no other psychoanalytical practitioner who has ever received such royal treatment. During the tea, Marion spoke to me about a welter of topics, but I particularly remember her childlike pleasure in revealing that, often, during sessions with her own patients, she would "doodle" (Milner, 1986b), drawing copious squiggle-like figures on pieces of paper. I could not help but wonder whether such Winnicottian doodling actually enhanced her capacity to concentrate on her patients' free associations or whether such activity might have distracted her.

Over the successive years, I had the pleasure of encountering Marion on several more occasions, not only at the Freud Museum, and at various psychoanalytical parties and book launches, but, most frequently, at meetings of The Squiggle Foundation. On one occasion, in 1991, I attended a lecture delivered by a very senior colleague, Dr Martin James, a great friend to Donald Winnicott and a close colleague to Anna Freud. Marion sat in the front row, keen to hear Dr James' thoughts on Winnicott's relationship to psychiatry. At the start of his very interesting talk, James (1991) singled out Milner for special recognition, which pleased me greatly. I suspect that the frequent Saturday meetings of The Squiggle Foundation gave Marion some important structure to her week as well as some richly deserved celebrity status.

Marion had become such a devotee of The Squiggle Foundation that the editors of *Winnicott Studies: The Journal of the Squiggle Foundation* published a special edition of this periodical in Marion's honour, complete with lovely tributes from such distinguished colleagues as Mrs Sadie Gillespie (1988), Dr William Gillespie (1988), and Mrs Frances Tustin (1988).

In her final years, Milner began to lose her eyesight, and towards the very end, she became almost completely blind. In order to amuse herself, she would sit in her armchair and cut up some of the paintings that she had made in previous years, and she would then rearrange the segments into lovely collages (Walters, 2000). For her very last public outing, she visited Imperial College, part of the University of London, in order to study the newly unveiled bust of her deceased brother, Professor Patrick

Blackett, the distinguished Nobel Laureate physicist, who, in 1969, had become Baron Blackett, of Chelsea in Greater London.

Although quite a few of us presumed that Marion might well reach her one hundredth birthday—and she had talked to her friends and associates about the possibility of a centenary—she died peacefully on Friday, 29th May, 1998, at the age of ninety-eight years, at her long-standing residence, 12, Provost Road, in Chalk Farm, in North-West London. Marion may perhaps have lived longer than every other clinical psychoanalyst in the entire history of the profession at that point in time. Some years later, Dr Hyman Spotnitz, an American psychoanalyst, would pass away in 2008, only months before his one hundredth birthday, and then, in 2014, Professor Martin Bergmann, also an American-based practitioner and scholar, would die only days before his one hundred and first birthday. But certainly, among British psychoanalysts, Marion Milner might well be the queen of longevity.

Needless to say, Marion remained very much in the minds of the many whose lives she had touched, long after her decease. On one occasion, during my ongoing oral history interviews with members of the British psychoanalytical community, I happened to speak to one of Marion's earliest training patients (Anonymous, 2010). This gentleman, now deceased, told me that, while lying on Milner's couch in Provost Road, he developed a profoundly erotic passion for her and asked whether the two of them could have a sexual affair. As this man related that compelling story to me, I could not help but wonder how Mrs Milner might have responded to this unusual request from a patient. In such clinical circumstances, it would be only too easy to render an interpretation about the erotic transference or to attack and shame the patient for his sadistic wish to destroy the boundaries of the psychoanalysis by turning the treatment relationship into a sexual one.

This former patient, who subsequently became an extremely senior mental health professional in his own right, told me, "Marion could not have replied in a classier way. She simply said to me, 'But that is not what we agreed'" (quoted in Anonymous, 2010), implying that he had every right to experience an erotic attraction and to verbalise his fantasies, but that the enactment of this wish would not be at all possible in a psychoanalytical context.

I appreciate that many clinicians might have responded in a rather different way, but this former analysand found Milner's rather independent, unique, idiosyncratic style of reply to be extremely helpful. This story has remained in my mind very powerfully indeed.

As a young psychologist, impassioned by psychoanalytical ideas and keen to work in this field, and as someone obsessed with the rich history of this profession, meeting Marion Milner proved to be a tremendous pleasure and a memorable honour. It never occurred to me that I would ever encounter someone who, as a young woman, had studied with, or fraternised with, some of the most significant pioneers in this field, including, Professor John C. Flügel, one Great Britain's very earliest psychoanalysts, who knew Sigmund Freud personally; Dr Irmarita Putnam, who became Milner's first psychoanalyst and who had herself undergone analysis with both Professor Sigmund Freud and Dr Carl Gustav Jung; Dr William Healy, one of the pioneers of child psychiatry; Dr Sylvia Payne, one of the queens of British psychoanalysis, who became Milner's second psychoanalyst; not to mention those senior figures who had served as her supervisors, namely, Mrs Melanie Klein, Mrs Joan Riviere, and Miss Ella Freeman Sharpe, let alone her subsequent psychoanalysts, Dr Donald Winnicott and Dr Clifford Scott (Dragstedt, 1998). Essentially, Marion Milner knew virtually all of the founders and she shared her reminiscences and the wisdom which she had internalised from these honorary mothers and fathers with a deeply open heart.

I consider myself immensely fortunate to have had the opportunity to spend time in the presence of such a truly lovely woman.

CHAPTER EIGHT

Enid Eichholz Balint: The Birth of Couple Psychoanalysis in England

The Prehistory of Couple Psychoanalysis

In 2012, the actors Meryl Streep and Tommy Lee Jones starred in a Hollywood film entitled *Hope Springs*—a touching story about a long-standing couple whose marriage had become somewhat anaemic, and who, after several sessions with a therapist, portrayed by the comedian Steve Carrell, begin to enjoy a more lively intimacy once again. Clearly, couple therapy has become a fixture in popular culture; and in view of the increasingly frequent portrayals of this modality in such mainstream television programmes as *The Sopranos*, *House of Cards*, and innumerable others, the image of the modern-day couple psychotherapist now threatens to eclipse that of the old-fashioned Viennese psychoanalyst, seated in a leather chair, while an individual patient free-associates on the couch.

Indeed, couple psychotherapists have not only become characters in television dramas but, moreover, several real-life couple practitioners have now appeared on reality television series as themselves. These programmes include the American series, *Couples Therapy*, first broadcast in 2012, on the cable network VH1, hosted by the psychotherapist Dr Jenn Mann, as well as a completely different series, also entitled *Couples Therapy*, first broadcast in 2019, on Showtime, hosted by the psychologist and psychoanalyst Dr Orna Guralnik.

But how did couple psychotherapy and couple psychoanalysis originate? And by what means, especially in Great Britain—a country historically renowned for its reluctance to speak about intimate matters—did couple work become such an increasingly visible modality? *Who invented British couple psychoanalysis?*

For centuries, most troubled couples simply suffered in silence, or turned, perhaps, to prayer. Even seasoned psychiatric pioneers offered little comfort to spouses in distress.

In 1919, the famous ballet dancer Vaslav Nijinsky became psychotic, and his wife arranged a consultation at the Burghölzli asylum in Switzerland with Professor Eugen Bleuler (1911), renowned for having invented the German-language term *"Schizophrenie"*, better known in English as "schizophrenia". Sadly, Bleuler provided little hope for the dancer's recovery or for the couple's happiness; and damningly, he offered the following soul-destroying prescription to Nijinsky's wife: "Now, my dear, be very brave. You have to take your child away; you have to get a divorce. Unfortunately, I am helpless. Your husband is incurably insane" (quoted in Nijinsky, 1933, p. 410). In desperation, Madame Romola Nijinsky also consulted Professor Sigmund Freud, Dr Carl Gustav Jung, Dr Alfred Adler, and Dr Sándor Ferenczi (Nijinsky, 1933; Ansbacher, 1981); yet none of these psychoanalysts provided any substantial support for either member of this troubled marital couple, and consequently, Nijinsky spent much of the next thirty-one years in a catatonic stupor while his wife embarked upon a series of lesbian affairs (Kahr, 1987; Nijinsky, 1991).

Indeed, on the rare occasions when the early psychoanalysts *did* attempt to grapple with marital issues, they would do so by treating the members of the couple *separately*, rather than *together*. In Vienna, Professor Sigmund Freud offered individual treatment to the American physician Dr Ruth Mack Brunswick and, also, to her husband, the composer Mr Mark Brunswick. But after lengthy analyses with Freud, conducted in parallel, the couple divorced (Roazen, 1995). To the best of our knowledge, this struggling marital pair never met with Freud for sessions at the same time. Freud treated many other couples in this fashion, with the husband attending at one hour and the wife at another; and those who participated in this arrangement often separated or ended up in sexless marriages.

This particular model of treating spouses separately remained the gold standard for much of the first half of the twentieth century. Psychoanalysts had simply not yet developed the idea of providing psychological therapy for both members of the couple *simultaneously*, in the same room at the same time.

Fortunately, throughout the middle years of the twentieth century, a seismic shift erupted in the clinical lens of psychotherapists and psychoanalysts alike due, in large measure, to the devastations of global warfare. As a result of the Second World War, many British soldiers lost their lives in combat, as indeed did many civilians, from bombings during the Blitz, leaving countless spouses abruptly widowed, as well as untold numbers of children bereaved of one parent or orphaned of both.

When the war ended, the fighting forces returned home to mainland Great Britain, and one can only begin to imagine the complexities of integrating the veterans back into their families. Many would have suffered from post-traumatic illness or would have contracted sexually transmitted diseases from acts of infidelity with prostitutes or mistresses abroad. Innumerable children failed to recognise their fathers whom they had not seen for years and, in some cases, had never met at all; and many other children became depressed from having had to endure evacuation to the countryside or even overseas (Bowlby, Miller, and Winnicott, 1939). Likewise, numerous wives may have taken lovers or may have harboured tremendous hatred towards their spouses for having left them to fend for themselves amid the privations and dangers on the home front. Those marriages which had, in fact, survived the war, did so under the greatest of strain.

Unsurprisingly, between 1939 and 1945, the number of petitions for the dissolution of marriages filed in England and Wales trebled, and continued to rise thereafter, on grounds of adultery, desertion, cruelty, lunacy, or the presumption of decease (*Statistical Digest of the War: Prepared in the Central Statistical Office*, 1951). With an impoverished treasury, a blitzed country, and a malnourished population which had endured death, loss, abandonment, and traumatisation, marriages continued to crumble. British couples needed rescue, but to whom, if anyone, could they turn?

Enid Eichholz and the Ravages of War

At some point during the 1940s, a woman called Enid Eichholz decided to do something proactive for troubled families and, in particular, for dysfunctional, traumatised marital couples.

Born in Hampstead, in North-West London, on 12th December, 1903, Enid Flora Albu attended school locally and then matriculated to Cheltenham Ladies' College and, ultimately, to the London School of Economics and Political Science in the University of London, where she obtained a BSc degree in economics in 1925 (Hopkins, 2004). She married Robert Nathaniel Eichholz, a lawyer (Rycroft, 1996), and soon became a mother. Round about 1934, one of her husband's German cousins came to visit and spoke of the horrors of Adolf Hitler's regime. Desperate to help, Mrs Eichholz established a school for German-Jewish refugee children. Through her work with these youngsters, she eventually expanded her efforts in order to provide assistance to adult refugees as well, some of whom came to live in her home (Rudnytsky, 2000).

Eventually, mid-war, Eichholz took up a posting at the Family Welfare Association, a charitable organisation which provided practical assistance for needy people in distress (Mowat, 1961); and she inaugurated a series of citizens advice bureaux in London. In this capacity, she visited the homes of the distressed, whom she described in later years as "people who had serious problems—relatives being killed, losing their limbs and their children" (quoted in Rudnytsky, 2000, p. 1). Mrs Eichholz had a mandate to advise these families about the benefits to which they would be entitled under the War Damages Act 1943. But family members surprised her by wishing to speak, not about financial remuneration but, rather, about their private tragedies. Enid Eichholz approached her work at the Family Welfare Association with considerable trepidation, deeply conscious of "my lack of knowledge about human relations and how people wanted to talk" (quoted in Rudnytsky, 2000, p. 2). Nevertheless, in spite of her inexperience, she hoped that she might still be of use.

But how on earth could a lone woman, with only a bachelor's degree and with no clinical training of any kind, begin to create a paradigm shift which would lay the groundwork for a new mental health profession, namely couple psychotherapy?

Eichholz's plan to develop an intervention for troubled couples and families did not, however, unfold in a historical vacuum. Her quest to offer support emerged amid the dissatisfactions with Great Britain's wartime administration.

Although Winston Churchill had served as an inspiring Prime Minister throughout the Second World War, devoting his energies to the War Department and to the Defence Committee, after V-E Day, Britons began to tire of his warmongering and his passion for crushing foreign enemies, and sought, instead, a far less bellicose leader (Harrington and Young, 1978); and, to the surprise of many, Clement Attlee, Deputy Prime Minister with special responsibility for the Home Front, took control of the government with a majority of 146 seats (Beckett, 1997), thus ousting the incumbent Churchill. A former social worker in Stepney, in London's East End (Attlee, 1920), the new Prime Minister ushered in an overtly socialist government which prioritised welfare over warfare, and improvements at home rather than victories overseas (Attlee, 1954).

The new Prime Minister devoted himself with tremendous zeal to the creation of a Post-War Settlement, designed to improve the quality of daily life for Britons by counteracting the food shortages, high taxes, fuel shortages, economic ruin, and the termination of American Lend-Lease aid. In point of fact, in an effort to improve both living and working conditions, Attlee's government passed no fewer than 347 Acts, thus masterminding the transition from a wartime to a peacetime economy, through the introduction of a profound system of social welfare (Burridge, 1985).

The National Health Service, inaugurated in 1948, became the flagship of Attlee's government, providing free health care for all (Hodgkinson, 1967). During its first year of operation alone, some 8,500,000 Britons received dental treatment, and some 5,000,000 people obtained spectacles. In total, physicians wrote approximately 187,000,000 prescriptions, often for long-standing health problems previously neglected due to the prohibitive costs of private medicine (Pearce, 1996). Attlee's government guaranteed not only physical well-being but, also, through the passage of the National Insurance Act 1946, government pensions, payment of funeral costs, fees to widows and to the handicapped, as well as increased unemployment benefits. Attlee's democratic socialism allowed many to seek a range of assistance for domestic needs, thus foregrounding the family explicitly for the very first time (Marwick, 1982).

Yet, in spite of Attlee's heroic efforts, the government did not directly tackle the serious crisis within marriages during the post-war period.

Those who did require help generally turned to religion in the hope that God would deliver them from abusive husbands and unfaithful wives. Several forward-thinking clergymen did, however, collaborate with physicians steeped in psychological medicine in an effort to create a more enlightened form of intervention for troubled marital relationships. For instance, in 1938, Reverend Herbert Gray, a Presbyterian minister, and Dr Edward Fyfe Griffith, a physician, founded the Marriage Guidance Council, which offered sexual and contraceptive advice to married couples (Griffith, 1981). And in 1946, a group of clerics established the Catholic Marriage Advisory Council, which provided support for couples through prayer (Harris, 2015).

But Enid Eichholz recognised that a *different* type of space might be helpful: one which provided couples, quite simply, with permission to speak privately, in unrestricted fashion and in a secular setting, much as Sigmund Freud had done with adult patients more than half a century previously.

With the blessing of Mr Benjamin Astbury, the General Secretary of the Family Welfare Association, Mrs Eichholz organised a formal meeting on 22nd January, 1946, at 11.00 a.m., to mark the inauguration of the newly constituted Marriage Guidance Council and, also, to discuss the formation of a series of "Marriage Guidance Centres", in which those with troubled spousal relationships could be offered consultations. The Marriage Guidance Council recognised that the valiant workers at its many citizens advice bureaux would not be sufficiently competent to undertake marital support, and, consequently, decided to engage qualified social workers, albeit few in number in Great Britain at that time. Ordinarily, male professionals—whether physicians or clergymen—provided most of the psychological treatment during the 1930s and 1940s; indeed, at the Tavistock Clinic in London, female doctors could not work with male patients, only female ones (Rushforth, 1984). But Eichholz's new and enlightened Marriage Guidance Council conceded that, "A male interviewer should not be a necessity each session" (Marriage Guidance Council, 1946).

Thus, Eichholz and her colleagues forged a path through which female workers could begin to engage with distressed marital couples. Those female staff members, referred to as "secretaries", in spite of their social work qualifications, would hold meetings with family members, and would thus be charged with the task of "diagnosing the trouble" (Marriage Guidance Council, 1946, p. 2).

Buoyed by the possibilities ahead of them, Mrs Eichholz and the members of the Marriage Guidance Council launched an ambitious scheme to open several marriage guidance centres in London, in February, 1946, with units in some of the capital's most impoverished areas, namely, Bethnal Green, East Lewisham, North Islington, Shoreditch, St Pancras, Wandsworth and, also, more centrally, in Westminster (Marriage Guidance Council, 1946). Soon thereafter, the Marriage Guidance Council changed its name to the Marriage Guidance Committee, and then, later on in 1946, altered its name once more to the Marriage Guidance Centres Committee (Marriage Guidance Council, 1946).

Most of the brief histories of couple psychotherapy in Great Britain claim that a woman called Enid *Balint* founded the first therapeutic organisation for troubled marriages—the Family Discussion Bureau—in 1948 (Gray, 1970; Woodhouse, 1990); but the documentary evidence reveals quite compellingly that Enid *Eichholz* (not yet married to her second husband Dr Michael Balint) did so, and *not* in 1948 but, rather, in 1946. Thus, contemporary practitioners can now date our foundation two years earlier to a fledgling organisation known, not as the Family Discussion Bureau but, rather, as the Marriage Guidance Council, then as the Marriage Guidance Committee, and subsequently, as the Marriage Guidance Centres Committee.

Eichholz's newly launched centres certainly met a need within the local communities. By December, 1946, the unit in Lewisham had attracted some six new cases, that in Shoreditch three cases, and the one in Wandsworth four more (Marriage Guidance Centres Committee: Monday, December 9th, 1946, 1946).

Alas, we know very little about the precise nature of the interviews undertaken by these "secretaries", nor the theoretical lens—if any—through which these women facilitated marital consultations in 1946. Furthermore, it remains very unclear to what extent Mrs Eichholz herself actually undertook the day-to-day clinical work; in fact, we have no surviving documentary evidence that she worked with couples or families in a direct way at all at that point in time. But certainly, she supported her "secretaries" and she maintained strong relationships with the hierarchy of the Family Welfare Association to ensure that her marriage centres would grow and prosper.

Enid Eichholz eventually came to recognise that, in spite of her remarkable capacities as an administrator and, moreover, as the progenitor of path-breaking projects, she needed more help to provide a robust and systematic clinical foundation for the work undertaken by the secretaries. Having already admitted to her "lack of knowledge about human relations" (quoted in Rudnytsky, 2000, p. 2), Eichholz knew that she would need to collaborate with some other person or persons who possessed a far greater understanding of the intimacies of family life.

The Marriage of Social Welfare and Psychoanalysis

At some point, probably during 1946 or 1947, Enid Eichholz had the opportunity to meet Dr Archibald Thomson Macbeth Wilson, one of the psychiatrists at the Tavistock Clinic. The encounter between these two individuals sparked a remarkable revolution in the marital guidance movement.

Tommy Wilson had studied medicine at the University of Glasgow in Scotland, and then, after a period of teaching physiology in London, he became a Rockefeller Research Fellow at the Tavistock Clinic, ultimately joining its medical staff in 1939 (Dicks, 1970). During the Second World War, Colonel Wilson worked in both the Directorate of Army Psychiatry as a commanding psychiatrist (Ahrenfeldt, 1958; Dicks, 1970) and, also, on the staff of the Directorate of Biological Research. After the war, he began to train at the Institute of Psycho-Analysis (Wilson, 1949).

A neglected figure in the history of psychoanalysis, Dr Wilson stood out from his colleagues as someone interested in working on the widest possible canvas. Unlike other practising Freudian analysts of the period who devoted themselves exclusively to five-times-weekly treatment of individual patients, Tommy Wilson had already pioneered psychosomatic medicine in Great Britain, applying psychoanalytical ideas to the understanding of physical symptomatology (Davies and Wilson, 1937). Moreover, Dr Wilson (1946) studied the psychological consequences of servicemen returning home to Great Britain.

Mrs Eichholz could not have attached herself to a more energetic and creative physician, and she regarded her meeting with Tommy Wilson as rather "lucky" (quoted in Rudnytsky, 2000, p. 3). He introduced her more formally to the works of Sigmund Freud (Rudnytsky, 2000); and he invited her to meet with his clinical colleagues, offering her an *entrée* into the thriving post-war community at the Tavistock Clinic. Before long, Mrs Eichholz became friendly with most, if not all, of the senior Tavistock staff.

As a formal medical organisation destined to join the incipient British National Health Service in 1948, the Tavistock Clinic could not receive donations of money from charitable organisations, nor could it, at that point, commission large-scale research projects; thus, a group of forward-thinking psychological practitioners and social scientists within the clinic community created the Tavistock Institute of Human Relations (TIHR) as a "twin" which could work alongside the Tavistock Clinic to promote psychodynamic thinking on a wider, non-clinical, applied scale (Dicks, 1970). Tommy Wilson became the first chairman of the Management Committee of the TIHR, and, in this capacity, he had the power to support projects such as Mrs Eichholz's Marriage Guidance Centres.

Eichholz soon began to attend seminars at the Tavistock Clinic, then located in its new post-war home at 2, Beaumont Street, in Central London, very close to Harley Street—the headquarters of the nation's elite, private medical district. Founded in 1920 by the pioneering medical psychologist Dr Hugh Crichton Miller, the Tavistock Clinic for Functional Nervous Disorders (later known simply as the Tavistock Clinic) championed the so-called "New Psychology" (Dicks, 1970, p. 1)—a non-sectarian catch-all for the ideas of Freud, Jung, Adler, and others (Crichton Miller, 1921, 1922). Unlike the British Psycho-Analytical Society, which promulgated only Freudian theories, the Tavistock Clinic enjoyed a more eclectic and open-spirited approach to the treatment of the neuroses, and actively sought to provide psychotherapy for those who could not afford private fees (Dicks, 1970), describing itself as a veritable "Harley Street for the anxious poor" (Anonymous, 1934, quoted in Kahr, 2000b, p. 399). Although Ernest Jones sternly forbade any members of the British Psycho-Analytical Society from teaching at the Tavistock Clinic (Kahr, 1984), the "Tavi", as it came to be known, encouraged the widest possible collaboration and facilitated its staff to develop outward-looking links.

Hugh Crichton Miller's successor, Dr John Rawlings Rees, fostered an even greater spirit of open-mindedness. Remembered as a "genial" (Dicks, 1970, p. 58) pipe smoker with an "American personality" (Dicks, 1970, p. 59), J. R. Rees enjoyed bringing newcomers into the larger Tavistock Clinic family. Indeed, in 1933, he wrote that, "We give the warmest welcome to every sound new venture in this field of psychiatry" (quoted in Dicks, 1970, p. 60).

During the Second World War, Brigadier Rees became the chief psychiatrist for the British army; consequently, he co-opted many of his clinical staff members and appointed them to key posts (Ahrenfeldt, 1958). As the "Tavi" psychiatrists returned to civilian life in 1945 and to their staff consultancies on Beaumont Street, many of them had already experimented with group psychotherapy and therapeutic communities (Bion, 1948; Gray, 1970)—new discoveries which developed from the sheer wartime necessity of processing large numbers of traumatised soldier-patients; consequently, the Tavi staff greeted Mrs Eichholz's efforts to work with marital couples and with families in a very appreciative manner. Indeed, the post-war Tavistock Clinic, headed initially by Dr Wilfred Bion as Chair of the Interim Medical Committee, had already planned, quite explicitly, to grapple with "problems of engagement and marriage" (Dicks, 1970, p. 143), as well as with the "anxieties of the newly married in relation to home-making" (Dicks, 1970, p. 143).

In 1948, Mrs Eichholz applied to train as a psychoanalyst in her own right at the Institute of Psycho-Analysis, and she became accepted to do so. She chose as her training analyst the venerable Quaker physician, Dr John Rickman, a pioneer of psychoanalysis and medical psychology and, also, a sometime analysand of Professor Sigmund Freud. Renowned for his openness and for his creative range of interests (Rickman, 1926a, 1926b, 1947; King, 2003a), not least for his work at the War Office Selection Board, applying psychological thinking to the screening of military personnel (Rickman, 1943; cf. King, 2003b), this much-admired man, John Rickman, possessed a great capacity to encourage his students in the most generous of manners.

Miss Pearl King (2001b), one of Rickman's analysands during the late 1940s, told me that Rickman used to urge his patients to speak in the fullest voice possible, not only figuratively but, also, literally. When, for instance, Miss King had begun to experience anxiety prior to delivering her very first paper, Rickman instructed her to visualise a physical barricade across the lecture room and insisted that she must work hard to project her voice over that barricade so that people at the back could hear her! Thus, one imagines that he helped his patients to become maximally vocal and impactful in their efforts and that Eichholz would have benefited hugely from having such a man as her training analyst.

Forging "Marital" Links: Enid Eichholz as Collaborator

Thus far, the Family Welfare Association's citizens advice bureaux had become transformed, first, into the Marriage Guidance Council, then into the Marriage Guidance Committee and, ultimately, into the Marriage Guidance Centres Committee. Circa 1948, Enid Eichholz's organisation changed its name once again, adopting the title of Marriage Welfare Committee. Eichholz herself served as the Secretary, and she co-opted Dr Tommy Wilson to serve alongside her, as well as a young Scottish woman, Miss Isabel Menzies, a social scientist who also worked at TIHR (Lyth, Scott, and Young, 1988). Brilliantly, Eichholz had surrounded herself with a formidable group of outward-looking and forward-thinking men and women who had devoted themselves to bringing health—in all its manifestations—out of the clinic and into the community.

By 26th February, 1948, the Family Welfare Association agreed that all new branches would be known hereafter as "Marriage Welfare Centres" (Extract from Minutes of A.C.: 26th. Feb. 1948, 1948). Only later that year did Eichholz begin to refer to her new experiment by yet another new name—its sixth designation—namely, the Family Discussion Bureaux (with "Bureaux" spelled in the plural, rather than in the singular).

Eichholz also co-opted the fifty-year-old Mrs Lily Pincus, a Jewish refugee, to serve as her day-to-day right-hand woman, administering to the minutiae of Eichholz's growing series of projects (Marriage Welfare Centres Committee: Monday, May 31st. 1948 at 10.30 a.m., 1948). Born in 1898 as Lily Lazarus, in the Austro-Hungarian city of Karlsbad, she distinguished herself as an administrative secretary in Potsdam, in Germany, and then, in 1939, fled with her husband, Herr Fritz Pincus, to London. Mrs Pincus would ultimately prove to be Mrs Eichholz's greatest institutional partner.

By mid-1948, Enid Eichholz (1948c) assumed the title of "Chairman" of the "Marriage Welfare Committee" (Eichholz, 1948c), and she began to describe herself and her female colleagues not as "secretaries" but, rather, as "social workers" (Eichholz, 1948c). Even though not all of the clinicians had graduated from a recognised social work training, the adoption of such a title proved to be very common at that time, in view of the dearth of recognised social work practitioners. By the summer of 1948, the "Marriage Welfare Committee" became rebranded as the "Marriage Welfare Sub-Committee"; and, on the morning of 14th June, 1948, Enid Eichholz, aided by Dr Tommy Wilson, convened a group of esteemed colleagues for yet another landmark meeting with the express purpose of discussing "the specialist services which can be arranged in connection with Marriage Welfare work to be undertaken by the Association" (General Secretary, 1948).

The invitees included Dr Tommy Wilson and Miss Isabel Menzies, both from the Tavistock Institute of Human Relations; Dr Thomas Forrest Main, the Medical Director of the Cassel Hospital for Functional Nervous Disorders; and, also, Dr John Bowlby (General Secretary, 1948).

One of Great Britain's most influential child psychiatrists, and a passionate enthusiast for healing troubled families (Bowlby, 1949a), Dr John Bowlby had, of late, become a keen supporter of Enid Eichholz's efforts to work with turbulent marriages. As Director of the Children's Department of the Tavistock Clinic since 1946, he had already begun to offer consultations to parents in the hope of alleviating the psychopathology of their children; consequently, he warmly supported the plan, which he described as one of "considerable importance" (Marriage Welfare Committee: Meeting Held at the Tavistock Institute of Human Relations on Monday June 14th. 1948 at 10 o'clock, 1948). In fact, Bowlby became so smitten by the project that he lobbied strongly for the establishment of a marriage welfare centre in Hendon, in North-West London, where he consulted on two afternoons per week.

Extraordinarily, within the space of only two years, Enid Eichholz had cultivated important links with some of the nation's leading mental health professionals and with at least three seminal psychological institutions: the Tavistock Clinic, the Tavistock Institute of Human Relations, and also the Cassel Hospital for Functional Nervous Disorders (Memorandum on Visit to the Cassel Hospital on Monday, 28th June 1948, by Mr. Astbury, Miss Menzies and Mrs Eichholz, 1948). With such support behind her, the Family Welfare Association agreed to fund the establishment of a number of better developed marital centres to replace the more makeshift ones first established in Bethnal Green, St Pancras, Wandsworth, and other communities, back in 1946. And on 20th September, 1948, a certain Mrs Reynolds—whose forename eludes us—commenced her employment at the first properly funded and properly staffed marriage welfare centre at 21, Kempson Road, in Walham Green, in Fulham, in South-West London, which opened to the public in early October, 1948 (Eichholz, 1948d).

With the launch of the marriage welfare centre at Kempson Road, Great Britain now boasted a formal institution—albeit a small one— which could provide fledgling psychological treatment for couples in distress. While the Catholic Marriage Advisory Council and the Marriage Guidance Council offered spiritual advice, medical information, and lessons in contraception, Enid Eichholz had created a space in which couples could talk about their private emotional lives for the very first time and could begin to have an experience of being listened to by specialist social workers or caseworkers. And by late 1948, the Family Welfare Association had established Marriage Welfare Centres in North Islington, South Islington, Kensington, Paddington, and St Pancras (Eichholz, 1948e).

By 1949, these individual centres became known as family discussion bureaux (FDB), and Eichholz (1949a) gradually began to describe her centres as the "F.D.B. of the FWA"[1]—the Family Discussion Bureau of the Family Welfare Association. This pilot experiment proved highly successful, and Eichholz discovered that the application of a psychoanalytical approach to the study of marital distress resulted in the betterment of the couple relationship and, also, in an improvement in the health of the children of couples who presented for treatment (Anonymous, n.d.).

Although the surviving archival materials from the years 1946 to 1949 offer a great deal of pertinent information about the development of the Family Discussion Bureau as an institution, they fail to offer much insight into the precise nature of clinical practice at that time. We do know, however, that Eichholz and her team worked with some very challenging marital patients. For instance, when Eichholz took some of the FDB cases to Dr Millicent Dewar's firm at the Cassel Hospital for Functional Nervous Disorders for discussion and consultation, Eichholz reported that Dr Dewar's team could make very clear, if not dismissive, pronouncements. For instance, in reference to the case of a certain married woman, Eichholz (1950a) wrote, "they thought that she had too slight a therapeutic drive and did not like this case"; and with reference to a certain male patient, Eichholz (1950a) recorded, "they did not like this, thought the case was too bad from my report of it and would not consider for triage".

Nevertheless, cheered no doubt by the establishment of the various branches of the Family Discussion Bureau and by her increasing sophistication in psychoanalysis, Eichholz called upon many of the senior staff at the Tavistock Clinic for further assistance. In 1948, she drafted a letter to the Medical Officer of Health of Middlesex County Council (Eichholz, 1948a), asking for support of her "piece of experimental social work", and of her plan to provide "intensive case work on a small number of cases" (Eichholz, 1948a), offered by "highly trained social workers" (Eichholz, 1948a). She explained that she and the staff at her pilot centres endeavoured to research "some of the reasons leading to marriage break-down, and following from that they will hope to develop more effective methods of prevention and treatment" (Eichholz, 1948a). In true pioneering fashion, Mrs Eichholz (1948a) explained to the Medical Officer of Health that she wished to engage in "preventive work", in the hope of treating cases "at an early stage before break-down occurs" (Eichholz, 1948a). In this respect, Eichholz positioned herself, perhaps unwittingly, as a champion of preventative mental health services, a concept which would not become more standard until approximately half a century later.

Such a forward-thinking approach to mental health work appealed greatly to John Bowlby, who had already begun to devote himself wholeheartedly to the documentation of the adverse effects of early deprivations and separations and to the strengthening of family ties (Bowlby, 1940b; cf. Kahr, 2015b). In an effort to be of assistance, Dr Bowlby kindly offered to comment upon Mrs Eichholz's (1948b) draft document to the Medical Officer of Health. In 1949, Eichholz (1949i) expressed a strong desire to collaborate with Bowlby directly at the Tavistock Clinic, but, alas, due to staff shortages in his department, Bowlby (1949b), to his regret, could do no more than support her "important work" when he could. But, happily, he did arrange most helpfully for Eichholz to undertake supervision with Miss Noël Hunnybun, one of his cherished social workers.

Eichholz thus found herself in supervision with a woman of exceptional skill and experience in mental health matters. Some fourteen years older than Mrs Eichholz, the warm-hearted Noël Hunnybun—a pioneer of psychiatric social work—provided a great deal of nurture. On 11th August, 1949, Hunnybun (1949) wrote to her new supervisee, "I shall look forward to our work together and hope that you will find it helpful. I must admit to some qualms at the prospect of supervising so experienced a worker as yourself, but anyway it will be fun I think, and very interesting, and I expect to learn from the experience." After having studied and collaborated with Hunnybun for some time, Eichholz (1950c) wrote, "I feel that the charges you make shew in no way the amount of work I get from contact with you and supervision of my cases."

After a year of formal supervision, the two women stopped referring to one another as "Miss Hunnybun" and "Mrs Eichholz", and began to speak more informally as Noël and Enid. One senses that Hunnybun's benign supervision of Eichholz proved most deeply valuable at a time when Eichholz, as "mother" to the social workers and caseworkers at the growing marriage welfare centres, had to give so much.

Sensibly, Eichholz sought further training and supervision not only for herself but, also, for her Family Discussion Bureaux staff. As a young trainee psychoanalyst, she had become a student once again and, consequently, she encouraged her new team members to do likewise. In 1951, Noël Hunnybun organised a course—very possibly the first full-time, year-long psychoanalytical postgraduate training for psychiatric social workers and caseworkers—based in the Child Guidance Department of the Tavistock Clinic. With lectures by Dr John Bowlby and by Dr Elliott Jaques, this course proved irresistible (Syllabus for the Advanced Course for Post Graduate Case Workers, 1951); and Mrs Eichholz sent two of her relatively new staffers to participate in this landmark training.

Miss Hunnybun (1951) honoured Mrs Eichholz and the team at the Family Discussion Bureau by suggesting that not only might FDB students train at the "Tavi", but that perhaps Tavi students might also begin to participate in FDB seminars as well—no doubt a profound validation of the work that Enid Eichholz had begun to undertake. As Hunnybun (1951) wrote, "May I say how pleased we are to extend this invitation to your students and some time I should like to discuss with you the suggested reciprocation, whereby our case work students in the Advanced Course might be able to join in a discussion on advanced case work with your group."

With a number of active branches of the Family Discussion Bureaux, and with a small but sturdy staff team in place, as well as supervision from Noël Hunnybun, and support from such figures as Tommy Wilson and John Bowlby, and, also, fortified by her own training at the Institute of Psycho-Analysis, Enid Eichholz had, by late 1949, truly created something from nothing.

A Home in Chandos Street: Towards Solid Foundations

Enid Eichholz's developmental work and her forging of rich professional alliances continued in an unrelenting fashion throughout 1949 and 1950. But Eichholz also began to undertake research and to apply for external funding. On 14th March, 1949, Eichholz (1949a) sketched out her intentions to commission a "Research Project into the Social Structure and Social Needs of Communities", in which she explained, "The help needed by individuals in families from social workers is very undefined. That there are needs for help in family + community living there seems little doubt. What the needs are, and how, and by whom they can be met can only be discovered by research." Consequently, she proposed a study of the landscape of individual and family requirements, which would be undertaken by psychologists, social caseworkers, and "socioanthropologists" (Eichholz, 1949a), and that, together, such a team could investigate the healthy families versus the unhealthy families, in an effort to understand their "storm centres" (Eichholz, 1949a). Ideally, this research project would come to discover "how to prevent + how to cure family disturbance, and how to plan communities which are helpful to individual + family growth + maturation" (Eichholz, 1949a).

By 1950, Enid Eichholz no longer positioned herself as the untrained female social worker who needed to align herself with potent male physicians for support. Colleagues came to recognise her as an independent expert in her own right and respected her hugely for what she had begun to achieve. For instance, in 1950, Tommy Wilson asked Eichholz to provide assistance to the distinguished psychiatrist Dr Alfred Torrie who hoped to establish a group for expectant mothers. In fact, she could state quite proudly that she and her team had *already* created such a group for post-natal mothers at the Fulham Maternity Hospital where "we hear quite a lot about their feelings before the birth of the baby and during their time in hospital" (Eichholz, 1950b).

At one point, during the late 1940s, while attending seminars at the Tavistock Clinic, Enid Eichholz met a most unusual man from Hungary.

Dr Michael Balint, a physician and psychoanalyst, worked in the Adult Department at Beaumont Street. Analysed not by one but, in fact, by two, of Freud's closest disciples—Dr Sándor Ferenczi in Budapest, and Dr Hanns Sachs in Berlin—Michael Balint developed a reputation as a man of deep intelligence and charisma; and Enid wasted no time in recruiting him to offer seminars to her staff team. On 25th March, 1949, she expressed her gratitude to Dr Balint, noting, "I am sure you know without my telling you how helpful we are finding the seminars and how much we appreciate your being able to spare us so much of your time and interest" (Eichholz, 1949f). Before long, Enid had begun to consult with Balint about the growth of the organisation and about how to handle her staff members (Eichholz, 1949b, 1949g); and by the summer of that year, she confessed, "I felt encouraged by our talk and look forward to finding out what we can do between us" (Eichholz, 1949h).

This remarkable theoretician and practitioner, Michael Balint, maintained a particular interest in the vicissitudes of adult sexuality, as opposed to infantile sexuality, and had recently published a seminal paper, "On Genital Love" (Balint, 1948), in which he wrote about the importance of treating one's lover with tenderness and respect, and without any greediness, denigration, or humiliation. In March, 1952, Enid arranged for Balint to deliver a seminar on adult sexuality (Eichholz, 1952b).

In spite of having separated from her husband Robert Eichholz, Enid and her estranged spouse had not yet divorced. Although still technically a married woman, Enid began to experience a frisson towards Dr Balint, and he seems to have shared these sentiments. Interestingly, when Enid struggled to obtain sufficient funds to pay for Michael Balint's seminars, he graciously told her that she must not worry about such matters (Eichholz, 1949c). The affection between Mrs Eichholz and Dr Balint blossomed, and gradually the two began to enjoy an extramarital affair. Her growing relationship with Dr Balint, both professionally and personally, would open up enormous collaborative vistas for Mrs Eichholz in years to come.

By 1951, Enid Eichholz had, in only half a decade, assembled an impressive staff team of social workers and caseworkers, and had recruited senior psychiatrists, social workers, and psychoanalysts to offer supervision and training, and, moreover, had enlisted the services of researchers in anthropology and social psychology. She had forged collaborative links with the Tavistock Clinic, the Tavistock Institute of Human Relations, the Cassel Hospital for Functional Nervous Diseases (Eichholz, 1949d, 1949e; Weddell, 1949), and other organisations. She had elicited funding from the Home Office and from the Nuffield Foundation (Eichholz, 1950d). And she had helped to inaugurate a stream of publications (Menzies, 1949; Wilson, 1949; Wilson, Menzies, and Eichholz, 1949). Above all, she had incorporated psychoanalytical ideas into traditional social welfare casework for troubled marriages, families, and even children, and, moreover, had begun to transform the marriage guidance profession, which had, hitherto, emphasised sex education and contraceptive advice, into a new profession of marital psychoanalysis.

By late 1951, Eichholz and her staff team could no longer squeeze into the offices of the Family Welfare Association on Vauxhall Bridge Road, near London's Victoria Station; and so, Eichholz arranged to lease premises in the heart of Central London, at 4, Chandos Street, quite close to Harley Street. In doing so, she endeavoured to position the work as a clinical discipline, on a par with psychiatry and medicine more generally.

In October, 1951, the new organisation opened its doors and began conducting approximately one hundred clinical interviews per month. Indeed, between 1st April, 1951 and 1st March, 1952, the Family Discussion Bureaux staff had facilitated as many as 1,175 interviews, with each case receiving on average five consultations (Eichholz, 1952a). The clientele consisted predominantly of married couples, but the FDB also treated premarital couples, adolescents, as well as parents concerned about their children.

By late 1952, Enid had become so very deeply ensconced in her psychoanalytical training and, also, in her extramarital relationship, that she decided to resign as head of FDB, and she surrendered her post to her stalwart deputy Lily Pincus. And on 2nd January, 1953, Enid and Michael married (Hopkins, 2004), and the staff of FDB sent them a bowl (Balint and Balint, 1953).

From 1953 onwards, Lily Pincus undertook yeoman work to develop the sturdy and impressive foundations established by her predecessor. Dr John Sutherland (1955), the Tavi's new Medical Director, praised the Family Discussion Bureau for treating clients like people: "I certainly have a strong impression that for the F.D.B. all of their clients are very much people + not bits of psychopathology". Indeed, he lamented that, "I personally have a strong feeling that what has gone out of psychoanalysis is 'love'. We really produce high-powered interpreting machines whereas the F.D.B. group have retained enough of their direct spontaneous feelings with the clients despite the attempt to understand the dynamics" (Sutherland, 1955). Enid Balint could not have asked for greater recognition.

Though no longer the reigning leader of the Family Discussion Bureau, Enid Balint remained a vibrant presence in the British mental health community. She not only collaborated extensively with her new husband on the application of psychodynamic ideas in the field of general medical practice (e.g., Balint and Balint, 1961; Balint, Balint, Gosling, and Hildebrand, 1966; cf. Balint, 1973), but she also became a much coveted training analyst at the Institute of Psycho-Analysis, as well as a teacher, lecturer, and administrator (Balint, 1993). She became so much in demand that, even in her seventies, she worked between sixty and seventy hours per week (Balint, 1974).

No doubt Enid Balint enjoyed watching the constant growth of the organisation, which included the launch of a book-length publication, in 1955, on the psychodynamic approach to marital treatment (Bannister, Lyons, Pincus, Robb, Shooter, and Stephens, 1955), as well as, in 1956, the transfer of the FDB to the Tavistock Institute of Human Relations, and a change of name—yet again—to become the Institute of Marital Studies. In 1959, the organisation relocated from Chandos Street to the Tavistock Clinic headquarters on Beaumont Street, and then, ultimately, in 1967, to the Tavi's new home in Belsize Park, becoming very much a central core of British psychoanalytical life. After *five* further name changes, from the Institute of Marital Studies, to the Tavistock Institute of Marital Studies, to the Tavistock Marital Studies Institute, to the Tavistock Centre for Couple Relationships, to Tavistock Relationships, the organisation and the profession it represents has developed robustly, providing relief for untold thousands upon thousands of couples and families for more than three quarters of a century.

A Tale of Two Roof Tops

Those of us who have followed in the footsteps of Enid Eichholz Balint have a great deal to learn from this bold and visionary woman. In spite of a dearth of clinical qualifications, she could, nevertheless, from the mid-1940s until the early 1950s, through sheer force, passion, and perseverance, make an outstanding contribution to the betterment of private life in Great Britain. And she created couple therapy through her brilliance at forging couple alliances with carefully selected colleagues—whether Wilson or Bowlby or Hunnybun or Balint or Sutherland or Pincus. Each of these professional "marriages" contributed hugely to the foundations of couple psychoanalytical work today.

Over the last forty years, I have conducted numerous interviews with senior mental health professionals on several continents, collecting reminiscences about our foremothers and forefathers in the psychotherapeutic field. Over the course of these interviews, I have heard many deeply unflattering, indeed ugly, stories about the great pioneers of our field. But it may be significant that of the many people who graciously shared with me their memories of Enid Balint, not a single person had anything nasty to say about her whatsoever. In fact, her former patients and colleagues always described her as warm, as maternal, as generous, and as gracious. One of my interviewees even characterised her to me, in no uncertain terms, as "the only compassionate person" (Welldon, 2015) in the entire Institute of Psycho-Analysis! No doubt her basic mental health allowed her to form partnerships easily and pleasurably. A mad woman, it seems to me, could not have founded the field of marital mental health.

But to idealise Enid Eichholz Balint as kind and sweet would be rather too simplistic. She could, by her own admission, be nasty and aggressive (Rudnytsky, 2000), and she possessed cunning, wiliness, and even sexual charm. Indeed, Dr Estela Welldon (2015) explained that virtually every man who met Enid Balint soon became rather "smitten". Undoubtedly this sexual allure may have facilitated the development of her professional partnerships with some of the Tavistock Clinic's most sturdy men and even women.

While leading psychiatrists and psychoanalysts such as Dr Wilfred Bion and Dr Siegmund Foulkes treated British soldiers during the Second World War, Enid decided that she would look after the wives, whose emotional needs had remained neglected. When the men returned home, she defied all gender restrictions and cared not only for the women and the husbands but, also, for the families. From the ravages of World War II, Enid created something moving and touching amid such unparalleled destruction.

It would be tempting to regard couple psychoanalysis as a mere extension of individual psychoanalysis, but this would be inaccurate. Sigmund Freud, though savvy about the cruel psychodynamics of intimate relationships and about the infantile origins of sexual conflicts, did not distinguish himself as a clinical practitioner for marital couples. Indeed, in 1891, Pauline Theiler Silberstein, the nineteen-year-old spouse of Freud's long-standing friend Eduard Silberstein, came to Vienna for a consultation with Freud; sadly, after having spoken with the future creator of psychoanalysis, she threw herself from an upper storey of his home at 8 Maria-Theresienstrasse and plunged to her death (Vieyra, 1989).

Enid Eichholz Balint did rather better at rooftop consultations. As a schoolgirl at the Cheltenham Ladies' College in Gloucestershire, the young Enid Flora Albu had developed a reputation for being sensitive and sensible. When, on a cold night, one of Enid's fellow schoolmates sought refuge on the roof of one of the buildings and none of the teachers could persuade this depressed and possibly suicidal girl to come back indoors, they sent Enid out to sit with her. Apparently, Enid perched herself neither too close to the girl nor too far away, and waited patiently until, in due course, the troubled student decided to return inside, much to everyone's relief (Balint, n.d.).

Perhaps irrespective of one's training and influences, one also needs a very particular internal core and a zest for healing. Certainly, Enid Flora Albu Eichholz Balint (eventually known as Enid Balint-Edmonds) possessed just such capacities.

Enid Balint created partnerships. She nurtured partnerships. And she healed partnerships. Her collaborative model of innovation and of leadership remains an inspiration to us all.

PART V

THE BAD BOYS
OF BRITISH PSYCHOANALYSIS

CHAPTER NINE

Rajah on the Couch: The Magnificence and Misery of Masud Khan

The Film Star of Psychoanalysis

In 2020, the global television platform Netflix aired a special eight-part series entitled *Freud*—a fanciful dramatisation of the life of the father of psychoanalysis. Although I watched these episodes with an open mind, and although I appreciated the high quality of the acting and of the production values, I found the series to be deeply inaccurate from a historical perspective and not at all compelling.

Although one day a skilful cinematographer might well create a more richly engaging film about the life and work of Professor Sigmund Freud, it might be that I could save a budding Cecil B. DeMille or an up-and-coming Steven Spielberg a great deal of time by recommending that he or she should begin to research a far more engaging, far more theatrical, far more captivating, and far more shocking story than the tale of Freud. In fact, of all the many characters who have inhabited the world of psychoanalysis over the last one hundred years or more, none would inspire a greater film or television series or play or opera or, indeed, ballet, than the Indian-born Masud Khan, arguably the most engaging, wise, compelling, seductive, and, also, *dangerous* figure in the entire profession.

Unlike the majority of Freudian psychoanalysts in Great Britain, who beavered away quietly in Hampstead, in North-West London, Khan, by contrast, led rather a more glamorous lifestyle, ensconced in a luxurious home, located in Knightsbridge, in cosmopolitan South-West London, only a stone's throw away from Harrod's department store. His flat boasted an extensive collection of expensive Impressionist and Post-Impressionist paintings (Paterson, 1991), as well as works of art by Georges Braque and Alberto Giacometti (Khan, 1988a). Indeed, Masud Khan and his second wife, Svetlana Beriozova, a prima ballerina at the Royal Ballet, lived next door to the famous Redgrave acting family (e.g., Sir Michael Redgrave, as well as his daughter Vanessa Redgrave), and he socialised with such celebrities as the actress and singer Julie Andrews, the film director Mike Nichols, and the dancer Rudolf Nureyev (Hopkins, 2006).

As a young student of psychology, I stumbled upon one of Khan's essays while browsing in my university library, namely, his excellent clinical paper on "Silence as Communication", which I came to regard as a very original, very sensitive examination of how patients communicate not only by what they verbalise but, also, by what they do not (cf. Kahr, 2022a). Not long thereafter, I began to read several of Khan's impressively written clinical books. I breezed through his first published compendia, *The Privacy of the Self* (Khan, 1974), and I found the essays rather scholarly, straightforward and, also, most intelligent, even a little drab at times. I then dipped into his second book, *Alienation in Perversions* (Khan, 1979a), which I regarded as solid and sturdy. And likewise, his third title, *Hidden Selves: Between Theory and Practice in Psychoanalysis* (Khan, 1983), impacted upon me in a similar way.

But, on the whole, as a baby undergraduate with no personal connections to the British psychoanalytical community, I knew absolutely nothing about Masud Khan as an individual, and I had heard no gossip about him at all. From my naive and inexperienced perspective, I regarded him simply as a London-based Freudian practitioner who wrote books and papers which seemed quite sensible.

However, my relationship to Masud Khan changed completely when, on 9th June, 1985, I delivered a lecture in London—one of my very first public talks—to a small organisation. After I presented my paper, I sat down for a most pleasant lunch with some of the audience members, including Mrs Judy Cooper, a very experienced psychotherapist who had trained at the British Association of Psychotherapists. During our meal, Mrs Cooper became aware of my growing interest in the history of depth psychology, and, in trusting fashion, generously revealed that, years previously, she had undergone a rather successful analysis with Masud Khan from 1967 until 1973 (Cooper, 1991a, 1993). Throughout our conversation, she spoke about her former psychoanalyst with great affection and gratitude.

Although I had already begun to interview many elderly psychoanalysts since 1982, very few had made much mention of Masud Khan. True, during my afternoon tea with Mrs Marion Milner on 16th February, 1985, she did reveal that she and Khan used to attend painting classes together, and that, in later years, he struggled with alcoholism and, more recently, that he had become very ill with cancer of the lung (Kahr, 1985c). But Judy Cooper spoke to me about Masud Khan in a much more fulsome way than Marion Milner had done, and I became deeply intrigued by this most unusual man.

As my friendship with Judy Cooper grew across the 1980s, I came to learn a great deal about her admiration for Khan as he had proved himself to be a loyal and excellent psychoanalyst who helped her to flourish in many ways. But, during our conversations, she also revealed that Khan would, at times, practise in a most unusual manner, and would sometimes ask her to perform errands for him. I remember learning that, on one occasion, Khan requested that his young patient should fetch some theatre tickets for him from the box office, although, in fact, she never obliged (Cooper, 2020). I must confess that I found this vignette rather perplexing, even a bit shocking. Why, I wondered, would a psychoanalyst send a patient on an errand?

By the late 1980s, I began to develop a profound interest in the work of the famous British psychoanalyst Dr Donald Winnicott, and, in 1991, I received an invitation to write a book about his life and contributions. I embarked upon this project with much gusto and, over the next few years, I began to interview anyone and everyone, recording their memories of this great hero of British Freudianism. As Masud Khan had enjoyed a close relationship with Winnicott, first as a teacher and supervisor, and later, as his very own personal psychoanalyst, my interest in this Indian-born man became more and more pronounced.

Judy Cooper tried valiantly, on *many* occasions, to arrange a meeting on my behalf with Khan, but, alas, owing to his debilitating cancer, we could not manage to speak directly, and, sadly, on 7th June, 1989, he died at the age of sixty-four years (Cooper, 1993; Hopkins, 2006).

Shortly before his death, Khan (1988a) published his final book, a collection of case studies entitled *When Spring Comes: Awakenings in Clinical Psychoanalysis*. Shockingly, this volume, although written by an experienced author, nevertheless contained several grotesquely anti-Semitic comments about one of Khan's Jewish patients. Many of us found these remarks deeply horrifying and perplexing. How could such a brilliant, experienced psychoanalyst, who had trained with some of the greatest members of the profession, including Donald Winnicott, publish an overtly anti-Semitic case history? I suspect that many people simply assumed that Khan had already become somewhat mentally unwell as a result of his invasive cancer treatment, and therefore, in consequence, many ignored this volume as the misguided rantings of a man on the verge of death.

As I persevered with my research about the life of Donald Winnicott, the name of Masud Khan emerged in quite a number of my interviews. In total, I spoke with approximately sixty-three individuals who knew Khan personally, and I also discovered much unpublished correspondence between Khan and Winnicott in the various archives on both sides of the Atlantic Ocean.

Over time, my knowledge of Masud Khan increased. Mrs Judy Cooper kindly permitted me to read through Khan's private diaries as he had bequeathed copies to her. Miss Pearl King, the founder of the Archives of the British Psycho-Analytical Society, graciously granted me permission to read through Khan's unpublished letters. Also, at this time, Mrs Cooper (1993) published her own book on Khan—the very first biography of this unusual figure—and this excellent text shed even more light upon both the genius and the shadows of Khan as a man and as a clinician.

As the next decade unfolded, Khan became a subject of increasing controversy as numerous stories began to emerge not only about his workaholism and his brilliance but, also, about his alcoholism and his deeply unethical behaviour. Khan would sometimes instruct his patients to perform chores for him, and would humiliate patients with anti-Semitic comments, but, even more strikingly, he transgressed other boundaries as well, and, unsurprisingly, rumours percolated throughout the London psychoanalytical community about Khan's many sexual affairs with some of his female patients.

Needless to say, many of Khan's contemporaries had known of his transgressive behaviour for years. As early as 14th January, 1977, the Council of the British Psycho-Analytical Society met to discuss removing Khan from its membership roster, but, owing to his newly diagnosed cancer, they took pity on him and allowed him to remain as a practising psychoanalyst (Hopkins, 2006). But, in the summer of 1988, after the publication of *When Spring Comes: Awakenings in Clinical Psychoanalysis* (Khan, 1988a)—the book which contained those overtly anti-Semitic remarks—the British Psycho-Analytical Society finally deleted him from its membership roster (King, 2005a; Hopkins, 2006).

With Khan ejected from his professional organisation in disgrace, and, then deceased, not long thereafter, from alcoholism and cancer, he became an increasingly marginalised figure. But with the completion of Cooper's biography in 1993, and with the publication of reminiscences from another one of Khan's patients in 2001 (Godley, 2001a, 2001b, cf. Godley, 2004), followed by two extended biographies in 2005 (Willoughby, 2005) and 2006 (Hopkins, 2006), the controversy surrounding Khan became increasingly pronounced and remains so to this day.

More and more shocking stories about Khan began to emerge. For instance, one of the biographers revealed that, on 13th June, 1962, at 3.00 p.m., the police arrested Khan at his London home, transported him to Chelsea Police Station, and fingerprinted him for having assaulted his houseboy, Antonio (Khan, 1962b; cf. Willoughby, 2005). We also learned that, on 21st August, 1976, Dr Hanna Segal, the noted psychoanalyst who, at that time chaired the Education Committee of the Institute of Psycho-Analysis in London, met with Khan to discuss the allegations of sexual impropriety with the wife of one of the trainee psychoanalysts (cf. Willoughby, 2005). Moreover, we came to discover that, on 22nd June, 1979, in the early hours of the morning, Khan (1979b) attempted to commit suicide, having tried to cut his throat with several blunt knives (cf. Kahr, 1996d; Hopkins, 2006).

Gradually, everyone began to develop a viewpoint about Khan, exposing the criminal side of this otherwise impressive and brilliant psychoanalytical practitioner and author (e.g., Sandler, 2004). I, too, published a small contribution to the literature by having written a paper about Khan's own analysis with Winnicott (Kahr, 2002a, 2003). I endeavoured to explore what impact it might have had on Khan's deterioration that all three of his British psychoanalysts—Miss Ella Freeman Sharpe, Dr John Rickman, and Dr Donald Winnicott—died in the middle of his treatment. Indeed, I attempted to explore the role of traumatic bereavement upon Khan's increasingly forensic enactments.

Thus far, I have revealed very few of the Masud Khan anecdotes to which I have become privy over the years. But, now, several decades later, the vast majority of those whom I had interviewed have since passed away, and thus I have decided that it might be of some interest to fellow mental health professionals and to fellow psychoanalytical historians to share some of this overtly gossipy material, in the hope of creating a fuller picture. Having now interviewed one of Khan's wives (Kahr, 2009d), as well as the husband of one of the women with whom Khan engaged in illicit sex (and whose name I shall not disclose),[1] I now have access to a great deal of material which may help to inform future biographical scholarship and, above all, may assist those of us who have devoted our lives to ethical clinical practice with patients to understand more fully how a practitioner of Khan's distinction could have engaged in such violent behaviour for so many years, and whether a man of this character should ever have received permission to train as a psychoanalyst in the first place.

A Plethora of Unpublished Anecdotes

On 21st July, 1924, Mohammed Masud Raza Khan, son of an elderly, wealthy feudal landowner, Fazal Dad Khan,[2] and his young wife Khursheed Begum Khan, entered the world on the family estate in Jhelum, in the Punjab, in India (Cooper, 1993; Willoughby, 2005; Hopkins, 2006). Masud Khan grew up in a complex family constellation with a father nearly sixty years older than his mother (Cooper, 1991a, 1993). Moreover, Khursheed Khan had once served as a courtesan in her teenage years (Cooper, 1993) and had already delivered a child out of wedlock (Cooper, 1991a, 1993).

Sadly, in 1942, Masud Khan's beloved sister, Mahmooda Khan, died at the age of sixteen years, due to an overdose of medication—mistakenly prescribed—intended as treatment for her tuberculosis. Not long thereafter, in 1943, Fazal Dad Khan—the father—died from grief (Cooper, 1991a, 1993). And in the wake of these two bereavements, the adolescent Khan (1988c), not yet twenty years of age, became deeply depressed. Fortunately, Khan enjoyed a period of psychotherapy or psychoanalysis from an Indian practitioner, who had trained in the United States of America, Dr Israel Latif (Cooper, 1991a, 1993), but this process did not last for very long and Khan came to regard him as a "a caring scoundrel" (quoted in Cooper, 1993, p. 11).

In 1946, Masud Khan arrived in London from his native India, keen to pursue a career in psychoanalysis. He underwent a formal interview with Dr Sylvia Payne, one of the grandees of both the British Psycho-Analytical Society and its training body, the Institute of Psycho-Analysis, which accepted his application. Years later, he reminisced to Dr Payne, "I shall always treasure the memory of my first meeting with you as a prospective candidate, nervous, terrified, and yet unyieldingly arrogant because of the tradition of his nurture, and you with your extraordinary sagacity and kindness immediately made allowance for all that complex of reactivity in me" (Khan, 1970).

Encouraged by Sylvia Payne, the young, ambitious Masud Khan began training as a psychoanalyst in London, later that year, shortly after the end of the Second World War. At the recommendation of Dr Payne, Khan undertook his first training analysis with none other than Miss Ella Freeman Sharpe, a noted teacher who had studied in Berlin under the psychoanalytical tutelage of the esteemed Dr Hanns Sachs, one of Professor Sigmund Freud's most loyal disciples. Thus, Khan could, quite legitimately, have regarded himself as an honorary great-grandchild of the father of modern psychology.

Miss Sharpe clearly found Khan not only engaging but, also, culturally challenging, and, on 7th November, 1946, she wrote to Dr Donald Winnicott, her former supervisee, "I am just starting the analysis of an Indian (a *candidate*). I can think no one more than yourself would enjoy the constant need I have to shift out of ruts and see the world through other eyes than Western ones!" (Sharpe, 1946). Khan certainly gained much from this work. Indeed, sometime later, he reminisced, "Only after

20 years what I learnt from her about the nature of metaphor is beginning to fructify into expressive thought" (Khan, 1967).

Throughout his training, Khan studied with some of the most distinguished progenitors of psychoanalysis, including Professor John Flügel, Dr William Gillespie, Dr Paula Heimann, Dr Willi Hoffer, Mrs Marion Milner, Dr John Rickman, Mrs Joan Riviere, and Dr Herbert Rosenfeld. And, as part of his training as a psychoanalyst of adults, Khan underwent supervision with Miss Anna Freud and Mrs Melanie Klein—the two queens of British psychoanalysis (Cooper, 1991a, 1993)—and, for his training in child psychoanalysis, he chose not only Marion Milner as a supervisor, but, also, Dr Clifford Scott and Dr Donald Winnicott (Cooper, 1993).

Khan could not have benefited from a more distinguished group of people. And he certainly endeared himself to many of these psychoanalysts of the older generation. Indeed, in one of Sylvia Payne's (1965) unpublished letters to Khan, she praised him, noting, "You are one of the few analysts that have a creative mind!"

Before long, Masud Khan had made himself indispensable within the British Psycho-Analytical Society as a hard-working, erudite candidate, and, upon qualification, as a valued colleague. He received permission to use the library at the Tavistock Clinic, then located on Beaumont Street in London, and he imbibed the collection of books and periodicals with thoroughness (King, 1991a). He read extensively and, following the recommendation of John Rickman, Khan ploughed through every issue of *The International Journal of Psycho-Analysis*, while travelling on the London Underground to his daily psychoanalytical sessions (Cooper, 1991a).

Even prior to qualifying as a psychoanalyst in 1950, Khan had become one of the Students' Representatives to the Library Committee of the British Psycho-Analytical Society, along with Dr Judith Waterlow, and, in this role, he undertook an enormous amount of voluntary labour, preparing subject indexes of some of the major English-language psychoanalytical periodicals. He also produced an index of the Reprints Collection in the organisation's library. The joint Librarians, Dr Liselotte Frankl and Dr Charles Rycroft (1951, p. 43), praised him warmly in their annual report, noting, "Almost all the work on both these projects has been done by Mr. Masud Khan."

In due course, Khan received an appointment as the Honorary Librarian of the organisation and, over time, he contributed hugely to the complex editorial process of *The International Journal of Psycho-Analysis*. Moreover, he became utterly indispensable to Dr Donald Winnicott (e.g., Winnicott, 1954b, 1958a, 1958b; Kahr, 2003), for whom he served as an editor of many of his books and papers. He also provided editorial assistance for his colleague Dr Charles Rycroft (Khan and Sutherland, 1968) as well as for Mrs Marion Milner (1969). Additionally, Khan helped to prepare a new edition of Ella Freeman Sharpe's classic book on dream analysis (Sharpe, 1978)—originally published in 1937 (Sharpe, 1937)—for which Khan (1978) wrote an introduction. Likewise, he assisted another less-well known colleague, Dr Robert Shields, with his own writings. As Shields (1962, pp. 13–14) wrote in the "Preface" to his papers on working with maladjusted children, "I am particularly grateful to Mr Masud R. Khan for endless encouragement throughout the preparation of the manuscript, for his constructive and helpful criticism, and for many helpful suggestions which have been incorporated in the text."

Apparently, throughout much of this time, the young Khan suffered from a sleep disorder and often worked into the small hours of the morning on behalf of the British Psycho-Analytical Society. As Pearl King (1991c, p. 19) once underscored to Masud Khan, "The Society doesn't realize how much they owe to your difficulties in sleeping".

Khan not only collaborated quite generously with his colleagues, but, rather early on in his career, he began to publish book reviews (e.g., Khan, 1954, 1955a, 1955b), as well as papers and chapters of his own (e.g., Khan, 1960a, 1960b, 1962a, 1963, 1964). In due course, he became a book-writer and teacher and hard-working administrator within both the British and the international psychoanalytical communities.

Just as Judy Cooper (1985, 1991a, 1993) reminisced—both personally and, also, in print—about her affection and gratitude to Masud Khan, so, too, did many other psychoanalytical practitioners who had enjoyed pleasant and educative encounters with this deeply experienced clinician and theoretician. For instance, Dr Gerald Wooster (2011), a venerable British psychoanalyst, told me that, during his training at the Institute of Psycho-Analysis, Khan exerted a powerful impact. Wooster explained that out of all of his tutors, many of whom induced a certain drowsiness, Khan, by contrast, "kept me awake".

Of all the colleagues whom I interviewed about Masud Khan, few knew him better than the venerable Pearl King, a one-time psychologist who trained alongside Khan during the late 1940s and who eventually became one of the world's most significant and most loved psychoanalysts. King (1991b, p. 14) rated Khan very highly, especially during his younger years, and she described him as "a nice lad". Additionally, King noted that, owing to Khan's wealth, he did not have to pursue a full-time job and, hence, unlike other candidates, he had lots of spare time in which to study the works of Sigmund Freud; and this deep immersion in scholarship permitted Khan to develop his intellectual excellence. Khan read widely and quickly. In fact, he once revealed to his colleague Robert Shields, "I try to read the whole of Freud once a year" (quoted in Kahr, 1996d). According to Shields, Khan also boasted an erudite knowledge of both English and Persian literature and he enjoyed a particularly fine familiarity with the works of William Shakespeare. Indeed, Shields described Khan to me as undoubtedly the most clever man associated with the Institute of Psycho-Analysis (Kahr, 1996d).

Quite understandably, Pearl King, when commenting on the quality of Khan's mind, recalled, "Of course he was good" (quoted in Kahr, 2005).

I regret to report that, in spite of having uncovered many little-known letters in the Archives of the British Psychoanalytical Society and in the Wellcome Library in London, and in spite of having interviewed fans of Khan, such as Pearl King and Gerald Wooster, the vast majority of the people with whom I spoke described him in a rather less flattering way.

Apparently, during his early years as a psychoanalyst, Khan seems to have worked hard and to have made many contributions, but, as time unfolded, he had to endure the death of his first psychoanalyst in Great Britain, Miss Ella Freeman Sharpe, followed not long thereafter by the decease of his second psychoanalyst, Dr John Rickman, and, ultimately, by the passing of his third psychoanalyst, Dr Donald Winnicott. As I have already underscored, these multiple bereavements contributed greatly to Khan's emotional deterioration (Kahr, 2003). And sadly, after the loss of Winnicott in 1971, Khan regressed significantly, and he became increasingly alcoholic, vituperative, unethical, and, even, violent. Indeed, as Pearl King (2005b) once explained, "There's more than one Masud."

As early as 1955, Dr Roger Money-Kyrle, a noted British psychoanalyst, wrote to Dr Donald Winnicott, expressing concerns that a new colleague with pointedly psychopathological characteristics had recently become elected to the membership of the British Psycho-Analytical Society. Although he did not mention Khan by name, the timing of the letter and its contents reveal that rumours had already begun to spread that Khan might well be a "potentially aggressive type of hypo-paranoid" (Money-Kyrle, 1955).

As Khan became better known within the psychoanalytical community, the tales became more and more troubling.

Dr John Evans, a psychiatrist and psychoanalyst, explained to me that he found Masud Khan to be "particularly nervous" (quoted in Kahr, 2010a). Others focused on his grandiosity. Mrs Isabel Menzies Lyth, also a psychoanalyst, reminisced about having studied under Khan in the 1950s at the Institute of Psycho-Analysis, during her candidacy (under the name Miss Isabel Menzies). Apparently, Khan always berated students who did not read as much of the clinical literature as he would have hoped. As Miss Menzies had to work hard to earn a living, she did not have much reading time and she resented Khan hugely for having set such a high, unrealistic bar (Kahr, 1995d).

Many of the people whom I interviewed over the years reported that Khan would often convey himself in a grandiose, princely manner. For instance, Mrs Barbara Dockar-Drysdale, one of Donald Winnicott's disciples and one of the leaders of the child mental health profession, told me that Masud Khan created quite a scandal during the congress of the International Psycho-Analytical Association, held in Vienna, Austria, in 1971. Whereas all of the other delegates arrived at the conference hall by car or by foot, Khan paraded through the streets on horseback, and many regarded this as upstaging and offensive (Kahr, 1991b).

Dr Brendan MacCarthy, a quondam President of the British Psycho-Analytical Society, knew Masud Khan across many decades. Although Dr MacCarthy rarely spoke ill of his colleagues, he did confess that he had never met anyone more insufferably narcissistic and exhibitionistic than Khan; he even admitted that Masud Khan reminded him in many ways of the American gangster Al Capone. MacCarthy recalled that Khan often strode into the room in a regal fashion; moreover, he would frequently boast about his knowledge of Freud in an obsessional fashion, attempting to impress people by citing the particular page number on which they might locate a certain Freud quotation. Although a gentleman of the highest magnitude, MacCarthy (2002) admitted to me, "I couldn't stand him."

Khan would insist that other people should refer to him as the "Prince of Kathar" (Paterson, 1991, p. 109) or as a "Rajah", claiming that he had grown up in an aristocratic family. In fact, in one of his publications, he signed his name "Prince Masud Khan" (Khan, 1987, p. xvii); and, shortly thereafter, the inside back flap of the jacket of his final book (Khan, 1988a) would describe him as both "Prince Masud Khan" and as "Prince Khan". Dr Jonathan Pedder, a noted British psychoanalyst, recalled that Khan also insisted upon being addressed in public as "Your Excellency" (quoted in Kahr, 1996j). But, according to Dr Charles Rycroft (1996), *The New York Times* had conducted an investigation into his presumptive aristocratic status and concluded that Khan had no right to style himself in such a manner.

According to the London-based psychoanalyst Dr Abrahão Brafman, who had studied with Masud Khan at the Institute of Psycho-Analysis, his teacher could be quite verbally violent. Brafman recalled that, during one of Khan's seminars, an Irish-born candidate named Dr Ronald St. Blaize-Molony once grazed his knee against the edge of a table, which Khan interpreted as a sign of great rudeness. Consequently, Khan exploded and shouted violently at St. Blaize-Molony (Kahr, 2002b).

To many, Khan seemed quite mad at times.

Ms Susie Orbach (later Dr Susie Orbach) and her colleague Ms Luise Eichenbaum visited Khan at his office in London in the hope of receiving clinical supervision. Apparently, in the middle of the conversation, Khan explained that he had once cut off the head of a dog with a sabre and he then attempted to demonstrate this act of savagery with his hands. He also presented these two young women with copies of a book written by none other than the Marquis de Sade. Needless to say, neither of those psychotherapists returned to Khan for further supervision (Orbach, 1994; cf. Orbach, 1997).[3] Although Khan did not physically assault either Orbach or Eichenbaum in any way, his enactment of a presumed beheading of a canine offered a true glimpse into the potentially forensic aspects of Khan's character structure (Kahr, 2020a).

The Forensic Side of Masud Khan

Although the vast majority of mental health practitioners will never, ever act-out their aggression in such a shocking manner and will never commit an actual crime, Masud Khan not only flirted with dangerousness across much of his life, especially during the 1970s and 1980s, but, moreover, he may well have qualified as a "forensic" patient, namely, an individual whose mental illness or mental struggle with aggression and violence cannot be contained and who will, therefore, engage in full-fledged criminality.

Certainly, Khan could exaggerate. But he could also lie. Indeed, during one of my later conversations with Judy Cooper (2005), she revealed that Khan had told her that he grew up in pre-partition India on a very large estate. But Khan never offered a consistent narrative about his family home, and, on certain occasions, he claimed that the estate spread across 4,500 acres; yet, at other times, he insisted that his father's land sprawled over as many as 17,500 acres. Cooper (2005) also revealed that Khan would violate the confidentiality of his patients and would often make very derogatory comments about their private lives (cf. Kahr, 2002b).

Khan would publicly insult not only some of his patients but, also, his former psychoanalyst, Winnicott. Indeed, Professor Andrew Samuels (2015) reminisced that, in 1975, while attending the seventieth birthday party of one of Great Britain's leading Jungian analysts, Dr Michael Fordham, Khan publicly lambasted Winnicott—one of Fordham's longstanding friends—and insisted that Winnicott suffered from sexual impotence! Apparently, Khan became so drunk at Fordham's birthday party that one of the other guests, Dr Rosemary Gordon, had to force him to stop his outburst (Samuels, 2019).

Several of my interviewees underscored that Masud Khan had repeated this same accusation about Winnicott's erectile difficulties on many different occasions. Dr Jonathan Pedder recalled that, while chairing a public meeting about Winnicott's work on behalf of the

British Psycho-Analytical Society, a member of the audience asked why Winnicott had never become a father. Khan butted in and cried out, "I'll tell you why. It's simple. He wasn't a man" (quoted in Kahr, 1996j).

Apparently, Khan had no difficulty violating the privacy of others. Not only would he insult people publicly and reveal their private thoughts and secrets but, also, he would read the sealed correspondence of others. According to Mrs Jenny Pearson (2009), the widow of the famous psychoanalyst Dr Charles Rycroft, the infamous Masud Khan would actually steam open Rycroft's private letters.

As the years progressed, Khan's thievery became more and more pronounced. Often, he would stroll into the famous psychoanalytical bookshop, H. Karnac (Books), located on the Gloucester Road in London, and he would steal various volumes. The original owner of the shop, Mr Harry Karnac, one of Khan's patients, would tolerate this thievery. Even after Karnac sold the business to Mr Cesare Sacerdoti, Khan persisted with book theft, and Sacerdoti, as the new owner, became very aggrieved that an eminent psychoanalyst would actually pilfer in this way. Sacerdoti told me that he wrote to Khan, insisting upon payment for the stolen titles. Khan replied by accusing Sacerdoti of being little more than a "Jewish shopkeeper" (quoted in Sacerdoti, 2001). Eventually, however, Khan did settle his account. Sacerdoti (2005) felt rather injured and betrayed by Khan for his technically criminal behaviour, and, in future years, whenever he happened to see Khan in the street, he would cross over to other the side of the road to avoid any contact with the man.

According to my many interviewees, Khan would not only shame his patients and his former analyst in public, as well as lie and steal, but he could also be quite sexually irresponsible. Dr Estela Welldon (2007), an Argentinian-born psychiatrist and psychotherapist, enjoyed a supper with Masud Khan during her younger years, along with her friends, Donald Ogden Stewart—a noted Academy Award-winning Hollywood screenwriter—and his wife, Ella Winter. Apparently, Khan comported himself in such a lascivious manner throughout the supper that, afterwards, the Stewarts telephoned Welldon and pleaded with her that she must never have an affair with Khan ... *ever*. In a subsequent conversation with Estela Welldon (2020)—now Profesora Welldon— she confirmed the details of this story and underscored that at least one other friend—a well-known film actress—had also attended this dinner party and that she, too, phoned Welldon afterwards to warn her about Khan.

Apparently, many people found Khan to be quite handsome. As the late Dr Peter Bruggen, a distinguished psychiatrist who knew Khan, recalled, "He looked lovely and knew it" (quoted in Kahr, 2010b). Hence, he had no difficulty attracting potential lovers. But he certainly did not treat them all with respect. According to Mr Mark Paterson, a literary agent who worked with Khan in managing the estate of none other than Sigmund Freud, the handsome psychoanalyst could be physically abusive. As Paterson (1991, p. 111) reported, "I once had to restrain him from frequently slapping his girlfriend."

In later years, Khan became involved sexually with several of his female patients. One of my interviewees, the aforementioned Robert Shields, recalled that, years previously, Masud Khan appeared at Shields' home in Dulwich in South-East London, one morning at approximately 2.00 a.m., having arrived in his Jaguar. Shields welcomed Khan at this late hour and listened as Khan confessed that he had slept with several of his patients and had even impregnated one of these women. The two men talked until just before 7.00 a.m., when Shields' first patient would arrive at the house (Kahr, 1996d).

Masud Khan also embarked upon a very passionate affair with the wife of one of the male trainees at the Institute of Psycho-Analysis. This resulted in much gossip and much scandal. According to Profesora Estela Welldon (2020), who knew the couple in question, the wife—one of Khan's patients—once returned home at 4.00 a.m. When the husband enquired where she had spent the evening, she attempted to convince him that she and Khan had a particularly late-night analytical session and that they spent many hours talking about her mind! Eventually, in 1975, the Institute of Psycho-Analysis stripped Khan of his status as a training analyst, thus forbidding him to psychoanalyse any formal candidates in future (Cooper, 1993); but they did not prevent him from maintaining his professional membership in the interlinked sibling organisation, namely, the British Psycho-Analytical Society. Needless to say, in spite of his guilt, Khan nevertheless felt ashamed and furious that his colleagues had demoted him in this way; and, according to Mrs Lydia James, a long-standing psychoanalytical practitioner in

London, Khan actually threatened to blow up the headquarters of the Institute of Psycho-Analysis, then located on New Cavendish Street in Central London (Kahr, 1996i).

In terms of sexuality, Khan not only engaged in misconduct with adult females, but, according to some of my interviewees, he also cheated with male lovers as well. Mr Edward Lucie-Smith, an art historian who often socialised with both Masud Khan and his wife Svetlana Beriozova, explained that Khan engaged in sexual conduct with several of his own houseboys, who tended to his home in Knightsbridge. According to Lucie-Smith, one of these young men eventually contracted the HIV virus and died from AIDS years later. Lucie-Smith characterised Khan as highly seductive and he granted me permission to reveal that he and Khan came but a hair's breadth from having sex with one another (Kahr, 2010d).

Although we certainly do not have sufficient data, or, indeed, the authorisation to comment upon the sexual life of Masud Khan with comprehensive understanding, I can report that, in addition to his extramarital affairs with both adult women and adult men, Khan made sexual advances to teenagers. One man whom I interviewed, who knew Khan well, told me that, during his younger years, the famous psychoanalyst had groped him sexually and, also, did likewise with his teenage sister. For reasons of discretion, I have chosen to protect the name of this person, but I can report that this gentleman spoke with clarity and conviction. Needless to say, I cannot prove this accusation of the sexual fondling of two teenagers to be true, but, in view of Khan's many other transgressions, we might well consider such a possibility.

Needless to say, the complexity and diversity of Khan's sexual life soon became increasingly well known within the confines of the psychoanalytical community, resulting in a sense of shock and outrage. Indeed, when, in 2009, I had the privilege of interviewing Masud Khan's first wife, Mrs Jane Shore Nicholas (formerly Mrs Jane Khan), she told me that, during the 1950s, whenever her husband and his psychoanalytical colleagues gathered for dinner parties, they always spoke extensively about sexual perversions (Kahr, 2009d).

Apparently, not everyone who engaged in sexual relations with Khan felt sullied. My colleague Dr Valerie Sinason (2020) told me that, back in 1993, she met a woman at a professional meeting who admitted that she had once enjoyed an extramarital affair with Khan. That person simply could not understand why Khan had come to evoke so much criticism and derision, because she described her own sexual encounters with him as among the most satisfying experiences of her entire life.

As the years unfolded, Khan became more and more vituperative, even violent. My interviewees told me stories aplenty of Khan becoming involved in physical brawls, and one of my American colleagues, the psychoanalyst Dr James Raney (1995), reminisced to me that Khan had once obtained an actual gun and fired a shot at a very eminent British psychoanalyst, whom Khan hated. Raney explained that he had learned about this incident from that very psychoanalyst himself who, thankfully, survived the assault and did not, apparently, press criminal charges. Although I never had the opportunity to interview this gunshot victim and cannot, therefore, offer official confirmation of the reality of the story, Khan certainly became conceptualised as a true, criminal forensic patient, namely, one who enacts his psychological turbulence through violent activities.

In addition to his sexual transgressions, his alcoholism, his thefts, his physical violence, his threatening behaviour, and his arguably pathological grandiosity, Khan also conveyed his anti-Semitic sentiments in an all too noticeable fashion. When, in 2010, I interviewed the elderly psychoanalyst, Professor Richard Michael—one of Khan's former clinical supervisees—he explained that he came to regard Khan not only as an essentially nice man and as a good mentor, but, also, as a person who actually hated Jews (Kahr, 2010c). Indeed, in her biography of Khan, his former patient, Judy Cooper, revealed that Khan had violated the confidentiality of a fellow analysand—a Jewish homosexual patient who underwent treatment with Khan—and that he had referred to that man as having a "dirty Jewish arse" (quoted in Cooper, 1993, p. 33).

Various commentators have offered divergent perspectives on Khan's ostensible anti-Semitic attitudes. Certainly, many have reported that Khan often verbalised his complicated views about Jewish people. As Khan explained to Judy Cooper, "What makes Jews insufferable is that in order to love themselves they have to be hated by others first" (quoted in Cooper, 1993, p. 33). And the aforementioned Robert Shields, a long-standing psychoanalytical colleague, told me that Khan believed that the Arabs should drive the Jews into the sea (Kahr,

1996d). But, by contrast, Mark Paterson (1991, p. 110), the literary agent who managed Sigmund Freud Copyrights, explained that he found Khan's anti-Semitic comments to be "curiously unconvincing", not least in view of the fact that Khan enjoyed warm friendships with a great many Jewish men and women.

Eventually, as Khan aged, he suffered from a debilitating lung cancer, and, in consequence, had to undergo the surgical removal of both his larynx and his trachea and, also, had to endure surgery on his eyes (Cooper, 1991a, 1993), and, moreover, quite terrifyingly, the removal of one of his lungs as well (Kahr, 1985c; Paterson, 1991). His voice—once very powerful—literally began to fade, and his long-standing colleague, Marion Milner, could barely understand him at times (Kahr, 1985c, 2023d).

And as Khan had to deal with the shame and the fall-out from being stripped of his status as a training analyst, he began to reveal his anti-Semitism more publicly and, also, more viciously. Quite shockingly, in 1988, he published the aforementioned *When Spring Comes: Awakenings in Clinical Psychoanalysis* (Khan, 1988a), in which he spoke in an unquestionably disgusting manner about a Jewish patient.

In contemporary terms, Khan's description of this patient, "Mr Luis", would be regarded not only as anti-Semitic but, also, as racist, not least as he referred to this man as a "bastard" (Khan, 1988a, p. 92) and, also, as "rather swarthy of taint" (Khan, 1988a, p. 92).

Certainly, Khan's (1988a, pp. 92–93) most shocking paragraph demands to be quoted in full:

> I warned Mr Luis: "One more personal remark about me, my wife, my staff or my things, and I will throw you out, you accursed nobody Jew. Find your own people then. Shoals of them drift around, just like you. Yes, I am anti-Semitic. You know why, Mr Luis? Because I am an Aryan and had thought all of you Jews had perished when Jesus, from sheer dismay—and he was one of you—had flown up to Heaven, leaving you in the scorching care of Hitler, Himmler and the crematoriums. Don't fret, Mr Luis; like the rest of your species, you will survive and continue to harass others, and lament, and bewail yourselves. Remarkable how Yiddish/Jewish you are. Vintage quality, too. Only you have gathered too much moss on your arse. Face you can mask with paints. Do you hear me,

Mr Luis? It is not that difficult to splurge obscenities and outrageousness. Now, is it? I can be a deft hand with it at times, when provoked. But what will be the point of that, with you? Playing your dirty games your way. Still, I am giving you one more hearing and shall decide then. Goodbye again, Mr Luis. Don't hang around in the hall, please. Try, or at least pretend, to respect the privacy and rights of others. Goodbye, Mr. Luis, till we meet again. If we meet!"

Judy Cooper (1991a, 1993) attempted to explain Khan's anti-Jewish diatribe as an envious attack on his healthy Jewish colleagues within the British Psycho-Analytical Society who did not have cancer. But whatever the extent of his anti-Semitic feelings and whatever his motivation for writing such shocking comments about his patient, Khan's professional colleagues finally leapt into action, outraged by this publication which the psychoanalyst Dr Eric Rayner (1993, p. xiii) considered to be "overtly racist".

In view of all of the horrors associated with Masud Khan, the senior members of the British Psycho-Analytical Society who, hitherto, had merely removed his status as training analyst, finally decided that he had brought the profession into disrepute and would have to be expelled from his clinical membership within the organisation. Dr Earl Hopper (2007), whom I had the pleasure of interviewing, served on the Council of the British Psycho-Analytical Society, and recalled in great detail the evening in which he and his colleagues elected to terminate Khan's membership. Strikingly, Mr Raymond Shepherd, one of the fellow Council members, abstained during the voting, but the rest agreed to the plan. Dr Hopper insisted that the minutes of the meeting should reflect the fact that although Khan had certainly acted in a grossly anti-Semitic fashion, it could not be overlooked that other practitioners within the British Psycho-Analytical Society also harboured such anti-Jewish sentiments—a reality that the organisation would have to confront.

Over recent decades, the subject of Khan's last book has emerged many times in conversations among psychoanalytical practitioners and sympathists. Not only have many of us wondered why Khan chose to publish such ghastly comments about Jews but, perhaps, even more shockingly, why his distinguished publisher, Chatto & Windus, an extremely classy and venerable firm, founded in the nineteenth century, had agreed to produce such a book in the first place. Professor Robert Stoller, the noted American psychoanalyst, expressed his shock to the British psychoanalytical bookseller, Mr Harry Karnac, wondering, "What induced Chatto to publish this?" (quoted in Karnac, 1992, p. 29).

In her extremely well researched and magnificently written biography of Khan, Dr Linda Hopkins (2006), the American psychoanalyst, has offered some revealing insight into the thinking behind the publication of *When Spring Comes: Awakenings in Clinical Psychoanalysis*, including the fact that Mr John Fraser Charlton, the director of Chatto & Windus, and its subsidiary, the Hogarth Press, had earlier produced two of Khan's previous books, namely, *Alienation in Perversions* (Khan, 1979a) and, also, *Hidden Selves: Between Theory and Practice in Psychoanalysis* (Khan, 1983). Hence, the two men had already forged a long-standing relationship.

But the deeper reasons may be even more complex.

When, in 1996, I spoke to Cesare Sacerdoti (1996), the gentleman who succeeded Harry Karnac as the owner and publisher of H. Karnac (Books), I learned something more incriminating about the inside story. Apparently, Sacerdoti knew John Charlton, the director of Chatto & Windus, quite well, through their overlapping roles in the field of book production. Naturally, as a Jew (and, moreover, as a refugee from Nazi-occupied Italy during the Second World War), Sacerdoti confronted Charlton and asked for an explanation.

Apparently, Charlton had worked closely with Khan over many years in relation to the special monograph series of the British Psycho-Analytical Society, published by the Hogarth Press, a subsidiary of Chatto & Windus. As a member of the Publications Committee of the British Psycho-Analytical Society, Khan played an important role in shaping the volumes which Charlton and his team would sanction. As Charlton (n.d., p. 136) once reminisced, "Masud did all the real thinking on the Publications Committee for years."

It seems that Charlton had contracted Khan to write his book *When Spring Comes: Awakenings in Clinical Psychoanalysis*, as early as 1986 (Hopkins, 2006). When Khan submitted the typescript sometime thereafter, it became quite clear that the book contained some shockingly unprofessional and anti-Semitic comments. But, Charlton still wished to proceed with publication. Indeed, according to Sacerdoti, Charlton resented some of the members of the British Psycho-Analytical Society, especially in view of the fact that, round about the time that Charlton had commissioned Khan's new book, the Publications Committee of that psychoanalytical organisation had decided that they would not renew their multi-year contract with the Hogarth Press, and that they would no longer publish the famous monograph series, The International Psycho-Analytical Library, but that, instead, they would launch a new series, The New Library of Psychoanalysis (spelled without a hyphen), which would now be released by the rival press, Tavistock Publications. John Charlton—a loyal friend to the British Psycho-Analytical Society and a director of both Chatto & Windus and, also, of the Hogarth Press, felt betrayed. Thus, as Sacerdoti explained, when Khan arrived with a book which might bring psychoanalysis into disrepute, Charlton seemed to have supported the plan.

I subsequently discovered an unpublished letter written by Masud Khan to Mrs Clare Winnicott, the widow of Dr Donald Winnicott, in which he revealed that he and Charlton had worked together since 1967. As he noted, "I trust his judgment totally" (Khan, 1977). Thus, when Khan submitted his text to Charlton, these two men had already enjoyed a twenty-year collaboration.

By the time Khan's book appeared in print, his world had become permanently soiled.

In the wake of the publication of this outrageous and troubled volume, the British Psycho-Analytical Society finally terminated Khan's membership. This resulted in the loss of many of his lifelong friendships, not least with Pearl King, who had trained alongside Khan approximately forty years previously. As King recalled, "People in the British Society said goodbye to Masud when he wrote the book, not when he died. We thought, 'We've forgiven Masud a lot, but this we won't forgive'" (quoted in Hopkins, n.d., p. 366).

Following his expulsion from membership in the British Psycho-Analytical Society, an organisation to which Khan had maintained extremely close ties for roughly four decades, his cancer continued to metastasise. Approximately eleven months prior to his death, Khan granted an audience to the Indian-born, American-based psychoanalyst, Professor Salman Akhtar (2022, p. 147), who recalled, "The encounter, while informative, left me distressed and disillusioned. Here was a man ravaged by cancer, alcoholism, moral decay, and social ostracism." This evocative statement truly encapsulates the tragedy of Khan's most unfortunate decline.

Sadly, on 7th June, 1989, Masud Khan died at the London Clinic, at the age of sixty-four years (Cooper, 1993; Hopkins, 2006).

The Struggle to Understand

In view of Masud Khan's seemingly privileged life, full of wealth and intelligence and opportunity, how on earth did this man end up in such a state of deterioration, especially as he had spent many years, early on in his career, demonstrating his skill, his intelligence, his competence, his scholarliness, and so much more?

As Mrs Judy Cooper (1993), Dr Roger Willoughby (2005), and Dr Linda Hopkins (2006) have written thorough and intelligent biographies of Masud Khan, I shall not attempt to provide a comprehensive overview of the gradual and complex process of his deterioration. For those who wish to learn more of his extraordinary life history, I warmly recommend all three of these carefully researched tomes.

If Masud Khan happened still to be alive today, one can only begin to imagine how he might understand the tragedy of his life story. But as a psychoanalyst, he would have possessed at least a certain amount, if not a great deal, of insight. Indeed, in 1977, he had confessed to Clare Winnicott, the widow of his once-beloved mentor, "having lived in acute pain myself, I know how pain corrodes morale, and one has to fight that all the way" (Khan, 1977).

Certainly, Khan endured a lot of trauma during his lifetime, which included the death of his beloved sister and his father, while still a teenager, and, subsequently, the death of his mother. But, in addition, he also lost three psychoanalysts, two of whom—Sharpe and Rickman—died in the midst of treatment, and one of whom—Winnicott—passed away in the middle of a close and intimate comradeship and collaboration.

In a public lecture, first delivered in 1994 (Kahr, 1994b) and published, subsequently, in more extended form nearly a decade thereafter (Kahr, 2002a, 2003), I argued that the death of all three of Khan's psychoanalysts—Ella Freeman Sharpe, John Rickman, and Donald Winnicott—impacted hugely upon this much bereaved man and contributed quite significantly to his deterioration during the 1970s and 1980s.

Shortly after his acceptance as a candidate at the Institute of Psycho-Analysis, Khan embarked upon his official training analysis with Ella Freeman Sharpe, but she died on 1st June, 1947, at the age of seventy-two years, not long after Khan had become her analysand. Whether a woman of Sharpe's age should have taken on a new training patient while in her seventies remains a matter of contention. But, certainly, her death will have affected Khan greatly.

In order to continue both his psychoanalysis and his clinical training, Khan sought out further treatment from John Rickman, not long thereafter. Khan and Rickman enjoyed an unusually close—arguably *unhelpfully* close—relationship. Indeed, according to Pearl King—one of Rickman's other analysands—Khan would often drink coffee with his second British psychoanalyst after sessions, thus extending their time together (Kahr, 2005). But, before Khan could complete his treatment, Rickman dropped dead of a heart attack, under a mulberry tree in London's Regent's Park, on 1st July, 1951, at the age of only sixty years (King, 2001a). Thus, within four years, Masud Khan had lost two psychoanalysts. And, after Rickman's decease, Khan began to consult with his third psychoanalyst, Donald Winnicott. Although it remains uncertain how long Khan attended for formal sessions with this iconic man, he certainly maintained extremely close and regular contact with Winnicott and made great progress as a result (Kahr, 2002a, 2003). But, on 25th January, 1971, Donald Winnicott died, also from heart disease, at the age of seventy-four years (Kahr, 1996a). In fact, all three of Khan's British psychoanalysts suffered from coronary illness. In consequence, Khan must have experienced considerable heartbreak of his own.

Donald Winnicott occupied an immensely important role in the life of Masud Khan. In fact, Khan worshipped Winnicott and referred to him as godlike (Kahr, 1996d). Moreover, according to Robert Shields, the affinity between the elderly Winnicott and the youthful Khan became so powerful that many people regarded them as rather akin to a mother and son (Kahr, 1996d).

Tragically, Khan had experienced many threats during his childhood. According to Edward Lucie-Smith, Khan's half-brothers had actually attempted to kill him (Kahr, 2010d)! Therefore, the kindness and calm of Winnicott would have proven quite a transformative remedy. Indeed, Winnicott may have made Khan feel quite bodily safe for the first time in his life. Masud Khan even confessed to his friend and colleague Pearl King that he would often fall asleep during his psychoanalytical sessions with Winnicott, not because he found them boring but, rather, because he felt sufficiently comfortable to do so in the presence of another man (Kahr, 2005).

Unsurprisingly, after the death of Winnicott, Khan really began to deteriorate. In fact, the two men had discussed the possibility of Winnicott's death. One of my teachers at the Portman Clinic in London, the psychoanalyst Dr Elif Gürisik (1996), told me that, during one of her conversations with Masud Khan, he talked to her about Winnicott's passing. He revealed that, apparently, Winnicott had already begun to prepare him for this loss and predicted that his death would be a regrettable persecution for Khan.

Virtually all of the forensic stories about Khan's grandiosity, ethical breaches, physical violence, and anti-Semitism occurred *after* the death of Winnicott in 1971. Undoubtedly, Winnicott's passing triggered not only the loss of his previous psychoanalysts, all of whom had died in the saddle, but, also, the deaths of his beloved sister and his tyrannical father. The decease of Winnicott triggered an explosion of unsafety in Khan. Indeed, Mrs Baljeet Mehra (1992, p. 25), a London-based psychoanalyst who knew Khan well, underscored that, in the wake of Winnicott's death, "the dams burst."

Traumatic losses during his youth, combined with displacement from his feudal Indian upbringing, exacerbated by the decease of Sharpe, Rickman, and Winnicott, all put Khan at a much higher risk for destructive enactments in later life.

Sadly, not long after the death of Winnicott, Khan's mother passed away on 10th June, 1971 (Willoughby, 2005; Hopkins, 2006). Thus, Khan endured two huge losses within months of one another.

It may also be the case that Khan survived even more profound tragedies during his childhood than we may realise. Many years ago, I conducted an interview with one of Khan's sometime analysands, a person whose name I shall not reveal, owing to reasons of confidentiality. This informant—a woman—told me that she had once questioned Khan about his early years in more detail. Apparently, he revealed to his former patient that, as a little child, a group of older boys who lived nearby had bullied him cruelly. Masud Khan then reported this abuse to his father, Fazal Dad Khan—an elderly feudal Rajah—who instructed several of his male servants to capture the local hoodlums and then sodomise those youngsters as a powerful punishment.

No wonder Masud Khan (1988b, p. 10) revealed to Judy Cooper that his father could be "a very caring man but could be very cruel".

Needless to say, we cannot possibly confirm the reality of this story. It might well have happened. It could perhaps represent an exaggeration or even a fantasy. But, what if the feudal Fazal Dad Khan *had*, indeed, forced his servants to commit such a paedophilic act? After all, at that time—probably in the late 1920s or early 1930s—few people knew anything about child abuse *per se*, and very few countries prohibited such activities by law. Moreover, one cannot help but wonder whether Masud Khan had suffered from some sort of sexual abuse himself. Certainly, such trauma might help to explain his promiscuity in adult life, his attraction to both women and, also, men, and, moreover, his attempts to fondle not only a teenage girl but, also, a teenage boy (as I indicated earlier in this essay), each of whom I interviewed many decades ago.

Whatever the truth about Masud Khan's early years, whatever the real nature of his private life, and whatever he might or might not have done in the consulting room, this man clearly led a difficult, challenging life, hidden by glamour, wealth, and, also, intellectual brilliance. No wonder Khan had hoped to write an autobiography entitled *Try Being Me* (Cooper, 1991a).

In her obituary of Masud Khan, Judy Cooper (1991a) revealed in print, probably for the first time, that Khan had entered the world in 1924 with a deformed right ear (cf. Cooper, 1993). The symbolism of a future psychoanalyst with a disabled ear requires little elaboration. No wonder Dr Charles Rycroft (1992, p. 30), one of Khan's colleagues at the British Psycho-Analytical Society, referred to him as "the Damaged Archangel". Profesora Estela Welldon, who devoted many decades to the study of the forensic patient, dared to describe Khan in a less poetic manner than Rycroft had done. With great conviction, Welldon (2020) insisted that Khan met all of the diagnostic criteria for a true, full-fledged "psychopath".

Interestingly, while researching the biography of Donald Winnicott, I happened to discover an unpublished letter that Khan's psychoanalyst had written in 1952 to the noted British plastic surgeon Sir Harold Gillies. Apparently, Winnicott had arranged for Gillies to operate on Khan's damaged ear. This occurred not long after the death of John Rickman, and not long after Khan had embarked upon his psychoanalysis with Donald Winnicott. Gillies, a man of tremendous skill (e.g., Pound, 1964), undertook the task with considerable professionalism and success; and, afterwards, Winnicott (1952) wrote to Gillies, praising him for his expert work: "I feel that even you with your high standards will be entirely satisfied with what you have accomplished."

This episode from Khan's medical history, underscored by his immense gratitude to, and dependence on, Winnicott's interventions, certainly forces us to pose the question: can a psychoanalyst with a damaged ear be healed, or should the Institute of Psycho-Analysis have interviewed a candidate with a damaged ear (metaphorically speaking) far more carefully?

* * *

Does this exploration of Khan's filmic character and life history bequeath to us any key lessons that will assist those of us who work in the mental health profession, or should we regard these anecdotes—many previously unpublished and unknown—as mere gossip about a captivating and provocative personality?

No doubt each of us will use this material in a different fashion. But for me, the case of Khan underscores the sheer complexity of the human psyche and serves as an important reminder that one can be both "enchanting" (Cooper, 1993, p. xx) as well as "demonic" (Cooper, 1993, p. xx), and, moreover, that one can lead a life of "monastic austerity" (Cooper, 1993, p. 3) as well as that of a "wealthy playboy" (Cooper, 1993, p. 3). Mark Paterson (1991, p. 109) summed up the complexity of Khan in two concise and comprehensive sentences: "Masud Khan, prince of princes as he described himself, art collector, womanizer, anti-Semite, snob, charmer, cancer victim. He was all these things and more, and surely one of the most colourful, charismatic and controversial figures of his time." Paterson (1991, p. 111) underscored further that, "Knowing him was an experience not to be missed."

Extraordinarily, in spite of his many professional transgressions and his personal abuses, Masud Khan really did help a great number of patients in quite a profound way. In spite of his "aristocratic hauteur" (Cooper, 1993, p. 88) and his "imperious manner" (Cooper, 1993, p. 89), he made quite an impact upon many individuals. According to his colleague Dr Eric Rayner (1992, p. 86), "He had a magical understanding of people and a feeling for them. The real gratitude that patients had to Khan was not to be sneezed at." And Dr Charles Rycroft (1991) reported that two of Khan's sometime patients revealed that no one had ever understood them better.

Eric Rayner (1991, p. 92) summed up the complexity of this extraordinary man most concisely when he wrote, "It could be said that Khan's theory came from the Gods and his behaviour from the Devil."

Although most of us will lead far more straightforward lives than Khan and most of us will wish to distance ourselves from the forensic aspects of this man, he cannot help but remind us of the tremendous nuance of human beings, and of the impact of trauma, and of the depth of the unconscious mind. In many ways, the complicated nature of Khan underscores the sheer importance of the work of Sigmund Freud and his successors, who have demonstrated that the depth-psychological understanding of a human being might require a great deal of slow and careful study over a very long period of time.

I hope that one day a clever filmmaker will transform Khan's life into a great movie which will not only entertain us but, also, educate us about the compelling nature of this controversial character and provide us with further insight into the mind of a man whom one reviewer described—quite rightly so—as "*too* fascinating" (Cooper, 1991b, p. 113), thus upstaging all of his patients.

CHAPTER TEN

R. D. Laing's Missing Tooth: The Secret Roots of Genius and Madness

> There's hell, there's darkenes, there is the ſulphurous pit.
> —"Lear", in William Shakespeare, *The Tragedie of King Lear*, c. 1603–1606, First Folio, Actus Quartus, Scena Quinta, lines 138–139

> Are not there little chapters in everybody's life, that seem to be nothing, and yet affect all the rest of the history?
> —William Makepeace Thackeray, *Vanity Fair: A Novel without a Hero*, 1848, Chapter VI (Thackeray, 1848, p. 46)

> The clay snake fell to pieces. I am in pieces. I am dead.
> —"Hubert", age eight

Ronald Laing and Psychoanalysis

In 1983, during my tenure as a Research Officer at the Littlemore Hospital in Oxfordshire, I decided that I would organise a weekly series of lectures on psychoanalytical topics. Although Oxford now boasts the highly analytically orientated Oxford Psychotherapy Society, back then, nothing of this kind existed, and I undertook to invite distinguished practitioners of psychoanalysis and psychotherapy to Oxford on a regular basis in an attempt to introduce psychodynamic ideas into a culture dominated by organic psychiatry and behaviourist psychology (cf. Kahr, 1985a). Dr Muriel Gardiner, the distinguished American psychoanalyst, who had trained with Dr Ruth Mack Brunswick in Vienna in the 1920s, delivered the inaugural lecture on 7th October, 1983, to this newly constituted group which I christened as The Oxford Psycho-Analytical Forum; and only four and a half weeks later, Dr Ronald Laing, the perennial gadfly of traditional British psychiatry, addressed the fledgling organisation as well.

Like most younger clinicians, I had always admired the work of Dr Laing immensely, especially his first book, *The Divided Self: A Study of Sanity and Madness* (Laing, 1960), which helped me a very great deal in my interactions with chronic, hospitalised patients who had received the dreaded diagnosis of "schizophrenia". As an aspiring clinical practitioner, I found Laing's writings highly compatible with those of Sigmund Freud and the other pioneers of psychoanalysis. Of course, Laing did choose to underpin his texts with extensive references to various Continental philosophers, such as Martin Heidegger, Maurice Merleau-Ponty, Jean-Paul Sartre, Paul Tillich, and others, figures who have had virtually no impact on practitioners in the psychoanalytically orientated community; but, in spite of Laing's penchant for existential philosophy, I regarded him as a true grandson of Freud. After all, Laing spent his career demonstrating two important facts:

1. Madness can be understood.
2. Madness develops in the bosom of the nuclear family.

In this respect, Laing placed himself quite centrally in the tradition of Freud, a man who also spent his long lifetime advancing these very ideas as well.

I did not doubt Dr Laing's Freudian credentials for one moment. After all, he underwent a personal analysis with Dr Charles Rycroft, as part of his training at the Institute of Psycho-Analysis; and he participated in clinical supervision with Mrs Marion Milner, another reputable psychoanalytical practitioner. Furthermore, Laing worked at the Tavistock Clinic in London, a veritable haven for psychoanalytically inclined psychotherapists and researchers. If anybody deserved an invitation to speak to the audience at The Oxford Psycho-Analytical Forum, surely, it would be R. D. Laing.

And yet, one afternoon, I found myself browsing through some old psychoanalytical journals in the Medical Library at Littlemore Hospital, and I stumbled upon two shocking book reviews of Laing's (1960) *opus classicus*, namely, *The Divided Self: A Study of Sanity and Madness*. Dr Marjorie Brierley, a senior member of the British Psycho-Analytical Society, and the author of an influential textbook on *Trends in Psycho-Analysis* (Brierley, 1951), reviewed Laing's book for *The International Journal of Psycho-Analysis*. Laing's treatise must have caused this woman a certain amount of anxiety, because she expressed a fear that he might be in danger of engaging in a change of focus within the field which might "lead to the discarding of any of the basic findings of psycho-analysis, as too often happens with the introduction of 'new' ideas" (Brierley, 1961, p. 291). Likewise, Dr Thomas Freeman, a highly regarded psychoanalyst who worked closely with Anna Freud, and who would eventually publish a number of substantial volumes on psychoanalytical psychiatry (e.g., Freeman, Cameron, and McGhie, 1965; Freeman, 1988), reviewed the book for *The British Journal of Medical Psychology*. Freeman (1961, p. 80) also wrote a somewhat hostile appraisal, chastising Laing for his neglect of the role of unconscious motivation in psychosis, and noting that, "Apart from the terminology there is nothing in Dr Laing's presentation which is not recognized daily by the practising psychoanalyst." In other words, the classically orientated clinicians regarded Laing as both dangerously creative and predictably pedestrian.

Some twenty-three years after the publication of Dr Laing's first book, it occurred to me that Laing had genuinely fulfilled the intuitions proffered by each of the reviewers. Brierley worried that he might introduce shockingly novel ideas and thus depart from the world of psychoanalysis, and, indeed, Laing did precisely that, severing his formal links with the Institute of Psycho-Analysis. And Freeman lamented that Laing had done no more than remind us of what every analyst already knew about the psychoses, an observation with which I would heartily concur (e.g., Freud, 1911; Laforgue, 1936; Rosenfeld, 1952; cf. Karon and VandenBos, 1981). I became increasingly baffled as to how Ronald Laing could be both antipathetic to psychoanalysis, and yet remain one of the most loyal adherents to psychodynamic ideas. With these confusions in the forefront of my mind, I thus invited Laing to address The Oxford Psycho-Analytical Forum about the precise nature of his relationship to the psychoanalytical community. Laing accepted the opportunity to deliver a talk on 14th November, 1983, and offered a rather uninspired title for his presentation, namely, "Theoretical Influences: From Klein to Bion".

The Tooth Falls Out

As soon as I announced Laing's imminent lecture, tickets for the event began to sell with alarming enthusiasm. Laing had not appeared in Oxford for quite some time, and the audience yearned to listen to this living legend of anti-psychiatry. As the date of the talk approached, many colleagues warned me that Laing could not be trusted to honour his public engagements. He had become intermittently alcoholic, and he often failed to appear unless one fetched him in person and then transported him bodily to the venue. Miss Mary Barnes, the great survivor of Dr Laing's experiment in community living at Kingsley Hall, in East London (Barnes and Berke, 1971), spoke to our group on 7th November, 1983, exactly one week before Laing's scheduled talk. As she departed, Miss Barnes told me that she had communicated with "Ronnie", reminding him—indeed, *urging* him—to honour his forthcoming commitment to speak at The Oxford Psycho-Analytical Forum. In the end, I became too anxious that Laing might not materialise, and so, on the day in question, a colleague and I drove to North-West London and collected him from his home at 2, Eton Road, in Chalk Farm. When we arrived, we discovered that Laing had already started drinking, and he seemed quite giddy and intoxicated. In the car ride to Oxford, he then proceeded to produce a large cigarette from his coat pocket, containing special Lebanese marijuana, and, to my utter shock, Laing then smoked this in an insouciant manner, after which he began to swig some strong Calvados! I should have urged him to drink some water instead, but I suspect that he would not have responded to that suggestion with any seriousness.

Shortly before the appointed time, I escorted Laing to the lecture theatre in the large University of Oxford building which housed both the Department of Experimental Psychology and the Department of Zoology, where an audience of roughly two hundred colleagues and admirers waited with bated breath. Before the lecture began, Laing greeted a familiar figure in the front row, Professor Shamai Davidson, the noted Israeli psychoanalyst, on sabbatical in Oxford in 1983–1984. Although Professor Davidson lived most of his life in Israel, he had actually known Laing in Scotland, many, many years beforehand. He and Laing had not seen each other for some time, and so, I invited Davidson and his wife, Mrs Jenny Davidson, to join us at the small party, scheduled to begin after the talk.

I then introduced Dr Laing to thunderous applause, and I sat in the front row, next to Shamai Davidson. I expected Laing to start lecturing straightaway, as all speakers tend to do, but instead of addressing the audience, Laing began to pace up and down the front of the hall in utter silence. We kept waiting for him to begin, but he simply shuffled to and fro, without uttering a single word. After several minutes, Professor Davidson nudged me, and whispered, "Do something!" As the chairperson, I suppose I could have intervened, yet I felt rather inhibited. After all, I could hardly say to this man, more than thirty years my senior, "Er, Dr Laing, could you please start speaking." Eventually, after what seemed an interminable period of silence, Laing proceeded to talk. He began by casting some brief aspersions against the Kleinian psychoanalysts, and then, to my surprise, he actually put his hand in his mouth, and he started to fiddle with one of his teeth.

We all gawped at this spectacle in utter amazement. Laing continued to jiggle his tooth and, eventually, he pulled it out of his mouth. I believe he then put it in his pocket and signalled to me that he wished to end the lecture at this point. He had already informed me that he did not wish to answer any questions, and, quite surprisingly, after having concluded his brief talk so abruptly, he begged me to whisk him away from the lecture theatre at once, before the crowd descended upon him with queries and requests for autographs. As he looked at me, this towering figure seemed more than unusually vulnerable.

We then retired to the home of Professor Godelieve Spaas, a most hospitable Belgian woman who taught French literature at the Roehampton Institute (later known as the University of Roehampton), and who maintained a very sympathetic attitude to psychoanalysis. As we waited for the supper which she had kindly prepared, Dr Laing began to pontificate about the power of medical doctors, boasting that physicians can do anything they choose with a patient's body. I believe that I remember his exact words when he boasted, "You can even remove somebody's brain from their head if you want to." We then sat down to dine and, before long, our distinguished guest asked the hostess for a copy of the Bible. Unquestioningly, Professor Spaas produced a Bible and handed it to R. D. Laing. He then told us that he had not brought his glasses with him, and he thus needed to borrow a pair in order to read from this ancient text. The obliging Professor Spaas lent him her reading glasses, which seemed to suit his eyes. Laing opened the Bible to the story of Jonah and, to our complete astonishment, he then began to chant the entire tale of Jonah and the whale in a very drunken and slurred voice.

After this memorable dinner party, Laing wished to go to a pub for more drinking. He became quite sullen and cross when I told him that the public houses in Oxford had already closed for the evening. He then became most irate and, eventually, he decided to create a more lively party for himself. Having no intention of catching the last train back to London, Laing took a taxi to the little village of Stadhampton in Oxfordshire, and he descended upon the residents of the Ascott Farmhouse, one of the community homes inhabited by former psychiatric patients and sponsored by the Philadelphia Association, an organisation dedicated to the promotion of Laing's work. At the Ascott Farmhouse, he drank and caroused for several hours more and, somehow, he managed to return to London in due course in order to see his patients the following day.

I did not accompany Laing through the night. I thanked him for his talk, wished him farewell, and then went to bed, thoroughly exhausted and quite disillusioned after meeting one of my long-standing heroes who had surprised me by his state of deterioration. Early the next morning, I received a frantic telephone call from our generous hostess, Professor Spaas, who delivered the *coup de grâce*. Apparently, R. D. Laing had returned to London and had taken her reading glasses with him!

The Inability to Think about Disintegration

Needless to say, my encounter with R. D. Laing unsettled me a great deal. Perhaps Laing had intended to do just that. But whatever his motivations, his visit exerted quite a strong impact on me and on those who had attended his talk.

I identified four clusters of reactions from our audience members:

1. Feelings of exploitation.
2. Aggression.
3. Humour.
4. Pathologisation.

Many people certainly felt quite exploited by Laing. They had paid money to hear him deliver a talk, and yet, the speech consisted of little more than a series of slanderous remarks about his teachers, interspersed with discomforting bouts of silence; and this made quite a number of people very angry and aggressive. Laing's mini-lecture also gave rise to a considerable amount of anxious humour, as several attendees ridiculed him for acting so strangely. Finally, many of us slid into the temptation to pathologise Laing by crowning him with any number of psychiatric labels as a rather flimsy means of briskly explaining away his seemingly odd behaviour. Only now, many long years after the event, have I come to the conscious realisation that this quartet of reactions, namely exploitation, aggression, humour, and pathologisation, constitute precisely that set of reactions which "schizophrenic" individuals can generate. Some people tend to laugh at such patients, call them names, become angry when they sense their neediness, and feel exploited by them when such troubled people unburden themselves in our care. Dr Donald Winnicott (1949b) identified a comparable phenomenon in his classic paper "Hate in the Counter-Transference".

In retrospect, I can now appreciate how I put my own internal world before Laing's in my feeble attempt to understand such an extraordinary encounter. At that time, many decades ago, I found myself quite preoccupied with two sets of affects. First, I felt sad that I had disappointed the many people who bought tickets to the talk. After all, I invited them in good faith to hear a serious presentation by an intelligent psychiatrist; instead, the audience paid hard-earned money and received only the merest shell. Second, I found myself struggling with the aftermath of watching one of my idols crash to the ground and shatter into a million tiny shards. I had always admired Laing's writings, but the man himself disappointed me very much. I suppose I harboured the phantasy that Laing's visit to Oxford might help to inject a more enlightened approach into the steeliness of the psychiatric sector, but, in fact, Laing's visit merely confirmed everyone's worst views about people who dabble in psychoanalysis or anti-psychiatry. Laing discredited both schools of thought in just one short half hour.

And yet, amid my own feelings of disappointment and embarrassment, it never occurred to me to *think* about Laing and his plight. I suppose I attributed his outlandish behaviour of pulling on his tooth and chanting the story of Jonah to the effects of the Lebanese marijuana and the Calvados, and to his general state of madness. At that time, I do not think it occurred to me to wonder *why* his tooth fell out, or why he chose to abuse himself and others in such a fashion. I found myself processing the visit of R. D. Laing in a *psychiatric* mode, rather than in a *psychoanalytical* or *psychotherapeutic* mode, as though all of Laing's insights about the origins of madness and the meanings of madness had evaded me.

Mad Behaviour as a Metaphor

In 1992, nearly one full decade after my encounter with Laing in Oxford, I attended a meeting of the Society for Existential Analysis in London—an organisation whose members had embraced the work of Laing more seriously. By that time, my conscious thinking about the seemingly strange case of this extraordinarily complicated man began to shift immeasurably. I do not usually travel in existential circles, so I have not often had an opportunity to talk to people who knew Dr Laing well and who still found him of interest. (The contemporary psychoanalysts would rarely ever refer to him.) But, at that gathering, I began to tell my R. D. Laing story, first to Dr Steven Gans, a philosopher and psychotherapist who knew Laing for many years, and then to Dr Stephen Ticktin, a psychiatrist who worked very extensively with Laing. Both Dr Gans (1992) and Dr Ticktin (1992) revealed to me that, shortly before the infamous talk in Oxford, Laing became embroiled in a fracas with a rather well-known mental health professional. Laing comported himself in a very obstreperous and insulting manner, and, in retaliation, this other man slugged Laing in the mouth, thus loosening the tooth which would eventually drop out during the Oxford lecture. Suddenly, I came to realise that the missing tooth could not simply be dismissed as an oddity of behaviour.

This unusual moment had a *history* and a *meaning*, and one could locate its history and meaning in a prior experience of interpersonal violence. Over the next few days, I began to rethink that entire Oxford evening in a more understanding and more symbolic way.

Previously, it had not occurred to me to wonder *why* Laing's tooth had become dislodged. After the Lebanese marijuana and the Calvados, it seemed somehow natural. I found myself trapped in the realm of the bizarre, rather than in the world of the thoughtful or the conceptual. But once I discerned the day residue of the mystery of the missing tooth, other aspects of this episode eventually began to make more sense. In a flash, two more bizarre components of the story suddenly acquired a rich meaning, namely, the chanting of the tale of Jonah, and the theft of Professor Spaas' reading glasses. I now began to think of those pieces of behaviour as metaphors, or as symptoms which convey powerful and rich personal meanings. After all, why did Laing choose to sing to us about *Jonah*? Why had he not regaled us with the story of Abraham and Isaac, or with that of Joseph and his coat of many colours? And why did Laing walk away with a pair of *glasses* instead of the Bible, or indeed a spoon or fork from the table?

I should like to suggest that R. D. Laing had experienced a recent trauma in two stages. First, a celebrated colleague from the mental health community had physically assaulted him, and, moreover, had humiliated him in front of other people. According to Dr Stephen Ticktin (1992), Laing certainly provoked the assault, but the punch and the embarrassment must have stung, nevertheless. Second, Laing lost a tooth in a public gathering. Perhaps this activated further feelings of shame, but, even more so, I suspect that the falling tooth stimulated quite primitive affects of bodily disintegration and death anxiety. After all, grown men of Laing's age do not usually lose teeth during their maturity. He must have wondered to what extent his body had actually begun to collapse. As we know from the work of trauma specialists (e.g., Herman, 1992), we try to cope with traumatic events through some sort of mastery. I wish to propose that by chanting the saga of Jonah, and by pilfering those reading glasses, Ronald Laing had unconsciously attempted to neutralise the trauma of having been assaulted, and then of losing his tooth as a consequence. The tale of Jonah involves a man entering the *mouth* of a whale and, inside the mouth, Jonah would have encountered large numbers of gigantic teeth. I wonder whether Laing wished to compensate for the loss of a body part by preoccupying himself with a story about a man who goes into an oral cavity and finds plenty of teeth to alleviate the anxiety of bodily disintegration. I would also hypothesise that the reading glasses represented a comparable attempt to master the two-pronged trauma of being punched in the face and of losing a tooth. Glasses can be conceptualised as extensions that one can place on the body, to guard against the loss of eyesight; furthermore, a prevalent tradition of long standing dictated that one must never punch a man who wears glasses, presumably because such well-read academic characters with poor eyesight might not be able to defend themselves physically against brawnier men who do not read. By stealing Spaas' spectacles, Laing not only added another piece to his body, but, perhaps, he protected himself in phantasy from being punched again.

The Childhood Origins of Bizarre Behaviour

Basically, I wish to postulate that, by examining the *details* of such ostensibly bizarre behaviours, one will achieve a better sense of comprehension. But the interpretation does not end here; after all, traumatic events inevitably reactivate earlier experiences.

I found myself wondering about the role of Professor Shamai Davidson in all of this. Davidson lived and worked in Israel, providing psychoanalytical treatment for survivors of the Holocaust. But, before he emigrated, he had known Ronnie when both men lived in Glasgow. Did the sudden reappearance of this old friend reactivate memories of Dr. Laing's Glaswegian childhood?

Laing's second son, Mr Adrian C. Laing, wrote an engaging memoir about his father's childhood entitled "R. D. Laing: The First Five Years" (Laing, 1991, p. 27), which contains the following poignant story concerning young Ronald and his mother, Mrs Amelia Kirkwood Laing:

> The toys which came his way were exceptional treats. There was a wooden horse, for example, which Amelia took away and destroyed when she felt wee Ronald had not only grown out of it but had become "too attached" to it. For the remainder of his days Ronnie was openly bitter about this wooden horse. To him the destruction

of his wooden horse, to which he really had grown very attached, was an act of unmitigated brutality by his mother. Wee Ronald was learning that there was more to his mother than met the eye. Another toy of wee Ronald's was a grand toy car. When this toy was broken Amelia decided to give it away, in its delapidated [*sic*] condition, to a less fortunate lady down the road for her boy to play with.

I wonder whether the presence of Shamai Davidson had lent a particular flavour to the experience of tooth loss, especially as Laing's Glasgow days consisted of the sudden loss of various physical objects.

As one delves deeper and deeper into a life history, suddenly, an infinite panoply of biographical clues becomes available in order to help us ascertain the layers of meaning. It did not take me long to discover that Mrs Amelia Laing had exerted very strict rules and regulations about young Ronald's intake of food and, more particularly, about the care of his teeth. Adrian Laing (1991, p. 28) reported that, "Wee Ronald's main crime in his early days was to disobey his mother's instructions about eating sweets and sweet things in general. There was no hiding such transgressions as Ronald's body would flare up into an acute form of eczema requiring money to be spent on ointments and bandages. It was for his own good." R. D. Laing himself wrote about his mother's control of his teeth, and about the ingestion of sugared and corrosive foods, on at least two occasions, first in his book, *The Politics of the Family and Other Essays* (Laing, 1971), and, subsequently, in his autobiography, *Wisdom, Madness and Folly: The Making of a Psychiatrist. 1927–1957* (Laing, 1985).

In the essay on "Rules and Metarules", published in his polemical 1971 collection of essays, Laing devoted considerable attention to the role of dental hygiene. He noted that,

> we may be instructed to keep our teeth and gums in good repair. It may be left to our discretion how we may do so. If our teeth get rotten, it may or may not be our fault, according to whether we have been instructed to regard this as our responsibility. However, if we are instructed to clean our teeth in a specific way, with a specific sort of toothbrush and a specific type of toothpaste, to eat certain things that are good for the teeth and not to eat other things that are bad for the teeth, together with other specific dos and don'ts, and if

we do the dos and don't do the don'ts—if, that is, we carry out our instructions to the letter—then, *if* our teeth fall out, it is not our fault. (Laing, 1971, p. 108)

This extraordinary passage certainly provides great insight into Laing's observation about the link between the loss of teeth and an infantile greedy desire to eat more naughty foods.

In his autobiography, Laing wrote at length about his mother's interdictions against such foods and beverages as margarine, sweets, and Coca-Cola. On young Ronald's first day at school, he violated Amelia's ban on cheap varieties of jam, and he gleefully tucked into a "large, very white roll with a thick layer of probably margarine and bright red jam in the middle" (Laing, 1985, p. 36). After having committed this nefarious deed, young Laing, roughly five years of age at the time, realised that he had perpetrated a grave offence. As Laing (1985, p. 36) recalled, "That was my first taste of that trashy jam that rots everyone's teeth and would ruin my mother in spending a fortune on ointments, cotton wool, white lint and pink lint and green waterproofing and bandages, one-inch and half-an-inch, if ever any of that poison got into my system." Upon returning home from school, Amelia Laing interrogated her son, and then, convinced that he had tasted the wicked jam, she dispatched him to his father, Mr David Laing, for some physical punishment. Laing (1985, p. 37) reminisced, "And that was that. When my father came home my mother told him and he gave me a 'sound' thrashing, one degree severer than a 'good' thrashing" (cf. Laing, 1991). Thus, we have now discovered the connection between the loss of teeth and physical violence.

As a young boy, Laing endured strict prohibitions against eating sweet foods. When he transgressed, however slightly, his mother threatened him that his teeth would fall out, and his father subjected him to ritualised beatings. But as a lad, his teeth did not actually fall out; his mother *told* him that they would do so. Yet in his mind, and in his experience, the beating came first, and then the anticipation of the tooth loss.

More than fifty years later, an *elder* man punched Laing for being a "naughty boy". Soon thereafter, in the midst of a lecture about his hated Kleinian psychoanalytical parents, his tooth came out of his mouth. I now realise that the tooth did not *fall* out of its own accord. Certainly, the punch had loosened the tooth, but only after jiggling it quite a bit did

Laing succeed in removing the tooth from his oral cavity, thus unconsciously proving to himself what Amelia had told him decades before, namely, that little boys who misbehave get beaten, and their teeth will fall out too.

I later discovered that Laing had a penchant for punching people in the mouth and that he had lost other teeth himself amid different brawls. Dr Stephen Ticktin discussed this matter on my behalf with Mrs Jutta Laing, the second of Laing's wives. She told Ticktin (1993) that Laing not only lost teeth but, also, that he had a false tooth, which he screwed in and out. This revelation lends further complexity to this mystery story, so much so that I cannot be certain whether Laing took a real tooth out of his mouth in Oxford, or a false one; and herein lie the pitfalls and the attractions of undertaking the necessary work of biographical reconstruction.

A New Perspective on Laing's Outrageousness

We now have a sufficient number of clues at our disposal in order to arrive at a more substantial interpretation of the episode of the disappearing tooth. Although Laing experienced a complex childhood, just as most humans will have done, the snapshot of mother and father threatening him and then beating him provides an insight into the abusive and controlling style of parenting which he endured throughout his early years. Such maternal and paternal behaviours will have occurred quite frequently during the 1920s and 1930s, characteristic of what the historian of childhood, Mr Lloyd deMause (1974, p. 52) had referred to as the *"Intrusive Mode"*, a form of parenting in which mothers and fathers would use physical punishments and threats in order to control the will of the child. Ronald Laing himself recognised that the intrusive maternal interdictions, which forced themselves upon his mind even as he ate a simple piece of bread and jam, contributed in large measure to his dour, melancholic style in adulthood. Laing (1971, p. 109) wrote that, "No one intended, when they told a little boy when and how to clean his teeth, and that his teeth would fall out if he was bad, together with Presbyterian Sunday School and all the rest of it, to produce forty-five years later the picture of a typical obsessive involutional depression. This syndrome is one of the specialities of Scotland."

This early childhood, crammed with bleakness and hostility, drove Laing into the field of psychiatry, and, in particular, onto the hospital wards where he could work with the silent catatonic patients who could not scream at him in the way that his mother had done. Upon entering a padded cell as a young psychiatrist, Laing (1985, p. 95) revealed, "I felt strangely at home there, lounging on the floor."

Yet as we know, creative work of the sort that Laing undertook in hospitals serves only as a temporary sublimation of one's own distress. Eventually, Laing underwent a personal psychoanalytical treatment with Dr Charles Rycroft, presumably in the hope that this encounter would alleviate his involutional disposition. Whether the treatment with Dr Rycroft helped Laing remains an open question; but, in view of Laing's subsequent alcoholism, philandering, broken marriages, and violent behaviours, one wonders how successfully Rycroft and Laing had worked together. Some time ago, I spoke to Dr Lawrence Goldie (1993), one of Laing's classmates at the Institute of Psycho-Analysis in the late 1950s. Goldie told me that Laing never wanted Rycroft as his psychoanalyst; instead, he had hoped to work with a Kleinian, perhaps even with Melanie Klein herself, but, for a variety of institutional reasons, this could not be arranged, and Laing felt very embittered. It may well be that this experience of rejection by the Kleinians contributed to Laing's extraordinarily vitriolic attitude towards Melanie Klein during the end of his life. In an interview with Klein's biographer, Professor Phyllis Grosskurth, Dr Laing described Melanie Klein as "an absolutely detestable person" (quoted in Grosskurth, 1982c, p. 446).

To recapitulate, in November, 1983, Laing participated in a violent affray with a senior colleague, and this caused a tooth to become loosened. Soon thereafter, he came to Oxford to speak about Melanie Klein and her followers, and during that talk about such a powerful woman whom he had come to perceive as "physically repellent" (Grosskurth, 1986, p. 447), he managed to prize the tooth from his mouth. In other words, Laing had been a naughty boy, quite verbally aggressive to the senior colleague, and this man punched him in response. And as we know, Amelia Laing always told her son that his teeth would fall out if he misbehaved. Thus, I suspect that Laing pulled out his own loose tooth *during* the lecture about the bad Kleinian mothers in order to fulfil this injunction from early childhood, thus proving that, in spite of his analysis with Rycroft, the voice of Amelia still held young Ronald in its grip. Boys who misbehave really do have to lose their teeth.

At the supper party which followed, in the presence of an old friend from Glasgow who specialised in victimology, Laing became aggressive and retaliatory, revelling in thoughts about removing someone's brain. He then chanted the biblical story of Jonah, and "accidentally" walked off with a pair of reading glasses, becoming increasingly belligerent and intoxicated as the evening wore on. I now understand this alcoholic binge and the talk about extracting brains as an attempt at a sort of *psychic leucotomy*. If only Laing could have rendered his own brain inactive, he would not have needed to think about the fight with his colleague, or about the loss of his tooth. But the missing tooth proved too upsetting, and, in an attempt to master the trauma, he magically transported himself into the mouth of a whale, replete with large, strong teeth.

Conclusion

In the preceding pages, I have endeavoured to offer a psychoanalytical, psychobiographical reconstruction of this particular moment from the life of R. D. Laing. I appreciate that various readers will no doubt have further formulations of this complex matter. I hope and trust that through conversation and communication, we can achieve even further elaboration and refinement. But nevertheless, more saliently, I wish to underscore several important points:

1. Bizarre behaviour stirs up powerful emotions, such as revulsion.
2. When we cannot think symbolically about the bizarre, we tend to distance ourselves through diagnosis and pathologisation.
3. Once we uncover biographical material, the bizarre suddenly becomes quite sensible.
4. Bizarre behaviour often results from a nexus of violent childhood events which become reactivated during specific moments in adult life.
5. Every detail of the bizarre behaviour has resulted from careful overdetermination.

6. Perhaps the most unthinkable bizarre behaviours follow in the aftermath of experiences in which actual bodily parts have become removed or have disappeared.

In a sense, these points serve merely as a reminder of what Freud had already taught us, and what Laing himself had restated so beautifully in *The Divided Self: A Study of Sanity and Madness*. Perhaps what disturbed me most about the evening with R. D. Laing may be the fact that he, a proven expert in the unravelling of the bizarre, had become so very entrapped in its vicious web. If only I had enjoyed a more sophisticated understanding of psychodynamics back in 1983, I might well have felt more charitably towards Dr Laing.

In the spirit of extending Laing's timeless work on schizophrenia, I wish to use his missing tooth and the anxieties which followed as a metaphor for the ubiquitous experience of fears of bodily disintegration in schizophrenic patients. Let us recall the eight-year-old boy to whom I have referred as "Hubert", quoted in the epigraph to this chapter. Hubert suffered from a childhood form of schizophrenia, and he experienced frequent, terrifying hallucinations of being murdered and abducted. During a pottery group, Hubert made a penile-like snake. After the clay hardened in the kiln, Hubert smashed the snake on the floor, whispering, "The clay snake fell to pieces. I am in pieces. I am dead." If Laing had not died so prematurely in 1989, he could have helped Hubert enormously, because this tragic communication about shattered snakes would not have frightened him. Laing would have regarded Hubert's speech not as a confirmation of a clinical diagnosis of schizophrenia but, rather, as a communication that needs to be addressed. In the wake of more recent psychoanalytical thinking on trauma and infancy, I tried to apply Laing's work by talking to Hubert about this experience of disintegration.

It soon emerged that Hubert's gesture of smashing the snake represented a wish to destroy the abusive penis that had actually buggered him; and it could also be understood at a more primitive level as a concretisation of the experience of being "dropped" during infancy, a series of painful moments which made him feel disintegrated and dead.

Ronald Laing has certainly gifted us many tools for understanding the most horrifying layers of psychotic fragmentation, and his life serves as a chilling reminder that in order to be of use to our schizophrenic patients and to other people suffering from extreme anguish, we must first relinquish the bizarre aspects of ourselves. Next, we must then acquire an unstinting capacity to bear someone else's disintegration and begin to *think* about that seemingly bizarre disintegration, rather than act it out, as Laing himself seems to have done. Once we have neutralised our own infantile anxieties, our teeth need not become dislodged before their time.

CONCLUSION

How to Be Intimate with a Corpse: The Role of Psychoanalytical Historiography

In this extremely digitalised modern era, full of computers and laptops and mobile telephones, as well as iPads and iPods and social media accounts such as Facebook and Twitter and Instagram, not to mention online banking and shopping and, moreover, untold numbers of emails and text messages and apps, why on earth would anyone wish to study ancient history?

After all, who in his or her right mind would dare to waste time reading the complete works of William Shakespeare in the First Folio Edition of 1623? Any savvy student of English literature could readily google a relevant Wikipedia page in a mere matter of seconds and thus not have to visit the British Library in order to plough through passage after passage of obscure, out-of-date language about people who lived hundreds and hundreds of years ago. Surely, youngsters today should devote their time instead to the reversal of climate change and to the eradication of discrimination and global terrorism. What good will it do to immerse ourselves in the lives of our ancestors?

Indeed, in this remarkably trendy, up-to-date moment in time, we need to craft modern solutions and prepare for the future, rather than drown ourselves in the past. For instance, I can think of no biomedical researchers, many of whom have toiled full-time to produce efficacious versions of a coronavirus vaccine, who would have devoted their days and nights during a pandemic lockdown to reading dusty copies of *The British Medical Journal* from the 1860s or issues of *The Lancet* from the 1890s. Modern scientists will concentrate instead on the most current, online publications from competitor laboratories across the planet. I have certainly not met any vaccinologists who prefer to spend their spare time trawling through the musings of the ancient Greek physician Hippocrates.

Certainly, I do appreciate that in order to navigate the twenty-first century, scientists and other professionals must be as up-to-date as possible.

But, although few physicians nowadays will be able to quote Hippocrates in the original ancient Greek, every single member of that profession must, nonetheless, adhere to the so-called "Hippocratic Oath" and must promise, first and foremost, that he or she will never harm his or her patients. In fact, the very heart of medical ethics and the high standards of professional practice can be traced back to ancient times; and our modern healthcare professionals would never have developed the capacity to interact in such a vigilant, patient-centred manner without having learned from the insights and the errors of those who will have preceded them.

Indeed, during the apex of the COVID-19 pandemic, which claimed the lives of millions upon millions of citizens worldwide in such a cruel manner, I experienced much daily regret that more people had not studied the works of the nineteenth-century, Hungarian-born physician, Dr Ignác Fülöp Semmelweis[1] (1861), who helped doctors to save the lives of their patients on obstetric wards by insisting upon meticulous hand-washing as a means of stopping the spread of deadly streptococcal infections (cf. Kahr, 2021a). Back then, few physicians scrubbed their hands thoroughly prior to medical examinations or surgical procedures and, hence, medics became the cause of death and not the cure!

Thus, we might well be able to learn a great deal about improving healthcare practice by immersing ourselves in the contributions of our predecessors ... but, *only* if we study history very carefully.

Although I would regard myself as a great admirer of modernity and cutting-edge science and would even describe myself as a "fan" of the very intelligent and original work undertaken nowadays, I also remain passionate about the need to return to history as well, so that we can still harvest the wisdom of the past and not repeat stupid errors again and again and again, as so many of our public health advisers and politicians seem to do daily as a matter of course (cf. Calvert and Arbuthnott, 2021).

Needless to say, scientists must work in the most present-day manner imaginable. Otherwise, without practitioners whom we might describe as being "on the ball", we may all be slaughtered by dangerous world leaders who recommend that we should imbibe bleach as a home remedy for COVID.

But what about those of us who work in the field of mental health, especially the small community of practitioners who have trained in the specialities known as psychoanalytical psychotherapy or psychoanalysis? Surely, we, too, must read the contemporary clinical and experimental literature, rather than drown ourselves in old copies of the *Internationale Zeitschrift für ärztliche Psychoanalyse* from the 1910s.

As a true, old-fashioned bibliophile, addicted to both reading and researching, I endeavour to absorb as much of the current mental health literature as possible. And I do my very best to learn about all of the new forms of psychotherapeutic styles and interventions which seem to be created here and there on a daily basis. This week alone I have encountered recent publications about such new forms of psychotherapy as cognitive hypnotherapy, commitment-assisted outpatient therapy, critical social justice therapy, dynamic-deconstructive psychotherapy, Mindful Interbeing Mirror Therapy, biodynamic psychotherapy, pluralistic therapy, radically-open dialectical behavioural therapy, right brain psychotherapy, foundational story psychotherapy, transdiagnostic cognitive behavioural therapy, exploratory goal corrected psychotherapy, Repetitive Visualisation Therapy, and far too many other versions.

The more I study such new ideas, the more I wonder, "Why on earth do these practitioners not simply read the works of Sigmund Freud?" After all, the late Professor Freud taught us long ago that if we sit quietly and listen carefully and study our patients' *histories*, then we will obtain all of the data that we need to stimulate a process of catharsis and insight, which will help to cure both the neuroses and the psychoses. In fact, in my estimation, every single psychoanalytical practitioner might well define himself or herself as a *clinical historian* of the mind, because those of us who work from a Freudian lens spend our days "taking histories", archiving data about our patients' infancies and childhoods, and learning from their pasts. Whatever our views about Hippocrates or Semmelweis, we have a professional clinical obligation to be as historically accurate and astute and interested in our patients as we can possibly be.

Many years ago, I had the opportunity to speak to a colleague who worked as an "integrative psychotherapist". This gentleman had never studied psychoanalysis formally; instead, he merely dabbled in the literature, and he spent most of his time congressing with humanistic psychotherapists, existential psychotherapists, body psychotherapists, and those of every shape and size. Moreover, he never read the foundational historical literature of the modern mental health profession. During his mid-seventies, this colleague confessed that he felt very guilty that he had never absorbed the works of Freud properly, and therefore, he decided that, prior to his death, he would treat himself to a complete set of Freud's works in English and that he would read each of the twenty-three volumes in turn (excluding, of course, the twenty-fourth volume, which comprises a meticulous index). Extraordinarily, this psychotherapist then did so and he confessed that he had, at long last, come to appreciate the true genius of Freud and that he deeply wished that he had imbibed these collected works many decades earlier.

When I began teaching psychoanalytical theory at a generalist college many years ago, my students expressed tremendous hesitation and, often, suspicion towards Freud: "Surely, Brett, he's rather old-fashioned? Hasn't he been proven to be incorrect? Shouldn't we read the more modern research literature?" Needless to say, I persevered with my teaching, and it pleases me to report that by having introduced my students to the biography of Freud—namely, to the gripping details of his challenging and inspiring life—they gradually began to fall in love with him as a person and then, ultimately, as a theoretician and clinician. Rather than having inaugurated my first lecture on Freud for students by defining the "id", the "ego", and the "superego", I would always describe instead, in much detail, precisely how Freud and his family had escaped from the Nazis in 1938. This approach certainly helped to humanise Freud and to draw the students into his world with a greater sense of interest and authenticity. Indeed, I learned very early on in my career that biographical studies and historical studies need not be dismissed as mere objects of geeky obsessionality but, rather, that such ancient data can truly help to humanise important figures and thus generate even more interest in their bodies of work.

In other words, I would like to believe that I taught my students how to become more intimate with corpses!

Throughout this book, *Hidden Histories of British Psychoanalysis: From Freud's Death Bed to Laing's Missing Tooth*, I have endeavoured to share some of my archival research, my oral history interviews, and my good old-fashioned readings of ancient, out-of-print published materials in order to bring some of these dead icons back to life. Rather than provide an entire history of psychoanalysis—a subject that would require multitudinous volumes—I have chosen, instead, to focus on some leading figures who, from their homes and offices in Great Britain, have gifted much wisdom to us all.

For instance, having examined the ways in which the open-minded, German-speaking Sigmund Freud transformed his practice in the wake of the First World War by studying English, in order to accept new referrals from both the United Kingdom and the United States of America, I learned that one can indeed expand one's working life in helpful and creative ways. If Freud had not begun to treat such influential individuals as the American-born William Bullitt—a noted diplomat and politician who helped Freud escape from Vienna—one doubts that he would have survived. Thus, by having studied Freud's "Anglicisation" of his practice, I believe that I learned more about how best to tolerate and, indeed, to flourish as well as possible during that unusually ugly chapter of history, which erupted in March, 2020, when I had to shut down my good old-fashioned "in-person" consulting room and turn it into a "virtual" one, having elected to speak with all of my patients by telephone throughout the course of the coronavirus pandemic (Kahr, 2021a). Although I certainly would have preferred to have continued working "in-person", rather than "remotely" during that time, I did draw upon Freud greatly; and although I could not sit close by to any of my analysands at the height of the upsurge of COVID-19, I did enjoy the fact that I own two rare statuettes of Sigmund Freud, which sit perched on my office table, and which I stare upon dozens and dozens of times per day.

The great British psychoanalysts (including the London-based Sigmund Freud of 1938–1939), whose lives and works I have examined in this volume, have always served as great sources of inspiration. Just as a young baby needs a good mother or a good father with whom he or she can identify, and whose health and strength and wisdom can serve as a source of positive identification, so, too, do we, as mental health workers, require impressive great-grandmothers and great-grandfathers who can function in our minds as role models. I know that, by having spent precious time with Enid Balint and John Bowlby and Marion Milner and their contemporaries, I have become a much more competent person, as these extraordinary individuals warmly shared their wisdom and their rich learning lessons in such a generous fashion.

As psychoanalytical practitioners, we know only too well how, as treatment progresses, our patients will begin to identify with us and will often become more like us in many respects (i.e., more reliable, more compassionate, more thoughtful, and so forth). But a healthy patient, spurred by a healthy psychoanalyst or psychotherapist, must also learn how to *dis-identify* as well, and should not be required to become a photocopy of us. Likewise, historical figures serve as great role models, not only about how to be but, also, about how *not* to be. And for that reason, I have included two chapters in this book about the so-called "Bad Boys" of British psychoanalysis, namely, Mohammed Masud Raza Khan and Ronald David Laing.

It pleases me to report that, across more than forty years of clinical practice, I have never engaged in a sexual affair with a patient, as Khan had done, nor have I ever arrived drunk or hung over in the consulting room, as Laing had done. Thankfully, almost none of our colleagues have ever slept with their analysands or become drunkards. Nevertheless, we must appreciate that such violations do occur from time to time and we cannot but regard those unethical practices as sources of deep concern and anguish and, indeed, shame for our entire professional community. But although most of us do not violate boundaries in that "bad boy" way, we all have much to learn from men such as Khan and Laing by recognising the dangerous consequences of their actions and by endeavouring to understand the *origins* of such forensic behaviours. Moreover, in spite of their ethical infractions, Khan and Laing continue to offer much wisdom, because, in their *non*-sexual, *non*-alcoholic states of mind, those two men wrote some brilliant books and papers about madness, which still have the potential to inspire us to this very day.

After having read the initial typescript of this book, our publisher, Mrs Kate Pearce (2021) of Phoenix Publishing House, shared a most relevant anecdote with me. She reminisced about a colleague who had once attended a lecture by R. D. Laing and who reported that Laing had ended that particular talk rather abruptly, after only a few minutes, just as he had done when addressing The Oxford Psycho-Analytical Forum, back in 1983. Kate Pearce's colleague recalled that the chairperson of this other brief Laingian lecture comforted the audience and reassured them that, in spite of the disruption of the talk, they should still feel grateful to have enjoyed the unique privilege of meeting a remarkable historical figure, if only for a brief period of time.

It may be that those men and women who had paid good money to listen to Laing in Oxford did, in fact, experience some gratitude. After Laing interrupted his tooth-driven lecture, I suspected that I would be inundated with requests for a refund. But, in fact, not a single member of the audience asked to be repaid. They appreciated that Laing had "broken down" in some way; they responded sympathetically; and they took some comfort from knowing that they had enjoyed the special experience of meeting this great genius in real life, if merely for a brief moment. And, I must underscore, in spite of Laing's shockingly unprofessional behaviour on that memorable day, his work as a critic of traditional psychiatry helped to transform modern mental health and, in fact, to champion the pathway for the growth of psychotherapy.

So, we all have much to learn from our ancestors, whether they behaved well or whether they behaved atrociously.

Having worked with many troubled patients over the years, I have done my best to offer as much insight and concern and care and support and reliability as possible. Happily, I acquired much of my clinical wisdom from my teachers and my colleagues, for which I remain eternally grateful. But I also had the privilege to benefit from my encounters with Mrs Balint and Dr Bowlby and so many hundreds of other great figures—all now deceased, alas—and thankfully, I know that I learned even more from these historical personalities and that I came to feel more genuinely immersed in this profession.

For instance, if I had not met Enid Balint—the founder of couple psychoanalysis in Great Britain—I might never have trained at the Tavistock Marital Studies Institute. And had I not done so, I would have pursued a much more restricted career in terms of the range of patients with whom I have worked and the numbers of dear colleagues whom I met, many of whom have become much-appreciated and loving friends to me and to my family. And had I not met John Bowlby, I doubt that I would have become involved in The Bowlby Centre—a clinical organisation that has brought me much professional satisfaction over the decades. When I first began to correspond with Mrs Balint, little did I realise that I would one day present the Twenty-First Enid Balint Memorial Lecture (Kahr, 2016b); likewise, when I first interviewed Dr Bowlby, I certainly could not have guessed that I would one day become a plenary speaker at more than one John Bowlby Memorial Conference (e.g., Kahr, 2007a, 2007b, 2014a, 2015c). These occasions certainly prompted me to write some of my more challenging papers (e.g., Kahr, 2012a, 2017a, 2022b), and I would never have done so without the magnificent experience of sitting at the feet of these incomparable great-grandparental figures while in my youth.

Speaking on an even more personal level, I remain immensely grateful to these ancient icons for a multitude of reasons. Not only had these superstars taught me so much about psychoanalysis and welcomed me so warmly into their orbits, and, moreover, helped me to understand their contributions more fully, I must report that at least one of the remarkable figures in this book actually changed my *private* life as well.

As a young boy, I studied not only history with great passion but, also, music, and I played the piano energetically for many long years. I never intended to become a professional pianist—that pathway never quite appealed to me—indeed, I always yearned to do something much more psychological, which might ease human distress. Of course, I appreciate that musicians do have the capacity to alleviate suffering by bringing hope and pleasure, and I respect that immensely. But I always wished to make a contribution through psychology rather than through the keyboard. Nevertheless, music remained an ongoing passion, not only the works of the classical geniuses such as

Wolfgang Amadeus Mozart and Ludwig van Beethoven but, also, the great composers of operettas and musical theatre as well. Therefore, one can only imagine my delight and surprise when, during a memorable conversation with Marion Milner (1987c), she revealed that her hero, Donald Winnicott, had always yearned to write an operetta in the style of Gilbert and Sullivan ... in his spare time. As a huge fan of "G. and S." in my own right, this revelation intrigued me tremendously and gave me permission to devote even more time to my own musical passions, even though I had already committed myself fully to a career in mental health.

I can reveal quite happily that, had Milner not granted me a quiet sense of permission to become even more musical, like the great Winnicott, I doubt that I would have socialised quite so much in musical circles during younger years and, had I not done so, I suspect that I would not have met one especially gifted professional singer who would, in due course, become my wife!

I hope and trust that this collection of essays about the history of British psychoanalysis will offer us all some nuggets of wisdom and inspiration and will prompt us to learn more from our predecessors than we have done thus far. I have never tired of reading and rereading the works of the many individuals mentioned in this book, and each time I study these ancient writings, I find that I absorb even more insights than I have done previously. As clinical historians who spend our days researching the early lives of our *patients*, let us also turn our attention to the early lives of our professional *ancestors* and incorporate as much of their great wisdom and playfulness as we possibly can.

Notes

Chapter Three

1. We cannot easily ascertain the precise number of patients with whom Dr Donald Winnicott worked across his long clinical career, but he certainly offered consultations to extremely large numbers. We do know that, in 1948, in the course of his address as Chair of the Medical Section of the British Psychological Society, Winnicott (1948b, p. 230), estimated that he had already treated "about 20,000 cases". If each of these 20,000 cases had one or two parents, it would not be unreasonable to estimate that Winnicott might have interviewed some 40,000 parents, not least as he still continued working up until his death in 1971 and would, therefore, have met with many more parental couples after 1948. In a letter to a colleague, written in 1949, Winnicott (1949d) noted that his specialist psychological department at the Paddington Green Children's Hospital processed an average of 3,000 cases per annum. And more than twenty years later, in 1971, his former patient and long-standing colleague Masud Khan (1971a, p. xviii) reported, in French, that, in fact, Winnicott worked with some *"soixante mille personnes environ"* ["around sixty thousand persons"]—including babies, children, mothers, fathers, parental couples, and grandparents—a figure then confirmed by Winnicott's

widow, Mrs Clare Winnicott (1979). I know of no other mental health clinician in history to have amassed such extensive experience.
2. In 1896, the year of Dr Donald Winnicott's birth, Plymouth had not yet achieved official city status; hence, it would be more appropriate to describe Plymouth as a town.
3. Unless otherwise specified, the biographical information contained in this essay derives either from my single-volume biography of Dr Donald Winnicott, published in 1996 (Kahr, 1996a), or, more often, from my extensive multi-volume study of Winnicott's life, currently in progress. Furthermore, in order to differentiate references between publications by Dr Donald Winnicott and Mrs Clare Winnicott, I have deployed the full name, "Clare Winnicott", when citing her writings.
4. In order to distinguish between the letters written by Mr James Strachey and those penned by his wife, Mrs Alix Strachey, I have deployed both their forenames and their surnames in the references.
5. As I revealed in 2011, Dr Donald Winnicott not only employed his secretary to undertake typing and administration, but he also offered this woman psychoanalytical sessions; therefore, in view of her status as a patient of sorts, I have elected to disguise her name for reasons of clinical confidentiality, and hence, she has become known by the pseudonymous designation of "Mrs Gladys Watson-Dixon" (Kahr, 2011).
6. In 1932, Dr Donald Winnicott and Mrs Alice Winnicott had moved from Surbiton in Surrey to Hampstead in North-West London.
7. Dr Donald Winnicott suffered several coronaries towards the end of his life, while married to his second wife. In 1968, during the midst of his lecture trip to New York City, he did succumb to a particularly massive coronary. Mrs Clare Winnicott, who accompanied her husband, cared for him with dedication and vigilance. Although Dr Lawrence Goldie (1994) did not provide a date of his conversation with Winnicott, it seems likely that the two men spoke some time prior to 1968.
8. I have reproduced Mrs Clare Winnicott's conversational speech exactly as it has appeared in the published version, in spite of the occasional repetition of words.
9. At the time of the launch party for *The Standard Edition of the Complete Psychological Works of Sigmund Freud*, twenty-three volumes had already appeared in print between 1953 and 1966 (Freud, 1953a, 1953b, 1953c, 1953d, 1955a, 1955b, 1955c, 1955d, 1957a, 1957b, 1958, 1959a, 1959b, 1960a, 1960b, 1961a, 1961b, 1962, 1963a, 1963b, 1964a, 1964b, 1966). The twenty-fourth volume, comprising the indices, would not be published until 1974 (Freud, 1974).

10. In his landmark textbook on *Marital Tensions: Clinical Studies Towards a Psychological Theory of Interaction*, Dr Henry V. Dicks (1967, p. 74), one of the progenitors of marital psychotherapy in Great Britain, spoke briefly of "the joint 'false self' of the couple", albeit without referring at all to the work of Dr Donald Winnicott. Nevertheless, Dicks wrote with prescience about the commonality of the "collusive marriage", in which each member of the couple invests a great deal of energy, "in the massive effort at dissociation or splitting required to keep it in being".

Chapter Four

1. During the course of my research on the life and work of Dr Donald Winnicott, I discovered several unpublished letters between Winnicott and the grandmother of The Piggle, in which these two concerned individuals corresponded about the case of a little boy whose parents had died in the Holocaust. Although while undertaking my historical investigations I always endeavour to provide detailed scholarly references to all facts, on this occasion, owing to confidentiality, I cannot readily reveal the source of these letters, as this would expose the true identity of The Piggle and her family, which Winnicott had worked so hard to preserve. The letters from which this material derives can be found in a public archive; however, I trust that fellow clinicians (as well as fellow historians) who might also come to discover this stash of correspondence will also honour the pledge of confidentiality.
2. Across the years, I have had the privilege of interviewing more than fifty of Dr Donald Winnicott's former analysands. In my publications, I have certainly never exposed their real names; however, one of my interviewees, Mrs Jane Shore Nicholas, the former Jane Khan—sometime wife of the psychoanalyst Mr Masud Khan—had already discussed her story in great detail with the American psychoanalyst and scholar, Dr Linda Hopkins (2006), and had granted Hopkins permission to print the story in full in her biography of Masud Khan; consequently, I have, on this occasion, referred to Jane Shore by her true name.
3. In the original version of this letter of 12th July, 1965, written solely to "Mrs Piggle", Dr Donald Winnicott (1965g) reported, "When I read your letter I do not feel absolutely in despair about the way things are going."
4. It would not be entirely unreasonable to hypothesise that Dr Donald Winnicott might have had to insert drops into his eyes in the midst of psychoanalytical sessions. Several decades ago, Ms Rosemarie Krausz,

then a trainee in the Department of Psychiatry at the Sir Mortimer B. Davis Jewish General Hospital in Montreal, Quebec, in Canada, received a diagnosis of Bell's palsy and had to use eye drops every thirty minutes, over a period of fourteen days, even while facilitating psychotherapy sessions (Brown and Krausz, 1984).

5. One could pontificate at length about the unconscious meanings of The Piggle's engagement with this particular toy. The fact that she enjoyed playing with a figurine of a little boy pulling a tiny girl on a sleigh might symbolise her capacity to tolerate two young children sharing the same space (i.e., working through the sibling rivalry). Alternatively, one might argue that The Piggle enjoyed the notion of the boy *pulling* the girl as a means of control.

6. Please refer to Endnote 1 of this chapter for more details about this piece of biographical data.

7. Needless to say, for reasons of confidentiality, I have used the designations of "Mr Piggle" and "Mrs Piggle". In the original letters, Dr Donald Winnicott addressed the parents by their titles and by their surnames at the outset of their correspondence.

8. In order to differentiate between publications by Dr Donald Winnicott and those written by his second wife, Mrs Clare Winnicott, I have, where necessary, inserted the name "Clare" into certain references, in order to provide greater clarity as to the authorship (cf. Endnote 3 to Chapter Three).

9. In the original American edition of the book, the typesetters misspelled the surname of Mr Raymond D. Shepherd, a member of the Winnicott Publications Committee, as "Shepard". Although the book renders his name correctly on the "Contents" page, one finds his surname misspelled as co-author of the "Preface". A member of the Independent Group of the British Psycho-Analytical Society, Shepherd devoted much of his life to the editing of many of Dr Donald Winnicott's posthumously published collections of papers, notably, *Deprivation and Delinquency* (Winnicott, 1984); *Home is Where We Start From: Essays by a Psychoanalyst* (Winnicott, 1986b); *Babies and Their Mothers* (Winnicott, 1987); *Human Nature* (Winnicott, 1988); *Psycho-Analytic Explorations* (Winnicott, 1989); *Talking to Parents* (Winnicott, 1993); and *Thinking About Children* (Winnicott, 1996).

10. In the original German version of Dr Muriel Gardiner's (1978, p. 66) memoir, she described her request for occasional sessions with Dr Ruth Mack Brunswick as "nur auf eigenes Ersuchen".

Chapter Five

1. In order to preserve space, I have abbreviated the full title of this document, which reads, in its unexpurgated form: *The Book of the Foundation of the Church of St. Bartholomew, London: Rendered into Modern English. From the Original Latin Version Preserved in the British Museum, Numbered Vespasian B. IX, by Mr. Humphrey H. King and Mr. William Barnard for Use in the 'Records of St. Bartholomew's Priory'.*
2. Professor William Osler's famous and influential textbook appeared in many, many editions. I have selected the fifth edition of 1905 (Osler, 1905)—published in the year of Osler's election as Regius Professor at the University of Oxford—and, also, the eleventh edition of 1930 (Osler and McCrae, 1930)—printed after Osler's death—for comparison, as these volumes framed the years of John Bowlby's childhood, youth, and early professional training. Osler's (1905, p. 1129) injunction that "Complaints of children should not be too seriously considered" appears completely unchanged in the later edition, published some twenty-five years hence (cf. Osler and McCrae, 1930, p. 1139). In view of this, we may better appreciate the truly stagnant nature of child mental health work during that time.
3. Theodore J. Faithfull, the Principal of The Priory Gate School, had trained in veterinary medicine and then became a member of the Royal College of Veterinary Surgeons. He maintained a long-standing interest in psychoanalysis, in depth psychology (e.g., Faithfull, 1927), and in Professor Sigmund Freud himself. In 1938, Faithfull (1938) published a book on *The Mystery of the Androgyne: Three Papers on the Theory and Practice of Psycho-Analysis*. A copy of this book still stands on the shelf of Freud's library at his London home, now the Freud Museum London at 20, Maresfield Gardens. One suspects that Faithfull had sent this to Freud, perhaps as an arrival present. Unfortunately, the book does not contain a personal inscription.
4. The Priory Gate School closed officially in 1930 (Faithfull, 1938). Hence, Dr John Bowlby had the good fortune to have worked there only a short while before it ceased formal operations.
5. Although Dr John Bowlby held Mrs Melanie Klein in considerable esteem as his sometime clinical supervisor, he also mocked her ferociously in private conversation (e.g., Kahr, 1984, 2009a, 2022b; cf. Bowlby, 1956). In a rare commentary, safely tucked away in a book which appeared in the year of Klein's death, Bowlby (1960, p. 46) dared to write, "Although I am in close sympathy with her general approach I do not find the details

of her formulation very convincing", and that, "In my view little progress will be made in the theoretical debates which have arisen around Melanie Klein's hypotheses until systematic observation, and where permissible experiments, are made on infants in their first year" (Bowlby, 1960, p. 46).

6. Dr Robert Karen (1994), author of a very useful study on the history of attachment theory, did not cite any publications by Dr John Bowlby prior to 1940 (e.g., Bowlby, 1940b), and, certainly, he made no reference to Bowlby's (1939a) chapter on childhood hysteria, or to his commentary on evacuation (Bowlby, Miller, and Winnicott, 1939). To compound matters, Bowlby himself made scant reference to his own papers of 1939. For instance, he never included any citation of his writings of 1939 in some of his classic works (e.g., Bowlby, 1940a, 1951a, 1969, 1973, 1980, 1988). To his great credit, however, the Dutch psychologist Dr Frank van der Horst (2011) has made a reference—albeit a brief one—to both of Bowlby's important contributions on the psychology of separation dating from 1939.

7. To my great surprise, several eminent, scholarly, senior British psychiatrists (including two child psychiatrists) have told me that they had never encountered Dr John Bowlby's (1939a) essay on "Hysteria in Children", nor had they even known of Dr Ronald Gordon's (1939) edited textbook, *A Survey of Child Psychiatry*. In view of the scarcity of copies of that important tome on child psychiatry, the family of Dr John Bowlby kindly granted me permission to arrange for the chapter on "Hysteria in Childhood" to be reprinted in a special edition of the journal *Attachment: New Directions in Psychotherapy and Relational Psychoanalysis* (Bowlby, 1939b; cf. Kahr, 2019c, 2019d, 2019e).

8. For further insight into this subject, I warmly recommend the following references: Isaacs, 1940; Bathurst, Brown, Bowlby, Bullen, Fairbairn, Isaacs, Mercer, Rooff, and Thouless, 1941; Winnicott, 1943, 1945b, 1948a; Dow and Brown, 1946; Jackson, 1985; Welshman, 2010; Summers, 2011.

9. One could, I suppose, argue that, in 1939, Dr John Bowlby also launched a third declaration of war through the publication of his first full-length book—rather too little known—entitled *Personal Aggressiveness and War* (Durbin and Bowlby, 1939). This text deserves a much more substantial analysis, but one can, nevertheless, summarise at least one aspect of its subversive importance by reminding ourselves that Bowlby wrote this book in concert with his great friend, the brilliant economist and budding politician Mr Evan Durbin who, in 1938, had served as best man at Bowlby's

wedding to Miss Ursula Longstaff (Ursula Bowlby, 1938). A brilliant attempt at divining the psychological origins of warfare, this book developed out of essays that each man had completed the previous year (Bowlby, 1938; Durbin, 1938), and which had appeared in another long-forgotten book entitled *War and Democracy: Essays on the Causes and Prevention of War* (Durbin, Bowlby, Thomas, Jay, Fraser, Crossman, and Catlin, 1938). I regard the publication of these works with Evan Durbin as a third salvo, not only because of their remarkable perceptivity but, also, because these contributions broke with psychoanalytical tradition. Previously, virtually every psychoanalyst who had ever published in concert with someone else had done so with a fellow Freudian (e.g., Freud, Ferenczi, Abraham, Simmel, and Jones, 1919; Ferenczi and Rank, 1924; Alexander and Staub, 1929; Hitschmann and Bergler, 1934; Klein and Riviere, 1937). But Bowlby dared to collaborate outside the psychoanalytical ghetto by working with an economist! In doing so, he very much underscored his independence of mind and his capacity to speak in his own voice, having no need to conform to the publication exigencies of colleagues within the British Psycho-Analytical Society.

10. In his interview with the journalist Mrs Rosemary Dinnage, for the magazine *New Society*, Dr John Bowlby repeated this very same claim about The Priory Gate School, noting that, "I've often said that everything I've done since stemmed from that six months" (quoted in Dinnage, 1979, p. 323).
11. Dr John Bowlby lamented not only the punitive pedagogy promoted by twentieth-century physicians such as Dr Truby King but, also, the advice of such nineteenth-century experts as Dr Daniel Gottlieb Moritz Schreber who promoted the use of restraints in the misguided hope of straightening children's bodies (Dinnage, 1979; cf. Niederland, 1959a, 1959b, 1963, 1974; Schatzman, 1973a, 1973b; Israëls, 1989a, 1989b; Lothane, 1992).

Chapter Six

1. Lady Prudence Pelham, born on 6th April, 1910, and thus three years John Bowlby's junior, could readily trace her aristocratic lineage to the twelfth century. Her ancestors included John Dudley, the duke of Northumberland, who engineered the usurpation of the English monarchy in 1553 by placing his daughter-in-law, Lady Jane Grey, upon the throne. Both Northumberland, and, subsequently his son, Guilford Dudley, and, also, his daughter-in-law, Lady Jane, would all be beheaded at the command

of Queen Mary. In many respects, Dr John Bowlby's courtship of Lady Prudence provides an indication of the gentrified circle in which Bowlby himself grew up, in part, as a result of being the child of the pre-eminent English surgeon Sir Anthony Bowlby, who had served the royal household of King George V. Lady Prudence Pelham ultimately married a younger man, Mr Guy Rawstron Branch, who eventually became a flying officer and fought in the Battle of Britain, and who died—killed in action—in 1940, while still in his twenties. Sadly, Lady Prudence also died young, at the age of forty-two years, on 13th October, 1952. Although I did not know this at the time, Lady Prudence, Bowlby's intended, had an indirect connection to Dr Donald Winnicott. Prior to her engagement to Bowlby, Lady Prudence enjoyed a relationship with the artist and poet Mr David Jones, a veteran of the Great War, who, after suffering from a serious breakdown, ultimately became someone with whom Winnicott met and corresponded on a multitude of occasions (e.g., Jones, 1943a, 1943b, 1943c, 1944; Kahr, 1996a). Interestingly, neither Sir Richard Bowlby (Richard Bowlby, 2015) nor Xenia, Lady Bowlby (Xenia Bowlby, 2015)—son and daughter-in-law of Dr John Bowlby—knew of this engagement.

2. Many years later, while studying Mrs Ursula Bowlby's desk diaries in the Rare Materials Rooms at the Wellcome Library in London, I discovered the following entry for Sunday, 29th January, 1995, at 10.00 a.m.:

"Winnicott / Riviére man ...
BRETT CARR"
(*1995*, 1995).

Mrs Bowlby had misspelled my surname, and had, also, inserted an unnecessary accent in Mrs Joan Riviere's surname.

3. Indeed, although we tend to think of Dr John Bowlby and Dr Donald Winnicott as working quite independently of one another, the two men had joined forces with fellow child psychiatrist Dr Emanuel Miller, the father of Sir Jonathan Miller, the polymathic physician and theatrical director, to write an important letter of concern to the *British Medical Journal*, warning against the potentially adverse consequences of the plan to evacuate London's children during World War II (Bowlby, Miller, and Winnicott, 1939; cf. Kahr, 2015b). Additionally, both Bowlby (1939a) and Winnicott (1939a) contributed important chapters to the very first British textbook on child psychiatry—a landmark publication—Dr Ronald Gordon's (1939) *A Survey of Child Psychiatry*. In spite of their many areas of collaboration, Winnicott and Bowlby could also be competitive

with one another. Certainly, when Bowlby discussed Winnicott with me in 1986, he managed to be both polite and superior about Winnicott at the same time (Kahr, 1986). And Winnicott, though a public admirer of Bowlby, also harboured certain reservations about his younger psychoanalytical colleague. Indeed, some years ago, I had the opportunity to inspect Winnicott's personal copy of *A Survey of Child Psychiatry* in the library at the Institute of Psychoanalysis in London, and I discovered, perusing the marginalia, that he had described Bowlby's chapter as "awfully disappointing"—one of Winnicott's handwritten comments.

4. Mrs Ursula Bowlby has referred to Dr Donald Winnicott's (1949a) pamphlet, based on his pioneering radio speeches for the British Broadcasting Corporation, entitled, in full, *The Ordinary Devoted Mother and Her Baby: Nine Broadcast Talks (Autumn 1949)*.

5. Dr Ernest Jones (1922, pp. 453–454) wrote to Professor Sigmund Freud about his analysis of Mrs Joan Riviere, "It is a case of typical hysteria, almost the only symptoms being sexual anaesthesia and unorganized Angst, with a few inhibitions of a general nature. Most of her neurosis goes into marked character reactions, which is one reason why I was not able to cure her. I am specially interested in the case, for as it is the worst failure I have ever had I have naturally learnt very much from her analysis. She came to me in 1916 and was with me till last June, with about a year's interruptions from tuberculosis and other causes. Seeing that she was unusually intelligent I hoped to win her for the cause, a mistake I shall never repeat. I underestimated the uncontrollability of her emotional reactions and in the first year made the serious error of lending her my country cottage for a week when I was not there, she having nowhere to go for a holiday. This led to a declaration of love and to the broken-hearted cry that she had never been rejected before (she has been the mistress of a number of men). From that time on she devoted herself to torturing me without any intermission and with considerable success and ingenuity, being a fiendish sadist."

6. Dr Athol Hughes (1995), the biographer of Mrs Joan Riviere, told me that this famous psychoanalyst had difficulty keeping servants. Dr Hanna Segal (1995) remembered that Riviere used to accuse her of "manic" behaviour whenever she arrived late for her supervision sessions and told Segal that she would not tolerate such nonsense!

7. Apparently, plans for the creation of the child psychotherapy curriculum at the Tavistock Clinic had begun as early as 1947. Indeed, on 29th October, 1947, Dr John Bowlby met with both Dr Esther Bick, and with the psychologist Miss Theodora Alcock—a specialist in the Rorschach ink

blot test—at the Tavistock Clinic's headquarters at 2, Beaumont Street, in Central London, in order to discuss this matter. Bowlby (1947) had also invited Dr Michael Balint and Dr Donald Winnicott to attend.

8. After having read this juvenile poem, Mrs Mary Gatling (2015), the eldest child of Mrs Ursula Bowlby, commented, "I feel the influence of the Dorset poet, William Barnes 1801–1886 who was greatly admired and read by her mother" (i.e., greatly admired and read by Mrs Dora Longstaff, mother of Ursula Longstaff Bowlby).

9. One cannot pay sufficient tribute to Mr Evan Durbin or to his role in the life of the Bowlby family in this context. Indeed, this remarkable man deserves a biographical salute of his own. Born on 1st March, 1906, approximately one year prior to John Bowlby, Evan Frank Mottram Durbin, son of a Baptist minister from Westcroft in Bideford, in the county of Devon, attended New College at the University of Oxford, where he read zoology, and then, subsequently, politics and economics. He continued his studies in economics at University College London, in the University of London, and eventually received a teaching post at the progressive, liberal-leaning London School of Economics and Political Science, also part of the University of London. Durbin and Bowlby became great friends and collaborators and, during the 1930s, they even shared a house. Their spouses, Mrs Marjorie Durbin and Mrs Ursula Bowlby, also became fond companions. The two young intellectuals would ultimately collaborate on the writing of a lengthy essay (John Bowlby, 1938; Durbin, 1938)—each authoring an extended section—and then, subsequently, would produce a more jointly integrated book (Durbin and Bowlby, 1939) on the causes of aggression, deeply steeped in both economic ideas and in psychological thought. A work of great majesty, *Personal Aggressiveness and War* examined the origins of cruelty across the species, and drew, *inter alia*, upon the latest animal research. This treatise would serve as a harbinger of many, if not all, of Bowlby's future writings. Consequently, this virtually forgotten publication deserves further study, often having become overshadowed by Bowlby's (1969, 1973, 1980) famous trilogy. In the "Preface" to the book-length version of their collaborative work, Durbin and Bowlby (1939, p. vii) explained that they would endeavour, "to describe and analyse the general psychological forces lying behind the timeless and ubiquitous urge to fight and kill". Durbin became increasingly involved in formal politics as both an economic adviser to Clement Attlee, the Deputy Prime Minister under Winston Churchill, and then subsequently as a Member of Parliament

in his own right, representing the constituency of Edmonton, in Greater London, between 1945 and 1948, on behalf of the Labour Party. Durbin eventually served as Parliamentary Private Secretary to Hugh Dalton, the Chancellor of the Exchequer in Clement Attlee's liberal administration, and then became Parliamentary Secretary to the Ministry of Works. Renowned for his progressive understanding of economics, Durbin helped to provide Prime Minister Attlee with the intellectual foundations of a post-war government along with other similarly intelligent and psychologically astute figures such as Richard Titmuss (e.g., Gowing, 1976), a fellow architect of democratic socialism. Blessed with a fine mind and with a very humane approach to government, Durbin authored quite a number of astute publications (e.g., Durbin, 1933, 1934, 1935, 1940, 1942, 1949); and many had expected that Durbin might well have become Prime Minister one day. But tragically, he died, on 3rd September, 1948, at the age of forty-two years, while saving one of his own daughters and another child from drowning off the coast at Strangles Beach, in Crackington Haven, near Bude, in Cornwall (Ellis, 2004). After Durbin's death, Clement Attlee (1949, p. vii), then Prime Minister, produced a glowing tribute, in which he wrote that, "The tragic death of Evan Durbin at the early age of forty-two deprived the nation and especially the Labour and Socialist Movement of a man of great distinction of mind and character who might well have given service for many years." Attlee (1949, p. viii) concluded his remarks with the touching sentiment: "I was privileged to enjoy his friendship and honoured to have had his help." If an incumbent Prime Minister of a large nation could take the time to prepare such a necrology, one can only imagine the affection and esteem that Durbin engendered, and the extent of the loss experienced by Bowlby himself.

10. As I indicated in Endnote 8 to Chapter Four, in order to differentiate between publications by Dr Donald Winnicott and Mrs Clare Winnicott, produced in the same year, I have, where necessary, referred to sources scripted by the less frequently cited Mrs Winnicott by deploying both her forename and her surname. Likewise, with regard to certain writings by Mrs Ursula Bowlby, I have used her full name in the citations in order to distinguish this member of the Bowlby family from her more frequently referenced husband, Dr John Bowlby; and furthermore, I have styled Sir Richard Bowlby (2015) and, also, Xenia, Lady Bowlby (2000, 2015), by using their full names in order to provide further differentiation. (Finally, with regard to the reference to Dr John Bowlby's (1938) appendix of 1938,

I have also cited his name in full in Chapter Six, Endnote 9, in order to distinguish this from Ursula Bowlby's (1938) letter of the same year).

Chapter Eight

1. In the original unpublished manuscript notes, Mrs Enid Eichholz (1949a) inserted full stops among the letters "F.D.B."—Family Discussion Bureau—but not among the initials of the Family Welfare Association, which she had rendered as "FWA".

Chapter Nine

1. Throughout this chapter, I have, wherever possible, provided a very full and transparent reference to all source materials. On a very small number of occasions, I have refrained from furnishing the name of certain individuals who had revealed extremely intimate pieces of knowledge about Mr Masud Khan, thus respecting the privacy of those persons. In all cases, the stories involved sexual allegations. While I appreciate that I cannot substantiate such accusations in a forensic sense, I have recorded the recollections of my interviewees with full accuracy.
2. Two of Mr Masud Khan's biographers have spelled the forename of his father as "Fazaldad" (Cooper, 1993, p. 5; Hopkins, 2006, p. 4), and one has referred to this man as "Fazal Dad" (Willoughby, 2005, p. 1).
3. I had the privilege of communicating with Ms Susie Orbach (1994, 1997) (subsequently Professor Orbach and, later, Dr Orbach), on several occasions, about her experience of meeting Rajah Masud Khan. Dr Linda Hopkins (1998a) also spoke with Orbach and with her American colleague Ms Luise Eichenbaum (Hopkins, 1998b) and published a similar version of their reminiscences in her outstanding biography of Masud Khan (Hopkins, 2006).

Conclusion

1. In the text of this chapter, I have referred to this famous physician and researcher as Dr Ignác Fülöp Semmelweis—the original Hungarian spelling of his names. But in the "References", readers will note that Semmelweis published his iconic 1861 textbook under the more traditional Austrian spelling: Ignaz Philipp Semmelweis.

Original Sources of Chapters

Introduction

This material appears here in print for the very first time.

Chapter One

An earlier version of this short article first appeared in *Athene: Magazine 2021/2022*, the annual magazine of the Freud Museum London (Kahr, 2021–2022). I express my deep gratitude to Mrs Monica Law, the museum's Marketing and Development Manager, for her kind invitation to contribute this brief essay.

Chapter Two

A previous incarnation of this short communication about Professor Sigmund Freud's death bed first appeared in *Athene: Magazine 2019*, a publication of the Freud Museum London (Kahr, 2019g). Once again, I offer my warm appreciation to Mrs Monica Law and to all of the staff at the Freud Museum London, for producing such beautiful publications. Likewise, I thank Ms Bryony Davies, then the Assistant Curator and Photo Library Manager—and now the full curator—of the Freud Museum London, for her generosity in having granted permission to include photographs of the Maresfield Gardens death bed.

Chapter Three

I presented an earlier rendition of this chapter at the Autumn Conference on "Winnicott and the Couple", sponsored by Tavistock Relationships, at the Tavistock Institute of Medical Psychology, in London, on 11th November, 2017. Ms Marion O'Connor organised this excellent conference at the helpful suggestion of Ms Susanna Abse. I owe warm appreciation to Mr Andrew Balfour, the Chief Executive Officer of Tavistock Relationships, for having chaired the day so splendidly, and I extend my thanks to Ms Krystle Houston, the Training Coordinator at that time, and to her colleague, Mr Isaac Moores, for their kind technological assistance with the display of visual images. The chapter appeared in a special edition of the journal *Couple and Family Psychoanalysis*, then under the editorship of Mrs Molly Ludlam (Kahr, 2019b). I thank Mrs Kate Pearce, the publisher of Phoenix Publishing House, for her kind permission to include an updated version of that article in this new book. I could not have written this chapter without the generous interviews afforded to me by members of Dr Donald Winnicott's family, not least two of his nephews and two of his nieces, to whom I owe incomparable appreciation (e.g., Kahr, 1995e, 1995f, 1996e, 1996f).

Chapter Four

I published an earlier and, indeed, shorter, version of this chapter (Kahr, 2021b), in a book edited by our American colleague, Dr Corinne Masur (2021), about Dr Donald Winnicott's celebrated patient, entitled, *Finding the Piggle: Reconsidering D.W. Winnicott's Most Famous Child Case*. I express my warmest thanks not only to Dr Masur—a most convivial collaborator—but, also, once again, to our publisher, Mrs Kate Pearce of Phoenix Publishing House, for having produced such an elegant volume. I congratulate Dr Masur for having received a Gradiva Award from the National Association for the Advancement of Psychoanalysis in 2021 for this very riveting book. Above all, I owe the most immense thanks to "The Piggle" herself, without whom I certainly could not have written this chronicle. The Piggle very kindly read several drafts and offered helpful comments and clarifications. Through the generosity and trust of The Piggle, I enjoyed the immense privilege of having studied her numerous family documents and photographs. I must also offer my appreciation to "Mr Piggle", the father, and to the late "Mrs Piggle", the mother, for their kind communications and reminiscences. Additionally, I would like to thank the sister of The Piggle, who generously granted permission for me to study

"'The Piggle' Papers"—a most unique archive which will, in future years, prove indispensable to historians of psychoanalysis.

Chapter Five

I delivered a very abbreviated edition of this chapter on 19th September, 2015, at the conference on "Attachment Theory: How John Bowlby Revolutionised Our Understanding of Human Relationships. Where is the Revolution Now? What Are the Future Directions?", part of The John Bowlby 25th Anniversary Event, An International Conference in Celebration of John Bowlby's Work, sponsored by The Bowlby Centre, London, and held in The Kennedy Lecture Theatre of the Wellcome Trust Building at the Institute of Child Health, University College London, in the University of London. I wish to express my thanks to Ms Kate White and our colleagues at The Bowlby Centre for their kind invitation to participate in this happy occasion commemorating Dr John Bowlby and his legacy. I also wish to offer my gratitude to John Bowlby's children, Mrs Mary Gatling and Sir Richard Bowlby, and to his daughter-in-law, Xenia, Lady Bowlby, and to his niece, Dr Juliet Hopkins, for their encouraging responses to this paper. And I convey further gratitude to Professor Arnon Bentovim, Dr. med. Karl-Heinz Brisch, Dr Christopher Clulow, Professor Mary Hepworth, Professor Jeremy Holmes, Dr Bob Marvin, Dr Susie Orbach, Dr Valerie Sinason, Professor Howard Steele, and Professor Miriam Steele, for their helpful comments about this research. An expanded version of my lecture subsequently appeared in the journal *Attachment: New Directions in Psychotherapy and Relational Psychoanalysis*, then under the editorship of Kate White (Kahr, 2015b). Once again, I extend my deep appreciation to Phoenix Publishing House for permission to include much of this original material. I have subsequently written more extensively about this topic (Kahr, 2019c, 2019d, 2019e). I wish to salute the late Dr Bowlby, whom I had the honour to meet on many occasions during the 1980s and from whom I learned so very much.

Chapter Six

My study of the late Mrs Ursula Longstaff Bowlby first appeared in the journal *Attachment: New Directions in Psychotherapy and Relational Psychoanalysis* (Kahr, 2016a), due to the warm encouragement of the incumbent editor, Ms Kate White. Once again, I express my thanks to the staff at Phoenix Publishing House for their kind permission to reprint this essay in an updated version. A considerably abbreviated tribute to the late Mrs Bowlby first appeared in *The Psychotherapy Review* (Kahr, 2000a), under the editorship of Mr Ian Jones-Healey. Without the expert archival care of the many staff members of the Wellcome Library who catalogued the Bowlby family papers and who continue to preserve them, I simply could not have completed this study. I owe much gratitude to the literally dozens of archivists at the Wellcome Library who have assisted me over many years of historical research, but I owe my greatest thanks to the staff in the Rare Materials Room and, in particular, to Dr Lesley Hall and Dr Jennifer Haynes, who undertook the bulk of the cataloguing of these precious items. Ms Crestina Forcina of the Wellcome Library graciously assisted with the duplication of some photographic material, for which I convey much gratitude. The Bowlby family supported this project with characteristic generosity of heart and spirit. Without the friendly receptivity of all the Bowlby children, this project would never have materialised. Mrs Mary Gatling—Ursula's Bowlby's elder daughter and, also, literary executor—and Sir Richard Bowlby and Xenia, Lady Bowlby—the elder son and daughter-in-law—read this essay and offered helpful encouragement. Mrs Pia Duran and Mr Robert Bowlby—the two younger children—expressed warm support of this work, for which I extend my appreciation. I also offer my deep thanks to Dr Juliet Hopkins and Professor Sophie Bowlby—two of Ursula Bowlby's nieces—for their welcome assistance. I thank all of the members of the Bowlby family for entrusting me with the task of studying and reporting on the life of their dear mother or mother-in-law or aunt. Mary Gatling, in particular, granted me a very extended interview about her mother in great detail (Kahr, 2014c). She also offered many helpful comments about this essay. I thank her for her deep generosity and for her wisdom, and I wish to convey warm appreciation to both Mary Gatling and her husband, Mr Tony Gatling, for having welcomed me so warmly into their home.

Chapter Seven

A somewhat abbreviated version of this chapter about the great Mrs Marion Milner (Kahr, 2023d) first appeared in a Festschrift edited by Dr Margaret Boyle Spelman and Professor Joan Raphael-Leff, entitled *The Marion Milner Tradition: Lines of Development. Evolution of Theory and Practice Over the Decades.* I express my warm gratitude not only to Dr Spelman and Professor Raphael-Leff but, also, to Ms Susannah Frearson, the publisher for mental health books at Routledge / Taylor and Francis Group, based in London and, also, in Abingdon, in Oxfordshire, for having released such a splendid tribute

ORIGINAL SOURCES OF CHAPTERS   251

to this remarkable woman and, moreover, for having kindly granted formal permission for me to publish an expanded version of that chapter in this current book. Above all, I wish to convey my immense thanks to the late Mrs Milner for her many acts of kindness to me over the years.

Chapter Eight

I first lectured about the late Mrs Enid Balint and the birth of couple psychoanalysis in the United Kingdom on 26th February, 2016, having had the privilege of delivering the Twenty-First Enid Balint Memorial Lecture at the Tavistock Centre for Couple Relationships at the Tavistock Institute of Medical Psychology in London, under the chairpersonship of my colleague Ms Susanna Abse, then Chief Executive Officer and Consultant Couple Psychotherapist at this venerable institution. Likewise, I wish to extend my deep appreciation to Dr Nicholas Pearce and to the trustees of the Tavistock Institute of Medical Psychology for having awarded me the post of Senior Fellow, with responsibility for documenting the history of our profession. Additionally, I owe kind thanks to the staff in the Rare Materials Room in the Wellcome Library, London, where I had the privilege of studying the unpublished archives of the Tavistock Centre for Couple Relationships. Numerous colleagues offered interviews or reminiscences about some of the key personalities described in this paper, whom I shall acknowledge more fully in an extended version of this chapter, currently in preparation. But at this point, in particular, I must thank Enid Balint's daughter, Mrs Barbara Clark, and granddaughter, Mrs Susan Lawlor, who granted me most gracious interviews (Kahr, 2016c, 2016d). I published an earlier incarnation of that talk in the journal *Couple and Family Psychoanalysis*, under the editorship of Mrs Molly Ludlam (Kahr, 2017a). I then presented a further, more historically contextualised iteration of this material at the conference on "When We Talk About Love: Celebrating the First 70 Years of Tavistock Relationships—Learning from Experience, Innovating for the Future", sponsored by Tavistock Relationships, part of the Tavistock Institute of Medical Psychology, held in the Great Hall of the King's Building, at King's College London in the University of London, on 30th November, 2018, under the chairpersonship of Dr Nicholas Pearce, and at the kind invitation of Mr Andrew Balfour. Not long thereafter, I offered yet another iteration of this chapter as a video contribution, filmed in Professor Sigmund Freud's consulting room at the Freud Museum London by Ms Karolina Urbaniak, and broadcast during two sessions as part of the conference on "The Balints and Their World: Object Relations and Beyond", held on 8th December, 2018, at the Freud Museum London, in association with

Birkbeck, University of London, in Central London, and Imago International, and, also, the British Psychoanalytical Society. I thank Mr Ivan Ward for the opportunity to participate in this conference. Yet another version appeared in the *Journal of the Balint Society* under the editorship of Dr Tom McAnea (Kahr, 2019f). I thank the entire staff team at Phoenix Publishing House for their kind permission to reprint this article. Above all, I wish to convey my appreciation to the late Mrs Enid Balint, whom I had the privilege of meeting in 1993. Little did I know then that one day, more than twenty years hence, I would come to write her history. If only I had had the foresight to have asked her many more questions.

Chapter Nine

My chapter on Rajah Masud Khan has not appeared in print previously. I wrote this piece especially for inclusion in this collection of chapters on the history of British psychoanalysis.

Over many decades, I had the privilege of speaking, often at great length, with quite a large number of people who knew Masud Khan extremely well. I wish to express my deepest thanks to the following sixty-four colleagues and acquaintances for their kind assistance with my oral history research, especially, the late Leo Abse, MP, the late Dr Bernard Barnett, Professor Arnon Bentovim, Dr Harold Bourne, Sir Richard Bowlby, the late Dr Abrahão Brafman, the late Dr Lilian Brafman, the late Dr Peter Bruggen, the late Dr Perry Calwell, Ms Victoria Caplin, the late Mrs Joyce Coles, Mrs Judy Cooper, the late Mrs Barbara Dockar-Drysdale, the late Professor Robert Dorn, Dr John Evans, the late Professor Peter Giovacchini, the late Professor Wynne Godley, Dr Elif Gürisik, Dr Earl Hopper, Dr Judith Issroff, the late Dr Colin James, the late Mrs Lydia James, Dr Oliver James, Mrs Ann Jameson, the late Mr Harry Karnac, the late Miss Pearl King, Mrs Ruth Brook Klauber, the late Dr Robert Langs, Mrs Susan Lawlor, Mr Edward Lucie-Smith, Dr Jeffrey Masson, the late Dr Isabel Menzies Lyth, the late Dr Brendan MacCarthy, the late Dr Joyce McDougall, Mrs Anne Michael, Professor Richard Michael, the late Mrs Marion Milner, Mrs Lucy Mosse, Dr Michael Neve, the late Mrs Jane Shore Nicholas, OBE, the late Mr William Nicholas, Dr Susie Orbach, Dr Andrew Paskauskas, Mr Mark Paterson, Mrs Jenny Pearson, the late Dr Jonathan Pedder, Dr James Raney, the late Dr Eric Rayner, the late Dr Katharine Rees, Mrs Ruth Rosen, the late Dr Charles Rycroft, the late Mr Cesare Sacerdoti, Professor Andrew Samuels, the late Ms Jean Scarlett, Ms Ann Scott, the late Mr Raymond Shepherd, the late Dr Robert Shields, Dr Peter Shoenberg, the late Count Andrew Skarbek, Mr Malcolm Smith, Mrs Mary Smith, Mrs Susan Vas Dias, Profesora Estela Welldon, and Dr Gerald Wooster.

Of these many good-hearted people, who shared their reminiscences quite generously, I must also thank several other individuals whom I met, who had undergone a personal psychoanalysis or a training psychoanalysis with Masud Khan, but who, unlike Judy Cooper, did not wish to share their experiences publicly. Nonetheless, these individuals offered me confirmation of many of the vignettes contained within this chapter and provided further glimpses into the life and work of Khan. Additionally, I wish to express my respect to the man who, many decades previously, filed a complaint against Khan, with the Institute of Psycho-Analysis, for having had an affair with his wife. He spoke with full candour about the awful chapter that he and his family had to navigate in consequence. For obvious reasons, I shall refrain from revealing the name of this person.

I owe special thanks to several individuals who assisted me in many, many ways. First and foremost, I must reiterate my gratitude to Mrs Judy Cooper for having introduced me to the world of Masud Khan back in 1985. I wish, also, to express my deep appreciation to the late Mrs Jane Shore Nicholas— the former Mrs Jane Khan—for her kindness in having welcomed me into her home and for having shared her memories with such kindness. The late Miss Pearl King, one of my dearest mentors and one of my heroines in the field of the history of psychoanalysis, very kindly granted me special permission to study the unpublished correspondence in The Masud Khan Archives, part of the Archives of the British Psychoanalytical Society, sequestered in the British Psychoanalytical Society's headquarters in Byron House, in Maida Vale, in West London. Owing to the notoriety which ensued after the publication of Professor Wynne Godley's (2001a, 2001b) condemnatory revelations about Masud Khan, Miss King and her colleagues closed that archive of papers to researchers, so I feel particularly privileged that Pearl had arranged for me to have access to this unique set of documents during my tenure as the Winnicott Clinic Senior Research Fellow in Psychotherapy, supported by The Winnicott Clinic of Psychotherapy, London.

I wish to convey further thanks to Dr Linda Hopkins (2006), whose thorough and meticulous and diplomatic biography of Masud Khan remains, in my mind, the very best study of a psychoanalytical personality ever written. I have enjoyed multiple conversations with Dr Hopkins on many occasions across the 1990s, 2000s, 2010s, and, into the present day. Through Dr Hopkins, I also had the pleasure to embark upon a very stimulating correspondence with Dr Steven Kuchuck, who collaborated with Dr Hopkins to prepare an excellent edition of Masud Khan's (2022) famous diaries, known as the "Work Books". I owe both Linda Hopkins and Steven Kuchuck much affection for their shrewd insights into the dynamics of Masud Khan.

Happily, on 14th July, 2022, during the final proofing of this book, I had the privilege of attending a special talk on "Remembering Masud Khan: Paradox, Hidden Selves and the Relationship with Anna Freud", delivered by both Dr Hopkins and Dr Kuchuck to the Anna Freud Centre Academic Faculty for Psychoanalytic Research, part of the Anna Freud National Centre for Children and Families, at The Kantor Centre of Excellence, in King's Cross, London, and affiliated with University College London, University of London, in London—albeit via Zoom—splendidly chaired by Professor Joan Raphael-Leff. During this memorable event, hosted on Zoom, four distinguished colleagues, namely, Mrs Dilys Daws, Dr Earl Hopper, Professor Joan Raphael-Leff, and Ms Ann Scott, offered many more personal reminiscences of their encounters with Masud Khan, which I found to be quite informative, and which resulted in a very rich discussion about the true complexities of the human personality. Dr Hopper (2022a, 2022b) then kindly recalled further memories and reflections with me in a personal correspondence.

And I wish to express additional thanks to Dr Valerie Sinason for having shared a most compelling story about Masud Khan, even though she had not met him personally.

Chapter Ten

I delivered a very brief version of this chapter, on 26th March, 1993, under the title, "R. D. Laing's Missing Tooth: Schizophrenia and Fears of Bodily Disintegration", to The Friday Forum, part of the Society for Existential Analysis, based at Regent's College, in the Inner Circle of Regent's Park, in London, thanks to the kind invitation of Ms Lucia Moja-Strasser and her colleagues. A shortened encapsulation of that lecture appeared in the *Journal of the Society of Existential Analysis* (Kahr, 1994a). I express my thanks to the late Dr Ronald Laing, who had kindly accepted my invitation to lecture at The Oxford Psycho-Analytical Forum, many years previously, in 1983. Although he comported himself in a troubled and complex manner, I do feel privileged that I had the occasion to meet this man whose work remains truly vital to the humanisation of psychiatry.

Conclusion

This material appears here in print for the very first time.

Acknowledgements

I wish to convey my warmest thanks to the many hundreds upon hundreds of psychoanalysts whom I interviewed over the years, who kindly shared their reminiscences about the early days of this profession. In particular, I offer my huge appreciation to the late Mrs Enid Balint-Edmonds, the late Dr John Bowlby, the late Mrs Ursula Bowlby, the late Dr Ronald D. Laing, the late Mrs Marion Milner, and so many others who feature in this collection of tributes and explorations.

As ever, I owe immense gratitude to the entire staff team at Phoenix Publishing House who produced my book *How to Flourish as a Psychotherapist* (Kahr, 2019a) some years previously. I extend deepest affection to the Publisher, Mrs Kate Pearce—a truly noble and warm-hearted woman—and to her loyal and honourable colleague, Mr Fernando Marques. I had the privilege of working with both Mrs Pearce and Mr Marques during their tenure at the old Karnac Books many years ago, and I have taken great pleasure in watching them flourish in their own creative ways as time has unfolded. I also wish to express my thanks to Ms Sophie-Jo Gavin, the Publishing Assistant, for her reliable and friendly contributions. Since the submission of this typescript, originally commissioned by Phoenix Publishing House, the press has now become incorporated into the newly relaunched Karnac Books, with Kate Pearce as its Publisher, a source of great pleasure to us all.

Additionally, I offer deepest plaudits to Mr James Darley, one of the very best copy editors in the world, with whom I had the privilege of working on my aforementioned book, *How to Flourish as a Psychotherapist*. He has always proved himself to be the most diligent and responsive of people. And, moreover, I extend my tremendous admiration to Mr Gilbert Courbanally for having designed such a compelling cover for this book, and, also, to Mr Nick Downing, the meticulous proof-reader. As ever, I thank the incomparably collaborative and professional Mrs Anita Mason, the new head of production of Karnac Books, for her ever iconic work.

It pleases me hugely that this book appears as part of the "Freud Museum London Series". I wish to underscore my tremendous affection and my deepest gratitude to all of the staff at Freud Museum London, especially Ms Carol Seigel, the former Director of the museum, who first approved the series in 2021. More recently, I have truly enjoyed the opportunity to collaborate with our new Director, Dr Giuseppe Albano, and with our Research Manager, Mr Tom DeRose, each of whom has provided wonderful support for this monograph series.

I extend sincere appreciation to all of my teachers of history and, also, my instructors and supervisors in psychology, psychotherapy, and psychoanalysis, as well as my colleagues, my friends, and, of course, my family for their warm support of my research.

Above all, I wish to communicate my deepest gratitude and respect to all of the patients with whom I have collaborated over the decades, each of whom has permitted me to share the historical wisdom of our ancestors in the course of our psychotherapeutic sessions. I remain very touched indeed that many of them can still quote verbatim from the writings of Professor Sigmund Freud and Dr Donald Winnicott, both of whom remain tremendous sources of great insight and pure inspiration.

References

Ackroyd, Peter (2002). *Dickens: Public Life and Private Passion.* London: BBC / BBC Worldwide.

Ahrenfeldt, Robert H. (1958). *Psychiatry in the British Army in the Second World War.* London: Routledge and Kegan Paul.

Ainsworth, Mary D. (1962). The Effects of Maternal Deprivation: A Review of Findings and Controversy in the Context of Research Strategy. In Mary D. Ainsworth, Robert G. Andry, Robert G. Harlow, Serge Lebovici, Margaret Mead, Dane G. Prugh, and Barbara Wootton. *Deprivation of Maternal Care: A Reassessment of its Effects*, pp. 97–165. Geneva: World Health Organization.

Akhtar, Salman (2022). *Tales of Transformation: A Life in Psychotherapy and Psychoanalysis.* Bicester, Oxfordshire: Phoenix Publishing House.

Alexander, Franz, and Staub, Hugo (1929). *Der Verbrecher und seine Richter: Ein psychoanalytischer Einblick in die Welt der Paragraphen.* Vienna: Internationaler Psychoanalytischer Verlag.

Andrewes, Christopher H. (1921). Note on a Case of Malignant Melanoma of the Vulva. *St. Bartholomew's Hospital Journal, 28,* 58.

Anonymous (1896). Healthy, Happy Nurseries. *The Lady.* 9th April, p. 498.

Anonymous (1934). A "Harley Street" for the Anxious Poor: Treatment of "Frightening Illnesses". *Banffshire Advertiser.* 17th May, n.p. Box 1. Folder 1. Tavistock Clinic Archives. Library, Tavistock Centre, Tavistock and Portman NHS Trust, Belsize Park, London.

Anonymous [Gershy Hepner] (1961). A Personal View—10: Donald Winnicott. *St. Mary's Hospital Gazette*, *67*, 137–138.

Anonymous (2000). Personal Communication to the Author. 15th February.

Anonymous (2010). Interview with the Author. 10th February.

Anonymous (2022). John Bowlby. Wikipedia. [https://en.wikipedia.org/wiki/John_Bowlby; accessed on 1st May, 2022].

Anonymous (n.d.). Notes: The Institute of Marital Studies, Formerly the Family Discussion Bureau. The Development of a Non-Medical Path into Work with Marital and Related Family Problems. Unpublished Typescript. SA/TCC/A/1/11. Tavistock Centre for Couple Relationships. Archives and Manuscripts, Rare Materials Room, Wellcome Library, Wellcome Collection, The Wellcome Building, London.

Ansbacher, Heinz L. (1981). Discussion of Alfred Adler's Preface to The Diary of Vaslav Nijinsky. *Archives of General Psychiatry*, *38*, 836–841.

Appendix to First Report of Commissioners: Mines. Part I. Reports and Evidence from Sub-Commissioners (1842). London: Her Majesty's Stationery Office.

Appendix to First Report of Commissioners: Mines. Part II. Reports and Evidence from Sub-Commissioners (1842). London: Her Majesty's Stationery Office.

Appleby, Mary (1967). Letter to Donald W. Winnicott. 4th April. Box 6. File 6. Donald W. Winnicott Papers. Archives of Psychiatry, The Oskar Diethelm Library, The DeWitt Wallace Institute of Psychiatry: History, Policy, and the Arts, Department of Psychiatry, Joan and Sanford I. Weill Medical College, Cornell University, The New York Presbyterian Hospital, New York, New York, U.S.A.

Armstrong-Jones, Robert (1917). Dreams and Their Interpretation. *The Practitioner*. March, pp. 201–219.

Arnold, Catharine (2018). *Pandemic 1918: The Story of the Deadliest Influenza in History*. London: Michael O'Mara Books.

Attlee, Clement R. (1920). *The Social Worker*. London: G. Bell and Sons.

Attlee, Clement R. (1949). Foreword: An Appreciation of E.F.M. Durbin by The Rt. Hon. C.R. Attlee. In Evan F.M. Durbin. *Problems of Economic Planning: Papers on Planning and Economics*, pp. vii–viii. London: Routledge and Kegan Paul.

Attlee, Clement R. (1954). *As it Happened*. London: William Heinemann.

Augenfeld, Felix (1974). Letter to Hans Lobner. 8th February. Cited in Michael Molnar (1992). Notes and References, p. 278. In Sigmund Freud. *The Diary of Sigmund Freud: 1929-1939. A Record of the Final Decade*. Michael Molnar (Ed. and Transl.), pp. 271–308. New York: Charles Scribner's Sons, and Toronto: Maxwell Macmillan Canada, and New York: Maxwell Macmillan

International/Maxwell Publishing Company, Maxwell Communication Group of Companies.

Balint, Enid (1973). Epilogue. In End Balint and Jacob S. Norell (Eds.). *Six Minutes for the Patient: Interactions in General Practice Consultation*, pp. 161–164. London: Tavistock Publications.

Balint, Enid (1974). Letter to Douglas Woodhouse. 27th June. SA/TCC/B/3/1. Tavistock Centre for Couple Relationships. Archives and Manuscripts, Rare Materials Room, Wellcome Library, Wellcome Collection, The Wellcome Building, London.

Balint, Enid (1993). *Before I Was I: Psychoanalysis and the Imagination*. Juliet Mitchell and Michael Parsons (Eds.). London: Free Association Books, and New York: Guilford Press, Guilford Publications.

Balint, Enid (n.d.). The Girl on the Roof, or Listening to Strangers (Unfinished and Unpublished). Cited in Jennifer Johns (2012). The Enid Files, p. 98. In Judit Szekacs-Weisz and Tom Keve (Eds.). *Ferenczi for Our Time: Theory and Practice*, pp. 91–99. London: Karnac Books.

Balint, Enid, and Balint, Michael (1953). Letter to Family Discussion Bureau. 17th January. SA/TCC/A/2/1. Tavistock Centre for Couple Relationships. Archives and Manuscripts, Rare Materials Room, Wellcome Library, Wellcome Collection, The Wellcome Building, London.

Balint, Michael (1948). On Genital Love. *International Journal of Psycho-Analysis*, 29, 34–40.

Balint, Michael, and Balint, Enid (1961). *Psychotherapeutic Techniques in Medicine*. London: Tavistock Publications.

Balint, Michael; Balint, Enid; Gosling, Robert, and Hildebrand, Peter (1966). *A Study of Doctors: Mutual Selection and the Evaluation of Results in a Training Programme for Family Doctors*. London: Tavistock Publications.

Balzac, Honoré de (n.d. [1920]). *La Peau de chagrin: Roman philosophique*. Vienna: Manz, Éditeur.

Bannister, Kathleen; Lyons, Alison; Pincus, Lily; Robb, James; Shooter, Antonia, and Stephens, Judith (1955). *Social Casework in Marital Problems: The Development of a Psychodynamic Approach. A Study by a Group of Caseworkers*. London: Tavistock Publications.

Barnes, Mary, and Berke, Joseph (1971). *Mary Barnes: Two Accounts of a Journey Through Madness*. London: MacGibbon and Kee.

Barry, John M. (2004). *The Great Influenza: The Epic Story of the Deadliest Plague in History*. New York: Viking/Penguin Group, Penguin Group (USA).

Bathurst, Georgina; Brown, Sibyl Clement; Bowlby, John; Bullen, G.A.; Fairbairn, Nancy; Isaacs, Susan; Mercer, N.S., Rooff, Madeline, and Thouless, Robert H. (1941). *The Cambridge Evacuation Survey: A Wartime Study in Social Welfare and Education*. Susan Isaacs, Sibyl Clement Brown, and Robert H. Thouless (Eds.). London: Methuen and Company.

Battiscombe, Georgina (1974). *Shaftesbury: A Biography of the Seventh Earl. 1801–1885*. London: Constable/Constable and Company.

Beckett, Francis (1997). *Clem Attlee*. London: Richard Cohen Books.

Berke, Joseph H. (1977). *Butterfly Man: Madness, Degradation and Redemption*. London: Hutchinson of London/Hutchinson and Company (Publishers).

Berthelsen, Detlef (1987). *Alltag bei Familie Freud: Die Erinnerungen der Paula Fichtl*. Hamburg: Hoffmann und Campe Verlag.

Bion, Wilfred R. (1948). Experiences in Groups: I. *Human Relations, 1*, 314–320.

Birt, Doris (1964). Letter to Donald W. Winnicott. 17th February. Box 4. File 12. Donald W. Winnicott Papers. Archives of Psychiatry, The Oskar Diethelm Library, The DeWitt Wallace Institute of Psychiatry: History, Policy, and the Arts, Department of Psychiatry, Joan and Sanford I. Weill Medical College, Cornell University, The New York Presbyterian Hospital, New York, New York, U.S.A.

Blanton, Smiley (1971). *Diary of My Analysis with Sigmund Freud*. New York: Hawthorn Books.

Bleuler, Eugen (1911). *Dementia Praecox oder Gruppe der Schizophrenien*. In Gustav Aschaffenburg (Ed.). *Handbuch der Psychiatrie: Spezieller Teil. 4. Abteilung, 1. Hälfte*, pp. vii–420. Vienna: Franz Deuticke.

Bourne, Geoffrey (1963). *We Met at Bart's: The Autobiography of a Physician*. London: Frederick Muller.

Bowlby, John (1938). Appendix: An Examination of the Psychological and Anthropological Evidence. In Evan F.M. Durbin, John Bowlby, Ivor Thomas, Douglas P.T. Jay, Robert B. Fraser, Richard H.S. Crossman, and George Catlin. *War and Democracy: Essays on the Causes and Prevention of War*, pp. 51–150. London: Kegan Paul, Trench, Trubner and Company.

Bowlby, John (1939a). Hysteria in Children. In Ronald G. Gordon (Ed.). *A Survey of Child Psychiatry*, pp. 80–94. London: Humphrey Milford/Oxford University Press.

Bowlby, John (1939b). Hysteria in Children. Brett Kahr (Ed.). (2019). *Attachment: New Directions in Psychotherapy and Relational Psychoanalysis, 13*, 152–163.

Bowlby, John (1940a). *Personality and Mental Illness: An Essay in Psychiatric Diagnosis*. London: Kegan Paul, Trench, Trubner and Company.

Bowlby, John (1940b). The Influence of Early Environment in the Development of Neurosis and Neurotic Character. *International Journal of Psycho-Analysis, 21*, 154–178.

Bowlby, John (1944a). Forty-Four Juvenile Thieves: Their Characters and Home-Life. *International Journal of Psycho-Analysis*, 25, 19–53.

Bowlby, John (1944b). Forty-Four Juvenile Thieves: Their Characters and Home-Life (II). *International Journal of Psycho-Analysis*, 25, 107–128.

Bowlby, John (1945–1946). Childhood Origins of Recidivism. *Howard Journal*, 7, 30–33.

Bowlby, John (1946). *Forty-Four Juvenile Thieves: Their Characters and Home-Life*. Covent Garden, London: Baillière, Tindall and Cox.

Bowlby, John (1947). Letter to Donald W. Winnicott. 14th October. PP/DWW/C/1/1. Donald Woods Winnicott Collection. Archives and Manuscripts, Rare Materials Room, Wellcome Library, Wellcome Collection, The Wellcome Building, London.

Bowlby, John (1949a). The Study and Reduction of Group Tensions in the Family. *Human Relations*, 2, 123–128.

Bowlby, John (1949b). Letter to Enid Eicholz [sic] [Enid Eichholz]. 28th November. SA/TCC/A/2/2. Tavistock Centre for Couple Relationships. Archives and Manuscripts, Rare Materials Room, Wellcome Library, Wellcome Collection, The Wellcome Building, London.

Bowlby, John (1951a). *Maternal Care and Mental Health: A Report Prepared on Behalf of the World Health Organization as a Contribution to the United Nations Programme for the Welfare of Homeless Children*. Geneva: World Health Organization.

Bowlby, John (1951b). Maternal Care and Mental Health. *Bulletin de l'Organisation Mondiale de la Santé/Bulletin of the World Health Organization*, 3, 355–533.

Bowlby, John (1953). *Child Care and the Growth of Love*. Margery Fry (Ed.). London: Penguin Books/Pelican Books.

Bowlby, John (1956). Letter to Melanie Klein. 14th February. PP/BOW/G.1/4. (Edward) John (Mostyn) Bowlby (1907–1990) Collection. Archives and Manuscripts, Rare Materials Room, Wellcome Library, Wellcome Collection, The Wellcome Building, London.

Bowlby, John (1957). Symposium on the Contribution of Current Theories to an Understanding of Child Development: I. An Ethological Approach to Research in Child Development. *British Journal of Medical Psychology*, 30, 230–240.

Bowlby, John (1958). The Nature of the Child's Tie to His Mother. *International Journal of Psycho-Analysis*, 39, 350–373.

Bowlby, John (1960). Comments on Professor Piaget's Paper. In James M. Tanner and Bärbel Inhelder (Eds.). *Discussions on Child Development: A Consideration of the Biological, Psychological, and Cultural Approaches*

to the Understanding of Human Development and Behaviour. Volume Four. The Proceedings of the Fourth Meeting of the World Health Organization Study Group on the Psychobiological Development of the Child. Geneva 1956, pp. 35–47. London: Tavistock Publications.
Bowlby, John (1969). *Attachment and Loss: Volume I. Attachment.* London: Hogarth Press and the Institute of Psycho-Analysis.
Bowlby, John (1973). *Attachment and Loss: Volume II. Separation. Anxiety and Anger.* London: Hogarth Press and the Institute of Psycho-Analysis.
Bowlby, John (1979). *The Making and Breaking of Affectional Bonds.* London: Tavistock Publications.
Bowlby, John (1980). *Attachment and Loss: Volume III. Loss. Sadness and Depression.* London: Hogarth Press and the Institute of Psycho-Analysis.
Bowlby, John (1984). Personal Reminiscences on the Dev[t] of Child Analysis in the British Society: 1935–1960. Unpublished Lecture Notes. PP/BOW/G.1/7. (Edward) John (Mostyn) Bowlby (1907–1990) Collection. Archives and Manuscripts, Rare Materials Room, Wellcome Library, Wellcome Collection, The Wellcome Building, London.
Bowlby, John (1985). Notes on Members of The British Psychoanalytical Society: 1935–1945. (Written in May, 1985), pp. 31–39. In Brett Kahr (Ed.). (2012). Reminiscences by John Bowlby: Portraits of Colleagues, 1935–1945. (Previously Unpublished). *Attachment: New Directions in Psychotherapy and Relational Psychoanalysis*, 6, 27–49.
Bowlby, John (1988). *A Secure Base: Clinical Applications of Attachment Theory.* London: Routledge.
Bowlby, John (1990). *Charles Darwin: A Biography.* London: Hutchinson.
Bowlby, John; Ainsworth, Mary; Boston, Mary, and Rosenbluth, Dina (1956). The Effects of Mother-Child Separation: A Follow-Up Study. *British Journal of Medical Psychology*, 29, 211–247.
Bowlby, John; Miller, Emanuel, and Winnicott, Donald W. (1939). Evacuation of Small Children. *British Medical Journal.* 16th December, pp. 1202–1203.
Bowlby, John, and Robertson, James (1953). A Two-Year-Old Goes to Hospital. *Proceedings of the Royal Society of Medicine*, 46, 425–426.
Bowlby, Richard (2015). Personal Communication to the Author. 19th September.
Bowlby, Ursula (1938). Letter to John Bowlby. n.d. In Ursula Bowlby (1938–1939). *Ursula's Letters to John: Vol: 2. 1938–1939.* PP/BOW/P.4/6/2. (Edward) John (Mostyn) Bowlby (1907–1990) Collection. Archives and Manuscripts, Rare Materials Room, Wellcome Library, Wellcome Collection, The Wellcome Building, London.

REFERENCES

Bowlby, Ursula (c. 1948a). ULB Book: Pt 1. PP/BOW/M.1. (Edward) John (Mostyn) Bowlby (1907–1990) Collection. Archives and Manuscripts, Rare Materials Room, Wellcome Library, Wellcome Collection, The Wellcome Building, London.

Bowlby, Ursula (c. 1948b). ULB Book: Pt 2. PP/BOW/M.2. (Edward) John (Mostyn) Bowlby (1907–1990) Collection. Archives and Manuscripts, Rare Materials Room, Wellcome Library, Wellcome Collection, The Wellcome Building, London.

Bowlby, Ursula (1957). Letter to Donald W. Winnicott. 8th March. Box 1. File 1. Donald W. Winnicott Papers. Archives of Psychiatry, The Oskar Diethelm Library, The DeWitt Wallace Institute of Psychiatry: History, Policy, and the Arts, Department of Psychiatry, Joan and Sanford I. Weill Medical College, Cornell University, The New York Presbyterian Hospital, New York, New York, U.S.A.

Bowlby, Ursula (1962). *Ursula's Worlds: Chapters 1, 2, 3*. [Revised 1992]. PP/BOW/P.4/2/1. (Edward) John (Mostyn) Bowlby (1907–1990) Collection. Archives and Manuscripts, Rare Materials Room, Wellcome Library, Wellcome Collection, The Wellcome Building, London.

Bowlby, Ursula (1992). *Picket Notes*. PP/BOW/P.4/4/1. (Edward) John (Mostyn) Bowlby (1907–1990) Collection. Archives and Manuscripts, Rare Materials Room, Wellcome Library, Wellcome Collection, The Wellcome Building, London.

Bowlby, Ursula L. (1994). Letter to the Author. 1st October.

Bowlby, Xenia (2000). Personal Communication to the Author. 28th March.

Bowlby, Xenia (2015). Personal Communication to the Author. 19th September.

Bradshaw, Anthony (1996). Personal Communication to the Author. 23rd March.

Breuer, Josef (1882). Krankengeschichte Bertha Pappenheim. Unpublished Typescript. Box 33A. Freud Museum London, Swiss Cottage, London.

Breuer, Josef (1895). Beobachtung I. Frl. Anna O … In Josef Breuer and Sigmund Freud. *Studien über Hysterie*, pp. 15–37. Vienna: Franz Deuticke.

Breuer, Josef, and Freud, Sigmund (1895). *Studien über Hysterie*. Vienna: Franz Deuticke.

Brierley, Marjorie (1951). *Trends in Psycho-Analysis*. London: Hogarth Press and the Institute of Psycho-Analysis.

Brierley, Marjorie (1961). Book Review of Ronald D. Laing. *The Divided Self: A Study of Sanity and Madness*. International Journal of Psycho-Analysis, 42, 288–291.

Brown, Ronald D., and Krausz, Rosemarie (1984). The Patient's Unconscious Perceptions of the Therapist's Disruptions. In James Raney (Ed.). *Listening and Interpreting: The Challenge of the Work of Robert Langs*, pp. 21–35. New York: Jason Aronson.

Burlingham, Michael John (1989). *The Last Tiffany: A Biography of Dorothy Tiffany Burlingham*. New York: Atheneum/Macmillan Publishing Company.

Burridge, Trevor (1985). *Clement Attlee: A Political Biography*. London: Jonathan Cape.

Caine, Sydney (1964). Letter to Donald W. Winnicott. 7th July. Box 5. File 4. Donald W. Winnicott Papers. Archives of Psychiatry, The Oskar Diethelm Library, The DeWitt Wallace Institute of Psychiatry: History, Policy, and the Arts, Department of Psychiatry, Joan and Sanford I. Weill Medical College, Cornell University, The New York Presbyterian Hospital, New York, New York, U.S.A.

Calvert, Jonathan, and Arbuthnott, George (2021). *Failures of State: The Inside Story of Britain's Battle with Coronavirus*. London: Mudlark/HarperCollins Publishers.

Cambridge University Reporter (1917). 16th June.

Cameron, Hector C. (1955). *The British Paediatric Association: 1928–1952*. London: British Paediatric Association/Hospital for Sick Children.

Cameron, Laura, and Forrester, John (1999). 'A Nice Type of the English Scientist': Tansley and Freud. *History Workshop Journal*, 48, 62–100.

Cautley, Edmund (1910). *The Diseases of Infants and Children*. London: Shaw and Sons.

Cautley, Edmund (1932). Book Review of Donald W. Winnicott. *Clinical Notes on Disorders of Childhood*. British Journal of Children's Diseases, 29, 75–76.

Charlton, John (n.d.). Personal Communication to Linda Hopkins. n.d. In Linda Hopkins (2006). *False Self: The Life of Masud Khan*, p. 136. New York: Other Press.

Cooper, Judy (1985). Personal Communication to the Author. 9th June.

Cooper, Judy (1991a). Masud Khan (1924–1989): A Personal Tribute. *Free Associations*, 2, Number *21*, 91–98.

Cooper, Judy (1991b). Book Review of M. Masud R. Khan. *When Spring Comes: Awakenings in Clinical Psychoanalysis*. Free Associations, 2, Number *21*, 113–114.

Cooper, Judy (1993). *Speak of Me as I Am: The Life and Work of Masud Khan*. London: Karnac Books/H. Karnac (Books).

Cooper, Judy (2005). Personal Communication to the Author. 15th November.

Cooper, Judy (2020). E-Mail to the Author. 12th July.

Crichton Miller, Hugh (1921). *The New Psychology and the Teacher*. London: Jarrolds Publishers.

Crichton Miller, Hugh (1922). The Outlook for Analytical Psychology in Medicine. *Medical Press and Circular*. 14th June, pp. 409–411.

Davies, Bryony (2019). *Sigmund Freud's Collection: Highlights from the Freud Museum London*. London: Freud Museum London.

Davies, Daniel T., and Wilson, A. Thomson Macbeth (1937). Observations on the Life-History of Chronic Peptic Ulcer. *The Lancet*. 11th December, pp. 1353–1360.

Deacon, Richard (1985). *The Cambridge Apostles: A History of Cambridge University's Élite Intellectual Secret Society*. London: Robert Royce.

deMause, Lloyd (1974). The Evolution of Childhood. In Lloyd deMause (Ed.). *The History of Childhood*, pp. 1–73. New York: Psychohistory Press.

deMause, Lloyd (1990). The History of Child Assault. *Journal of Psychohistory*, 18, 1–29.

deMause, Lloyd (1991). The Universality of Incest. *Journal of Psychohistory*, 19, 123–164.

Despert, J. Louise (1965). *The Emotionally Disturbed Child: Then and Now*. New York: Robert Brunner.

Dicks, Henry V. (1967). *Marital Tensions: Clinical Studies Towards a Psychological Theory of Interaction*. London: Routledge and Kegan Paul.

Dicks, Henry V. (1970). *Fifty Years of the Tavistock Clinic*. London: Routledge and Kegan Paul.

Dinnage, Rosemary (1979). John Bowlby. *New Society*. 10th May, pp. 323–325.

Dorsey, John M. (1976). *An American Psychiatrist in Vienna, 1935–1937, and His Sigmund Freud*. Detroit, Michigan: Center for Health Education.

Dow, James F., and Brown, Marjorie A. (1946). *Evacuation to Westmorland from Home and Europe: 1939–1945*. Kendal, Westmorland: Westmorland Gazette.

Dragstedt, Naome Rader (1998). Creative Illusions: The Theoretical and Clinical Work of Marion Milner. *Journal of Melanie Klein and Object Relations*, 16, 425–536.

Durbin, Evan F.M. (1933). *Purchasing Power and Trade Depression: A Critique of Under-Consumption Theories*. London: Jonathan Cape.

Durbin, Evan F.M. (1934). *Purchasing Power and Trade Depression: A Critique of Under-Consumption Theories*. New and Revised Edition. London: Jonathan Cape.

Durbin, Evan F.M. (1935). *The Problem of Credit Policy*. London: Chapman and Hall.

Durbin, Evan F.M. (1938). Personal Aggressiveness and War. In Evan F.M. Durbin, John Bowlby, Ivor Thomas, Douglas P.T. Jay, Robert B. Fraser, Richard H.S. Crossman, and George Catlin. *War and Democracy: Essays on the Causes and Prevention of War*, pp. 1–50. London: Kegan Paul, Trench, Trubner and Company.

Durbin, Evan F.M. (1940). *The Politics of Democratic Socialism: An Essay on Social Policy*. London: George Routledge and Sons.

Durbin, Evan F.M. (1942). *What Have We to Defend?: A Brief Critical Examination of the British Social Tradition*. London: Labour Book Service.

Durbin, Evan F.M. (1949). *Problems of Economic Planning: Papers on Planning and Economics*. London: Routledge and Kegan Paul.

Durbin, Evan F.M., and Bowlby, John (1939). *Personal Aggressiveness and War*. London: Kegan Paul, Trench, Trubner and Company.

Durbin, Evan F.M.; Bowlby, John; Thomas, Ivor; Jay, Douglas P.T.; Fraser, Robert B.; Crossman, Richard H.S., and Catlin, George (1938). *War and Democracy: Essays on the Causes and Prevention of War*. London: Kegan Paul, Trench, Trubner and Company.

Ehrenzweig, Anton (1949). The Origin of the Scientific and Heroic Urge: (The Guilt of Prometheus). *International Journal of Psycho-Analysis*, 30, 108–123.

Ehrenzweig, Anton (1953). *The Psycho-Analysis of Artistic Vision and Hearing: An Introduction to a Theory of Unconscious Perception*. London: Routledge and Kegan Paul.

Ehrenzweig, Anton (1967). *The Hidden Order of Art: A Study in the Psychology of Artistic Imagination*. London: Weidenfeld and Nicolson.

Eichholz, Enid (1948a). Draft Letter to Medical Officer of Health, Middlesex County Council. n.d. SA/TCC/A/2/2. Tavistock Centre for Couple Relationships. Archives and Manuscripts, Rare Materials Room, Wellcome Library, Wellcome Collection, The Wellcome Building, London.

Eichholz, Enid (1948b). Letter to John Bowlby. 19th July. SA/TCC/A/2/2. Tavistock Centre for Couple Relationships. Archives and Manuscripts, Rare Materials Room, Wellcome Library, Wellcome Collection, The Wellcome Building, London.

Eichholz, Enid (1948c). Letter to P.S. Main [sic] [Thomas Main]. 21st July. SA/TCC/A/2/3. Tavistock Centre for Couple Relationships. Archives and Manuscripts, Rare Materials Room, Wellcome Library, Wellcome Collection, The Wellcome Building, London.

Eichholz, Enid (1948d). Letter to William Morison McIntyre. 15th September. SA/TCC/A/2/3. Tavistock Centre for Couple Relationships. Archives and

Manuscripts, Rare Materials Room, Wellcome Library, Wellcome Collection, The Wellcome Building, London.

Eichholz, Enid (1948e). Letter to John Sutherland. 26th October. SA/TCC/A/2/8. Tavistock Centre for Couple Relationships. Archives and Manuscripts, Rare Materials Room, Wellcome Library, Wellcome Collection, The Wellcome Building, London.

Eichholz, Enid (1949a). Research Project into the Social Structure and Social Needs of Communities. Unpublished Manuscript Notes. SA/TCC/A/2/9. Tavistock Centre for Couple Relationships. Archives and Manuscripts, Rare Materials Room, Wellcome Library, Wellcome Collection, The Wellcome Building, London.

Eichholz, Enid (1949b). Staffing Plans. Unpublished Memorandum. SA/TCC/A/2/1. Tavistock Centre for Couple Relationships. Archives and Manuscripts, Rare Materials Room, Wellcome Library, Wellcome Collection, The Wellcome Building, London.

Eichholz, Enid (1949c). Note. n.d. SA/TCC/A/2/1. Tavistock Centre for Couple Relationships. Archives and Manuscripts, Rare Materials Room, Wellcome Library, Wellcome Collection, The Wellcome Building, London.

Eichholz, Enid (1949d). Letter to Doreen Widdell [sic] [Doreen Weddell]. 14th January. SA/TCC/A/2/3. Tavistock Centre for Couple Relationships. Archives and Manuscripts, Rare Materials Room, Wellcome Library, Wellcome Collection, The Wellcome Building, London.

Eichholz, Enid (1949e). Letter to Doreen Weddell. 24th February. SA/TCC/A/2/3. Tavistock Centre for Couple Relationships. Archives and Manuscripts, Rare Materials Room, Wellcome Library, Wellcome Collection, The Wellcome Building, London.

Eichholz, Enid (1949f). Letter to Michael Balint. 25th March. SA/TCC/A/2/1. Tavistock Centre for Couple Relationships. Archives and Manuscripts, Rare Materials Room, Wellcome Library, Wellcome Collection, The Wellcome Building, London.

Eichholz, Enid (1949g). Letter to Michael Balint. 18th July. SA/TCC/A/2/1. Tavistock Centre for Couple Relationships. Archives and Manuscripts, Rare Materials Room, Wellcome Library, Wellcome Collection, The Wellcome Building, London.

Eichholz, Enid (1949h). Letter to Michael Balint. 9th August. SA/TCC/A/2/1. Tavistock Centre for Couple Relationships. Archives and Manuscripts, Rare Materials Room, Wellcome Library, Wellcome Collection, The Wellcome Building, London.

Eichholz, Enid (1949i). Letter to John Bowlby. 9th August. SA/TCC/A/2/2. Tavistock Centre for Couple Relationships. Archives and Manuscripts, Rare Materials Room, Wellcome Library, Wellcome Collection, The Wellcome Building, London.

Eichholz, Enid (1950a). Visit by Mrs. Eichholz. Unpublished Note. SA/TCC/A/2/3. Tavistock Centre for Couple Relationships. Archives and Manuscripts, Rare Materials Room, Wellcome Library, Wellcome Collection, The Wellcome Building, London.

Eichholz, Enid (1950b). Letter to A. Thomson M. Wilson. 5th January. SA/TCC/A/2/9. Tavistock Centre for Couple Relationships. Archives and Manuscripts, Rare Materials Room, Wellcome Library, Wellcome Collection, The Wellcome Building, London.

Eichholz, Enid (1950c). Letter to Noël Hunnybun. 8th February. SA/TCC/A/2/5. Tavistock Centre for Couple Relationships. Archives and Manuscripts, Rare Materials Room, Wellcome Library, Wellcome Collection, The Wellcome Building, London.

Eichholz, Enid (1950d). Letter to Millicent Dewar. 27th February. SA/TCC/A/2/4. Tavistock Centre for Couple Relationships. Archives and Manuscripts, Rare Materials Room, Wellcome Library, Wellcome Collection, The Wellcome Building, London.

Eichholz, Enid (1952a). Memorandum on the Work of the Family Discussion Bureaux for the Period April 1951 to March 1952. Unpublished Typescript. SA/TCC/B/1/3/2. Tavistock Centre for Couple Relationships. Archives and Manuscripts, Rare Materials Room, Wellcome Library, Wellcome Collection, The Wellcome Building, London.

Eichholz, Enid (1952b). Letter to Noël K. Hunnybun. 7th March. SA/TCC/A/2/5. Tavistock Centre for Couple Relationships. Archives and Manuscripts, Rare Materials Room, Wellcome Library, Wellcome Collection, The Wellcome Building, London.

Eissler, Kurt R. (1952). *Interview with Dr. Adolph Stern: November 13, 1952.* Unpublished Transcript. Box 122. Folder 10. Sigmund Freud Papers. Sigmund Freud Collection. Manuscript Reading Room, Room 101, Manuscript Division, James Madison Memorial Building, Library of Congress, Washington, D.C., U.S.A.

Eissler, Kurt R. (1953). *Sonoband No. 17: Sir Arthur Tansley. Summer 1953.* Unpublished Transcript. Box 122. Folder 12. Sigmund Freud Papers. Sigmund Freud Collection. Manuscript Reading Room, Room 101, Manuscript Division, James Madison Memorial Building, Library of Congress, Washington, D.C., U.S.A.

Elkan, Irmi (1995). Personal Communication to the Author. 26th May.
Ellis, Catherine (2004). Durbin, Evan Frank Mottram (1906–1948). In H. Colin G. Matthew and Brian Harrison (Eds.). *Oxford Dictionary of National Biography: In Association with the British Academy. From the Earliest Times to the Year 2000. Volume 17. Drysdale-Ekins*, pp. 390–393. Oxford: Oxford University Press.
Elmhirst, Susanna Isaacs (1996a). Personal Communication to the Author. 25th January.
Elmhirst, Susanna Isaacs (1996b). Personal Communication to the Author. 7th March.
Extract from Minutes of A.C.: 26th. Feb. 1948 (1948). Minutes. In Marriage Guidance Centres: Agenda and Minutes. From: 22.1.46 (1946–1956). SA/TCC/A/3/1/7. Tavistock Centre for Couple Relationships. Archives and Manuscripts, Rare Materials Room, Wellcome Library, Wellcome Collection, The Wellcome Building, London.
Faithfull, Theodore J. (1927). *Bisexuality: An Essay on Extraversion and Introversion*. London: John Bale, Sons and Danielsson.
Faithfull, Theodore J. (1938). *The Mystery of the Androgyne: Three Papers on the Theory and Practice of Psycho-Analysis*. London: Forum Publishing Company.
Ferenczi, Sándor, and Rank, Otto (1924). *Entwicklungsziele der Psychoanalyse: Zur Wechselbeziehung von Theorie und Praxis*. Vienna: Internationaler Psychoanalytischer Verlag.
Fichtl, Paula (n.d.). Personal Communication to Jack J. Spector. n.d. Cited in Jack J. Spector (1972). *The Aesthetics of Freud: A Study in' Psychoanalysis and Art*, p. 15. New York: Praeger Publishers.
Field, Joanna (1934). *A Life of One's Own*. London: Chatto and Windus.
Field, Joanna (1950). *On Not Being Able to Paint*. London: William Heinemann.
Fielding, John, and Newman, Alexander (1988). Editorial. *Winnicott Studies*, 3, 3.
First Report of the Commissioners: Mines (1842). London: Her Majesty's Stationery Office.
Forrester, John, and Cameron, Laura (1999). 'A Cure with a Defect': A Previously Unpublished Letter by Freud Concerning 'Anna O'. *International Journal of Psychoanalysis*, 80, 929–942.
Forrester, John, and Cameron, Laura (2017). *Freud in Cambridge*. Cambridge: Cambridge University Press.
Forsyth, David (1920). Psycho-analysis of a Case of Early Paranoid Dementia. *Proceedings of the Royal Society of Medicine*, Section of Psychiatry, *13*, 65–81.

Forsyth, David (1922). *The Technique of Psycho-Analysis*. London: Kegan Paul, Trench, Trubner and Company.

Frank, Claudia (1999). *Melanie Kleins erste Kinderanalysen: Die Entdeckung des Kindes als Objekt sui generis von Heilen und Forschen*. Stuttgart Bad Cannstatt: Frommann-Holzboog/Friedrich Frommann Verlag/Günther Holzboog.

Frankl, Liselotte, and Rycroft, Charles (1951). Report of the Joint Librarians. *The Institute of Psycho-Analysis and the British Psycho-Analytical Society Report for the Year Ending 30th June 1951*, p. 43. London: Institute of Psycho-Analysis.

Freeman, Erika (1971). *Insights: Conversations with Theodor Reik*. Englewood Cliffs, New Jersey: Prentice-Hall.

Freeman, Lucy (1972). *The Story of Anna O*. New York: Walker and Company.

Freeman, Thomas (1961). Book Review of Ronald D. Laing. *The Divided Self: A Study of Sanity and Madness*. British Journal of Medical Psychology, 34, 79–80.

Freeman, Thomas (1988). *The Psychoanalyst in Psychiatry*. London: H. Karnac (Books).

Freeman, Thomas; Cameron, John L., and McGhie, Andrew (1965). *Studies on Psychosis: Descriptive, Psycho-Analytic, and Psychological Aspects*. London: Tavistock Publications.

Freud, Anna (1927). *Einführung in die Technik der Psychoanalyse*. Vienna: Internationaler Psychoanalytischer Verlag.

Freud, Anna (1928). *Introduction to the Technic of Child Analysis*. L. Pierce Clark (Transl.). New York: Nervous and Mental Disease Publishing Company.

Freud, Anna (1968). Letter to Donald W. Winnicott. 30th October. Box 7. File 2. Donald W. Winnicott Papers. Archives of Psychiatry, The Oskar Diethelm Library, The DeWitt Wallace Institute of Psychiatry: History, Policy, and the Arts, Department of Psychiatry, Joan and Sanford I. Weill Medical College, Cornell University, The New York Presbyterian Hospital, New York, New York, U.S.A.

Freud, Martin (1957). *Glory Reflected: Sigmund Freud—Man and Father*. London: Angus and Robertson.

Freud, Sigmund (1905a). Bruchstück einer Hysterie-Analyse. [Part I]. *Monatsschrift für Psychiatrie und Neurologie*, 18, 285–309.

Freud, Sigmund (1905b). Bruchstück einer Hysterie-Analyse. [Part II]. *Monatsschrift für Psychiatrie und Neurologie*, 18, 408–467.

Freud, Sigmund (1909a). Analyse der Phobie eines 5jährigen Knaben. *Jahrbuch für psychoanalytische und psychopathologische Forschungen*, 1, 1–109.

Freud, Sigmund (1909b). Bemerkungen über einen Fall von Zwangsneurose. *Jahrbuch für psychoanalytische und psychopathologische Forschungen*, 1, 357–421.

Freud, Sigmund (1910). Beiträge zur Psychologie des Liebeslebens: I. Über einen besonderen Typus der Objektwahl beim Manne. *Jahrbuch für psychoanalytische und psychopathologische Forschungen*, 2, 389–397.

Freud, Sigmund (1911). Psychoanalytische Bemerkungen über einen autobiographisch beschriebenen Fall von Paranoia (Dementia Paranoides). *Jahrbuch für psychoanalytische und psychopathologische Forschungen*, 3, 9–68.

Freud, Sigmund (1913). Weitere Ratschläge zur Technik der Psychoanalyse: I. Zur Einleitung der Behandlung. *Internationale Zeitschrift für ärztliche Psychoanalyse*, 1, 1–10.

Freud, Sigmund (1914a). Weitere Ratschläge zur Technik der Psychoanalyse: II. Erinnern, Wiederholen und Durcharbeiten. *Internationale Zeitschrift für ärztliche Psychoanalyse*, 2, 485–491.

Freud, Sigmund (1914b). Remembering, Repeating and Working-Through: (Further Recommendations on the Technique of Psycho-Analysis. II). Joan Riviere and James Strachey (Transls.). In Sigmund Freud (1958). *The Standard Edition of the Complete Psychological Works of Sigmund Freud: Volume XII. (1911–1913). The Case of Schreber. Papers on Technique and Other Works*. James Strachey, Anna Freud, Alix Strachey, and Alan Tyson (Eds. and Transls.), pp. 147–156. London: Hogarth Press and the Institute of Psycho-Analysis.

Freud, Sigmund (1916a). Einige Charaktertypen aus der psychoanalytischen Arbeit. *Imago*, 4, 317–336.

Freud, Sigmund (1916b). Some Character-Types Met with in Psycho-Analytic Work. In Sigmund Freud (1957). *The Standard Edition of the Complete Psychological Works of Sigmund Freud: Volume XIV. (1914–1916). On the History of the Psycho-Analytic Movement. Papers on Metapsychology and Other Works*. James Strachey, Anna Freud, Alix Strachey, and Alan Tyson (Eds. and Transls.), pp. 311–333. London: Hogarth Press and the Institute of Psycho-Analysis.

Freud, Sigmund (1918). Aus der Geschichte einer infantilen Neurose. In *Sammlung kleiner Schriften zur Neurosenlehre: Vierte Folge*, pp. 578–717. Vienna: Hugo Heller und Compagnie.

Freud, Sigmund (1919a). Letter to Ernest Jones. 18th April. In Sigmund Freud and Ernest Jones (1993). *The Complete Correspondence of Sigmund Freud and Ernest Jones: 1908–1939*. R. Andrew Paskauskas (Ed.). Frauke Voss

(Transl.), pp. 340–341. Cambridge, Massachusetts: Belknap Press of Harvard University Press.

Freud, Sigmund (1919b). Letter to Max Eitingon. 12th October. In Sigmund Freud and Max Eitingon (2004). *Briefwechsel: 1906–1939. Erster Band.* Michael Schröter (Ed.), pp. 163–165. Tübingen: edition diskord.

Freud, Sigmund (1919c). Letter to Karl Abraham. 2nd November. In Sigmund Freud and Karl Abraham (2009). *Briefwechsel 1907–1925: Vollständige Ausgabe. Band 2: 1915–1925.* Ernst Falzeder and Ludger M. Hermanns (Eds.), pp. 632–633. Vienna: Verlag Turia und Kant.

Freud, Sigmund (1920a). Letter to Ernest Jones. 13th May. In Sigmund Freud and Ernest Jones (1993). *The Complete Correspondence of Sigmund Freud and Ernest Jones: 1908–1939.* R. Andrew Paskauskas (Ed.). Frauke Voss (Transl.), pp. 379–380. Cambridge, Massachusetts: Belknap Press of Harvard University Press.

Freud, Sigmund (1920b). Letter to Karl Abraham. 31st October. In Sigmund Freud and Karl Abraham (2009). *Briefwechsel 1907–1925: Vollständige Ausgabe. Band 2: 1915–1925.* Ernst Falzeder and Ludger M. Hermanns (Eds.), pp. 672–673. Vienna: Verlag Turia und Kant.

Freud, Sigmund (1932). Letter to Arthur Tansley. 20th November, p. 930. In John Forrester and Laura Cameron (1999). 'A Cure with a Defect': A Previously Unpublished Letter by Freud Concerning 'Anna O'. *International Journal of Psychoanalysis, 80*, 929–942.

Freud, Sigmund (1933). *Neue Folge der Vorlesungen zur Einführung in die Psychoanalyse.* Vienna: Internationaler Psychoanalytischer Verlag.

Freud, Sigmund (1939). Diary Entry. 1st August. In Sigmund Freud (1992). *The Diary of Sigmund Freud: 1929–1939. A Record of the Final Decade.* Michael Molnar (Ed. and Transl.), p. 41. New York: Charles Scribner's Sons, and Toronto: Maxwell Macmillan Canada, and New York: Maxwell Macmillan International, and New York: Charles Scribner's Sons/Macmillan Publishing Company, Maxwell Communication Group of Companies, and Don Mills, Ontario: Maxwell Macmillan Canada.

Freud, Sigmund (1953a). *The Standard Edition of the Complete Psychological Works of Sigmund Freud: Volume IV. (1900). The Interpretation of Dreams. (First Part).* James Strachey, Anna Freud, Alix Strachey, and Alan Tyson (Eds. and Transls.). London: Hogarth Press and the Institute of Psycho-Analysis.

Freud, Sigmund (1953b). *The Standard Edition of the Complete Psychological Works of Sigmund Freud: Volume V. (1900–1901). The Interpretation of Dreams. (Second Part) and On Dreams.* James Strachey, Anna Freud, Alix

Strachey, and Alan Tyson (Eds. and Transls.). London: Hogarth Press and the Institute of Psycho-Analysis.

Freud, Sigmund (1953c). *The Standard Edition of the Complete Psychological Works of Sigmund Freud: Volume VII. (1901–1905). A Case of Hysteria. Three Essays on Sexuality and Other Works.* James Strachey, Anna Freud, Alix Strachey, and Alan Tyson (Eds. and Transls.). London: Hogarth Press and the Institute of Psycho-Analysis.

Freud, Sigmund (1953d). *The Standard Edition of the Complete Psychological Works of Sigmund Freud: Volume XIII. (1913–1914). Totem and Taboo and Other Works.* James Strachey, Anna Freud, Alix Strachey, and Alan Tyson (Eds. and Transls.). London: Hogarth Press and the Institute of Psycho-Analysis.

Freud, Sigmund (1955a). *The Standard Edition of the Complete Psychological Works of Sigmund Freud: Volume II. (1893–1895). Studies on Hysteria.* James Strachey, Anna Freud, Alix Strachey, and Alan Tyson (Eds. and Transls.). London: Hogarth Press and the Institute of Psycho-Analysis.

Freud, Sigmund (1955b). *The Standard Edition of the Complete Psychological Works of Sigmund Freud: Volume X. (1909). Two Case Histories ('Little Hans' and the 'Rat Man').* James Strachey, Anna Freud, Alix Strachey, and Alan Tyson (Eds. and Transls.). London: Hogarth Press and the Institute of Psycho-Analysis.

Freud, Sigmund (1955c). *The Standard Edition of the Complete Psychological Works of Sigmund Freud: Volume XVII. (1917–1919). An Infantile Neurosis and Other Works.* James Strachey, Anna Freud, Alix Strachey, and Alan Tyson (Eds. and Transls.). London: Hogarth Press and the Institute of Psycho-Analysis.

Freud, Sigmund (1955d). *The Standard Edition of the Complete Psychological Works of Sigmund Freud: Volume XVIII. (1920–1922). Beyond the Pleasure Principle. Group Psychology and Other Works.* James Strachey, Anna Freud, Alix Strachey, and Alan Tyson (Eds. and Transls.). London: Hogarth Press and the Institute of Psycho-Analysis.

Freud, Sigmund (1957a). *The Standard Edition of the Complete Psychological Works of Sigmund Freud: Volume XI. (1910). Five Lectures on Psycho-Analysis, Leonardo da Vinci and Other Works.* James Strachey, Anna Freud, Alix Strachey, and Alan Tyson (Eds. and Transls.). London: Hogarth Press and the Institute of Psycho-Analysis.

Freud, Sigmund (1957b). *The Standard Edition of the Complete Psychological Works of Sigmund Freud: Volume XIV. (1914–1916). On the History of the Psycho-Analytic Movement, Papers on Metapsychology and Other Works.*

James Strachey, Anna Freud, Alix Strachey, and Alan Tyson (Eds. and Transls.). London: Hogarth Press and the Institute of Psycho-Analysis.

Freud, Sigmund (1958). *The Standard Edition of the Complete Psychological Works of Sigmund Freud: Volume XII. (1911–1913). The Case of Schreber. Papers on Technique and Other Works*. James Strachey, Anna Freud, Alix Strachey, and Alan Tyson (Eds. and Transls.). London: Hogarth Press and the Institute of Psycho-Analysis.

Freud, Sigmund (1959a). *The Standard Edition of the Complete Psychological Works of Sigmund Freud: Volume IX. (1906–1908). Jensen's 'Gradiva' and Other Works*. James Strachey, Anna Freud, Alix Strachey, and Alan Tyson (Eds. and Transls.). London: Hogarth Press and the Institute of Psycho-Analysis.

Freud, Sigmund (1959b). *The Standard Edition of the Complete Psychological Works of Sigmund Freud: Volume XX. (1925–1926). An Autobiographical Study, Inhibitions, Symptoms and Anxiety, The Question of Lay Analysis and Other Works*. James Strachey, Anna Freud, Alix Strachey, and Alan Tyson (Eds. and Transls.). London: Hogarth Press and the Institute of Psycho-Analysis.

Freud, Sigmund (1960a). *The Standard Edition of the Complete Psychological Works of Sigmund Freud: Volume VI. (1901). The Psychopathology of Everyday Life*. James Strachey, Anna Freud, Alix Strachey, and Alan Tyson (Eds. and Transls.). London: Hogarth Press and the Institute of Psycho-Analysis.

Freud, Sigmund (1960b). *The Standard Edition of the Complete Psychological Works of Sigmund Freud: Volume VIII. (1905). Jokes and Their Relation to the Unconscious*. James Strachey, Anna Freud, Alix Strachey, and Alan Tyson (Eds. and Transls.). London: Hogarth Press and the Institute of Psycho-Analysis.

Freud, Sigmund (1961a). *The Standard Edition of the Complete Psychological Works of Sigmund Freud: Volume XIX. (1923–1925). The Ego and the Id and Other Works*. James Strachey, Anna Freud, Alix Strachey, and Alan Tyson (Eds. and Transls.). London: Hogarth Press and the Institute of Psycho-Analysis.

Freud, Sigmund (1961b). *The Standard Edition of the Complete Psychological Works of Sigmund Freud: Volume XXI. (1927–1931). The Future of an Illusion. Civilization and its Discontents and Other Works*. James Strachey, Anna Freud, Alix Strachey, and Alan Tyson (Eds. and Transls.). London: Hogarth Press and the Institute of Psycho-Analysis.

Freud, Sigmund (1962). *The Standard Edition of the Complete Psychological Works of Sigmund Freud: Volume III. (1893–1899). Early Psycho-Analytic*

Publications. James Strachey, Anna Freud, Alix Strachey, and Alan Tyson (Eds. and Transls.). London: Hogarth Press and the Institute of Psycho-Analysis.

Freud, Sigmund (1963a). *The Standard Edition of the Complete Psychological Works of Sigmund Freud: Volume XV. (1915–1916). Introductory Lectures on Psycho-Analysis. (Parts I and II).* James Strachey, Anna Freud, Alix Strachey, and Alan Tyson (Eds. and Transls.). London: Hogarth Press and the Institute of Psycho-Analysis.

Freud, Sigmund (1963b). *The Standard Edition of the Complete Psychological Works of Sigmund Freud: Volume XVI. (1916–1917). Introductory Lectures on Psycho-Analysis. (Part III).* James Strachey, Anna Freud, Alix Strachey, and Alan Tyson (Eds. and Transls.). London: Hogarth Press and the Institute of Psycho-Analysis.

Freud, Sigmund (1964a). *The Standard Edition of the Complete Psychological Works of Sigmund Freud: Volume XXII. (1932–1936). New Introductory Lectures on Psycho-Analysis and Other Works.* James Strachey, Anna Freud, Alix Strachey, and Alan Tyson (Eds. and Transls.). London: Hogarth Press and the Institute of Psycho-Analysis.

Freud, Sigmund (1964b). *The Standard Edition of the Complete Psychological Works of Sigmund Freud: Volume XXIII. (1937–1939). Moses and Monotheism. An Outline of Psycho-Analysis and Other Works.* James Strachey, Anna Freud, Alix Strachey, and Alan Tyson (Eds. and Transls.). London: Hogarth Press and the Institute of Psycho-Analysis.

Freud, Sigmund (1966). *The Standard Edition of the Complete Psychological Works of Sigmund Freud: Volume I. (1886–1899). Pre-Psycho-Analytic Publications and Unpublished Drafts.* James Strachey, Anna Freud, Alix Strachey, and Alan Tyson (Eds. and Transls.). London: Hogarth Press and the Institute of Psycho-Analysis.

Freud, Sigmund (1974). *The Standard Edition of the Complete Psychological Works of Sigmund Freud: Volume XXIV. Indexes and Bibliographies.* James Strachey, Anna Freud, Alix Strachey, Alan Tyson, and Angela Richards (Eds.). London: Hogarth Press and the Institute of Psycho-Analysis.

Freud, Sigmund; Ferenczi, Sándor; Abraham, Karl; Simmel, Ernst, and Jones, Ernest (1919). *Zur Psychoanalyse der Kriegsneurosen.* Vienna: Internationaler Psychoanalytischer Verlag.

Friedman, Leonard J. (1962). *Virgin Wives: A Study of Unconsummated Marriages.* London: Tavistock Publications, and Springfield, Illinois: Charles C Thomas, Publisher.

Gabriel, Pam (1965a). Letter to Donald W. Winnicott. 5th July. Box 5. File 3. Donald W. Winnicott Papers. Archives of Psychiatry, The Oskar Diethelm

Library, The DeWitt Wallace Institute of Psychiatry: History, Policy, and the Arts, Department of Psychiatry, Joan and Sanford I. Weill Medical College, Cornell University, The New York Presbyterian Hospital, New York, New York, U.S.A.

Gabriel, Pam (1965b). Letter to Donald W. Winnicott. 5th October. Box 5. File 3. Donald W. Winnicott Papers. Archives of Psychiatry, The Oskar Diethelm Library, The DeWitt Wallace Institute of Psychiatry: History, Policy, and the Arts, Department of Psychiatry, Joan and Sanford I. Weill Medical College, Cornell University, The New York Presbyterian Hospital, New York, New York, U.S.A.

Gaddini, Renata (1996). Personal Communication to the Author. 2nd May.

Gamwell, Lynn (1989). The Origins of Freud's Antiquities Collection. In Lynn Gamwell and Richard Wells (Eds.). *Sigmund Freud and Art: His Personal Collection of Antiquities*, pp. 21–32. London: Thames and Hudson, and Binghamton, New York: State University of New York, and London: Freud Museum.

Gans, Steven (1992). Personal Communication to the Author. 5th December.

Gardiner, Juliet (2005). *The Children's War: The Second World War Through the Eyes of the Children of Britain*. London: Portrait/Piatkus Books/Imperial War Museum.

Gardiner, Muriel (1978). In Wien vom 12. Februar 1934 bis zum Anschluß. In Muriel Gardiner and Joseph Buttinger. *Damit wir nicht vergessen: Unsere Jahre 1934–1947 in Wien, Paris und New York*, pp. 31–72. Vienna: Verlag der Wiener Volksbuchhandlung.

Gardiner, Muriel (1983). *Code Name "Mary": Memoirs of an American Woman in the Austrian Underground*. New Haven, Connecticut: Yale University Press.

Gatling, Mary (2015). E-Mail to the Author. 24th July.

General Secretary (1948). Letter to P.S. Maine [sic] [Thomas Main]. 3rd June. SA/TCC/A/2/3. Tavistock Centre for Couple Relationships. Archives and Manuscripts, Rare Materials Room, Wellcome Library, Wellcome Collection, The Wellcome Building, London.

Gillespie, Sadie (1988). Marion. *Winnicott Studies*, 3, 61–62.

Gillespie, William H. (1971). Donald W. Winnicott. *International Journal of Psycho-Analysis*, 52, 227–228.

Gillespie, William (1988). Mrs Marion Milner. *Winnicott Studies*, 3, 60.

Gitelson, Maxwell (1963). Letter to Donald W. Winnicott. 30th October. PP/DWW/M.2/1. Donald Woods Winnicott Collection. Archives and Manuscripts, Rare Materials Room, Wellcome Library, Wellcome Collection, The Wellcome Building, London.

Godley, Wynne (2001a). Saving Masud Khan. *London Review of Books.* 22nd February, pp. 3, 5-7.

Godley, Wynne (2001b). My Lost Hours on the Couch. *The Times.* Section 2. 23rd February, pp. 2-5.

Godley, Wynne (2004). Commentary. *International Journal of Psychoanalysis*, 85, 42-43.

Goldie, Lawrence (1993). Personal Communication to the Author. 9th January.

Goldie, Lawrence (1994). Personal Communication to the Author. 1st May.

Gordon, Ronald G. (Ed.). (1939). *A Survey of Child Psychiatry.* London: Humphrey Milford/Oxford University Press.

Gowing, Margaret (1976). Richard Morris Titmuss: 1907-1973. *Proceedings of the British Academy*, 61, 401-428. London: British Academy/Oxford University Press.

Gray, Sidney G. (1970). The Tavistock Institute of Human Relations. In Henry V. Dicks. *Fifty Years of the Tavistock Clinic*, pp. 206-227. London: Routledge and Kegan Paul.

Griffith, Edward F. (1981). *The Pioneer Spirit.* Upton Grey, Basingstoke, Hampshire: Green Leaves Press.

Grinker, Roy R. (1940). Reminiscences of a Personal Contact with Freud. *American Journal of Orthopsychiatry*, 10, 850-854.

Grosskurth, Phyllis (1981). Interview with Clare Winnicott. 18th September. Cited in Phyllis Grosskurth (1986). *Melanie Klein: Her World and Her Work*, p. 481, n. 21. New York: Alfred A. Knopf.

Grosskurth, Phyllis (1982a). Interview with Susanna Isaacs Elmhirst. 24th January. Cited in Phyllis Grosskurth (1986). *Melanie Klein: Her World and Her Work*, p. 479, n. 43. New York: Alfred A. Knopf.

Grosskurth, Phyllis (1982b). Interview with Arthur Hyatt Williams. 12th February. Cited in Phyllis Grosskurth (1986). *Melanie Klein: Her World and Her Work*, p. 479, n. 44. New York: Alfred A. Knopf.

Grosskurth, Phyllis (1982c). Interview with Ronald D. Laing. 18th March. Cited in Phyllis Grosskurth (1986). *Melanie Klein: Her World and Her Work*, p. 480, n. 16. New York: Alfred A. Knopf.

Grosskurth, Phyllis (1984). Melanie Klein in Berlin. *Journal of the Melanie Klein Society*, 2, Number 2, 3-43.

Grosskurth, Phyllis (1986). *Melanie Klein: Her World and Her Work.* New York: Alfred A. Knopf.

Guntrip, Harry (n.d.). Obituary: Donald Woods Winnicott. Unpublished Typescript. PP/DWW/G/6/2. Donald Woods Winnicott Collection. Archives and Manuscripts, Rare Materials Room, Wellcome Library, Wellcome Collection, The Wellcome Building, London.

Gürisik, Elif (1996). Personal Communication to the Author. 5th December.
Guthrie, Leonard G. (1907). *Functional Nervous Disorders in Childhood*. London: Henry Frowde/Oxford University Press, and Hodder and Stoughton.
H.D. [Hilda Doolittle] (1945a). Writing on the Wall. [Part I]. *Life and Letters To-Day*, 45, 67–98.
H.D. [Hilda Doolittle] (1945b). Writing on the Wall: (Continued). [Part II]. *Life and Letters To-Day*, 45, 137–154.
H.D. [Hilda Doolittle] (1945c). Writing on the Wall: (To Sigmund Freud). [Part III]. *Life and Letters and The London Mercury and Bookman*, 46, 72–89.
H.D. [Hilda Doolittle] (1945d). Writing on the Wall: (To Sigmund Freud). [Part IV]. *Life and Letters and The London Mercury and Bookman*, 46, 136–151.
H.D. [Hilda Doolittle] (1946). Writing on the Wall: (To Sigmund Freud). [Part V]. *Life and Letters and The London Mercury*, 48, 33–45.
H.D. [Hilda Doolittle] (1956). *Tribute to Freud: With Unpublished Letters by Freud to the Author*. New York: Pantheon/Pantheon Books.
Harrington, William, and Young, Peter (1978). *The 1945 Revolution*. London: Davis-Poynter.
Harris, Alana (2015). Love Divine and Love Sublime: The Catholic Marriage Advisory Council, the Marriage Guidance Movement and the State. In Alana Harris and Timothy Willem Jones (Eds.). *Love and Romance in Britain, 1918–1970*, pp. 188–224. Houndmills, Basingstoke, Hampshire: Palgrave Macmillan.
Hart, Edward (1963). Letter to Donald W. Winnicott. 2nd May. Box 4. File 1. Donald W. Winnicott Papers. Archives of Psychiatry, The Oskar Diethelm Library, The DeWitt Wallace Institute of Psychiatry: History, Policy, and the Arts, Department of Psychiatry, Joan and Sanford I. Weill Medical College, Cornell University, The New York Presbyterian Hospital, New York, New York, U.S.A.
Hellmuth, Hermine (1912). "Versprechen" eines kleinen Schuljungen. *Zentralblatt für Psychoanalyse*, 2, 603–604.
Hepner, Gershy (1961). Letter to Donald W. Winnicott. 11th November. PP/DWW/A/J. Folder 1. Donald Woods Winnicott Collection. Archives and Manuscripts, Rare Materials Room, Wellcome Library, Wellcome Collection, The Wellcome Building, London.
Herman, Judith Lewis (1992). *Trauma and Recovery*. New York: Basic Books.
Hitschmann, Eduard, and Bergler, Edmund (1934). *Die Geschlechtskälte der Frau: Ihr Wesen und ihre Behandlung*. Vienna: Verlag der "Ars Medici".

Hodder, Edwin (1886a). *The Life and Work of the Seventh Earl of Shaftesbury, K.G.: Vol. I*. London: Cassell and Company.
Hodder, Edwin (1886b). *The Life and Work of the Seventh Earl of Shaftesbury, K.G.: Vol. II*. London: Cassell and Company.
Hodder, Edwin (1886c). *The Life and Work of the Seventh Earl of Shaftesbury, K.G.: Vol. III*. London: Cassell and Company.
Hodgkinson, Ruth G. (1967). *The Origins of the National Health Service: The Medical Services of the New Poor Law, 1834–1871*. London: Wellcome Historical Medical Library.
Hollander, Bernard (1916). *Abnormal Children: (Nervous, Mischievous, Precocious, and Backward). A Book for Parents, Teachers, and Medical Officers of Schools*. London: Kegan Paul, Trench, Trubner and Company.
Hopkins, Linda (1998a). Interview with Luise Eichenbaum. n.d. Cited in Linda Hopkins (2006). *False Self: The Life of Masud Khan*, p. 347. New York: Other Press.
Hopkins, Linda (1998b). Interview with Susie Orbach. n.d. Cited in Linda Hopkins (2006). *False Self: The Life of Masud Khan*, p. 347. New York: Other Press.
Hopkins, Linda (2006). *False Self: The Life of Masud Khan*. New York: Other Press.
Hopkins, Linda (n.d.). Interview with Pearl King. Quoted in Linda Hopkins (2006). *False Self: The Life of Masud Khan*, p. 366. New York: Other Press.
Hopkins, Philip (2004). Balint, Michael Maurice [*formerly* Mihaly Bergsmann] (1896–1970). In H. Colin G. Matthew and Brian Harrison (Eds.). *Oxford Dictionary of National Biography: In Association with the British Academy. From the Earliest Times to the Year 2000. Volume 3. Avranches-Barnewall*, pp. 550–553. Oxford: Oxford University Press.
Hopper, Earl (2007). Personal Communication to the Author. 4th June.
Hopper, Earl (2022a). E-Mail to the Author. [E-Mail Number 1]. 15th July.
Hopper, Earl (2022b). E-Mail to the Author. [E-Mail Number 2]. 15th July.
Horney, Karen (1942). *Self-Analysis*. New York: W.W. Norton and Company.
Howard, Maurice F., and Houghton, Geoffrey C. (Eds.). (1991). *The Handbook and Directory of the Leys School: Twentieth Edition. Brought Up to December 31, 1990*. Sawston, Cambridge: Crampton and Sons.
Hug-Hellmuth, Hermine (Ed.). (1919). *Tagebuch eines halbwüchsigen Mädchens*. Vienna: Internationaler Psychoanalytischer Verlag.
Hug-Hellmuth, Hermine (1922). Correspondence. *British Journal of Psychology: Medical Section*, 2, 257.

Hughes, Athol (1991). Joan Riviere: Her Life and Work. In Athol Hughes (Ed.). *The Inner World and Joan Riviere: Collected Papers. 1920-1958*, pp. 1-43. London: H. Karnac (Books).

Hughes, Athol (1995). Personal Communication to the Author. 3rd November.

Hughes, Judith M. (1989). *Reshaping the Psychoanalytic Domain: The Work of Melanie Klein, W.R.D. Fairbairn, and D.W. Winnicott.* Berkeley, California: University of California Press.

Hunnybun, Noël K. (1949). Letter to Enid Eicholz [sic] [Enid Eichholz]. 11th August. SA/TCC/A/2/5. Tavistock Centre for Couple Relationships. Archives and Manuscripts, Rare Materials Room, Wellcome Library, Wellcome Collection, The Wellcome Building, London.

Hunnybun, Noël K. (1951). Letter to Enid Eichholz. 24th August. SA/TCC/A/2/5. Tavistock Centre for Couple Relationships. Archives and Manuscripts, Rare Materials Room, Wellcome Library, Wellcome Collection, The Wellcome Building, London.

Isaacs, Susan (1940). The Uprooted Child. In John Rickman (Ed.). *Children in War-Time: The Uprooted Child, the Problem of the Young Child, the Deprived Mother, Foster-Parents, Visiting, the Teacher's Problems, Homes for Difficult Children*, pp. 5-19. London: New Education Fellowship.

Israëls, Han (1989a). *Schreber: Vader en Zoon: Historisch-kritische opmerkingen over een psychoanalytisch beschreven geval van paranoia.* Amsterdam: Historische Uitgeverij Groningen/Omslagontwerp Gerard Hadders/Schiedam.

Israëls, Han (1989b). *Schreber: Father and Son.* H.S. Lake (Transl.). Madison, Connecticut: International Universities Press.

Jackson, Carlton (1985). *Who Will Take Our Children?* London: Methuen/Methuen London.

James, Martin (1965). Letter to Donald W. Winnicott. 1st December. Box 5. File 4. Donald W. Winnicott Papers. Archives of Psychiatry, The Oskar Diethelm Library, The DeWitt Wallace Institute of Psychiatry: History, Policy, and the Arts, Department of Psychiatry, Joan and Sanford I. Weill Medical College, Cornell University, The New York Presbyterian Hospital, New York, New York, U.S.A.

James, Martin (1991). Lecture on "Has Winnicott Become a Winnicottian?: The Importance of Psychiatry". The Squiggle Foundation, Primrose Hill, London, at the Primrose Hill Community Centre, Primrose Hill, London. 16th February.

Jones, David (1943a). Postcard to Harold S. Ede. 10th March. Kettle's Yard Archives. Kettle's Yard, University of Cambridge, Cambridge, Cambridgeshire.

Jones, David (1943b). Letter to Harold S. Ede. 27th March. Kettle's Yard Archives. Kettle's Yard, University of Cambridge, Cambridge, Cambridgeshire.

Jones, David (1943c). Letter to Harold S. Ede. 17th May. Kettle's Yard Archives. Kettle's Yard, University of Cambridge, Cambridge, Cambridgeshire.

Jones, David (1944). Letter to Harold S. Ede. 13th March. Kettle's Yard Archives. Kettle's Yard, University of Cambridge, Cambridge, Cambridgeshire.

Jones, Ernest (1919). Letter to Sigmund Freud. 1st July. In Sigmund Freud and Ernest Jones (1993). *The Complete Correspondence of Sigmund Freud and Ernest Jones: 1908–1939*. R. Andrew Paskauskas (Ed.). Frauke Voss (Transl.), p. 350. Cambridge, Massachusetts: Belknap Press of Harvard University Press.

Jones, Ernest (1922). Letter to Sigmund Freud. 22nd January. In Sigmund Freud and Ernest Jones (1993). *The Complete Correspondence of Sigmund Freud and Ernest Jones: 1908–1939*. R. Andrew Paskauskas (Ed.), pp. 453–454. Cambridge, Massachusetts: Belknap Press of Harvard University Press.

Jones, Ernest (1944). Letter to Donald W. Winnicott. 26th January. PP/DWW/B/A/16. Donald Woods Winnicott Collection. Archives and Manuscripts, Rare Materials Room, Wellcome Library, Wellcome Collection, The Wellcome Building, London.

Jones, Ernest (1950). Letter to Donald W. Winnicott. 3rd October. PP/DWW/B/A/16. Donald Woods Winnicott Collection. Archives and Manuscripts, Rare Materials Room, Wellcome Library, Wellcome Collection, The Wellcome Building, London.

Jones, Ernest (1953). *The Life and Work of Sigmund Freud: Volume 1. The Formative Years and the Great Discoveries. 1856–1900*. New York: Basic Books.

Jones, Ernest (1957). *The Life and Work of Sigmund Freud: Volume 3. The Last Phase. 1919–1939*. New York: Basic Books.

Jones, Mervyn, and Ferris, Paul (1959). *Dr. Ernest Jones: Portrait Assembled from Reminiscences of People Who Knew Him*. Radio Broadcast. 15th March. Tape T30130. B.B.C. Home Service. B.B.C. Sound Archives, National Sound Archives, London.

Kahr, Brett (1984). Interview with John Bowlby. 20th February.

Kahr, Brett E. (1985a). Psycho-Analysis in Oxford: A Study in Heresy. *British Journal of Psychotherapy*, *1*, 293–294.

Kahr, Brett (1985b). Marion Milner Interview: Saturday, 16th February, 1985. Unpublished Typescript.

Kahr, Brett (1985c). Interview with Marion Milner. 16th February.

Kahr, Brett (1985d). Interview with Margaret Little. 25th May.

Kahr, Brett (1986). Interview with John Bowlby. 30th October.

Kahr, Brett (1987). Lecture on "Nijinsky's Madness: A Psychoanalytic Study". Discussion Group on "The Nature of the Creative Process". Fall Meeting, American Psychoanalytic Association, at the Waldorf Astoria Hotel, New York, New York, U.S.A. 18th December.

Kahr, Brett (1991a). The Sexual Molestation of Children: Historical Perspectives. *Journal of Psychohistory*, 19, 191–214.

Kahr, Brett (1991b). Interview with Barbara Dockar-Drysdale. 13th July.

Kahr, Brett (1993). Interview with Charles Rycroft. 29th November.

Kahr, Brett (1994a). R.D. Laing's Missing Tooth: Schizophrenia and Bodily Disintegration. *Journal of the Society for Existential Analysis*, 4, 64–79.

Kahr, Brett (1994b). Lecture on "Masud Khan's Analysis with Donald Winnicott: On the Hazards of Befriending a Patient". First Sundays Public Lectures on "Psychoanalysis, Community and Culture". Philadelphia Association, Hampstead, London. 9th October.

Kahr, Brett (1994c). Interview with Michael Fordham. 13th February.

Kahr, Brett (1994d). Telephone Interview with Donald Campbell. 2nd May.

Kahr, Brett (1994e). Interview with Susanna Isaacs Elmhirst. 30th May.

Kahr, Brett (1994f). Interview with Malcolm Pines. 3rd October.

Kahr, Brett (1994g). Interview with Joyce Coles. 18th December.

Kahr, Brett (1995a). Letter to "Mrs. Piggle". 7th November. "The Piggle" Papers. London.

Kahr, Brett (1995b). Interview with Ursula Bowlby. 29th January.

Kahr, Brett (1995c). Interview with Agnes Wilkinson. 31st January.

Kahr, Brett (1995d). Interview with Isabel Menzies Lyth. 12th February.

Kahr, Brett (1995e). Interview with Anthony Bradshaw. 18th February.

Kahr, Brett (1995f). Interview with Betty Bradshaw. 18th February.

Kahr, Brett (1995g). Interview with Joyce Coles. 5th March.

Kahr, Brett (1995h). Telephone Interview with "Mrs. Piggle". 12th December.

Kahr, Brett (1996a). *D.W. Winnicott: A Biographical Portrait*. London: Karnac Books/H. Karnac (Books).

Kahr, Brett (1996b). Telephone Interview with Katharine Rees. 3rd January.

Kahr, Brett (1996c). Interview with Raymond Shepherd. 20th February.

Kahr, Brett (1996d). Telephone Interview with Robert Shields. 2nd March.

Kahr, Brett (1996e). Interview with Christopher Bradshaw. 4th March.

Kahr, Brett (1996f). Interview with Valiant Bradshaw. 4th March.

Kahr, Brett (1996g). Interview with "Arabella Bagshawe". 12th March.

Kahr, Brett (1996h). Interview with "The Piggle". 2nd April.

Kahr, Brett (1996i). Interview with Lydia James. 12th October.

Kahr, Brett (1996j). Interview with Jonathan Pedder. 22nd October.

Kahr, Brett (1997). Interview with "Edmund Fothergill". 3rd January.

Kahr, Brett (2000a). Ursula Bowlby. *Psychotherapy Review*, 2, 160.

Kahr, Brett (2000b). 'A Harley Street for the Anxious Poor': The Tavistock Clinic in the 1930s. *Psychotherapy Review*, 2, 397–399.

Kahr, Brett (2002a). Masud Khan's Analysis with Donald Winnicott: On the Hazards of Befriending a Patient. Human Nature. [http://www.human-nature.com].

Kahr, Brett (2002b). Interview with Abrahão Brafman. 17th July.

Kahr, Brett (2003). Masud Khan's Analysis with Donald Winnicott: On the Hazards of Befriending a Patient. *Free Associations*, 10, 190–222.

Kahr, Brett (2004a). A Personal Reminiscence of John Bowlby. In Kate White (Ed.). *Touch: Attachment and the Body. The John Bowlby Memorial Conference Monograph 2003*, pp. xiii–xvi. London: Karnac Books/Karnac (Books).

Kahr, Brett (2004b). Introduction of Sir Richard Bowlby: John Bowlby and Donald Winnicott. Collegial Comrades in Child Mental Health. In Richard Bowlby. *Fifty Years of Attachment Theory*, pp. 3–9. London: Karnac (Books), and Ruislip, Middlesex: Winnicott Clinic of Psychotherapy.

Kahr, Brett (2005). Interview with Pearl King. 20th October.

Kahr, Brett (2007a). Lecture on "The Infanticidal Origins of Psychosis: The Role of Trauma in Schizophrenia. Part 1". Centenary John Bowlby Memorial Conference 1907–2007 on "Shattered States: Disorganised Attachment and its Repair". Centre for Attachment-Based Psychoanalytic Psychotherapy, London, at The Kennedy Lecture Theatre, Institute of Child Health, University College London, University of London, London. 9th March.

Kahr, Brett (2007b). Lecture on "The Infanticidal Origins of Psychosis: The Role of Trauma in Schizophrenia. Part 2". Centenary John Bowlby Memorial Conference 1907–2007 on "Shattered States: Disorganised Attachment and its Repair". Centre for Attachment-Based Psychoanalytic Psychotherapy, London, at The Kennedy Lecture Theatre, Institute of Child Health, University College London, University of London, London. 9th March.

Kahr, Brett (2009a). Dr. John Bowlby: Personal Reminiscences of a Gentleman Psychoanalyst. *Attachment: New Directions in Psychotherapy and Relational Psychoanalysis*, 3, 362–371.

Kahr, Brett (2009b). Telephone Interview with Olive Stevenson. 16th June.

Kahr, Brett (2009c). Telephone Interview with Gershon Hepner. 5th August.

Kahr, Brett (2009d). Interview with Jane Shore Nicholas. 21st August.

Kahr, Brett (2010a). Telephone Interview with John Evans. 1st February.

Kahr, Brett (2010b). Interview with Peter Bruggen. 10th February.

Kahr, Brett (2010c). Interview with Richard Michael. 26th March.

Kahr, Brett (2010d). Interview with Edward Lucie-Smith. 30th November.

Kahr, Brett (2011). Winnicott's *"Anni Horribiles"*: The Biographical Roots of "Hate in the Counter-Transference". *American Imago*, 68, 173–211.

Kahr, Brett (2012a). The Infanticidal Origins of Psychosis: The Role of Trauma in Schizophrenia. In Judy Yellin and Kate White (Eds.). *Shattered States: Disorganised Attachment and its Repair. The John Bowlby Memorial Conference Monograph 2007*, pp. 7–126. London: Karnac Books.

Kahr, Brett (Ed.). (2012b). Reminiscences by John Bowlby: Portraits of Colleagues, 1935–1945. (Previously Unpublished). *Attachment: New Directions in Psychotherapy and Relational Psychoanalysis*, 6, 27–49.

Kahr, Brett (2014a). Lecture on "The Intra-Marital Affair: From Erotic Tumour to Conjugal Aneurysm". Conference on "The Couple in the Room, the Couple in Mind: Reflections from an Attachment Perspective". The 21st John Bowlby Memorial Conference 2014. The Bowlby Centre, Highbury East, London, at The Kennedy Lecture Theatre, Wellcome Trust Building, Institute of Child Health, University College London, University of London, Holborn, London. 4th April.

Kahr, Brett (2014b). Telephone Interview with Mary Gatling. 21st August.

Kahr, Brett (2014c). Interview with Mary Gatling. 11th October.

Kahr, Brett (2015a). Winnicott's *Anni Horribiles*: The Biographical Roots of "Hate in the Counter-Transference". In Margaret Boyle Spelman and Frances Thomson-Salo (Eds.). *The Winnicott Tradition: Lines of Development—Evolution of Theory and Practice Over the Decades*, pp. 69–84. London: Karnac Books.

Kahr, Brett (2015b). "Led Astray by Their Half-Baked Pseudo-Scientific Rubbish": John Bowlby and the Paradigm Shift in Child Psychiatry. *Attachment: New Directions in Psychotherapy and Relational Psychoanalysis*, 9, 297–317.

Kahr, Brett (2015c). Lecture on "Historical Introduction". Conference on "Attachment Theory: How John Bowlby Revolutionised Our Understanding of Human Relationships. Where is the Revolution Now? What Are the Future Directions?", John Bowlby 25th Anniversary Event. An International Conference in Celebration of John Bowlby's Work. The Bowlby Centre, London, at The Kennedy Lecture Theatre, Wellcome Trust Building, Institute of Child Health, University College London, University of London, Holborn, London. 19th September.

Kahr, Brett (2015d). Lecture on "The Roots of Mental Health Broadcasting". Afternoon Workshop on "Donald Winnicott, the Public Psychoanalyst:

Broadcasting Beyond the Consulting Room". International Conference on "Donald Winnicott and the History of the Present: A Celebration of the Collected Works of D.W. Winnicott". The Winnicott Trust, London, in association with the British Psychoanalytical Society, Byron House, Maida Vale, London, and the British Psychoanalytic Association, British Psychotherapy Foundation, London, and the Association of Independent Psychoanalysts, London, at the Board Room, Mary Ward House Conference and Exhibition Centre, Holborn, London. 21st November.

Kahr, Brett (2016a). Ursula Longstaff Bowlby (1916–2000): The Creative Inspiration Behind the Secure Base. *Attachment: New Directions in Psychotherapy and Relational Psychoanalysis*, 10, 223–242.

Kahr, Brett (2016b). Lecture on " 'How to Cure Family Disturbance': Enid Balint and the Creation of Couple Psychoanalysis". Enid Balint Memorial Lecture. Tavistock Centre for Couple Relationships, Tavistock Institute of Medical Psychology, London. 26th February.

Kahr, Brett (2016c). Interview with Barbara Clark. 15th March.

Kahr, Brett (2016d). Interview with Susan Lawlor. 18th March.

Kahr, Brett (2017a). "How to Cure Family Disturbance": Enid Balint and the Creation of Couple Psychoanalysis. Twenty-first Enid Balint Memorial Lecture 2016. *Couple and Family Psychoanalysis*, 7, 1–25.

Kahr, Brett (2017b). Winnicott's Banquet of 1966. OUPblog. Oxford University Press. [http://blog.oup.com/2017/01/winnicotts-banquet-of-1966/].

Kahr, Brett (2018). The Public Psychoanalyst: Donald Winnicott as Broadcaster. In Angela Joyce (Ed.). *Donald W. Winnicott and the History of the Present: Understanding the Man and His Work*, pp. 111–121. London: Karnac Books.

Kahr, Brett (2019a). *How to Flourish as a Psychotherapist*. Bicester, Oxfordshire: Phoenix Publishing House.

Kahr, Brett (2019b). The First Mrs Winnicott and the Second Mrs Winnicott: Does Psychoanalysis Facilitate Healthy Marital Choice? *Couple and Family Psychoanalysis*, 9, 105–131.

Kahr, Brett (Ed.). (2019c). Historical Section: Bowlby 1939: "Hysteria in Children" and the Birth of Attachment Theory. *Attachment: New Directions in Psychotherapy and Relational Psychoanalysis*, 13, 143–197.

Kahr, Brett (2019d). A Neglected Work of Genius: John Bowlby on "Hysteria in Children". *Attachment: New Directions in Psychotherapy and Relational Psychoanalysis*, 13, 144–151.

Kahr, Brett (2019e). John Bowlby and the Birth of Child Mental Health. *Attachment: New Directions in Psychotherapy and Relational Psychoanalysis*, 13, 164–180.

Kahr, Brett (2019f). Before Enid Was Enid: The Birth of Couple Psychoanalysis. *Journal of the Balint Society, 47,* 57–65.

Kahr, Brett (2019g). Freud's Death Bed: Notes on the 'Invalid Couch' at Maresfield Gardens. *Athene: Magazine 2019,* pp. 6–9.

Kahr, Brett (2020a). *Dangerous Lunatics: Trauma, Criminality, and Forensic Psychotherapy.* London: Confer/Confer Books.

Kahr, Brett (2020b). "I wish your life didn't have to be so difficult": Winnicott's Last Three Patients. Unpublished Typescript.

Kahr, Brett (2020c). Lecture on "How Donald Winnicott Survived the COVID of His Time". Anna Freud Centre Academic Faculty for Psychoanalytic Research, Anna Freud National Centre for Children and Families, The Kantor Centre of Excellence, King's Cross, London, and University College London, University of London, London. 30th June. [Via Zoom].

Kahr, Brett (2021a). *Freud's Pandemics: Surviving Global War, Spanish Flu, and the Nazis.* London: Karnac/Karnac Books, Confer.

Kahr, Brett (2021b). "The Piggle Papers": An Archival Investigation, 1961–1977. In Corinne Masur (Ed.). *Finding the Piggle: Reconsidering D.W. Winnicott's Most Famous Child Case,* pp. 41–100. Bicester, Oxfordshire: Phoenix Publishing House.

Kahr, Brett (2021c). Lecture on "Donald Winnicott's Pandemics: Surviving the Spanish Flu of 1918 and the Hong Kong Flu of 1968". Evening Meeting Programme 2021. Wessex Psychotherapy Society, Horizon Centre Western Community Hospital Site, Southampton, Hampshire. 17th March. [Via Zoom].

Kahr, Brett (2021d). Lecture on "Winnicott's Pandemics: Surviving the Spanish Flu of 1918 and the Hong Kong Flu of 1968". Parallel Session, Breakout Room 1, Online Conference 2021. Conference on "Winnicott: A Present for the Future". The Winnicott Trust, London, in association with the Squiggle Foundation, Harrow, London, The Independent Psychoanalysis Trust, London, and the British Psychoanalytic Association, London. 25th September. [Via Zoom].

Kahr, Brett (2021e). Lecture on "Donald Winnicott's Pandemics: Surviving the Spanish Flu of 1918 and the Hong Kong Flu of 1968". Fall 2021. The Richardson History of Psychiatry Research Seminar. DeWitt Wallace Institute of Psychiatry: History, Policy, and the Arts, Department of Psychiatry, Joan and Sanford I. Weill Medical College, Cornell University, The New York Presbyterian Hospital, New York, New York, U.S.A. 17th November. [Via Zoom].

Kahr, Brett (2021–2022). 'Zoom Psychoanalysis' in Old Vienna: How Freud Transformed His Career in 1919. *Athene: Magazine 2021/2022,* pp. 10, 12–14.

Kahr, Brett (2022a). Foreword. In Masud Khan. *Diary of a Fallen Psychoanalyst: The Work Books of Masud Khan. 1967–1972*. Linda Hopkins and Steven Kuchuck (Eds.), pp. vii–xii. London: Karnac/Karnac Books, Confer.

Kahr, Brett (2022b). Sigmund Freud as the Father of Attachment Theory. *Attachment: New Directions in Psychotherapy and Relational Psychoanalysis*, 16, 123–151.

Kahr, Brett (2023a). *How to Be Intimate with 15,000,000 Strangers: Musings on Media Psychoanalysis*. London: Routledge/Taylor and Francis Group, and Abingdon, Oxfordshire: Routledge/Taylor and Francis Group. [In Press].

Kahr, Brett (2023b). Winnicott's Anni Horribiles: *The Creation of 'Hate in the Counter-Transference'*. [In Preparation].

Kahr, Brett (2023c). *The Musical Psychoanalyst: From Freud's Ambivalence to Winnicott's Embrace*. [In Preparation].

Kahr, Brett (2023d). 'What a lovely woman': My Youthful Encounters with Marion Milner, (1985–1998). In Margaret Boyle Spelman and Joan Raphael-Leff (Eds.). *The Marion Milner Tradition: Lines of Development: Evolution of Theory and Practice Over the Decades*, pp. 34–50. London: Routledge/Taylor and Francis Group, and Abingdon, Oxfordshire: Routledge/Taylor and Francis Group.

Kardiner, Abram (1977). *My Analysis with Freud: Reminiscences*. New York: W.W. Norton and Company.

Karen, Robert (1994). *Becoming Attached: Unfolding the Mystery of the Infant-Mother Bond and Its Impact on Later Life*. New York: Warner Books/Time Warner Company.

Karnac, Harry (1992). Personal Communication to Judy Cooper. n.d. Cited in Judy Cooper (1993). *Speak of Me as I Am: The Life and Work of Masud Khan*, p. 29. London: Karnac Books/H. Karnac (Books).

Karon, Bertram P., and VandenBos, Gary R. (1981). *Psychotherapy of Schizophrenia: The Treatment of Choice*. New York: Jason Aronson.

Karpf, Anne (2014). Constructing and Addressing the 'Ordinary Devoted Mother'. *History Workshop Journal*, Number 78, 82–106.

Kay, James Phillips (1839). *The Training of Pauper Children: A Report Published by the Poor Law Commissioners in Their Fourth Annual Report*. London: William Clowes and Sons.

Khan, M. Masud R. (1954). Book Review of Robert Fliess. *The Revival of Interest in the Dream*, and Book Review of Géza Róheim. *The Gates of the Dream*. *British Journal of Medical Psychology*, 27, 266–267.

Khan, M. Masud R. (1955a). Book Review of Ralph W. Pickford. *The Analysis of an Obsessional*. *International Journal of Psycho-Analysis*, 36, 414.

Khan, M. Masud R. (1955b). Book Review of Bruno Bettelheim. *Symbolic Wounds: Puberty Rites and the Envious Male*. *International Journal of Psycho-Analysis*, 36, 416.

Khan, M. Masud R. (1960a). Regression and Integration in the Analytic Setting: A Clinical Essay on the Transference and Counter-Transference Aspects of These Phenomena. *International Journal of Psycho-Analysis*, 41, 130–146.

Khan, M. Masud R. (1960b). Clinical Aspects of the Schizoid Personality: Affects and Technique. *International Journal of Psycho-Analysis*, 41, 430–437.

Khan, M. Masud R. (1962a). The Theory of the Parent-Infant Relationship. *International Journal of Psycho-Analysis*, 43, 253–254.

Khan, M. Masud R. (1962b). Letter to Zoë Dominic. 14th June. Dominic Papers. London. Cited in Roger Willoughby (2005). *Masud Khan: The Myth and the Reality*, p. 274, n. 39. London: Free Association Books.

Khan, M. Masud R. (1963). Silence as Communication. *Bulletin of the Menninger Clinic*, 27, 300–313.

Khan, M. Masud R. (1964). The Role of Infantile Sexuality and Early Object Relations in Female Homosexuality. In Ismond Rosen (Ed.). *The Pathology and Treatment of Sexual Deviation: A Methodological Approach*, pp. 221–292. London: Oxford University Press.

Khan, M. Masud R. (1967). Letter to Sylvia M. Payne. 5th June. File 18.2. The Masud Khan Archives. Archives of the British Psychoanalytical Society, British Psychoanalytical Society, Byron House, Maida Vale, London.

Khan, M. Masud R. (1970). Letter to Sylvia M. Payne. 4th March. File 18.2. The Masud Khan Archives. Archives of the British Psychoanalytical Society, British Psychoanalytical Society, Byron House, Maida Vale, London.

Khan, M. Masud R. (1971a). Une Certaine intimité. In Donald W. Winnicott. *La Consultation thérapeutique et l'enfant*. Claude Monod (Transl.), pp. ix –xliv. Paris: Gallimard/Éditions Gallimard.

Khan, M. Masud R. (1971b). Letter to Alfred Flarsheim. 2nd February. Box 8. File 11. Donald W. Winnicott Papers. Archives of Psychiatry, The Oskar Diethelm Library, The DeWitt Wallace Institute of Psychiatry: History, Policy, and the Arts, Department of Psychiatry, Joan and Sanford I. Weill Medical College, Cornell University, The New York Presbyterian Hospital, New York, New York, U.S.A.

Khan, M. Masud R. (1973). Mrs Alix Strachey (1892–1973). *International Journal of Psycho-Analysis*, 54, 370.

Khan, M. Masud R. (1974). *The Privacy of the Self*. London: Hogarth Press and the Institute of Psycho-Analysis.

Khan, Masud (1977). Letter to Clare Winnicott. 26th July. PP/DWW/H/3/1. Donald Woods Winnicott Collection. Archives and Manuscripts, Rare Materials Room, Wellcome Library, Wellcome Collection, The Wellcome Building, London.

Khan, M. Masud R. (1978). Introduction. In Ella Freeman Sharpe. *Dream Analysis: A Practical Handbook for Psycho-Analysts*, pp. 9–10. London: Hogarth Press and the Institute of Psycho-Analysis.

Khan, M. Masud R. (1979a). *Alienation in Perversions*. London: Hogarth Press and the Institute of Psycho-Analysis.

Khan, M. Masud R. (1979b). Work Book Entry. 22nd June. Cited in Linda Hopkins (2006). *False Self: The Life of Masud Khan*, p. 479, n. 18. New York: Other Press.

Khan, M. Masud R. (1983). *Hidden Selves: Between Theory and Practice in Psychoanalysis*. London: Hogarth Press and the Institute of Psycho-Analysis.

Khan, Masud (1987). Foreword. In Anne Clancier and Jeannine Kalmanovitch (Eds.). *Winnicott and Paradox: From Birth to Creation*. Alan Sheridan (Transl.), pp. xvi–xvii. London: Tavistock Publications.

Khan, M. Masud R. (1988a). *When Spring Comes: Awakenings in Clinical Psychoanalysis*. London: Chatto and Windus.

Khan, Masud (1988b). Personal Communication to Judy Cooper. n.d. Quoted in Judy Cooper (1993). *Speak of Me as I Am: The Life and Work of Masud Khan*, p. 10. London: Karnac Books/H. Karnac (Books).

Khan, Masud (1988c). Personal Communication to Judy Cooper. n.d. Cited in Judy Cooper (1993). *Speak of Me as I Am: The Life and Work of Masud Khan*, p. 11. London: Karnac Books/H. Karnac (Books).

Khan, Masud (2022). *Diary of a Fallen Psychoanalyst: The Work Books of Masud Khan. 1967–1972*. Linda Hopkins and Steven Kuchuck (Eds.). London: Karnac/Karnac Books, Confer.

Khan, M. Masud R., and Sutherland, John D. (1968). Introduction. In Charles Rycroft. *Imagination and Reality: Psycho-Analytical Essays. 1951–1961*, pp. vii–ix. London: Hogarth Press and the Institute of Psycho-Analysis.

King, F. Truby (1916). *The Expectant Mother, and Baby's First Month: Hints to Fathers and Mothers*. Wellington: Marcus F. Marks.

King, Mary (1948). *Truby King: The Man*. London: George Allen and Unwin.

King, Pearl (1991a). Personal Communication to Judy Cooper. n.d. Cited in Judy Cooper (1993). *Speak of Me as I Am: The Life and Work of Masud Khan*, p. 13. London: Karnac Books/H. Karnac (Books).

King, Pearl (1991b). Personal Communication to Judy Cooper. n.d. Quoted in Judy Cooper (1993). *Speak of Me as I Am: The Life and Work of Masud Khan*, p. 14. London: Karnac Books/H. Karnac (Books).

King, Pearl (1991c). Personal Communication to Judy Cooper. n.d. Quoted in Judy Cooper (1993). *Speak of Me as I Am: The Life and Work of Masud Khan*, p. 19. London: Karnac Books/H. Karnac (Books).

King, Pearl (1997). Talk on Sept. 5, 1987 on the Twentieth Anniversary of the Founding of the Finnish Psycho-Analytical Society. In Aira Laine, Helena Parland, and Esa Roos (Eds.). *Psykoanalyysin uranuurtajat Suomessa*, pp. 161–168. Kemijärvi: LPT Lapin Painotuote Oy.

King, Pearl (2001a). Personal Communication to the Author. 27th August.

King, Pearl (2001b). Personal Communication to the Author. 4th November.

King, Pearl (2002). Personal Communication to the Author. 19th June.

King, Pearl (Ed.). (2003a). *No Ordinary Psychoanalyst: The Exceptional Contributions of John Rickman*. London: H. Karnac (Books).

King, Pearl (2003b). Introduction: The Rediscovery of John Rickman and His Work. In Pearl King (Ed.). *No Ordinary Psychoanalyst: The Exceptional Contributions of John Rickman*, pp. 1–68. London: H. Karnac (Books).

King, Pearl (2005a). Foreword. In Roger Willoughby. *Masud Khan: The Myth and the Reality*, pp. x–xix. London: Free Association Books.

King, Pearl (2005b). Personal Communication to the Author. 29th October.

King, Pearl, and Steiner, Riccardo (Eds.). (1991). *The Freud-Klein Controversies: 1941–45*. London: Tavistock/Routledge.

Klein, Melanie (1923). Die Rolle der Schule in der libidinösen Entwicklung des Kindes. *Internationale Zeitschrift für Psychoanalyse*, 9, 323–344.

Klein, Melanie (1924). The Rôle of the School in the Libidinal Development of the Child. *International Journal of Psycho-Analysis*, 5, 312–331.

Klein, Melanie (1927a). The Psychological Principles of Infant Analysis. *International Journal of Psycho-Analysis*, 8, 25–37.

Klein, Melanie (1927b). Symposium on Child-Analysis. *International Journal of Psycho-Analysis*, 8, 339–370.

Klein, Melanie (1928). Early Stages of the Oedipus Conflict. *International Journal of Psycho-Analysis*, 9, 167–180.

Klein, Melanie (1932a). *Die Psychoanalyse des Kindes*. Vienna: Internationaler Psychoanalytischer Verlag.

Klein, Melanie (1932b). *The Psycho-Analysis of Children*. Alix Strachey (Transl.). London: Hogarth Press and the Institute of Psycho-Analysis.

Klein, Melanie (1948). *Contributions to Psycho-Analysis: 1921–1945*. London: Hogarth Press and the Institute of Psycho-Analysis.

Klein, Melanie (1961). *Narrative of a Child Analysis: The Conduct of the Psycho-Analysis of Children as Seen in the Treatment of a Ten Year Old Boy*. London: Hogarth Press and the Institute of Psycho-Analysis.

Klein, Melanie, and Riviere, Joan (1937). *Love, Hate and Reparation: Two Lectures*. London: Leonard and Virginia Woolf at the Hogarth Press, and the Institute of Psycho-Analysis.

Kravis, Nathan (2017). *On the Couch: A Repressed History of the Analytic Couch from Plato to Freud*. Cambridge, Massachusetts: MIT Press.

Krugman, Steven (1987). Trauma in the Family: Perspectives on the Intergenerational Transmission of Violence. In Bessel A. van der Kolk (Ed.). *Psychological Trauma*, pp. 127–151. Washington, D.C.: American Psychiatric Press.

Laforgue, René (1936). A Contribution to the Study of Schizophrenia. *International Journal of Psycho-Analysis, 17*, 147–162.

Laing, Adrian C. (1991). R.D. Laing: The First Five Years. *Journal of the Society for Existential Analysis, 2*, 24–29.

Laing, Ronald D. (1960). *The Divided Self: A Study of Sanity and Madness*. London: Tavistock Publications.

Laing, Ronald D. (1961). *The Self and Others: Further Studies in Sanity and Madness*. London: Tavistock Publications.

Laing, Ronald D. (1971). *The Politics of the Family and Other Essays*. London: Tavistock Publications.

Laing, Ronald D. (1985). *Wisdom, Madness and Folly: The Making of a Psychiatrist. 1927–1957*. London: Macmillan London.

Laing, Ronald D., and Cooper, David G. (1964). *Reason and Violence: A Decade of Sartre's Philosophy. 1950–1960*. London: Tavistock Publications.

Law, Frank W. (1963). Letter to Donald W. Winnicott. 2nd July. Box 4. File 4. Donald W. Winnicott Papers. Archives of Psychiatry, The Oskar Diethelm Library, The DeWitt Wallace Institute of Psychiatry: History, Policy, and the Arts, Department of Psychiatry, Joan and Sanford I. Weill Medical College, Cornell University, The New York Presbyterian Hospital, New York, New York, U.S.A.

Leitch, J. Neil (1920a). A Simple Form of Rhythmic Interrupter. *The Lancet*. 24th July, p. 192.

Leitch, J. Neil (1920b). An Electrical Method of Treating Enuresis. *St. Bartholomew's Hospital Journal, 27*, 162.

Little, Margaret I. (1985). Winnicott Working in Areas Where Psychotic Anxieties Predominate: A Personal Record. *Free Associations*, Number 3, 9–42.

Longstaff, Ursula (1926). Untitled Poem. In Mary L. Longstaff (Ed.). *Poems by My Grandchildren*, p. 11. n.p.: n.p.

Lothane, Zvi (1992). *In Defense of Schreber: Soul Murder and Psychiatry*. Hillsdale, New Jersey: Analytic Press.

Lyth, Isabel Menzies; Scott, Ann, and Young, Robert M. (1988). Reflections on My Work: Isabel Menzies Lyth in Conversation with Ann Scott and Robert M. Young. In Isabel Menzies Lyth. *Containing Anxiety in Institutions: Selected Essays. Volume I*, pp. 1–42. London: Free Association Books.

MacCarthy, Brendan (2002). Personal Communication to the Author. 25th September.

Magnello, Eileen (2000). *A Century of Measurement: An Illustrated History of The National Physical Laboratory*. Bath: Canopus Publishing.

Marriage Guidance Centres Committee: Monday, December 9th, 1946 (1946). Minutes. In *Marriage Guidance Centres: Agenda and Minutes. From: 22.1.46* (1946–1956). SA/TCC/A/3/1/7. Tavistock Centre for Couple Relationships. Archives and Manuscripts, Rare Materials Room, Wellcome Library, Wellcome Collection, The Wellcome Building, London.

Marriage Guidance Council (1946). Minutes. In *Marriage Guidance Centres: Agenda and Minutes. From: 22.1.46* (1946–1956). SA/TCC/A/3/1/7. Tavistock Centre for Couple Relationships. Archives and Manuscripts, Rare Materials Room, Wellcome Library, Wellcome Collection, The Wellcome Building, London.

Marriage Welfare Centres Committee: Monday, May 31st. 1948 at 10.30 a.m. (1948). Minutes. In *Marriage Guidance Centres: Agenda and Minutes. From: 22.1.46* (1946–1956). SA/TCC/A/3/1/7. Tavistock Centre for Couple Relationships. Archives and Manuscripts, Rare Materials Room, Wellcome Library, Wellcome Collection, The Wellcome Building, London.

Marriage Welfare Committee: Meeting Held at the Tavistock Institute of Human Relations on Monday June 14th. 1948 at 10. o'clock (1948). Minutes. In *Marriage Guidance Centres: Agenda and Minutes. From: 22.1.46* (1946–1956). SA/TCC/A/3/1/7. Tavistock Centre for Couple Relationships. Archives and Manuscripts, Rare Materials Room, Wellcome Library, Wellcome Collection, The Wellcome Building, London.

Martin, Alexander Reid (1975). Untitled Oral History of Karen Horney. American Academy of Psychoanalysis. Cited in Susan Quinn (1987). *A Mind of Her Own: The Life of Karen Horney*, p. 445, n. 13. New York: Summit Books/Simon and Schuster.

Marwick, Arthur (1982). *British Society Since 1945*. London: Allen Lane/Penguin Books.

Masur, Corinne (Ed.). (2021). *Finding the Piggle: Reconsidering D.W. Winnicott's Most Famous Child Case*. Bicester, Oxfordshire: Phoenix Publishing House.

May, Ulrike (2006). Freuds Patientenkalender: Siebzehn Analytiker in Analyse bei Freud (1910–1920). *Luzifer-Amor*, 19, Number 37, 43–97.

May, Ulrike (2007a). Neunzehn Patienten in Analyse bei Freud (1910–1920): Teil I: Zur Dauer von Freuds Analysen. *Psyche, 61*, 590–625.
May, Ulrike (2007b). Neunzehn Patienten in Analyse bei Freud (1910–1920): Teil II: Zur Frequenz von Freuds Analysen. *Psyche, 61*, 686–709.
Mehra, Baljeet (1992). Personal Communication to Judy Cooper. n.d. Quoted in Judy Cooper (1993). *Speak of Me as I Am: The Life and Work of Masud Khan*, p. 25. London: Karnac Books/H. Karnac (Books).
Meltzer, Donald (1967). *The Psycho-Analytical Process*. London: William Heinemann Medical Books.
Memorandum on Visit to the Cassel Hospital on Monday, 28th June 1948, by Mr. Astbury, Miss Menzies and Mrs Eichholz (1948). Unpublished Memorandum. SA/TCC/A/2/3. Tavistock Centre for Couple Relationships. Archives and Manuscripts, Rare Materials Room, Wellcome Library, Wellcome Collection, The Wellcome Building, London.
Menaker, Esther (1988). Early Struggles in Lay Psychoanalysis: New York in the Thirties, Forties, and Fifties. *Psychoanalytic Review, 75*, 373–379.
Menaker, Esther (1989). *Appointment in Vienna: An American Psychoanalyst Recalls Her Student Days in Pre-War Austria*. New York: St. Martin's Press.
Menzies, Isabel E.P. (1949). Factors Affecting Family Breakdown in Urban Communities: A Preliminary Study Leading to the Establishment of Two Pilot Family Discussion Bureaux. *Human Relations, 2*, 363–373.
Miller, Alice (1979). The Drama of the Gifted Child and the Psycho-Analyst's Narcissistic Disturbance. *International Journal of Psycho-Analysis, 60*, 47–58.
Miller, Alice (1981). *Prisoners of Childhood*. Ruth Ward (Transl.). New York: Basic Books.
Milner, Marion (1969). *The Hands of the Living God: An Account of a Psycho-analytic Treatment*. London: Hogarth Press and the Institute of Psycho-Analysis.
Milner, Marion (Joanna Field) (1984). *On Not Being Able to Paint*. Reprint Edition. London: Heinemann London/William Heinemann Educational Books.
Milner, Marion (1985). Personal Communication to the Author. 5th January.
Milner, Marion (1986a). Letter to Judith M. Hughes. 8th April. Cited in Judith M. Hughes (1989). *Reshaping the Psychoanalytic Domain: The Work of Melanie Klein, W.R.D. Fairbairn, and D.W. Winnicott*, p. 202, n. 89. Berkeley, California: University of California Press.
Milner, Marion (1986b). Personal Communication to the Author. 27th October.
Milner, Marion (1987a). *Eternity's Sunrise: A Way of Keeping a Diary*. London: Virago Press.

Milner, Marion (1987b). *The Suppressed Madness of Sane Men: Forty-Four Years of Exploring Psychoanalysis*. London: Tavistock Publications.

Milner, Marion (1987c). Personal Communication to the Author. 24th October.

Milner, Marion (2012). *Bothered by Alligators*. London: Routledge/Taylor and Francis Group, and Hove, East Sussex: Routledge/Taylor and Francis Group.

Milner, Marion (n.d.). Letter to Donald W. Winnicott. 25th September. PP/DWW/B/A/21. Donald Woods Winnicott Collection. Archives and Manuscripts, Rare Materials Room, Wellcome Library, Wellcome Collection, The Wellcome Building, London.

Minne, Carine (2019). Personal Communication to the Author. 14th November.

Mitchell, Silas Weir (1877). *Fat and Blood: And How to Make Them*. Philadelphia, Pennsylvania: J.B. Lippincott.

Molnar, Michael (1992). Notes and References. In Sigmund Freud. *The Diary of Sigmund Freud: 1929–1939. A Record of the Final Decade*. Michael Molnar (Ed. and Transl.), pp. 271–308. New York: Charles Scribner's Sons, and Toronto: Maxwell Macmillan Canada, and New York: Maxwell Macmillan International/Maxwell Publishing Company, Maxwell Communication Group of Companies.

Money-Kyrle, Roger (1955). Letter to Donald W. Winnicott. 12th February. PP/DWW/B/A/17. Donald Woods Winnicott Collection. Archives and Manuscripts, Rare Materials Room, Wellcome Library, Wellcome Collection, The Wellcome Building, London.

Montessori, Mario M. (Ed.). (1968). Report of the 25th International Psycho-Analytical Congress, pp. 116–148. *Bulletin of the International Psycho-Analytical Association. International Journal of Psycho-Analysis*, 49, 116–157.

Mowat, Charles Loch (1961). *The Charity Organisation Society: 1869–1913. Its Ideas and Work*. London: Methuen and Company.

"Mr. Piggle" and "Mrs. Piggle" (1964a). Letter to Donald W. Winnicott. 4th January. In Donald W. Winnicott (1977). *The Piggle: An Account of the Psychoanalytic Treatment of a Little Girl*. Ishak Ramzy (Ed.), pp. 5–7. New York: International Universities Press.

"Mr. Piggle" and "Mrs. Piggle" (1964b). Letter to Donald W. Winnicott. n.d. In Donald W. Winnicott (1977). *The Piggle: An Account of the Psychoanalytic Treatment of a Little Girl*. Ishak Ramzy (Ed.), pp. 96–97. New York: International Universities Press.

"Mrs. Piggle" (1964). Letter to Donald W. Winnicott. n.d. In Donald W. Winnicott (1977). *The Piggle: An Account of the Psychoanalytic Treatment of a Little Girl*. Ishak Ramzy (Ed.), pp. 63–65. New York: International Universities Press.

"Mrs. Piggle" (n.d. [a]). Untitled Note. "The Piggle" Papers. London.

"Mrs. Piggle" (n.d. [b] [1965]). Letter to Donald W. Winnicott. n.d. In Donald W. Winnicott (1977). *The Piggle: An Account of the Psychoanalytic Treatment of a Little Girl*. Ishak Ramzy (Ed.), p. 161. New York: International Universities Press.

"Mrs. Piggle" (n.d. [c] [c. 1973]). Draft Letter to Ishak Ramzy. n.d. "The Piggle" Papers. London.

"Mrs. Piggle" (n.d. [d]). Draft Letter to Donald W. Winnicott. n.d. "The Piggle" Papers. London.

Neve, Michael (1983). Interview with Clare Winnicott, June 1983. In Peter L. Rudnytsky (1991). *The Psychoanalytic Vocation: Rank, Winnicott, and the Legacy of Freud*, pp. 180–193. New Haven, Connecticut: Yale University Press.

Newnham College Register: 1871–1950. Volume I. 1871–1923 (1963). n.p.: n.p.

Niederland, William G. (1959a). The "Miracled-Up" World of Schreber's Childhood. *Psychoanalytic Study of the Child*, 14, 383–413. New York: International Universities Press.

Niederland, William G. (1959b). Schreber: Father and Son. *Psychoanalytic Quarterly*, 28, 151–169.

Niederland, William G. (1963). Further Data and Memorabilia Pertaining to the Schreber Case. *International Journal of Psycho-Analysis*, 44, 201–207.

Niederland, William G. (1974). *The Schreber Case: Psychoanalytic Profile of a Paranoid Personality*. New York: Quadrangle/New York Times Book Company.

Nijinsky, Romola (1933). *Nijinsky*. Covent Garden, London: Victor Gollancz.

Nijinsky, Tamara (1991). *Nijinsky and Romola*. London: Bachman and Turner/ United Arts Publishers.

1995 [Untitled Diary] (1995). PP/BOW/P.5/36. (Edward) John (Mostyn) Bowlby (1907–1990) Collection. Archives and Manuscripts, Rare Materials Room, Wellcome Library, Wellcome Collection, The Wellcome Building, London.

Oberndorf, Clarence P. (1953). *A History of Psychoanalysis in America*. New York: Grune and Stratton.

Oberndorf, Clarence P. (1958). *An Autobiographical Sketch*. Ithaca, New York: Cornell University Infirmary and Clinic.

Orbach, Susie (1994). Personal Communication to the Author. 1st October.

Orbach, Susie (1997). Personal Communication to the Author. 2nd February.

Osler, William (1905). *The Principles and Practice of Medicine: Designed for the Use of Practitioners and Students of Medicine. Fifth Edition.* London: Sidney Appleton, and New York: D. Appleton and Company.

Osler, William, and McCrae, Thomas (1930). *The Principles and Practice of Medicine: Designed for the Use of Practitioners and Students of Medicine. Eleventh Edition Revised.* London: D. Appleton and Company.

Palmer, Vicki (1967). Letter to Joyce Coles. 20th September. Box 6. File 14. Donald W. Winnicott Papers. Archives of Psychiatry, The Oskar Diethelm Library, The DeWitt Wallace Institute of Psychiatry: History, Policy, and the Arts, Department of Psychiatry, Joan and Sanford I. Weill Medical College, Cornell University, The New York Presbyterian Hospital, New York, New York, U.S.A.

Pankhurst, E. Sylvia (1935). *The Life of Emmeline Pankhurst: The Suffragette Struggle for Women's Citizenship.* London: T. Werner Laurie.

Paterson, Mark (1991). Obituary: Masud Khan. *Free Associations*, 2, Number 21, 109–111.

Payne, Sylvia M. (1965). Letter to M. Masud R. Khan. 19th January. File 18.2. The Masud Khan Archives. Archives of the British Psychoanalytical Society, British Psychoanalytical Society, Byron House, Maida Vale, London.

Pearce, Kate (2021). Personal Communication to the Author. 21st October.

Pearce, Robert (1996). *Contemporary Britain: 1914–79.* Harlow, Essex: Longman/Addison Wesley Longman.

Pearson, Jenny (2009). Personal Communication to the Author. 19th September.

Pinchbeck, Ivy, and Hewitt, Margaret (1973). *Children in English Society: Volume II. From the Eighteenth Century to the Children Act 1948.* London: Routledge and Kegan Paul, and Toronto: University of Toronto Press.

Pollock, Linda A. (1983). *Forgotten Children: Parent-Child Relations from 1500 to 1900.* Cambridge: Cambridge University Press.

Poulton, Edward P., Symonds, Charles Putnam; Barber, Harold W., and Gillespie, Robert D. (1930). *Taylor's Practice of Medicine: Fourteenth Edition.* London: J. and A. Churchill.

Pound, Reginald (1964). *Gillies: Surgeon Extraordinary.* London: Michael Joseph.

Pyatt, Edward (1983). *The National Physical Laboratory: A History.* Bristol: Adam Hilger.

Ramzy, Ishak (1969a). Letter to Louise Carpenter. 14th January. Box 7. File 11. Donald W. Winnicott Papers. Archives of Psychiatry, The Oskar Diethelm Library, The DeWitt Wallace Institute of Psychiatry: History, Policy, and the Arts, Department of Psychiatry, Joan and Sanford I. Weill Medical College,

Cornell University, The New York Presbyterian Hospital, New York, New York, U.S.A.

Ramzy, Ishak (1969b). Letter to Donald W. Winnicott. 10th July. Box 7. File 16. Donald W. Winnicott Papers. Archives of Psychiatry, The Oskar Diethelm Library, The DeWitt Wallace Institute of Psychiatry: History, Policy, and the Arts, Department of Psychiatry, Joan and Sanford I. Weill Medical College, Cornell University, The New York Presbyterian Hospital, New York, New York, U.S.A.

Ramzy, Ishak (1971). Letter to Clare Winnicott. 26th March. PP/DWW/G/6/1. Folder 2. Donald Woods Winnicott Collection. Archives and Manuscripts, Rare Materials Room, Wellcome Library, Wellcome Collection, The Wellcome Building, London.

Ramzy, Ishak (1977a). Editor's Foreword. In Donald W. Winnicott. *The Piggle: An Account of the Psychoanalytic Treatment of a Little Girl*. Ishak Ramzy (Ed.), p. 145. New York: International Universities Press.

Ramzy, Ishak (1977b). Footnote 3. In Donald W. Winnicott. *The Piggle: An Account of the Psychoanalytic Treatment of a Little Girl*. Ishak Ramzy (Ed.), p. 145. New York: International Universities Press.

Ramzy, Ishak (1978). Editor's Foreword. In Donald W. Winnicott. *The Piggle: An Account of the Psychoanalytic Treatment of a Little Girl*. Ishak Ramzy (Ed.), pp. xi–xvi. London: Hogarth Press and the Institute of Psycho-Analysis.

Raney, James (1995). Personal Communication to the Author. 6th October.

Rayner, Eric (1991). Personal Communication to Judy Cooper. n.d. Quoted in Judy Cooper (1993). *Speak of Me as I Am: The Life and Work of Masud Khan*, pp. 91–92. London: Karnac Books/H. Karnac (Books).

Rayner, Eric (1992). Personal Communication to Judy Cooper. n.d. Quoted in Judy Cooper (1993). *Speak of Me as I Am: The Life and Work of Masud Khan*, p. 86. London: Karnac Books/H. Karnac (Books).

Rayner, Eric (1993). Foreword. In Judy Cooper. *Speak of Me as I Am: The Life and Work of Masud Khan*, pp. xi–xvi. London: Karnac Books/H. Karnac (Books).

Reed, John R. (2010). *Dickens' Hyperrealism*. Columbus, Ohio: Ohio State University Press.

Rickman, John (1926a). A Psychological Factor in the Aetiology of Descensus Uteri, Laceration of the Perineum and Vaginismus. *International Journal of Psycho-Analysis*, 7, 363–365.

Rickman, John (1926b). A Survey: The Development of the Psycho-Analytical Theory of the Psychoses. 1894–1926. *British Journal of Medical Psychology*, 6, 270–294.

Rickman, John (1943). The Psychiatric Interview in the Social Setting of a War Office Selection Board. In Pearl King (Ed.). (2003). *No Ordinary Psychoanalyst: The Exceptional Contributions of John Rickman*, pp. 132–139. London: H. Karnac (Books).

Rickman, John (1947). Psychology in Medical Education. *British Medical Journal*. 6th September, pp. 363–366.

Riviere, Joan (1936). Letter to Donald W. Winnicott. 30th December. PP/DWW/B/A/25. Donald Woods Winnicott Collection. Archives and Manuscripts, Rare Materials Room, Wellcome Library, Wellcome Collection, The Wellcome Building, London.

Riviere, Joan (1937a [sic] [1936]). Letter to Donald W. Winnicott. 4th January. PP/DWW/B/A/25. Donald Woods Winnicott Collection. Archives and Manuscripts, Rare Materials Room, Wellcome Library, Wellcome Collection, The Wellcome Building, London.

Riviere, Joan (1937b). Letter to Donald W. Winnicott. 8th September. PP/DWW/B/A/25. Donald Woods Winnicott Collection. Archives and Manuscripts, Rare Materials Room, Wellcome Library, Wellcome Collection, The Wellcome Building, London.

Riviere, Joan (1938). Letter to Donald W. Winnicott. 27th December. PP/DWW/B/A/25. Donald Woods Winnicott Collection. Archives and Manuscripts, Rare Materials Room, Wellcome Library, Wellcome Collection, The Wellcome Building, London.

Riviere, Joan (1958a). Letter to Donald W. Winnicott. 12th June. Box 1. File 13. Donald W. Winnicott Papers. Archives of Psychiatry, The Oskar Diethelm Library, The DeWitt Wallace Institute of Psychiatry: History, Policy, and the Arts, Department of Psychiatry, Joan and Sanford I. Weill Medical College, Cornell University, The New York Presbyterian Hospital, New York, New York, U.S.A.

Riviere, Joan (1958b). Letter to Donald W. Winnicott. 7th December. Box 1. File 13. Donald W. Winnicott Papers. Archives of Psychiatry, The Oskar Diethelm Library, The DeWitt Wallace Institute of Psychiatry: History, Policy, and the Arts, Department of Psychiatry, Joan and Sanford I. Weill Medical College, Cornell University, The New York Presbyterian Hospital, New York, New York, U.S.A.

Roazen, Paul (1990). Tola Rank. *Journal of the American Academy of Psychoanalysis*, 18, 247–259.

Roazen, Paul (1993). *Meeting Freud's Family*. Amherst, Massachusetts: University of Massachusetts Press.

Roazen, Paul (1995). *How Freud Worked: First-Hand Accounts of Patients*. Northvale, New Jersey: Jason Aronson.

Roazen, Paul (2000). *Oedipus in Britain: Edward Glover and the Struggle Over Klein.* New York: Other/Other Press.

Roberts, June (1994). Personal Communication to the Author. 20th June.

Robertson, James, and Bowlby, John (1952). Recent Trends in the Care of Deprived Children in the U.K. *Bulletin of the World Federation for Mental Health, 4*, 131–138.

Robinson, Kenneth (1965). Official Opening of the Conference. In *The Price of Mental Health*, pp. 4–12. London: National Association for Mental Health.

Rodman, F. Robert (2003). *Winnicott: Life and Work.* New York: Perseus Publishing/Perseus Books Group.

Rosenfeld, Herbert (1952). Notes on the Psycho-Analysis of the Super-Ego Conflict of an Acute Schizophrenic Patient. *International Journal of Psycho-Analysis, 33*, 111–131.

Royal Society of Medicine. Section of Paediatrics and Child Health. Symposium on the History of Paediatrics 2000 (2000). In *Early History of Paediatrics and Child Health in Britain: Royal College of Paediatrics and Child Health* (2004). [D.V.D]. London: Royal College of Paediatrics and Child Health.

Rudnytsky, Peter L. (2000). Enid Balint: The Broken Couch. In Peter L. Rudnytsky (Ed.). *Psychoanalytic Conversations: Interviews with Clinicians, Commentators, and Critics*, pp. 1–25. Hillsdale, New Jersey: Analytic Press.

Rushforth, Winifred (1984). *Ten Decades of Happenings.* London: Gateway Books.

Rycroft, Charles (1968a). *Anxiety and Neurosis.* London: Allen Lane/The Penguin Press.

Rycroft, Charles (1968b). *Imagination and Reality: Psycho-Analytical Essays. 1951–1961.* London: Hogarth Press and the Institute of Psycho-Analysis.

Rycroft, Charles (1991). Personal Communication to Judy Cooper. n.d. Cited in Judy Cooper (1993). *Speak of Me as I Am: The Life and Work of Masud Khan*, p. 86. London: Karnac Books/H. Karnac (Books).

Rycroft, Charles (1992). Letter to Judy Cooper. 27th December. Cited in Judy Cooper (1993). *Speak of Me as I Am: The Life and Work of Masud Khan*, pp. 30–31. London: Karnac Books/H. Karnac (Books).

Rycroft, Charles (1996). Personal Communication to the Author. 27th January.

Sacerdoti, Cesare (1996). Personal Communication to the Author. 18th March.

Sacerdoti, Cesare (2001). Personal Communication to the Author. 21st June.

Sacerdoti, Cesare (2005). Personal Communication to the Author. 29th October.

Samuels, Andrew (2015). Personal Communication to the Author. 5th October.

Samuels, Andrew (2019). Personal Communication to the Author. 1st April.

Sandler, Anne-Marie (2004). Institutional Responses to Boundary Violations: The Case of Masud Khan. *International Journal of Psychoanalysis*, 85, 27–42.

Schatzman, Morton (1973a). *Soul Murder: Persecution in the Family*. New York: Random House.

Schatzman, Morton (1973b). Paranoia or Persecution: The Case of Schreber. *History of Childhood Quarterly*, 1, 62–88.

Schur, Max (1972). *Freud: Living and Dying*. New York: International Universities Press.

Segal, Hanna (1995). Personal Communication to the Author. 3rd June.

Semmelweis, Ignaz Philipp (1861). *Die Aetiologie, der Begriff und die Prophylaxis des Kindbettfiebers*. Pest: C.A. Hartleben's Verlags-Expedition.

Senn, Milton (1977). John Bowlby Interview with Milton Senn, M.D. Joel Kanter (Ed.). (2007). *Beyond the Couch: The Online Journal of the American Association for Psychoanalysis in Clinical Social Work*, Number 2, [1–20].

Sharpe, Ella Freeman (1937). *Dream Analysis: A Practical Handbook for Psycho-Analysts*. London: Leonard and Virginia Woolf at the Hogarth Press, and the Institute of Psycho-Analysis.

Sharpe, Ella Freeman (1946). Letter to Donald W. Winnicott. 7th November. PP/DWW/B/A/27. Donald Woods Winnicott Collection. Archives and Manuscripts, Rare Materials Room, Wellcome Library, Wellcome Collection, The Wellcome Building, London.

Sharpe, Ella Freeman (1978). *Dream Analysis: A Practical Handbook for Psycho-Analysts*. London: Hogarth Press and the Institute of Psycho-Analysis.

Sherman, Murray H. (1983). Lytton and James Strachey: Biography and Psychoanalysis. In Norman Kiell (Ed.). *Blood Brothers: Siblings as Writers*, pp. 329–364. New York: International Universities Press.

Shields, Robert W. (1962). *A Cure of Delinquents: The Treatment of Maladjustment*. London: Heinemann Educational Books.

Sinason, Valerie (2020). Personal Communication to the Author. 21st June.

Skues, Richard A. (2006). *Sigmund Freud and the History of Anna O.: Reopening a Closed Case*. Houndmills, Basingstoke, Hampshire: Palgrave Macmillan.

Statistical Digest of the War: Prepared in the Central Statistical Office (1951). London: His Majesty's Stationery Office/Longmans Green and Company.

Stephen, Adrian (1909). Diary Entry. 1st July. In Jean MacGibbon (1997). *There's the Lighthouse: A Biography of Adrian Stephen*, pp. 63–65. London: James and James (Publishers).

Stern, Adolph (1922). Some Personal Psychoanalytical Experiences with Prof. Freud. *New York State Journal of Medicine*, 22, 21–25.

Stirland, John (1963). *The Leys School: Handbook and Directory. Sixteenth Edition. Brought Up to March 1963.* Sawston, Cambridge: Crampton and Sons.

Strachey, Alix (1924). Letter to James Strachey. 29th December. In James Strachey and Alix Strachey (1985). *Bloomsbury/Freud: The Letters of James and Alix Strachey. 1924–1925.* Perry Meisel and Walter Kendrick (Eds.), pp. 165–166. New York: Basic Books.

Strachey, James (1924). Letter to Alix Strachey. [11th November]. In James Strachey and Alix Strachey (1985). *Bloomsbury/Freud: The Letters of James and Alix Strachey. 1924–1925.* Perry Meisel and Walter Kendrick (Eds.), pp. 115–116. New York: Basic Books.

Summers, Julie (2011). *When the Children Came Home: Stories of Wartime Evacuees.* London: Simon and Schuster, Simon and Schuster UK/CBS Company.

Sutherland, John D. (1955). Letter to Lily Pincus. 11th October. SA/TCC/A/2/8. Tavistock Centre for Couple Relationships. Archives and Manuscripts, Rare Materials Room, Wellcome Library, Wellcome Collection, The Wellcome Building, London.

Syllabus for the Advanced Course for Post Graduate Case Workers (1951). SA/TCC/A/2/5. Tavistock Centre for Couple Relationships. Archives and Manuscripts, Rare Materials Room, Wellcome Library, Wellcome Collection, The Wellcome Building, London.

Taylor, James (1938). Letter to Donald W. Winnicott. 17th August. PP/DWW/B/A/8. Donald Woods Winnicott Collection. Archives and Manuscripts, Rare Materials Room, Wellcome Library, Wellcome Collection, The Wellcome Building, London.

Taylor, John (1941). Letter to Donald W. Winnicott. 21st July. PP/DWW/B/D/6. Donald Woods Winnicott Collection. Archives and Manuscripts, Rare Materials Room, Wellcome Library, Wellcome Collection, The Wellcome Building, London.

Taylor, John W. (1894a). On Some of the Less Common Diseases of the Vulva. [Part One]. *Birmingham Medical Review, 36,* 193–199.

Taylor, John W. (1894b). On Some of the Less Common Diseases of the Vulva. [Part Two]. *Birmingham Medical Review, 36,* 287–289.

Taylor, John W. (1894c). On Some of the Less Common Diseases of the Vulva. [Part Three]. *Birmingham Medical Review, 36,* 335–344.

Taylor, John W. (1895). On Some of the Less Common Diseases of the Vulva. [Part Four]. *Birmingham Medical Review, 37,* 20–26.

Taylor, Karen J. (1985). Venereal Disease in Nineteenth-Century Children. *Journal of Psychohistory, 12,* 431–463.

Thackeray, William Makepeace (1848). *Vanity Fair: A Novel without a Hero*. London: Bradbury and Evans.

The Book of the Foundation of the Church of St. Bartholomew, London: Rendered into Modern English. From the Original Latin Version Preserved in the British Museum, Numbered Vespasian B. IX, by Mr. Humphrey H. King and Mr. William Barnard for Use in the 'Records of St. Bartholomew's Priory' (1923). Edward A. Webb (Transl.). London: Humphrey Milford/Oxford University Press.

"The Piggle" (2017). Personal Communication to the Author. 25th January.

"The Piggle" (2020). Personal Communication to the Author. 23rd February.

Thomas, Ruth (1971). Letter to Clare Winnicott. 14th March. PP/DWW/G/6/1. Folder 2. Donald Woods Winnicott Collection. Archives and Manuscripts, Rare Materials Room, Wellcome Library, Wellcome Collection, The Wellcome Building, London.

Ticktin, Stephen (1992). Personal Communication to the Author. 5th December.

Ticktin, Stephen (1993). Personal Communication to the Author. 28th March.

Tizard, J. Peter M. (1971). Donald W. Winnicott. *International Journal of Psycho-Analysis*, 52, 226–227.

Tizard, J. Peter M. (1981). Donald Winnicott: The President's View of a Past President. *Journal of the Royal Society of Medicine*, 74, 267–274.

Tomalin, Claire (2011). *Charles Dickens: A Life*. London: Viking/Penguin Books, Penguin Group.

Training Ctte Minutes: 24.3.1926—29.10.1945 (1926–1945). Archives of the British Psychoanalytical Society. British Psychoanalytical Society, Byron House, Maida Vale, London.

Tustin, Frances (1988). A Personal Reminiscence. *Winnicott Studies*, 3, 57–59.

van der Horst, Frank C.P. (2011). *John Bowlby—From Psychoanalysis to Ethology: Unravelling the Roots of Attachment Theory*. Chichester, West Sussex: Wiley-Blackwell/John Wiley and Sons.

van Dijken, Suzan (1998). *John Bowlby: His Early Life. A Biographical Journey into the Roots of Attachment Theory*. London: Free Association Books.

Vieyra, Rosita Braunstein (1989). Biographical Notes on Dr. Eduard Silberstein, Compiled by his Granddaughter, Rosita Braunstein Vieyra. In Sigmund Freud. *Jugendbriefe an Eduard Silberstein: 1871–1881*. Walter Boehlich (Ed.), pp. 217–219. Frankfurt am Main: S. Fischer Verlag.

von Hug-Hellmuth, Hermine (1914). Kinderpsychologie, Pädagogik. *Jahrbuch der Psychoanalyse*, 6, 393–404.

Wagner, Gillian (1979). *Barnardo*. London: Weidenfeld and Nicolson.

Wakefield, Jerome C. (2007). Max Graf's "Reminiscences of Professor Sigmund Freud" Revisited: New Evidence from the Freud Archives. *Psychoanalytic Quarterly*, 76, 149–192.

Walker's Diary for 1929 (1929). PP/KLE/A.25. Melanie Klein Collection. Archives and Manuscripts, Rare Materials Room, Wellcome Library, Wellcome Collection, The Wellcome Building, London.

Walters, Margaret (2000). Lecture on "Marion Milner". Series on "The Pioneers of Psychoanalysis". Confer, London, at Fifth Floor Lecture Theatre, Tavistock Clinic, Tavistock Centre, Tavistock and Portman NHS Trust, Belsize Park, London. 19th July.

Waters, Catherine (2006). Reforming Culture. In John Bowen and Robert L. Patten (Eds.). *Palgrave Advances in Charles Dickens Studies*, pp. 155–175. Houndmills, Basingstoke, Hampshire: Palgrave Macmillan.

Weddell, Doreen (1949). Letter to Enid Eicholz [sic] [Enid Eichholz]. 25th February. SA/TCC/A/2/3. Tavistock Centre for Couple Relationships. Archives and Manuscripts, Rare Materials Room, Wellcome Library, Wellcome Collection, The Wellcome Building, London.

Welldon, Estela (2007). Personal Communication to the Author. 13th April.

Welldon, Estela (2015). Personal Communication to the Author. 15th May.

Welldon, Estela (2020). Personal Communication to the Author. 19th July.

Welshman, John (2010). *Churchill's Children: The Evacuee Experience in Wartime Britain*. Oxford: Oxford University Press.

Welter, Volker M. (2012). *Ernst L. Freud, Architect: The Case of the Modern Bourgeois Home*. New York: Berghan Books.

West, Charles (1848). *Lectures on the Diseases of Infancy and Childhood*. London: Longman, Brown, Green, and Longmans.

Williams, A.E. (1943). *Barnardo of Stepney: The Father of Nobody's Children*. London: George Allen and Unwin.

Willoughby, Roger (2005). *Masud Khan: The Myth and the Reality*. London: Free Association Books.

Wilson, A. Thomson M. (1946). The Serviceman Comes Home. *Pilot Papers*, 1, 9–28.

Wilson, A. Thomson M. (1949). Some Reflections and Suggestions on the Prevention and Treatment of Marital Problems. *Human Relations*, 2, 233–252.

Wilson, A. Thomson M., Menzies, Isabel, and Eichholz, Enid (1949). The Marriage Welfare Sub-Committee of the Family Welfare Association. *Social Work*, 6, 258–262.

Winnicott, Clare (1971). Note to "Mrs. Piggle" and "Mr. Piggle". n.d. February. "The Piggle" Papers. London.

Winnicott, Clare (1973a). Letter to "Mrs. Piggle" and "Mr. Piggle". 4th June. "The Piggle" Papers. London.

Winnicott, Clare (1973b). Letter to "Mrs. Piggle" and "Mr. Piggle". 5th September. "The Piggle" Papers. London.

Winnicott, Clare (1976). Letter to "Mrs. Piggle". 18th July. "The Piggle" Papers. London.

Winnicott, Clare (1977). Letter to "Mrs. Piggle". n.d. "The Piggle" Papers. London.

Winnicott, Clare (1978). D.W.W.: A Reflection. In Simon A. Grolnick, Leonard Barkin, and Werner Muensterberger (Eds.). *Between Reality and Fantasy: Transitional Objects and Phenomena*, pp. 17–33. New York: Jason Aronson.

Winnicott, Clare (1979). Letter to Phyllis Greenacre. 29th March. PP/DWW/H/3/1. Donald Woods Winnicott Collection. Archives and Manuscripts, Rare Materials Room, Wellcome Library, Wellcome Collection, The Wellcome Building, London.

Winnicott, Clare (1982). Letter to James W. Anderson. 23rd September. PP/DWW/H/3/1. Folder 2. Donald Woods Winnicott Collection. Archives and Manuscripts, Rare Materials Room, Wellcome Library, Wellcome Collection, The Wellcome Building, London.

Winnicott, Clare, and Shepard, Raymond D. [sic] [Shepherd, Raymond D.] (1977). Preface. In Donald W. Winnicott. *The Piggle: An Account of the Psychoanalytic Treatment of a Little Girl*. Ishak Ramzy (Ed.), pp. vii–ix. New York: International Universities Press.

Winnicott, Clare, and Shepherd, Raymond D. (1978). Preface. In Donald W. Winnicott. *The Piggle: An Account of the Psychoanalytic Treatment of a Little Girl*. Ishak Ramzy (Ed.), pp. vii–ix. London: Hogarth Press and the Institute of Psycho-Analysis.

Winnicott, Donald W. (1918a). "The Lumbar Puncture.". *St. Bartholomew's Hospital Journal*, 25, 94–95.

Winnicott, Donald W. (1918b). Hospital Staff in War Time. *St. Bartholomew's Hospital Journal*, 26, 19.

Winnicott, Donald W. (1919). Episodes of Ward-Life: "The Jolly Ronukers". *St. Bartholomew's Hospital Journal*, 26, 84–85.

Winnicott, Donald W. (1931a). *Clinical Notes on Disorders of Childhood*. London: William Heinemann (Medical Books).

Winnicott, Donald W. (1931b). A Clinical Note on Convulsions, p. 257. In Anonymous. British Paediatric Association: Proceedings of the Fourth Annual General Meeting. *Archives of Disease in Childhood*, 6, 255–258.

Winnicott, Donald W. (1932). Growing Pains; the Problem of Their Relation to Acute Rheumatism, p. 227. In Anonymous. British Paediatric Association:

Proceedings of the Fifth Annual General Meeting. *Archives of Disease in Childhood, 7*, 225–229.

Winnicott, Donald W. (1933). Pathological Sleeping. *British Journal of Children's Diseases, 30*, 205–206.

Winnicott, Donald W. (1935). The Manic Defence. In Donald W. Winnicott (1958). *Collected Papers: Through Paediatrics to Psycho-Analysis*, pp. 129–144. London: Tavistock Publications.

Winnicott, Donald W. (1937). Letter to H.J. Eley. 17th March. PP/DWW/B/A/23. Donald Woods Winnicott Collection. Archives and Manuscripts, Rare Materials Room, Wellcome Library, Wellcome Collection, The Wellcome Building, London.

Winnicott, Donald W. (1938). Letter to W. Clifford M. Scott. 12th September, p. 83. Cited in Patrick J. Mahony (1997). W.C.M. Scott and Otherness. In Michel Grignon (Ed.). *Psychoanalysis and the Zest for Living: Reflections and Psychoanalytic Writings in Memory of W.C.M. Scott*, pp. 81–85. Binghamton, New York: Esf Publishers.

Winnicott, Donald W. (1939a). The Psychology of Juvenile Rheumatism. In Ronald G. Gordon (Ed.). *A Survey of Child Psychiatry*, pp. 28–44. London: Humphrey Milford/Oxford University Press.

Winnicott, Donald W. (1939b). Letter to W. Clifford M. Scott. 16th October, p. 83. Cited in Patrick J. Mahony (1997). W.C.M. Scott and Otherness. In Michel Grignon (Ed.). *Psychoanalysis and the Zest for Living: Reflections and Psychoanalytic Writings in Memory of W.C.M. Scott*, pp. 81–85. Binghamton, New York: Esf Publishers.

Winnicott, Donald W. (1940). The Deprived Mother. In John Rickman (Ed.). *Children in War-Time: The Uprooted Child, the Problem of the Young Child, the Deprived Mother, Foster-Parents, Visiting, the Teacher's Problems, Homes for Difficult Children*, pp. 31–43. London: New Education Fellowship.

Winnicott, Donald W. (1942). Child Department Consultations. *International Journal of Psycho-Analysis, 23*, 139–146.

Winnicott, Donald W. (1943). Delinquency Research. *New Era in Home and School, 24*, 65–67.

Winnicott, Donald W. (1945a). Primitive Emotional Development. *International Journal of Psycho-Analysis, 26*, 137–143.

Winnicott, Donald W. (1945b). The Return of the Evacuated Child. In Donald W. Winnicott (1957). *The Child and the Outside World: Studies in Developing Relationships*. Janet Hardenberg (Ed.), pp. 88–92. London: Tavistock Publications.

Winnicott, Donald W. (1948a). Children's Hostels in War and Peace: A Contribution to the Symposium on "Lessons for Child Psychiatry". Given at a Meeting of the Medical Section of the British Psychological Society, 27 February 1946. *British Journal of Medical Psychology, 21,* 175–180.

Winnicott, Donald W. (1948b). Pediatrics and Psychiatry. *British Journal of Medical Psychology, 21,* 229–240.

Winnicott, Donald W. (1949a). *The Ordinary Devoted Mother and Her Baby: Nine Broadcast Talks (Autumn 1949).* London: C.A. Brock and Company.

Winnicott, Donald W. (1949b). Hate in the Counter-Transference. *International Journal of Psycho-Analysis, 30,* 69–74.

Winnicott, Donald W. (1949c). Letter to Ruth Usher. 11th February. PP/DWW/B/A/30. Donald Woods Winnicott Collection. Archives and Manuscripts, Rare Materials Room, Wellcome Library, Wellcome Collection, The Wellcome Building, London.

Winnicott, Donald W. (1949d). Letter to Noel Harris. 19th November. Box 8. File 1. Donald W. Winnicott Papers. Archives of Psychiatry, The Oskar Diethelm Library, The DeWitt Wallace Institute of Psychiatry: History, Policy, and the Arts, Department of Psychiatry, Joan and Sanford I. Weill Medical College, Cornell University, The New York Presbyterian Hospital, New York, New York, U.S.A.

Winnicott, Donald W. (1951). Letter to Dorothy E.M. Gardner. 4th January. PP/DWW/B/A/10. Donald Woods Winnicott Collection. Archives and Manuscripts, Rare Materials Room, Wellcome Library, Wellcome Collection, The Wellcome Building, London.

Winnicott, Donald W. (1952). Letter to Harold Gillies. 8th July. PP/DWW/B/A/11. Donald Woods Winnicott Collection. Archives and Manuscripts, Rare Materials Room, Wellcome Library, Wellcome Collection, The Wellcome Building, London.

Winnicott, Donald W. (1953). Psychoses and Child Care. *British Journal of Medical Psychology, 26,* 68–74.

Winnicott, Donald W. (1954a). Withdrawal and Regression. In Donald W. Winnicott (1958). *Collected Papers: Through Paediatrics to Psycho-Analysis,* pp. 255–261. New York: Basic Books.

Winnicott, Donald W. (1954b). Letter to M. Masud R. Khan. 6th December. PP/DWW/B/A/17. Donald Woods Winnicott Collection. Archives and Manuscripts, Rare Materials Room, Wellcome Library, Wellcome Collection, The Wellcome Building, London.

Winnicott, Donald W. (1955a). Metapsychological and Clinical Aspects of Regression within the Psycho-Analytical Set-Up. *International Journal of Psycho-Analysis, 36,* 16–26.

Winnicott, Donald W. (1955b). Foreword. In Medica (Dr. Joan Graham) [Joan Malleson]. *Any Wife or Any Husband: A Book for Couples Who Have Met*

Sexual Difficulties and for Doctors. Second Edition, p. v. London: William Heinemann Medical Books.

Winnicott, Donald W. (1956a). On Transference. *International Journal of Psycho-Analysis*, 37, 386–388.

Winnicott, Donald W. (1956b). The Antisocial Tendency. In Donald W. Winnicott (1958). *Collected Papers: Through Paediatrics to Psycho-Analysis*, pp. 306–315. London: Tavistock Publications.

Winnicott, Donald W. (1957a). *The Child and the Family: First Relationships*. Janet Hardenberg (Ed.). London: Tavistock Publications.

Winnicott, Donald W. (1957b). *The Child and the Outside World: Studies in Developing Relationships*. Janet Hardenberg (Ed.). London: Tavistock Publications.

Winnicott, Donald W. (1958a). *Collected Papers: Through Paediatrics to Psycho-Analysis*. London: Tavistock Publications.

Winnicott, Donald W. (1958b). Letter to M. Masud R. Khan. 28th November. Box 1. File 11. Donald W. Winnicott Papers. Archives of Psychiatry, The Oskar Diethelm Library, The DeWitt Wallace Institute of Psychiatry: History, Policy, and the Arts, Department of Psychiatry, Joan and Sanford I. Weill Medical College, Cornell University, The New York Presbyterian Hospital, New York, New York, U.S.A.

Winnicott, Donald W. (1960a). The Theory of the Parent-Infant Relationship. *International Journal of Psycho-Analysis*, 41, 585–595.

Winnicott, Donald W. (1960b). Ego Distortion in Terms of True and False Self. In Donald W. Winnicott (1965). *The Maturational Processes and the Facilitating Environment: Studies in the Theory of Emotional Development*, pp. 140–152. London: Hogarth Press and the Institute of Psycho-Analysis.

Winnicott, Donald W. (1961a). The Effect of Psychotic Parents on the Emotional Development of the Child. *British Journal of Psychiatric Social Work*, 6, 13–20.

Winnicott, Donald W. (1961b). The Paediatric Department of Psychology. *St. Mary's Hospital Gazette*, 67, 188–189.

Winnicott, Donald W. (1961c). La Théorie de la relation parent-nourrisson. Janine Massoubre (Transl.). *Revue Française de Psychanalyse*, 25, 7–26.

Winnicott, Donald W. (1961d). Loving. *New Statesman*. 5th May, pp. 722–723.

Winnicott, Donald W. (1961e). The Paediatric Department of Psychology. Typescript. PP/DWW/A/J. Folder 1. Donald Woods Winnicott Collection. Archives and Manuscripts, Rare Materials Room, Wellcome Library, Wellcome Collection, The Wellcome Building, London.

Winnicott, Donald W. (1961f). Letter to Gordon Levinson. 3rd July. Box 3. File 4. Donald W. Winnicott Papers. Archives of Psychiatry, The Oskar Diethelm

Library, The DeWitt Wallace Institute of Psychiatry: History, Policy, and the Arts, Department of Psychiatry, Joan and Sanford I. Weill Medical College, Cornell University, The New York Presbyterian Hospital, New York, New York, U.S.A.

Winnicott, Donald W. (1961g). Letter to Michael H. Harmer. 28th September. Box 3. File 3. Donald W. Winnicott Papers. Archives of Psychiatry, The Oskar Diethelm Library, The DeWitt Wallace Institute of Psychiatry: History, Policy, and the Arts, Department of Psychiatry, Joan and Sanford I. Weill Medical College, Cornell University, The New York Presbyterian Hospital, New York, New York, U.S.A.

Winnicott, Donald W. (1962a). Reply. *International Journal of Psycho-Analysis*, 43, 256–257.

Winnicott, Donald W. (1962b). La Première année de la vie: Conceptions modernes du développement affectif au cours de la première année de la vie (I). Jeannine Kalmanovitch and Janine Massoubre (Transls.). *Revue Française de Psychanalyse*, 26, 477–490.

Winnicott, Donald W. (1962c). Hayatin ilk yili. *Tipta yenilikler*, 7, 4–8.

Winnicott, Donald W. (1962d). Adolescence. *New Era in Home and School*, 43, 145–151.

Winnicott, Donald W. (1962e). Introduction. In Robert W. Shields. *A Cure of Delinquents: The Treatment of Maladjustment*, pp. 9–10. London: Heinemann Educational Books.

Winnicott, Donald W. (1962f). Ego Integration in Child Development. In Donald W. Winnicott (1965). *The Maturational Processes and the Facilitating Environment: Studies in the Theory of Emotional Development*, pp. 56–63. London: Hogarth Press and the Institute of Psycho-Analysis.

Winnicott, Donald W. (1962g). The Aims of Psycho-Analytical Treatment. In Donald W. Winnicott (1965). *The Maturational Processes and the Facilitating Environment: Studies in the Theory of Emotional Development*, pp. 166–170. London: Hogarth Press and the Institute of Psycho-Analysis.

Winnicott, Donald W. (1962h). A Personal View of the Kleinian Contribution. In Donald W. Winnicott (1965). *The Maturational Processes and the Facilitating Environment: Studies in the Theory of Emotional Development*, pp. 171–178. London: Hogarth Press and the Institute of Psycho-Analysis.

Winnicott, Donald W. (1963a). The Young Child at Home and at School. In William Roy Niblett (Ed.). *Moral Education in a Changing Society*, pp. 96–111. London: Faber and Faber.

Winnicott, Donald W. (1963b). Dependence in Infant Care, in Child Care, and in the Psycho-Analytic Setting. *International Journal of Psycho-Analysis*, 44, 339–344.

Winnicott, Donald W. (1963c). Symposium: Training for Child Psychiatry. *Journal of Child Psychology and Psychiatry and Allied Disciplines*, 4, 85–91.

Winnicott, Donald W. (1963d). Regression as Therapy Illustrated by the Case of a Boy Whose Pathological Dependence was Adequately Met by the Parents. *British Journal of Medical Psychology*, 36, 1–12.

Winnicott, Donald W. (1963e). The Development of the Capacity for Concern. *Bulletin of the Menninger Clinic*, 27, 167–176.

Winnicott, Donald W. (1963f). Symposium: Training for Child Psychiatry. *Journal of Child Psychology and Psychiatry and Allied Disciplines*, 4, 85–91.

Winnicott, Donald W. (1963g). Struggling Through the Doldrums. *New Society*. 25th April, pp. 8–11.

Winnicott, Donald W. (1963h). From Dependence Towards Independence in the Development of the Individual. In Donald W. Winnicott (1965). *The Maturational Processes and the Facilitating Environment: Studies in the Theory of Emotional Development*, pp. 83–92. London: Hogarth Press and the Institute of Psycho-Analysis.

Winnicott, Donald W. (1963i). Psychiatric Disorder in Terms of Infantile Maturational Processes. In Donald W. Winnicott (1965). *The Maturational Processes and the Facilitating Environment: Studies in the Theory of Emotional Development*, pp. 230–241. London: Hogarth Press and the Institute of Psycho-Analysis.

Winnicott, Donald W. (1963j). The Tree. In Adam Phillips (1988). *Winnicott*, p. 29. London: Fontana Press/Fontana Paperbacks, Collins Publishing Group.

Winnicott, Donald W. (1963k). The Tree. In F. Robert Rodman (2003). *Winnicott: Life and Work*, pp. 289–291. New York: Perseus Publishing/Perseus Books Group.

Winnicott, Donald W. (1964a). *The Child, the Family, and the Outside World*. Harmondsworth, Middlesex: Penguin Books.

Winnicott, Donald W. (1964b). The Neonate and His Mother. *Acta Paediatrica Latina*, 17, Supplement, 747–758.

Winnicott, Donald W. (1964c). The Concept of the False Self. In Donald W. Winnicott (1986). *Home is Where We Start From: Essays by a Psychoanalyst*. Clare Winnicott, Ray Shepherd, and Madeleine Davis (Eds.), pp. 65–70. Harmondsworth, Middlesex: Penguin Books/Pelican Books.

Winnicott, Donald W. (1964d). Letter to "Mrs. Piggle". 25th June. "The Piggle" Papers. London.

Winnicott, Donald W. (1964e). Letter to Michael Duane. 2nd November. Box 5. File 6. Donald W. Winnicott Papers. Archives of Psychiatry, The Oskar Diethelm Library, The DeWitt Wallace Institute of Psychiatry: History, Policy, and the Arts, Department of Psychiatry, Joan and Sanford I. Weill Medical

College, Cornell University, The New York Presbyterian Hospital, New York, New York, U.S.A.

Winnicott, Donald W. (1965a). *The Family and Individual Development*. London: Tavistock Publications.

Winnicott, Donald W. (1965b). *The Maturational Processes and the Facilitating Environment: Studies in the Theory of Emotional Development*. London: Hogarth Press and the Institute of Psycho-Analysis.

Winnicott, Donald W. (1965c). A Child Psychiatry Case Illustrating Delayed Reaction to Loss. In Max Schur (Ed.). *Drives, Affects, Behavior: Volume 2. Essays in Memory of Marie Bonaparte*, pp. 212–242. New York: International Universities Press.

Winnicott, Donald W. (1965d). The Price of Disregarding Research Findings. In *The Price of Mental Health*, pp. 34–41. London: National Association for Mental Health.

Winnicott, Donald W. (1965e). Letter to Roger Money-Kyrle. 14th May. Box 5. File 5. Donald W. Winnicott Papers. Archives of Psychiatry, The Oskar Diethelm Library, The DeWitt Wallace Institute of Psychiatry: History, Policy, and the Arts, Department of Psychiatry, Joan and Sanford I. Weill Medical College, Cornell University, The New York Presbyterian Hospital, New York, New York, U.S.A.

Winnicott, Donald W. (1965f). Letter to "Mr. Piggle" and "Mrs. Piggle". 12th July. In Donald W. Winnicott (1977). *The Piggle: An Account of the Psychoanalytic Treatment of a Little Girl*. Ishak Ramzy (Ed.), p. 145. New York: International Universities Press.

Winnicott, Donald W. (1965g). Letter to "Mrs. Piggle". 12th July. "The Piggle" Papers. London.

Winnicott, Donald W. (1965h). Letter to Ronald Markillie. 2nd August. Box 5. File 5. Donald W. Winnicott Papers. Archives of Psychiatry, The Oskar Diethelm Library, The DeWitt Wallace Institute of Psychiatry: History, Policy, and the Arts, Department of Psychiatry, Joan and Sanford I. Weill Medical College, Cornell University, The New York Presbyterian Hospital, New York, New York, U.S.A.

Winnicott, Donald W. (1965i). Letter to Pam Gabriel. 27th September. Box 5. File 3. Donald W. Winnicott Papers. Archives of Psychiatry, The Oskar Diethelm Library, The DeWitt Wallace Institute of Psychiatry: History, Policy, and the Arts, Department of Psychiatry, Joan and Sanford I. Weill Medical College, Cornell University, The New York Presbyterian Hospital, New York, New York, U.S.A.

Winnicott, Donald W. (1965j). Letter to "Mrs. Piggle". 10th November. "The Piggle" Papers. London.

Winnicott, Donald W. (1965k). Letter to "Mrs. Piggle". 5th December. "The Piggle" Papers. London.

Winnicott, Donald W. (1966a). A Psychoanalytic View of the Antisocial Tendency. In Ralph Slovenko (Ed.). *Crime, Law and Corrections*, pp. 102–130. Springfield, Illinois: Charles C Thomas, Publisher.

Winnicott, Donald W. (1966b). Comment on Obsessional Neurosis and 'Frankie'. *International Journal of Psycho-Analysis*, 47, 143–144.

Winnicott, Donald W. (1966c). Letter to John Davis. 14th February. Box 5. File 10. Donald W. Winnicott Papers. Archives of Psychiatry, The Oskar Diethelm Library, The DeWitt Wallace Institute of Psychiatry: History, Policy, and the Arts, Department of Psychiatry, Joan and Sanford I. Weill Medical College, Cornell University, The New York Presbyterian Hospital, New York, New York, U.S.A.

Winnicott, Donald W. (1967a). The Aetiology of Infantile Schizophrenia in Terms of Adaptive Failure. In Donald W. Winnicott (1996). *Thinking About Children*. Ray Shepherd, Jennifer Johns, and Helen Taylor Robinson (Eds.), pp. 218–223. London: H. Karnac (Books).

Winnicott, Donald W. (1967b). Letter to "Mrs. Piggle" and "Mr. Piggle". 17th March. "The Piggle" Papers. London.

Winnicott, Donald W. (1967c). Letter to Mary Appleby. 6th April. Box 6. File 6. Donald W. Winnicott Papers. Archives of Psychiatry, The Oskar Diethelm Library, The DeWitt Wallace Institute of Psychiatry: History, Policy, and the Arts, Department of Psychiatry, Joan and Sanford I. Weill Medical College, Cornell University, The New York Presbyterian Hospital, New York, New York, U.S.A.

Winnicott, Donald W. (1967d). Letter to "The Piggle". 21st April. "The Piggle" Papers. London.

Winnicott, Donald W. (1967e). Letter to "Mrs. Piggle" and "Mr. Piggle". 27th December. "The Piggle" Papers. London.

Winnicott, Donald W. (1968a). The Non-Pharmacological Treatment of Psychosis in Childhood. In Hermann Stutte and Hubert Harbauer (Eds.). *Concilium Paedopsychiatricum: Verhandlungen des 3. Europäischen Kongresses für Pädopsychiatrie. Wiesbaden, 4.—9. Mai 1967*, pp. 193–198. Basel: Verlag S. Karger.

Winnicott, Donald W. (1968b). The Squiggle Game. *Voices: The Art and Science of Psychotherapy*, 4, 98–112.

Winnicott, Donald W. (1968c). Letter to Richard Michael. 15th March. Box 7. File 5. Donald W. Winnicott Papers. Archives of Psychiatry, The Oskar Diethelm Library, The DeWitt Wallace Institute of Psychiatry: History, Policy, and the Arts, Department of Psychiatry, Joan and Sanford I. Weill Medical

College, Cornell University, The New York Presbyterian Hospital, New York, New York, U.S.A.

Winnicott, Donald W. (1969a). Foreword. In Marion Milner. *The Hands of the Living God: An Account of a Psycho-analytic Treatment*, pp. ix–x. London: Hogarth Press and the Institute of Psycho-Analysis.

Winnicott, Donald W. (1969b). James Strachey: 1887–1967. *International Journal of Psycho-Analysis*, 50, 129–131.

Winnicott, Donald W. (1969c). Letter to "The Piggle". 3rd March. "The Piggle" Papers. London.

Winnicott, Donald W. (1969d). Note to "Mr. Piggle" and "Mrs. Piggle". n.d. March. "The Piggle" Papers. London.

Winnicott, Donald W. (1971). *Therapeutic Consultations in Child Psychiatry*. London: Hogarth Press and the Institute of Psycho-Analysis.

Winnicott, Donald W. (1972). Fragment of an Analysis. Alfred Flarsheim (Annot.). In Peter L. Giovacchini (Ed.). *Tactics and Techniques in Psychoanalytic Therapy*, pp. 457–693. New York: Science House.

Winnicott, Donald W. (1977). *The Piggle: An Account of the Psychoanalytic Treatment of a Little Girl*. Ishak Ramzy (Ed.). New York: International Universities Press.

Winnicott, Donald W. (1978). *The Piggle: An Account of the Psychoanalytic Treatment of a Little Girl*. Ishak Ramzy (Ed.). London: Hogarth Press and the Institute of Psycho-Analysis.

Winnicott, Donald W. (1984). *Deprivation and Delinquency*. Clare Winnicott, Ray Shepherd, and Madeleine Davis (Eds.). London: Tavistock Publications.

Winnicott, Donald W. (1986a). *Holding and Interpretation: Fragment of an Analysis*. London: Hogarth Press and the Institute of Psycho-Analysis.

Winnicott, Donald W. (1986b). *Home is Where We Start From: Essays by a Psychoanalyst*. Clare Winnicott, Ray Shepherd, and Madeleine Davis (Eds.). Harmondsworth, Middlesex: Penguin Books/Pelican Books.

Winnicott, Donald W. (1987). *Babies and Their Mothers*. Clare Winnicott, Ray Shepherd, and Madeleine Davis (Eds.). Reading, Massachusetts: Addison-Wesley Publishing Company.

Winnicott, Donald W. (1988). *Human Nature*. Christopher Bollas, Madeleine Davis, and Ray Shepherd (Eds.). London: Free Association Books.

Winnicott, Donald W. (1989). *Psycho-Analytic Explorations*. Clare Winnicott, Ray Shepherd, and Madeleine Davis (Eds.). London: H. Karnac (Books).

Winnicott, Donald W. (1993). *Talking to Parents*. Clare Winnicott, Christopher Bollas, Madeleine Davis, and Ray Shepherd (Eds.). Reading, Massachusetts: Addison-Wesley Publishing Company.

Winnicott, Donald W. (1996). *Thinking About Children*. Ray Shepherd, Jennifer Johns, and Helen Taylor Robinson (Eds.). London: H. Karnac (Books).

Winnicott, Donald W. (n.d.). *Not Less Than Everything*. Cited in Clare Winnicott (1978). D.W.W.: A Reflection. In Simon A. Grolnick, Leonard Barkin, and Werner Muensterberger (Eds.). *Between Reality and Fantasy: Transitional Objects and Phenomena*, pp. 17–33. New York: Jason Aronson.

Woodhouse, Douglas (1990). The Tavistock Institute of Marital Studies: Evolution of a Marital Agency. In Christopher Clulow (Ed.). *Marriage: Disillusion and Hope. Papers Celebrating Forty Years of the Tavistock Institute of Marital Studies*, pp. 69–119. London: H. Karnac (Books).

Wooster, Gerald (2011). Personal Communication to the Author. 22nd June.

Wortis, Joseph (1940). Fragments of a Freudian Analysis. *American Journal of Orthopsychiatry*, 10, 843–849.

Wortis, Joseph (1954). *Fragments of an Analysis with Freud*. New York: Simon and Schuster.

Young-Bruehl, Elisabeth (1988). *Anna Freud: A Biography*. New York: Summit Books/Simon and Schuster.

Zetzel, Elizabeth (Ed.). (1964). The Finnish Study Group, p. 625. *125th Bulletin of the International Psycho-Analytical Association. International Journal of Psycho-Analysis*, 45, 618–625.

Index

"A Child Psychiatry Case" (Donald W. Winnicott), 55
A Life of One's Own (Joanna Field), 149
A Survey of Child Psychiatry (Ronald G. Gordon), 101, 240, 242–243
Abraham, 215
Abraham, Karl, 25, 241
Acta Paediatrica Latina, 64
Adult Department, Tavistock Clinic, London, 171
Africa, 69, 97
AIDS, 194
Ainsworth, Mary Salter, 106
Akhtar, Salman, 199–200
Albu, Enid Flora, *see* Balint, Enid
Alcock, Theodora, 243–244
Alcoholism, 141, 145, 181, 182, 183, 189, 195, 200, 210, 220, 221, 230–231
Alford, John, 99
Alienation in Perversions (M. Masud R. Khan), 180, 198
All Saints', Broad Chalke, Wiltshire, 121
All Souls College, University of Oxford, Oxford, Oxfordshire, 59
American Psychiatric Association, Washington, D.C., U.S.A., 66
Amsterdam, The Netherlands, 70, 82

Andrewes, Christopher, 22, 23
Andrews, Julie, 180
Angst, 243
"Anna O", *see* Pappenheim, Bertha
Anti-psychiatry, 130
Anti-Semitism, 182–183, 195–197, 198, 202, 204
Antonio, 183
Anxiety, 48, 53, 64, 76, 96, 100, 101, 127, 134, 164, 165, 209, 210, 213, 215, 216, 222, 223
Anxiety and Neurosis (Charles Rycroft), 134
Any Wife or Any Husband: A Book for Couples Who Have Met Sexual Difficulties and for Doctors. Second Edition (Medica (Dr. Joan Graham) [Joan Malleson]), 40
Applied Social Studies Course, London School of Economics and Political Science, University of London, London, 70
Archives and Manuscripts, Wellcome Library, Wellcome Collection, London, 60
Archives of Psychiatry, The Oskar Diethelm Library of the History of Psychiatry, New York Hospital—Cornell Medical Center, New York, New York, U.S.A., 112
Archives of the British Psycho-Analytical Society, British Psycho-Analytical Society, London, xiii, 78, 182

315

Archives of the British Psychoanalytical Society, British Psychoanalytical Society, London, 188, 253
Armstrong-Jones, Robert, 23–24
Ascott Farmhouse, Stadhampton, Oxfordshire, 212
Ashley, New Forest, Hampshire, 120
Ashley-Cooper, Anthony, 95
Association of Child Psychoanalysis, New York City, New York, U.S.A., 101
Association of Child Psychotherapists, London, 101
Association of Workers for Maladjusted Children, London, 66
Astbury, Benjamin, 160, 167
Atlantic Ocean, 3, 17, 37, 182
Attachment: New Directions in Psychotherapy and Relational Psychoanalysis, 240
Attachment theory, 93, 94, 100, 106, 107, 109, 110, 111, 116, 119, 124, 240
Attlee, Clement, 159, 244–245
Augenfeld, Felix, 150
Austria, xiii, xiv, 5, 7, 23, 189
Autism, 57, 79, 132

Babies and Their Mothers (Donald W. Winnicott), 238
"Bagshawe, Arabella", 88
Bakelite, 50
Balint, Enid, xii, xvi, 41, 42, 47, 155–176, 230, 232
Balint, Michael, xvi, 41, 46, 161, 171–172, 173, 244
Balint-Edmonds, Enid, *see* Balint, Enid
Balkányi, Charlotte, 137
Balzac, Honoré de, 11
Barnes, Mary, 210
Barnes, William, 244
Bart's, *see* St. Bartholomew's Hospital Medical College, University of London, London
Battle of Britain, 242
Beatles, 70
Beaumont Street, London, 163, 164, 171, 174, 186, 244
Belgrave Hospital for Children, London, 98
Belgravia, South-West London, London, 33, 47, 53, 60
Belsize Park, North-West London, London, 135, 174
Bento, Alexandre, 148
Benzie, Isa, 60

Berggasse, Vienna, Austria, 6, 20, 133
Bergmann, Martin, 152
Beriozova, Svetlana, 180, 194
Berkshire, England, 30, 32
Berlin, Germany, xiii, 25, 100, 171, 185
Bernays, Minna, 12
Bernfeld, Siegfried, 7
Beth Israel Hospital, Boston, Massachusetts, U.S.A., 55
Bethnal Green, London, 161, 167
Bible, 212, 215
Bick, Esther, 114, 243–244
Bideford, Devon, 244
Biodynamic psychotherapy, 227
Bion, Francesca, 46
Bion, Wilfred, 47, 175, 210
Blackett, Patrick, 151–152
Bleuler, Eugen, 156
Blitz, 157
Blitzkrieg, 30
Bloomsbury, London, 25, 114
Board of Extra-Mural Studies, University of Cambridge, Cambridge, Cambridgeshire, 66
Bonnard, Augusta, 149
Booth, Karen, 150
Borderline personality disorder, 139
Boston, Massachusetts, U.S.A., 55, 66, 79
Boston Psychoanalytic Society, Boston, Massachusetts, U.S.A., 55
Boston Society for Psychiatry and Neurology, Boston, Massachusetts, U.S.A., 66
Bowlby, Anthony, 242
Bowlby, John, xii, xv, xvi, xvii, 30, 46, 93–107, 109–118, 121, 124, 136, 166–167, 169, 170, 174, 230, 231, 232, 239, 240–241, 242–243, 244, 245
Bowlby, Richard, 115, 242, 245
Bowlby, Robert, 122
Bowlby, Ursula, xv, 106, 107, 109–124, 241, 242, 243, 244, 245
Bowlby, Xenia, 242, 245
Bradshaw, Anthony, 28
Brafman, Abrahão, 190
Branch, Guy Rawstron, 242
Braque, Georges, 180
Breuer, Josef, 78, 85, 102
Brierley, Marjorie, 209
British Association of Psychotherapists, London, 181
British Broadcasting Corporation, London, 60, 243

INDEX   317

British Library, London, 94, 225
British Medical Journal, 104, 105, 226, 242
British Paediatric Association, London, 56, 98
British Psycho-Analytical Society, London, xiii, 6, 24, 29, 36, 55, 59, 63, 64, 70, 73, 74, 78, 82, 86, 164, 182, 183, 186, 187, 189, 192, 193, 197, 198, 199, 203, 209, 238, 241
British Psychoanalytical Society, London, 188
British Psychological Society, London, 59, 235
Britton, Alison, 59
Britton, Celia, 59
Britton, Clare, *see* Winnicott, Clare
Britton, Elizabeth, 83
Broad Chalke, Wiltshire, 121
Bronx, New York, U.S.A., 55
Bruggen, Peter, 193
Brunswick, Mark, 156
Brunswick, Ruth Mack, 87, 156, 208, 238
Buckingham Palace, London, 33
Budapest, Hungary, 171
Bude, Cornwall, 245
Bullitt, William, 229
Burghölzli, near Zürich, Switzerland, 156

Cairo, Egypt, 81
Calvados, 210, 214, 215
Cambridge, Cambridgeshire, xvi, 18, 19, 22, 30, 65, 66, 83, 127, 129, 131, 132, 133, 135, 139, 146
Cambridge Psychoanalytical Society, University of Cambridge, Cambridge, Cambridgeshire, 217
Cambridge University Campaign for Nuclear Disarmament, University of Cambridge, Cambridge, Cambridgeshire, 65
Canada, 105, 238
Cancer, 10, 11, 26, 27, 141, 181, 182, 183, 196, 197, 199, 200, 204
Capone, Al, 190
Carcinoma, *see* Cancer
Cardiac disease, 32, 34, 56, 82
Carrell, Steve, 155
Carter, John, 11
Casework, 167, 169, 170, 171, 172
Cassel Hospital for Functional Nervous Disorders, Ham, Richmond, London, 166, 167, 168, 172
Catholic Marriage Advisory Council, London, 160, 167
Cautley, Edmund, 98

Central London, London, 10, 25, 30, 74, 163, 173, 194, 244
Central Training Council in Child Care, London, 59
Centre for Attachment-Based Psychoanalytic Psychotherapy, Hampstead, London, 110
Chalk Farm, North-West London, London, 30, 133, 135, 145, 152, 210
Chandos Street, London, 170, 173, 174
Charlton, John Fraser, 198–199
Chasseguet-Smirgel, Janine, 141
Chatto & Windus, London, 136, 197–198, 199
Chelsea, Greater London, London, 59, 152
Chelsea Police Station, London, 183
Cheltenham Ladies' College, Cheltenham, Gloucestershire, 158, 176
Chester Square, Belgravia, South-West London, London, 47, 49, 50, 51, 54, 56, 58, 60, 61, 63, 67, 71, 81, 83
Child Guidance Department, Tavistock Clinic, London, 170
Child mental health, xv, 49, 96, 101, 105, 107, 189, 239
Child Psychiatric Section, Royal Medico-Psychological Association, London, 64
Child psychiatry, xii, xv, 29, 52, 53, 54, 55, 56, 64, 73, 84, 86, 93–107, 115, 122, 153, 240, 242, 243
Child psychoanalysis, 29, 36, 41, 49, 52, 53, 75, 86, 100, 101, 186
Child psychology, 95, 111
Child psychotherapy, 75, 114
Children's Department, Home Office, London, 67
Children's Department, Tavistock Clinic, London, 166
Children's medicine, 6, 23, 24, 52, 95–96, 98, 99
Christ, 94
Christianity, 26
Christmas, 50, 68, 80, 83
Churchill, Winston, 159, 244
Clinical Notes on Disorders of Childhood (Donald W. Winnicott), 87, 99
Coca-Cola, 218
Cognitive hypnotherapy, 227
Coles, Joyce, xii, 32, 33, 47, 60, 64, 77
"Collusive marriage", 237
Commitment-assisted outpatient therapy, 227
"compulsion to repeat", 34
Confidentiality, 4, 35, 57, 78, 81, 88, 140, 191, 195, 203, 236, 237, 238

Connecticut, U.S.A., 56
Consulting room, xiii, xiv, 3, 7, 8, 9, 20, 24, 30, 33, 34, 37, 40, 47, 49, 50, 56, 57, 60, 61, 62, 71, 72, 133, 135, 149, 151, 203, 229, 230
Contemporary Medical Archives Centre, Archives and Manuscripts, Rare Materials Room, The Wellcome Library for the History and Understanding of Medicine, Wellcome Collection, The Wellcome Building, London, 116–117
"Controversial Discussions", 114
Cooper, David, 134
Cooper, Judy, 181, 182, 183, 187, 191, 195, 197, 200, 203
Copenhagen, Denmark, 70, 79
Cornwall, England, 245
Coronavirus, see COVID-19
Couch, xiv, 3, 5, 9–12, 25, 35, 38, 43, 61, 113, 114, 133, 140, 152, 155, 179
Council, British Psycho-Analytical Society, London, 183, 197
Couple psychoanalysis, xvi, 16, 20, 39, 40, 41, 42, 155–176, 232
Couple psychotherapy, 15, 16, 20, 40, 41, 155, 156, 158, 161
Couples Therapy (Showtime), 156
Couples Therapy (VH1), 155
COVID-19, 3, 4, 8, 226, 227, 229
Crackington Haven, near Bude, Cornwall, 245
Craxtons, 138
Crichton Miller, Hugh, 163, 164
"Crime: A Challenge", 59
Critical social justice therapy, 227

Dalton, Hugh, 245
Darwin, Charles, 93, 106, 107
Davidson, Jenny, 211
Davidson, Shamai, 211, 216, 217
Davidson, Sonny, 41
de Sade, Marquis [Donatien Alphonse François], 190
Death bed, xiv, xvi, 9–12, 229
Defence Committee, 159
Delusions, 128, 130, 136
deMause, Lloyd, 219
DeMille, Cecil B., 179
Denmark, 70, 79
Department of Experimental Psychology, University of Oxford, Oxford, Oxfordshire, 210

Department of Zoology, University of Oxford, Oxford, Oxfordshire, 210
Depression, 28, 98, 100, 144, 157, 176, 185, 219
Deprivation and Delinquency (Donald W. Winnicott), 238
Depth psychology, xi, 24, 41, 181, 239
Devon, England, 18, 19, 79, 244
Devonshire Place, London, 57
Dewar, Millicent, 168
Dicks, Henry, 237
Dinnage, Rosemary, 241
Directorate of Army Psychiatry, 162
Directorate of Biological Research, 162
"Discussion Around a Clinical Detail" (Donald W. Winnicott), 78
Ditton Hill Road, Surbiton, Surrey, 26
Division of Psychoanalytic Education, State University of New York, Bronx, New York, U.S.A., 55
Dockar-Drysdale, Barbara, 189
"Dora", 85
Dorset, England, 244
Dover's powder, 96
Duane, Michael, 67
Dudley, Guilford, 241
Dudley, John, 241
Dulwich, South-East London, London, 193
Durbin, Evan Frank Mottram, 121, 240–241, 244–245
Durbin, Marjorie, 244
Dynamic psychology, 52
Dynamic psychotherapy, 101
Dynamic-deconstructive psychotherapy, 227

East End, London, 105, 159
East Lewisham, London, 161
East London, London, 210
"Editor's Foreword" (Ishak Ramzy), 83
Edmonton, Greater London, London, 245
Education Committee, Institute of Psycho-Analysis, London, 183
Edward VIII, 31
(Edward) John (Mostyn) Bowlby (1907–1990) Collection, Archives and Manuscripts, Wellcome Library, Wellcome Collection, The Wellcome Building, London, 117
Ego, 228
Egypt, 81
Ehrenzweig, Anton, xvi, 144
Eichenbaum, Luise, 190–191, 246
Eichholz, Enid, see Balint, Enid

Eichholz, Robert Nathaniel, 158, 172
"Einige Charaktertypen aus der psychoanalytischen Arbeit" (Sigmund Freud), 102
Einstein, Albert, 93, 107
Electroconvulsive shock, 32, 138
Elizabeth II, 66
Elkan, Irmi, 30–31
Elmhirst, Susanna Isaacs, 131
Elsworthy Road, Primrose Hill, London, 9
England, xi, xiv, 20, 47, 54, 56, 79, 81, 95, 97, 141, 155, 157
Enid Balint Memorial Lecture, Tavistock Centre for Couple Relationships, Tavistock Institute of Medical Psychology, London, 232
Enuresis, 68, 97
Epstein, Brian, 70
Eternity's Sunrise: A Way of Keeping a Diary (Marion Milner), 136
Eton Road, Chalk Farm, North-West London, London, 210
Euston Road, London, 117
"Evacuation of Small Children" (John Bowlby, Emanuel Miller, and Donald W. Winnicott), 104
Evans, John, 189
"Example of a Therapeutic Consultation with a Child" (Donald W. Winnicott), 55
Exchequer, 245
Exploratory goal corrected psychotherapy, 227

F.D.B., Family Welfare Association, London, *see* Family Discussion Bureau, Family Welfare Association, London, 167, 168, 170, 173, 174
"Factors and Features of Early Compulsive Formation" (Ishak Ramzy), 82
Faithfull, Lucy, 49
Faithfull, Theodore, 82, 239
False self, 16, 19, 42, 59, 237
"false self marriage", 42
"false self-couple", 42
Family Discussion Bureau, Family Welfare Association, London, 161, 167, 168, 170, 173, 246
Family Discussion Bureaux, Family Welfare Association, London, 41, 165, 167, 169, 170, 173
Family Welfare Association, London, 41, 158, 160, 162, 165, 167, 172, 246
Fatal vulvo-vaginal disease, 27

Ferenczi, Sándor, 156, 171, 241
Field, Joanna, *see* Milner, Marion
Finchley Road, Swiss Cottage, London, 9
Finland, 55, 65
First Folio (William Shakespeare), 207, 225
First World War, *see* World War I
Fitzalan-Howard, Bernard, 66
Flügel, John, 153
Fordham, Michael, 31, 191
"Foreword" (Donald W. Winnicott), 40
Forrester, John, 131–132
Forsyth, David, xiv, 6
"Fothergill, Edmund", 56–57
Foulkes, Siegmund, 175
Foundational story psychotherapy, 227
"fractional analysis", 87
"Fractured Analysis", 87
"Fragment of an Analysis" (Donald W. Winnicott), 84
France, 55, 79
Frankl, Liselotte, 186
Fraser, Francis, 59
Freeman, Thomas, 209
Frensham, Surrey, 18
Freud (Netflix), 179
Freud, Anna, 12, 49, 86, 100, 148, 149, 151, 186, 209
Freud, Ernst, 9, 150
Freud, Martha, 9, 109, 118, 124, 150–151
Freud, Martin, 4
Freud, Sigmund, xii, xiii, xiv, xvi, xvii, 1, 3–8, 9–12, 20, 25, 28, 34, 36, 38, 43, 49, 53, 74, 85, 86, 87, 89, 93, 100, 101, 102, 109, 113, 114, 118, 133, 134, 135, 148, 149, 150, 151, 153, 156, 160, 163, 164, 171, 175, 179, 185, 188, 190, 193, 196, 205, 208, 222, 227, 228, 229, 230, 236, 239, 243
Freud Museum, Swiss Cottage, London, 148, 150–151
Freud Museum London, Swiss Cottage, London, 9, 12, 239
Frühanalyse, 100
Fulham, South-West London, London, 167, 171
Fulham Maternity Hospital, Fulham, South-West London, London, 171
FWA, London, *see* Family Welfare Association, London

"G. and S.", 233
Gabriel, Pam, 69

"Gabrielle", *see* "The Piggle"
Gaddini, Renata, 64
Gans, Steven, 214
Garden Hospital, Hendon, North-West London, London, 124
Gardiner, Muriel, 87, 136, 208, 238
Gardner, Dorothy, 41
Gatling, Mary, 106, 244
Geneva, Switzerland, 73, 87
George V, 242
Georgia, U.S.A., 56
Germany, 25, 79, 166
Giacometti, Alberto, 180
Gilbert, William Schwenck, 147–148, 233
Gillespie, Sadie, 141, 151
Gillespie, William, 98, 141, 151, 186
Gillies, Harold, 204
Gitelson, Maxwell, 65
Glasgow, Scotland, 162, 216, 217, 221
Gloucester Road, London, 192
Gloucestershire, 176
Glover, Edward, xv, 114
Golders Green, North-West London, London, 110
Goldie, Lawrence, 34, 220, 236
Gordon, Ronald, 101, 240, 242
Gordon, Rosemary, 191
Gordon Square, London, 25
Government Evacuation Scheme, 30
Graf, Herbert, 89
Graf, Max, 89
Graf, Olga Hönig, 89
Gray, Herbert, 160
Great Britain, xiv, xvi, 5, 7, 18, 20, 23, 29, 52, 63, 70, 79, 95, 101, 144, 147, 153, 156, 157, 159, 160, 161, 163, 166, 167, 174, 180, 188, 191, 229, 232, 237
Great Ormond Street, London, 95
Great Portland Street, London, 10
Great War, *see* World War I
Greater London, London, 152, 245
Green, André, 141–142
Grey, Jane, 241
Griffith, Edward Fyfe, 160
Grosskurth, Phyllis, 115, 220
Group psychotherapy, 164
Guralnik, Orna, 156
Gürisik, Elif, 202
Guthrie, Leonard George, 97
Guy's Hospital, London, 99

H. Karnac (Books), London, 192, 198
Hampshire, England, 79, 119, 120
Hampstead, North-West London, London, 32, 33, 53, 110, 112, 126, 135, 137, 158, 180
Happy Infancy (Ursula Bowlby), 107, 121–123
Hardenberg, Herman, 66
Harley Street, London, 18, 163, 164, 173
Harris, James Armstrong, 66
"Hate in the Counter-Transference" (Donald W. Winnicott), 32, 213
Headington, Oxfordshire, 140
Heal and Son, London, 29
"Healthy, Happy Nurseries" (Anonymous), 96
Healy, William, 153
Heidegger, Martin, 208
Heimann, Paula, 46, 71, 186
Helsinki, Finland, 55
Hendon, North-West London, London, 124, 167
Henry VIII, xi
Hepner, Gershon, 54
Herringham Hall, Regent's College, Inner Circle, Regent's Park, London, 110
Hertfordshire, England, 32, 79
Hidden Histories of British Psychoanalysis: Unearthing Freud's Death Bed and Laing's Missing Tooth (Brett Kahr), 229
Hidden Selves: Between Theory and Practice in Psychoanalysis (M. Masud R. Khan), 180, 198
Himalayas, 119
Himmler, Heinrich, 196
Hippocrates, 226, 228
"Hippocratic Oath", 226
Historiography, xii, xv, 225–233
Hitler, Adolf, 158, 196
HIV, 194
HMS Lucifer, 18
Hoffer, Willi, 186
Hogarth Press, London, 69, 83, 134, 136, 198, 199
Holding and Interpretation: Fragment of an Analysis (Donald W. Winnicott), 84
Holborn Viaduct, London, 11
"Holiday Feast", 82
Hollywood, California, U.S.A., 155, 192
Holocaust, 76, 216, 237
Home Front, 157, 159
Home is Where We Start From: Essays by a Psychoanalyst (Donald W. Winnicott), 238
Home Office, London, 59, 67, 172
Homosexuality, 25, 26, 195

INDEX   321

Hong Kong Flu, 80
Hope Springs, 155
Hopkins, Linda, 198, 200, 237
Hopper, Earl, 197
Horney, Karen, 87
Hospital for Sick Children, London, 95
House of Cards, 155
Howard League for Penal Reform, London, 66
"Hubert", 207
Hughes, Athol, 243
Hughes, Judith, 138
Human Nature (Donald W. Winnicott), 238
Hunnybun, Noël, 169, 170, 174
Hysteria, 96, 98, 101–104, 240, 243
"Hysteria in Children" (John Bowlby), 101–104, 240

Id, 228
Imagination and Reality: Psycho-Analytical Essays. 1951–1961 (Charles Rycroft), 134
Imperial College, University of London, London, 151
"Index" (Edward P. Poulton, Charles Putnam Symonds, Harold W. Barber, and Robert D. Gillespie), 99
India, 119, 141, 179, 181, 184, 185, 191, 199, 202
Institute for Self Analysis, Hampstead, London, 110
Institute for Self Analysis Centre for Attachment-Based Psychoanalytic Psychotherapy, Hampstead, London, 110
Institute of Child Health, University of London, London, 73
Institute of Education, University of London, London, 41, 55, 64, 70, 79
Institute of Marital Studies, Tavistock Institute of Human Relations, London, 174
Institute of Psycho-Analysis, London, xvi, 29, 30, 41, 69, 79, 81, 83, 111, 112, 121, 130, 134, 140, 145, 162, 164, 170, 173, 175, 183, 185, 187, 188, 189, 190, 193, 194, 201, 204, 208, 209, 220
Institute of Psychoanalysis, Maida Vale, London, 243
Institute of Youth Employment Officers, London, 66
Interim Medical Committee, Tavistock Clinic, London, 164
International Campaign for the Freud Museum, Freud Museum, Swiss Cottage, London, 148

International Psycho-Analytical Association, 65, 70, 82, 189
International Psycho-Analytical Congress, International Psycho-Analytical Association, Amsterdam, The Netherlands, 70, 82
International Psycho-Analytical Congress, International Psycho-Analytical Association, Vienna, Austria, 189
Internationale Zeitschrift für ärztliche Psychoanalyse, 227
"Introduction" (Donald W. Winnicott), 77
"*Intrusive Mode*", 219
Ireland, 109
Isaac, 215
Isaacs, Susanna, *see* Elmhirst, Susanna Isaacs
Italy, 73, 79, 198

J. and A. Carter, London, 10–11
Jaguar, 193
James, Lydia, 193
James, Martin, 69–70, 86, 151
Jaques, Elliott, 47, 170
Jazz for John Bowlby, 110
Jazzindo, 110
Jesus, 196
Jesus College, University of Cambridge, Cambridge, Cambridgeshire, 18, 30
"John", 88
John Bowlby Memorial Conference, The Bowlby Centre, London, 232
"Jonah", 212, 214, 215, 221
Jones, David, 242
Jones, Ernest, xv, 10, 24–25, 36, 46, 87, 113, 114, 164, 243
Jones, Tommy Lee, 155
Joseph, 215
Jung, Carl Gustav, 153, 156, 163

Karen, Robert, 240
Karlsbad, Austro-Hungarian empire, 166
Karnac, Harry, 192, 198
Kay, James Phillips, 95
Kempson Road, Walham Green, Fulham, South-West London, London, 167
Kent, England, 29, 47, 141
Kettner's, London, 50
Khan, Fazal Dad, 184, 246
Khan, Fazaldad, *see* Khan, Fazal Dad
Khan, Jane Shore, *see* Nicholas, Jane Shore
Khan, Khursheed Begum, 184

Khan, Mahmooda, 185
Khan, Mohammed Masud Raza, xiii, xvi, xvii, 59, 66, 83, 141, 144, 179–205, 230, 235, 237, 246
King, Pearl, vii, xiii, 71, 137, 164, 182, 187, 188, 189, 199, 201, 202
King, Truby, 107, 122–123, 241
Kingsley Hall, East London, London, 210
Klein, Melanie, xii, 15, 36, 38, 42, 46, 49, 61, 63, 84, 100, 101, 112, 113, 114, 115, 134, 138, 144, 153, 186, 210, 220, 239–240
"kleine Hans", see Graf, Herbert
Kleinians, 15, 36, 42, 49, 113, 115, 211, 218, 220, 221
Kops, Rose, 105
Krausz, Rosemarie, 237–238

La Peau de chagrin: Roman philosophique (Honoré de Balzac), 11
Lacan, Jacques, 135, 137, 142
Lacanians, 137, 142
Laing, Adrian, 216, 217
Laing, Amelia Kirkwood, 216–217, 218, 219, 220–221
Laing, David, 130, 218
Laing, Jutta, 219
Laing, Ronald, xii, xvi, xvii, 130, 134, 136, 145, 207–223, 229, 230–231
Latif, Israel, 185
Laurence the Martyr, 94
Law, Frank, 57
Lawrence, Thomas Edward, 27
Lawrence of Arabia, see Lawrence, Thomas Edward
Lazarus, Lily, see Pincus, Lily
"Lear", 207
Lebanese marijuana, 210
Leipzig, Germany, 54
Leitch, John Neil, 97–98
Lend-Lease, 159
Lenox Hill Hospital, Upper East Side, New York, New York, U.S.A., 80
Les Misérables (Alain Boublil, Claude-Michel Schönberg, John Caird, Herbert Kretzmer, Jean-Marc Natel, and Trevor Nunn), 46
Leucotomy, 32, 54, 221
Levinson, Gordon, 53
Lewisham, South-East London, London, 161
Leys School, Cambridge, Cambridgeshire, 18
Library Committee, British Psycho-Analytical Society, London, 186
Little, Margaret, xvi, 47, 66, 141

"Little Hans", see Graf, Herbert
Littlemore Hospital, Littlemore, Oxfordshire, 207, 209
Logan Airport, Boston, Massachusetts, U.S.A., 79
Lomas, Peter, 66
London, England, xiii, xiv, xvi, 6, 8, 9–12, 18, 21, 22, 24, 25, 29, 30, 32, 33, 41, 45, 47, 49, 53, 54, 55, 57, 59, 60, 62, 63, 64, 65, 67, 69, 70, 73, 74, 78, 79, 80, 81, 82, 83, 87, 94, 95, 97, 98, 99, 100, 104, 105, 110, 117, 119, 121, 124, 127, 130, 132, 133, 135, 140, 141, 143, 145, 148, 151, 152, 158, 159, 160, 161, 162, 163, 166, 167, 172, 173, 180, 183, 185, 186, 188, 190, 192, 193, 194, 200, 201, 202, 208, 210, 212, 214, 230, 236, 239, 242, 243, 244, 245
London Child Guidance Clinic, London, 104
London Clinic, London, 200
London Clinic of Psycho-Analysis, British Psycho-Analytical Society, London, 30
London School of Economics and Political Science, University of London, London, 55, 59, 64, 70, 73, 79, 158, 244
London Underground, London, 133, 145, 186
Longstaff, Dora Mary Hamilton Scott, 119, 244
Longstaff, Mary, 120
Longstaff, Tom George, 119
Longstaff, Ursula, see Bowlby, Ursula
Lord's Day, 94
Los Angeles, California, U.S.A., 55
Los Angeles Psychoanalytic Society, Los Angeles, California, U.S.A., 55
Love, Hate and Reparation: Two Lectures (Melanie Klein and Joan Riviere), 134
Lucie-Smith, Edward, 194, 202
"Luis, Mr", 196–197
Luftwaffe, 104
Lyth, Isabel Menzies, 165, 166, 167, 189

MacCarthy, Brendan, 189
Madness, xvi, 28, 94, 106, 112, 114, 134, 136, 175, 190, 207, 208, 209, 214–216, 217, 222, 231
Main, Thomas Forrest, 166
Management Committee, Tavistock Institute of Human Relations, London, 163
Manchester, England, 5
Manhattan, New York, U.S.A., 80, 112
Mann, Jenn, 155
Maresfield Gardens, Swiss Cottage, London, 9–12, 135, 148, 239
Maria-Theresienstrasse, Vienna, Austria, 176

Marital Tensions: Clinical Studies Towards a Psychological Theory of Interaction (Henry V. Dicks), 237
Markillie, Ronald, 70
Marlé, Anne, xii
Marriage Guidance Centres Committee, London, 161, 165
Marriage Guidance Committee, London, 161, 165
Marriage Guidance Council, London, 160, 161, 165, 167
Marriage Welfare Centres, London, 165, 167
Marriage Welfare Committee, London, 166
Marriage Welfare Sub-Committee, London, 166
Martin, Alexander Reid, 86
Mary, 242
Mary Ward Settlement, London, 73
Maryland, U.S.A., 56
Masochism, 37, 43, 145
Massachusetts, U.S.A., 55, 56, 66, 79
Massachusetts Society for Research in Psychiatry, Boston, Massachusetts, U.S.A., 66
Matte Blanco, Ignacio, 121, 137
Maxwell, Harold, 137
Mediastinal pleurisy, 23
Medical Library, Littlemore Hospital, Littlemore, Oxfordshire, 209
Medical psychology, 163, 164, 209
Medical Section, British Psychological Society, London, 59, 70, 235
Mehra, Baljeet, 202
Meltzer, Donald, 63, 134
Memory loss, 11
Menaker, Esther, 101
Menninger, Karl, 81
Menninger School of Psychiatry, Topeka, Kansas, U.S.A., 55
Mental health, xi, xiii, xv, xvii, 3, 8, 16, 17, 19, 39, 42, 47–48, 49, 51, 55, 58, 70, 73, 79, 81, 84, 90, 93, 96, 101, 105, 106, 107, 111, 144, 145, 152, 158, 167, 168–169, 173, 174, 175, 184, 189, 191, 204, 214, 215, 227, 228, 230, 231, 233, 236, 239
Menuhin, Yehudi, 66
Menzies, Isabel, *see* Lyth, Isabel Menzies
Merleau-Ponty, Maurice, 208
Messrs. Alfred Carter, London, 11
Messrs. Carter, London, 11
Michael, Richard, 195
Middlesex County Council, Middlesex, London, 168
Miller, Alice, 143–144

Miller, Emanuel, 101, 104, 242
Miller, Jacques-Alain, 142
Miller, Jonathan, 242
Milner, Dennis, 147
Milner, Marion, xii, xvi, xvii, 30, 46, 127–153, 181, 186, 187, 196, 208, 230, 233
Mindful Interbeing Mirror Therapy, 227
Mines and Collieries Act 1842, 95
Ministry of Works, 245
Mitchell, Silas Weir, 96
"modified analysis", 86
Money-Kyrle, Roger, 69, 189
Montreal, Quebec, Canada, 238
Mozart, Wolfgang Amadeus, 233
"Mr. Piggle", 49, 51, 71, 77, 80, 81, 83, 84, 88, 238
"Mrs. Piggle", 48, 49, 50, 51, 58, 62, 63, 68, 69, 71, 75, 76, 77, 80, 81, 82, 83, 84, 88, 237, 238
Myocardial infarction, 81

Namier, Lewis, 87
Napsbury Hospital, near London Colney, Hertfordshire, 32
Narcissism, 144, 189
Narrative of a Child Analysis: The Conduct of the Psycho-Analysis of Children as Seen in the Treatment of a Ten Year Old Boy (Melanie Klein), 84
National Association for Mental Health, London, 70, 73, 79
National Health Service, 56, 159, 163
National Insurance Act 1946, 159
National Physical Laboratory, Teddington, Middlesex, 26, 27
National Society for the Prevention of Cruelty to Children, London, 103
Nazism, 7, 9, 198, 228
Netflix, 179
Netherlands, The, 70, 73, 82
"Neurophysiological, Neuroclinical and Psychological Problems of the Full-Term and Premature Neonate", *see* "Problemi neurofisiologici, neuroclinici e psicologici del neonata a termine e prematuro"
Neuroses, 55, 70, 98, 100, 137, 163, 227, 243
Neve, Michael, 34
New Cavendish Street, London, 11, 74, 78, 194
New Forest, Hampshire, 119–120
"New Psychology", 163
New Society, 241
New York City, New York, U.S.A., 79, 80, 82, 83, 87, 236

New York, U.S.A., 55, 56, 101
New York Hospital – Cornell Medical Center, New York, New York, U.S.A., 112
New Zealand, 122
Newman, Alexander, 142–143
Newnham College, University of Cambridge, Cambridge, Cambridgeshire, 19
Nicholas, Jane Shore, 59, 141, 194, 237
Nichols, Mike, 180
Nijinsky, Vaslav, 156
Nile river, Egypt, 81
1952 Club, London, 134, 137
1914–1918 war, see World War I
Norfolk, Duke of, see Fitzalan-Howard, Bernard
North Islington, London, 161, 167
North London, London, 67
North-West London, London, 53, 110, 124, 152, 158, 167, 180, 210, 236
Northern New England District Branch, American Psychiatric Association, Boston, Massachusetts, U.S.A., 66
Nureyev, Rudolf, 180

Obsessional neurosis, 70
Obsessive involutional depression, 219
"Oliver Twist", 95
Olivier, Laurence, 66
"on demand", 63, 64, 66, 67, 73, 75, 78, 86, 87, 88, 89
"On Genital Love" (Michael Balint), 172
On Not Being Able to Paint (Joanna Field), 149
Optrex, 57, 71–73, 74
Orbach, Susie, 190–191, 246
Osler, William, 97, 237
Oxford, Oxfordshire, 49, 59, 63, 132, 133, 137, 140, 143, 145, 207, 210, 211, 212, 213, 214, 215, 219, 220, 231
Oxford Psychotherapy Society, Oxford, Oxfordshire, 207
Oxford Union Society, University of Oxford, Oxford, Oxfordshire, 59
Oxford University Mental Health Association, University of Oxford, Oxford, Oxfordshire, 55
Oxfordshire, England, 30, 32, 48, 49, 58, 63, 77, 79, 207, 212

Paddington, West London, London, 167
Paddington Green Children's Hospital, Paddington, West London, London, 18, 30, 49, 53, 54, 55, 56, 57, 66, 86–87, 97, 235
Paddington Station, Paddington, West London, London, 133, 145
Palace Theatre, London, 45
Pandemic, 3, 4, 5, 8, 23, 226, 229
Pappenheim, Bertha, 78, 85
Paris, France, 11, 55, 79
Paris Psycho-Analytical Society, Paris, France, see Société Psychanalytique de Paris, Paris, France
Park Lane, London, 98
Paterson, Mark, 193, 196, 204, 205
Pavor nocturnus, 97
Payne, Sylvia, 46, 153, 185, 186
Pearce, Kate, 231
Pearson, Jenny, 192
Pedder, Jonathan, 190, 191
Pelham, Jocelyn Brudenell, 109
Pelham, Prudence Mary, 109, 241–242
Pennsylvania, U.S.A., 56
Penrose, Lionel, 7
Penrose, Roger, 7
Pep-Web, see Psychoanalytic Electronic Publishing
Peredur Appeal, 66
Personal Aggressiveness and War (Evan F.M. Durbin and John Bowlby), 121, 240, 244
Peter Jones, London, 59
Philadelphia Association, London, 212
Phoenix Publishing House, Bicester, Oxfordshire, 231
Pilgrim's Lane, Hampstead, North-West London, London, 32
Pincus, Fritz, 166
Pincus, Lily, 165, 166, 173, 174
Play therapy, 67, 85
Playing, 18, 21, 22, 26, 28, 33, 34, 51, 62, 63, 67, 68, 72, 74, 75, 85, 89, 90, 120, 132, 136, 142, 148, 149, 217, 232, 233, 238
Pluralistic therapy, 227
Plymouth, Devon, 18, 19, 28, 79, 236
Portman Clinic, Belsize Park, London, 202
Post-War Settlement, 159
Potsdam, Germany, 166
Pratt, Frederick William Markham, 55
"Preface" (Robert W. Shields), 187
"Preface" (Clare Winnicott and Raymond Shepherd), 83
Primrose Hill, London, 9
"Problemi neurofisiologici, neuroclinici e psicologici del neonata a termine e prematuro", 64

Proceedings of the Royal Society of Medicine, 6
Provost Road, Chalk Farm, North-West
    London, London, 30, 133, 135, 137,
    139–140, 145, 147, 148, 152
"Psychiatric Snack Bar", 87
Psychiatry, xii, xv, xvi, 23, 29, 30, 32, 34, 41, 49,
    52, 53, 54, 55, 56, 60, 64, 66, 73, 74, 81, 84,
    85, 86, 87, 89, 93–107, 112, 115, 121, 122,
    130, 137, 144, 151, 153, 156, 162, 164, 166,
    169, 170, 171, 172, 173, 175, 189, 192, 193,
    208, 209, 210, 212, 213, 214, 217, 220, 231,
    238, 240, 242, 243
"*Psychic leucotomy*", 221
Psycho-Analytic Explorations (Donald W.
    Winnicott), 238
"Psycho-Neurosis in Childhood" (Donald W.
    Winnicott), 55
Psychoanalysis, xi–xvii, 3, 4, 5, 6, 7, 10, 11, 16,
    17, 19, 20, 21, 23, 24, 25, 29, 30, 31, 35, 36,
    37, 38, 39, 40, 41, 42, 43, 45, 46, 47, 49, 50,
    51, 52, 53, 54, 55, 59, 60, 63, 64, 65, 66, 67,
    69, 70, 71, 72, 73, 74, 75, 78, 79, 80, 81, 82,
    83, 84, 85, 86, 87, 88, 89, 93, 100, 101, 102,
    110, 111, 112, 113, 114, 115, 118, 119, 121,
    127, 129, 130, 131, 134, 135, 136, 137, 138,
    139, 140, 141, 142, 145, 147, 149, 150, 152,
    153, 155, 156, 157, 162, 163, 164, 169, 170,
    171, 172, 173, 175, 179, 180, 181, 182, 183,
    184, 185, 186, 187, 188, 189, 190, 191, 192,
    193, 194, 195, 196, 197, 198, 199, 200, 201,
    202, 203, 204, 207–210, 211, 214, 220, 227,
    228, 229, 230, 231, 232, 233, 237, 238, 239,
    240, 241, 243, 244
"psychoanalysis *partagé*", 88–89
Psychoanalytic Electronic Publishing, 103
Psychodrama, 143
Psychology, v, xi, xii, xv, xvi, 3, 4, 5, 7, 16, 19, 20,
    23, 24, 28, 30, 31, 32, 36, 38, 41, 51, 52, 54,
    55, 58, 59, 60, 61, 64, 70, 81, 85, 88, 90, 93,
    95, 97, 98, 99, 100, 101, 104, 105, 107, 111,
    112, 114, 115, 129, 137, 144, 153, 156, 157,
    160, 163, 164, 167, 170, 172, 180, 181, 185,
    188, 195, 205, 208, 209, 210, 232, 235, 236,
    237, 239, 240, 241, 243, 244, 245
Psychopathology, xii, 97, 100, 102, 145, 166,
    173, 189
Psychoses, 41, 63, 64–65, 86, 140, 156, 209,
    223, 227
Psychosomatic medicine, 65, 67, 163
Psychotherapy, xi, xii, 3, 4, 8, 15, 16, 17, 19, 20,
    40, 41, 57, 75, 86, 87, 88, 93, 94, 101, 103,
    106, 110, 116, 127, 142, 155, 156, 157, 158,
    161, 164, 175, 181, 185, 190, 192, 207, 208,
    214, 227, 228, 230, 231, 237, 238, 240, 243
Publications Committee, British Psycho-
    Analytical Society, London, 198, 199
Pulmonary oedema, 80
Putnam, Irmarita, 153

Queen Anne Street, London, 30, 33
Quebec, Canada, 238
Quigley, Janet, 60

"R.D. Laing: The First Five Years"
    (Adrian C. Laing), 216
Radically-open dialectical behaviour
    therapy, 227
Radlett, Hertfordshire, 79
Ramzy, Ishak, 81–83, 84
Raney, James, 195
Rank, Beata, 6
Rank, Otto, 6
Rapp, Miriam, 143
Rare Materials Room, Wellcome Library,
    Wellcome Building, The Wellcome
    Collection, London, 117, 242
"Rat Man", 85
Rayner, Eric, 197, 205
*Reason and Violence: A Decade of Sartre's
    Philosophy. 1950–1960* (Ronald D. Laing
    and David G. Cooper), 134
Redgrave, Michael, 180
Redgrave, Vanessa, 180
Rees, John Rawlings, 164
"References" (Ignaz Philipp Semmelweis), 246
Regency, 11
Regent's College, Inner Circle, Regent's Park,
    London, 110
Regent's Park, London, 45
Regent's University London, Inner Circle,
    Regent's Park, London, 110
Reik, Theodor, 87
Repetitive Visualisation Therapy, 227
Reprints Collection, Library, British Psycho-
    Analytical Society, London, 186
Rescue phantasy, 28
"Research Project into the Social Structure and
    Social Needs of Communities", 170
*Reshaping the Psychoanalytic Domain: The
    Work of Melanie Klein, W.R.D. Fairbairn,
    and D.W. Winnicott* (Judith Hughes), 138
"*Rettungsphantasie*", 28

Reynolds, Mrs., 167
Rhodesia, 69
Rickman, John, xiii, 41, 164–165, 184, 186, 188, 200, 201, 202, 204
"Ridgelands", Wimbledon, South-West London, London, 119
Right brain psychotherapy, 227
Ringwood, New Forest, Hampshire, 119
Ringwood Workhouse, Ashley, New Forest, Hampshire, 119–120
Risinghill School, North London, London, 67
Riviere, Joan, xiii, xv, 31, 35, 36–38, 42, 46, 112, 113, 134, 153, 186, 242, 243
"Robert A.", 103
Robertson, James, 106
Robertson, Joyce, 106
Robinson, Kenneth, 70
Roehampton Institute, London, 211
Rome, Italy, 56, 64, 65, 82
Rorschach ink blot test, 243–244
Rosenberg, Cyril, 47
Rosenblüth, Michael, 47
Rosenfeld, Herbert, 46, 71, 186
Royal Army Medical Corps, 100
Royal College of Paediatrics and Child Health, London, 23
Royal College of Physicians of London, London, 97
Royal College of Psychiatrists, London, 64, 101
Royal College of Surgeons, London, 97
Royal College of Veterinary Surgeons, London, 239
Royal Infirmary for Children, London, 95
Royal Medico-Psychological Association, London, 64, 101
Royal Naval Volunteer Reserve, 22
Rubinstein, Lothair, 41, 71
"Rules and Metarules" (Ronald D. Laing), 217
Rycroft, Charles, 37, 134, 186, 187, 190, 192, 203, 205, 208, 220, 221

Sacerdoti, Cesare, 192, 198, 199
Sachs, Hanns, 171, 185
Sadism, 16, 43, 140, 152, 243
Samuels, Andrew, 191
San Francisco Psychoanalytic Institute, San Francisco, California, U.S.A., 55
Sartre, Jean-Paul, 134, 208
Scandinavian Orthopsychiatric Congress, Helsinki, Finland, 55

Schilder, Paul, 86
Schizophrenia, 32, 127–128, 129, 130, 139, 144, 146, 156, 208, 213, 222, 223
"Schizophrenie", see Schizophrenia
Schreber, Daniel Gottlieb Moritz, 241
Schreber, Daniel Paul, 85
Schur, Max, 10, 11
Scotland, United Kingdom, 56, 95, 124, 162, 211, 219
Scott, Clifford, 38, 153, 186
Searles, Harold, 139
Second World War, see World War II
Segal, Hanna, 36–37, 46, 183, 243
Self-Analysis (Karen Horney), 87
Semmelweis, Ignác Fülöp, 226, 228, 246
Semmelweis, Ignaz Philipp, see Semmelweis Ignác Fülöp
Senn, Milton, 105
Separation, 99, 103, 104, 106, 107, 169, 240
Sevenoaks, Kent, 141
Shakespeare, William, 188, 207, 225
Sharpe, Ella Freeman, 153, 184, 185, 187, 188, 201
Shepherd, Raymond, 83, 197, 238
Shields, Robert, 187, 188, 193, 195, 201
Shoe Lane, London, 11
Shoreditch, London, 161
Showtime, 156
Sigmund Freud Copyrights, London, 196
Silberstein, Eduard, 175
Silberstein, Pauline Theiler, 175
"Silence as Communication" (M. Masud R. Khan), 180
Simpson, Wallis Warfield, 31
Sinason, Valerie, 194
Sir Mortimer B. Davis Jewish General Hospital, Montreal, Quebec, Canada, 238
Skynner, Robin, 136
Skype therapy, 63
Social work, xiv, 30–31, 49, 53, 101, 159, 160, 161, 166, 167, 168, 169, 170, 171, 172
Société Psychanalytique de Paris, Paris, France, 55
Society for Existential Analysis, London, 214
Society for Psychosomatic Research, London, 65
Society for the Study of Disease in Children, London, 98
Sohn, Leslie, 86
Solnit, Albert, 136
"Some Character-Types Met with in Psycho-Analytic Work" (Sigmund

Freud), *see* "Einige Charaktertypen aus der psychoanalytischen Arbeit" (Sigmund Freud)
South Islington, London, 167
South-East London, London, 193
South-West London, London, 33, 53, 119, 167, 180
Southern, Dorothy, 117
Spaas, Godelieve, 211–212, 215, 216
Spanish flu, 5, 23
Spielberg, Steven, 179
Spotnitz, Hyman, 152
Squiggle Foundation, London, *see* The Squiggle Foundation, London
Squiggles, 57
St. Albans, Hertfordshire, 32
St. Bartholomew's church, London, 94, 239
St. Bartholomew's Hospital, London, 23, 30, 59
St. Bartholomew's Hospital Journal, 23
St. Bartholomew's Hospital Medical College, University of London, London, 18, 22, 30
St. Blaize-Molony, Ronald, 190
St. Mary's Hospital Gazette, 54
St. Pancras, London, 161, 167
St. Thomas' Hospital, London, 119
Stadhampton, Oxfordshire, 212
Standlake, Oxfordshire, 79
State University of New York, Bronx, New York, U.S.A., 55
Stephen, Adrian, xv, 114
Stephen, Karin, xv, 114
Stepney, East End, London, 159
Stewart, Donald Ogden, 192
Stockholm, Sweden, 56
Stokes, Adrian, xvi, 144
Stoller, Robert, 198
Streep, Meryl, 155
Studien über Hysterie (Josef Breuer and Sigmund Freud), 102
Strachey, Alix Sargant-Florence, 7, 20, 25, 35, 236
Strachey, James, xiv, 7, 20, 25, 29, 30, 31, 35–36, 42, 46, 74, 236
Strangles Beach, Crackington Haven, near Bude, Cornwall, 245
"Suburbiton", 21
Sullivan, Arthur, 147–148, 233
Superego, 228
Supervision, 15, 16, 37, 82, 99, 169, 172, 186, 190, 208, 243
Surbiton, Surrey, 21, 26, 236

Surrey, England, 18, 21, 26, 236
"Susan" (patient of Marion Milner), 32, 129, 137–140
"Susan" (sister of "The Piggle"), 48, 50, 58, 62, 67, 75, 76
Sutherland, John, 173, 174
Sweden, 65
Swiss Cottage, North-West London, London, 9, 12, 135, 148
Switzerland, 73, 156
Syphilitic elephantiasis, 27

Talking to Parents (Donald W. Winnicott), 238
"Tavi", London, *see* Tavistock Clinic, London
Tavistock Centre for Couple Relationships, Tavistock Institute of Medical Psychology, Belsize Park, London, 15, 174
Tavistock Clinic, Tavistock Centre, Tavistock and Portman NHS Trust, Belsize Park, London, 15–16, 117, 160, 162–164, 166, 167, 168, 169, 170, 171, 172, 173, 174, 175, 186, 208, 243–244
Tavistock Clinic for Functional Nervous Disorders, London, 163
Tavistock Institute of Human Relations, London, 41, 163, 166, 167, 172, 174
Tavistock Institute of Marital Studies, Tavistock Institute of Medical Psychology, Belsize Park, London, 174
Tavistock Marital Studies Institute, Tavistock Institute of Medical Psychology, Belsize Park, London, 15, 174, 232
Tavistock Publications, London, 69, 136, 199
Tavistock Relationships, Tavistock Institute of Medical Psychology, London, 15, 21, 41, 174
Taylor, Alice Buxton, *see* Winnicott, Alice
Taylor, Florence Maberly, 27
Taylor, John, 26–27
Taylor, Mary, 27
Taylor, Pauline, 27
Taylor's Practice of Medicine (Edward P. Poulton, Charles Putnam Symonds, Harold W. Barber, and Robert D. Gillespie), 99
Teddington, Middlesex, 27
Thackeray, William Makepeace, 207
"The Aims of Psycho-Analytical Treatment" (Donald W. Winnicott), 42, 86
The Book of the Foundation of the Church of St. Bartholomew, London: Rendered into Modern English. From the Original

INDEX

Latin Version Preserved in the British Museum, Numbered Vespasian B. IX, by Mr. Humphrey H. King and Mr. William Barnard for Use in the 'Records of St. Bartholomew's Priory', 239

The Bowlby Centre, London, 110, 232

The British Journal of Medical Psychology, 209

The British Medical Journal, 104, 105, 226, 242

The Child and the Family: First Relationships (Donald W. Winnicott), 65, 112

The Child and the Outside World: Studies in Developing Relationships (Donald W. Winnicott), 65

The Child, the Family, and the Outside World (Donald W. Winnicott), 65

"The Concept of the False Self" (Donald W. Winnicott), 59

The Diseases of Infants and Children (Edmund Cautley), 98

The Divided Self: A Study of Sanity and Madness (Ronald D. Laing), 208, 209, 222

The Family and Individual Development (Donald W. Winnicott), 69, 77

The Hands of the Living God: An Account of a Psycho-analytic Treatment (Marion Milner), 127, 128, 137

The International Journal of Psycho-Analysis, 186, 187, 209

"The International Psycho-Analytical Library", 69, 83, 134, 199

The Lady, 96

The Lancet, 226

"The Manic Defence" (Donald W. Winnicott), 61

The Maturational Processes and the Facilitating Environment: Studies in the Theory of Emotional Development (Donald W. Winnicott), 69, 77

The Mystery of the Androgyne: Three Papers on the Theory and Practice of Psycho-Analysis (Theodore J. Faithfull), 239

"The Neonate and His Mother" (Donald W. Winnicott), 64

"The New Library of Psychoanalysis", 199

The New York Times, 190

The Ordinary Devoted Mother and Her Baby: Nine Broadcast Talks (Autumn 1949) (Donald W. Winnicott), 243

"The Origins of Violence" (Donald W. Winnicott), 65

The Oskar Diethelm Library of the History of Psychiatry, New York Hospital – Cornell Medical Center, New York, New York, U.S.A., 112

The Oxford Psycho-Analytical Forum, Corpus Christi College, University of Oxford, Oxford, Oxfordshire, 136, 208, 209, 210, 231

"The Paediatric Department of Psychology", Paddington Green Children's Hospital, Paddington, West London, London, 54

"The Piggle", xv, xvi, 45–90, 237, 238

The Piggle: An Account of the Psychoanalytic Treatment of a Little Girl (Donald W. Winnicott), 50, 57, 83, 89

The Piggle: Her Psycho-analytic Treatment (Donald W. Winnicott), 80

'"The Piggle" Papers', 45–90

The Politics of the Family and Other Essays (Ronald D. Laing), 217

"The Price of Disregarding Research Findings" (Donald W. Winnicott), 70

"The Price of Mental Health", 70

The Priory Gate School, near King's Lynn, Norfolk, 99, 105, 239, 241

The Privacy of the Self (M. Masud R. Khan), 180

The Psycho-Analytical Process (Donald Meltzer), 134

"The Psycho-Somatic Dilemma" (Donald W. Winnicott), 65

The Self and Others: Further Studies in Sanity and Madness (Ronald D. Laing), 134

The Sopranos, 155

The Squiggle Foundation, London, 131, 133, 141, 142, 146, 151

The Standard Edition of the Complete Psychological Works of Sigmund Freud (Sigmund Freud), 7, 36, 236

The Suppressed Madness of Sane Men: Forty-Four Years of Exploring Psychoanalysis (Marion Milner), 136

The Technique of Psycho-Analysis (David Forsyth), 6

The Tragedie of King Lear (William Shakespeare), 207

"Theoretical Influences from Klein to Bion" (Ronald D. Laing), 210

Thinking About Children (Donald W. Winnicott), 238

Thomas, Ruth, 38

Ticktin, Stephen, 214, 215, 219

Tillich, Paul, 208

Titmuss, Richard, 245

Tizard, Peter, 73

Topeka, Kansas, U.S.A., 55, 81
Topeka Psychoanalytic Society, Topeka, Kansas, U.S.A., 55
Tottenham Court Road, London, 29
Training Committee, Institute of Psycho-Analysis, London, 112
Transdiagnostic cognitive behavioural therapy, 227
Transference, 36, 75, 147, 152
Trends in Psycho-Analysis (Marjorie Brierley), 209
Trinity College, University of Cambridge, Cambridge, Cambridgeshire, 127, 129, 135, 146
Trisul, India, 119
True self, 16, 19, 42
"true self marriage", 42
Tustin, Frances, 151

Unconscious, 17, 26, 28, 32, 38, 39, 88, 102, 145, 205, 209, 215, 219, 238
Unconscious marital choice, 17
United Kingdom, xiv, 8, 15, 23, 41, 55, 146, 229
United States of America, xiv, 5, 86, 105, 185, 229
University College London, University of London, London, 244
University of Cambridge, Cambridge, Cambridgeshire, 18, 19, 22, 30, 65, 66, 83, 127, 131, 132
University of Edinburgh, Edinburgh, Scotland, 120
University of Glasgow, Glasgow, Scotland, 162
University of London, London, 41, 55, 70, 79, 80, 81, 151, 158, 244
University of Roehampton, London, 211
Upper East Side, New York, New York, U.S.A., 80

V-E Day, 159
van Beethoven, Ludwig, 233
van der Horst, Frank, 240
Vanity Fair: A Novel without a Hero (William Makepeace Thackeray), 207
Vauxhall Bridge Road, London, 172
Ventricular failure, 81
Vespasian, 94, 239
Veterinary medicine, 239
VH1, 155
Victimology, 221
Victoria Station, London, 172

Vienna, Austria, xiii, 3–8, 10, 11, 20, 25, 87, 100, 133, 156, 175, 189, 208, 229
Virago Press, London, 136
von Hug-Hellmuth, Hermine, 100
vulva, 26–27

Wales, United Kingdom, 138, 157
Walham Green, Fulham, South-West London, London, 167
Wandsworth, London, 161, 167
War and Democracy: Essays on the Causes and Prevention of War (Evan F.M. Durbin, John Bowlby, Ivor Thomas, Douglas P.T. Jay, Robert B. Fraser, Richard H.S. Crossman, and George Catlin), 241
War Damages Act 1943, 158
War Department, 159
War Office Selection Board, 164
Warneford Hospital, Headington, Oxfordshire, 140
Waterlow, Judith, 186
"Watson-Dixon, Gladys", 30, 236
Wellcome Building, London, 117, 119
Wellcome Collection, Wellcome Building, London, 60
Wellcome Library, Wellcome Collection, Wellcome Building, London, 60, 117, 118, 119, 122, 188, 242
Welldon, Estela, 175, 192–193, 203–204
Weltkrieg, see World War I
Wesleyan Methodism, 18, 28
West, Charles, 95–96
West End, London, 46
West London, London, 53
Westcroft, Bideford, Devon, 244
Weymouth Street, London, 18, 24
When Spring Comes: Awakenings in Clinical Psychoanalysis (M. Masud R. Khan), 182, 183, 196, 198
"white heat", 40
Wiesbaden, Germany, 79
Wikipedia, xi, 107, 225
Willoughby, Roger, 200
Wilson, Archibald Thomson Macbeth ("Tommy"), 162–163, 165, 166, 170, 171, 174
Wiltshire, England, 121
Wimbledon (tennis tournament), Wimbledon, South-West London, London, 39
Wimbledon (town), South-West London, London, 119

Winnicott, Alice, xiv, 15, 17–22, 24–29, 31–34, 36–38, 40, 42–43, 53, 112, 137–138, 236
Winnicott, Clare, xiv, 15, 17, 30–31, 33, 34, 35, 38–39, 40, 42–43, 49, 53, 59, 60, 67, 81, 82, 83, 84, 130, 136, 199, 200, 236, 238, 245
Winnicott, Donald W., xii, xiv, xv, xvi, xvii, 13, 15–43, 45–90, 96, 97, 99, 100, 101, 104, 110–113, 115, 117, 118, 123, 124, 130–131, 136, 137–138, 139, 141, 142, 143, 146, 147, 148, 151, 153, 181, 182, 184, 185, 186, 187, 188, 189, 191–192, 199, 200, 201–202, 204, 213, 233, 235, 236, 237, 238, 242–243, 244, 245
Winnicott, Elizabeth, 28
Winnicott, Frederick, 28, 31
Winnicott, Kathleen, 18
Winnicott, Violet, 18
Winnicott Publications Committee, 83
Winnicott Studies: The Journal of the Squiggle Foundation, 151
Winnicottiana, xiv, 13, 16
Winter, Ella, 192
Wisdom, Madness and Folly: The Making of a Psychiatrist. 1927–1957 (Ronald D. Laing), 217
"Wolf Man", 85

Woodhead, Barbara, 66
Wooster, Gerald, 187–188
World Boxing Federation, 39
World Health Organization, Geneva, Switzerland, 30, 106
World War I, xiv, 4, 5, 18, 22, 26, 52, 83, 143, 229, 242
World War II, 10, 30, 41, 49, 106, 114, 122, 157, 159, 162, 164, 175, 185, 198, 242
Wyldes Close Corner, Golders Green, North-West London, London, 116

Yale University, New Haven, Connecticut, U.S.A., 105
Yale University Press, New Haven, Connecticut, U.S.A., 136

Zagazig, Egypt, 81
Zoom, 3, 4, 5, 8
Zoom fatigue, 4
Zoom psychoanalysis, 4, 7
Zoom psychotherapy, 4, 63
Zoom therapy, *see* Zoom psychotherapy
"Zwang zur Wiederholung", *see* "compulsion to repeat"